LIFE OF BLESSED THOMAS MORE

Permissu Superiorum.

Nihil obstat.

EDUARD. O'LAVERTY, C.SS.R.,
Censor Deputatus.

Imprimatur.

HENRICUS EDUARDUS,
Card. Archiep. Westmon.

Feb. 6, 1891.

Tho: Moor L'Chancelour

A. BRAUN ET CIE DORNACH & PARIS

BLESSED THOMAS MORE

From Holbein's sketch made in the 50th year of the Martyr's age.

LIFE AND WRITINGS OF
BLESSED THOMAS MORE

LORD CHANCELLOR OF ENGLAND

AND

MARTYR UNDER HENRY VIII.

BY THE

REV. T. E. BRIDGETT

OF THE CONGREGATION OF THE MOST HOLY REDEEMER

THIRD EDITION

LONDON: BURNS & OATES, LIMITED
NEW YORK, CINCINNATI, CHICAGO: BENZIGER BROTHERS
1904

PREFACE.

In More's dedicatory letter to Thomas Ruthal of his translation into Latin of three of Lucian's dialogues, he complained that writers of the lives of saints sometimes indulge in falsehoods: "They have scarcely left a life of martyr or of virgin without foisting into it something untrue—piously, no doubt! for of course there was a danger lest truth, left to itself, should not be able to stand upright; so that it was necessary to prop it up with lies!"*

I may say that my first anxiety in composing this Life of the illustrious writer, chancellor and martyr, has been not to merit this reproach; to state nothing that I did not believe, and to accept nothing for which I had not historical evidence. My first care was to collate the biographies of More already in existence.

In giving some account of the principal of these, I shall be able at the same time to state the sources from which a correct and complete life of More can be drawn.

* Itaque nullam fere martyris, nullam virginis vitam prætermiserunt, in quam non aliquid hujusmodi mendaciorum inseruerint; pie scilicet, alioquin periculum erat ne veritas non posset sibi ipsa sufficere, nisi fulciretur mendaciis. This epistle is ascribed to Erasmus in the Leyden edition of his works; but wrongly. It is More's, and bears his name both in the original edition and in his collected works.

My own conclusion was, that such a Life still remained to be written ; and I have made a serious attempt to supply the want. My readers and critics must judge how far I have succeeded.

1. ERASMUS. In the letters of Erasmus there are descriptions of More so minute and full, though written during his lifetime, that Erasmus may almost be called his first biographer. There is also a large correspondence between the two friends. This source had already been well used by Stapleton ; but I have taken nothing at second-hand. It will be seen that the writings of Erasmus have supplied me with some of my best materials.*

2. ROPER. More's son-in-law, William Roper, resided with him for sixteen years. In the time of Queen Mary he wrote down his reminiscences, as well as details learnt from his wife, Margaret More. These reminiscences were not intended as a complete Life. They were notes supplied to Dr. Nicholas Harpsfield, Archdeacon of Canterbury, by whom they were worked up into a Life to be mentioned immediately. Roper, writing from memory twenty years after the death of More, makes a few mistakes in dates, but his narrative bears intrinsic evidence of the simple uprightness of the narrator and of his substantial accuracy, which is confirmed by historical documents. This Life, or rather these notes, were in circulation in MS. and were used by compilers of lives long before they were printed. They were first printed in Paris in 1626 ; then by

---

* I have used throughout the Leyden edition of Erasmus.

Hearne in 1716; and by Lewis in 1729, 1731, 1765, who added a valuable appendix of documents. The best edition is that of Singer in 1817, of which only 150 copies were printed. Roper's *Life of More* is also annexed to Mr. Lumley's edition of the *Utopia*.

3. HARPSFIELD. A *Life of More* was composed by Nicholas Harpsfield, Archdeacon of Canterbury, in the time of Queen Mary. In his dedication of it to William Roper, he says that he has used the materials supplied to him by Roper, but has been able to add something of his own. I have carefully collated the two, and I find that Harpsfield is far more diffuse than his original, but without much gain to the narrative. What he has added to the history is derived principally from the writings of More. This Life has not been printed. Several MS. copies exist.* I have used a careful transcript from Harpsfield's MS. in the British Museum, Harl. 6253, lent to me by the Rev. John Morris, S.J., F.S.A.

4. GEORGE LILLY, son of William Lilly, More's fellow-student, wrote some " Elogia virorum aliquot qui nostro sæculo eruditione et doctrina clari, memorabilesque fuerunt ". These were Colet, (William) Lilly, Grocyn, Linacre, Lupset, Pace, Fisher, More, and (William) Latimer. He gives about two pages to each, rather of general eulogy than facts. There is nothing of value for the Life of More.

---

* The copy in the Bodleian was seized by Topclif, the informer and priest-catcher, on 13th April, 1582, among the books of Thomas More, the Martyr's grandson. (Bodley, Rawlinson's letters 23.) There is a copy in Emmanuel Coll., Cambridge, and two in Lambeth.

5. MAURICE CHAUNCY'S *Historia aliquot nostri sæculi martyrum* (1550). This also is merely a short sketch.

6. Lodiocius Pacæus, a Spanish Dominican (apparently of English origin), a learned and eloquent man, took much pains in gathering materials for a Life of More. Death cut short the work (Stapleton).

7. RASTELL'S LIFE OF MORE. William Rastell, the son of John Rastell and Elizabeth, sister of Sir Thomas More, was born in London in 1508. He first followed his father's business as printer, and then studied the law at Lincoln's Inn. In the time of Edward VI. he went into exile, but returning in the reign of Mary, became serjeant-at-law and judge. He collected and edited the English works of his uncle and also wrote his Life, as Sander informs us. The latter fact has been denied by Burnet, but it does not rest merely on the assertion of Sander, though that would be sufficient evidence. In vol. 152 of the Arundel Collection in the British Museum are some "Notes from Rastell's *Life of More*," and in the same volume a fragment of a large work that had been divided into books and chapters. This fragment bears no title or name of author, but the careful reader will find that the "Notes" are taken from it, thus showing that it is a part of Rastell's *Life of More*. The extracts, however, only regard Fisher, having been copied for the description of the bishop's martyrdom, of which Rastell was an eye-witness. Unfortunately the rest of this work is not known to exist, nor do any of the writers of More's life appear to have used it. In the time of Elizabeth, Rastell again went into exile at Louvain. He died in 1565. As he

had married Winifred, daughter of John Clements and Margaret Gigs, More's adopted child, he had every means of obtaining authentic information. It is therefore greatly to be hoped that this Life may be yet found in some continental library.

8. STAPLETON'S TRES THOMÆ. By far the best Life of More is that of Thomas Stapleton, published at Douai in 1588. Stapleton was born in Sussex, in July, 1535, the year and month of the martyrdom of Blessed Thomas More. He was educated at Winchester and New College, Oxford, and was prebendary of Chichester in the reign of Mary. He left England at the accession of Elizabeth, and lived forty-two years in exile. He was regius professor of Holy Scripture in the University of Louvain and canon of St. Peter's in that city. No name probably stands higher than his as a controversialist. His book, *Tres Thomæ*, contains the lives of St. Thomas the Apostle, of St. Thomas of Canterbury, and of Thomas More. In his introduction he tells us that he had the help derived from long intimacy with Dr. John Clements, More's favourite scholar, and his wife, Margaret Gigs; as also with John Harris, More's secretary, and Dorothy Colly, his wife, who had been servant to Margaret Roper and had helped to bury Sir Thomas; with John Haywood, the epigrammatist, who was very intimate with William Rastell. During several years Stapleton gathered from all these their reminiscences and anecdotes, and committed them to paper at the time, with a view of one day writing a Life. This, happily, he lived to accomplish. He also studied carefully the Latin and English writings of More, and

the letters of Erasmus and other learned contemporaries.
Living in exile, he had, of course, no help from English
documents, but his friends and fellow-exiles, especially
John Harris, at the death of More had secured some of
his unpublished MSS., the knowledge of which we owe
to Stapleton.   It is certain, also, that he had a copy of
William Roper's notes.

Stapleton's *Life of More* has been frequently printed
in Latin ; it has been translated into French.   I am
not aware of any English translation.

9. In the Lambeth Library, together with a copy of
Harpsfield, there is a MS. *Life of More* (in the same
vol., 179), which has been printed by Dr. Wordsworth in
his *Ecclesiastical Biography* (vol. ii.).   An introductory
letter bears the date 1599. The Preface is signed " Ro-
Ba ". The author was a Catholic, and the Life is made
up from the Lives by Roper, Harpsfield, and especially
from Stapleton.   The compiler does not seem to have
added anything from other sources.

10. CRESACRE MORE'S LIFE. Between 1615-1620
another English *Life of More* was composed.   It was
printed in 1627, and bore the initials "M. T. M."   The
editor, M. C. M. E., attributes it to Thomas More, a
priest, and great-grandson of Sir Thomas.   Yet there was
abundant internal evidence that it was written by a
layman.   Hence the editor of the second edition of
1726 attributed it to Thomas More, *Esquire*.   A third
edition appeared in 1828, with a Preface by the Rev.
Joseph Hunter, F.S.A., clearing up the matter and
assigning the work to its real author, Cresacre More, of
More Place, Co. Herts, and Barnborough, in Yorkshire,

Esquire. This gentleman was the great-grandson of
Sir Thomas, and the youngest of thirteen children ;
but the inheritance had devolved on him by the death of
his elder brothers or by their entering religious orders.

This Life of Sir Thomas is much esteemed and often
quoted ; but after collating it carefully with Stapleton,
Roper and Harpsfield, I find that it contains very
little original matter. I have preferred, therefore, to
quote directly from the sources from which Cresacre
More drew.

II. VARIA. Of other Lives I need not say much.
The Mirror of Virtue (1626), *The History of the Life
and Death of More*, by J. H. (John Hoddesden),
are mere abridgments of Stapleton. Memoirs and
Lives, by Dr. Warner, Dibdin, Miss Taylor, and
articles in Cyclopædias do not profess to do more
than select and rearrange. The two volumes of the
Memoir of Sir T. More, by Sir A. Cayley (1808), are
principally taken up with an account of some of his
writings, particularly his poems, and contain some
interesting poetical translations by Archdeacon Wrangham. A book called *Philomorus*, of which the second
edition appeared in 1878, is almost exclusively given
to More's epigrams, as they illustrate his life and
character. In 1807 appeared *Lives of British Statesmen*,
by John Macdiarmid. These are More, Cecil, Went-
worth, and Hyde. The Right Hon. Sir James Mackintosh supplied a very interesting sketch of More's life
to the *Cabinet Cyclopedia ;* this was printed separately
in 1844. Mr. Foss, in his *Lives of the Judges*, and Lord
Campbell, in his *Lives of the Chancellors*, have con-

sidered Sir Thomas principally as a lawyer. Among
Catholics the Rev. W. J. Walter produced a good life
in America, reprinted in Dolman's Catholic Library
(2nd ed., 1840), and the accomplished authoress of *Christian Schools and Scholars* gave us a charming sketch in
her *Three Chancellors*, Wykeham, Waynfleet, and More
(Burns & Oates). Miss Stewart's *Life of More* is trivial
and inaccurate.

12. SEEBOHM'S OXFORD REFORMERS, of which the 3rd
edition appeared in 1887. By "Oxford Reformers" Mr.
Seebohm means, not reformers of Oxford, but three Oxford
scholars, Colet, More, and Erasmus, who were working
together at a deep reformation of the Church when
Luther's reformation came to hinder or divert their
work. I have read this work more than once on
account of the praise given to it, and I have taken
great pains to weigh and verify its statements. In
the course of the following Life I am obliged to contest
many of Mr. Seebohm's conclusions. I will merely say
here that I consider the whole book to be fantastic and
misleading, built up from conjectures and misunder-
standings, and by false deductions. As the story
breaks off with Dean Colet's death in 1519, More's
part is quite secondary as well as fragmentary. Mr.
Seebohm has given great care to questions of date,
especially as regards the early life and correspondence
of Erasmus.

13. MORE'S OWN WORKS have been my principal study.
Of these I shall give an account in the proper place.
There will be grounds for reproach to the Catholics of
England if, in the course of a few years, there is not a

complete and careful edition of all his works, both in
Latin and English. With the exception of the *Dialogue
of Comfort in Tribulation*, reprinted by Dolman, and the
translations of the *Utopia* and the *History of Richard
III.*, More's English writings are almost inac-
cessible.* Even in the British Museum there is but
one copy of the great black letter collection by William
Rastell of 1456 pages in double column. I gratefully
acknowledge the loan of a copy of this rare book from
C. T. Gatty, Esq., F.S.A., which has much facilitated
my labours. I have used the Francfort edition of
More's Latin works of 1689. There are some *opus-
cula* and many letters not contained in any (so-called)
Opera Omnia. I trust none of these has escaped my
attention.

Here let me say that were I writing the Life of one
whose works might be supposed to be in the hands of
my readers, or easily accessible to them, I should not
feel myself justified in quoting as I have done. I have
translated long passages from More's Latin works and
transcribed pages from his English writings, as freely as
if I were printing from unique MSS. in my own possession. For the same reason I have generally given his
letters and those addressed to him in full, instead of
incorporating the substance in my own narrative. My
readers will have to take nothing from me on trust.
They will have the very text of my "evidences" on
every point. I am aware that this method interferes

* More's translation of the *Life of Pico della Mirandula* has been re-
edited since the above was written (see *infra*, p. 78).

somewhat with the easy flow of the narrative, and perhaps doubles its length.   The compensating advantages
are that the reader can form his own judgment, and has
only to rely on the biographer for the accuracy and the
completeness of the record.   He gains also some knowledge of More as a writer.

One singular result is inevitable from this method of
presenting my materials.   More wrote both in Latin
and in English.   The English in the early part of the
sixteenth century has become antiquated, and thus presents a great contrast with the translations from Latin
into modern English.   More will, therefore, be found
speaking, as it were, two languages, or two very different
dialects of the same language—that of the first years of
the sixteenth century, and that of the last years of the
nineteenth.

If this is anomalous, it may serve to bring home to us
an important fact.   What we call the *quaint* words and
turns of old English make us regard the writers or
speakers of that language as themselves quaint, strange,
uncouth, rude, simple, or in some way unlike men and
women of the same class of society, the same talents
and education at the present day.   But if they wrote in
Latin, the delusion—for such it is—is dissipated.   Latin
is to us what it was to them.   It has not become antiquated or changed its form.   We find that they wrote
just as we should write, if we were as well versed in the
language as they were.   They thought just as we think.
We turn their words into our modern English, and all
quaintness has disappeared.   There is nothing odd or
unusual in their way of reasoning or in their modes of

feeling. As soon as they speak our own language in our own form or dialect, we judge of them for good or evil as we judge of our contemporaries; and we cease to *patronise* them, as if they were only clever boys or promising savages.

I have modernised the spelling, but I have been scrupulous not to alter a word in making extracts. My reason is that More was very precise in his choice of words and in their arrangement, whereas I can discover no rule in the spelling. Besides this, the spelling is not that of the author, but of the printer. By a comparison between the first and second editions of More's English works, it is clear that the type-setter was free to vary the spelling according to the exigence of the line, adding a final *e* or doubling a consonant where the modern type-setter would use a space. The following passage, amusing in itself, will explain what I mean by More's choice of exact words :—

No and Nay.

"I woulde not here note, by the way, that Tyndal here translateth ' no ' for ' nay,' for it is but a trifle and mistaking of the Englishe worde : saving that ye shoulde see that he whych in two so plain Englishe wordes, and so common as is naye and no, can not tell when he should take the tone and when the tother, is not, for translating into Englishe, a man very mete.

" For the use of those two wordes in answerring to a question is this : *Naye* * answereth the question framed

---

* Rastell has here put *no*, by an evident misprint.

by the affirmative. As, for example, if a manne should aske Tindall hymselfe: Ys an heretike mete to translate Holy Scripture into Englishe? Lo, to thys question, if he will aunswere trew Englishe, he must aunswere 'nay' and not 'no'. But and if the question be asked hym thus, lo: Is not an heretyque mete to translate Holy Scripture into English? To this question, lo, if he will aunswer true English, he must aunswer 'no' and not 'nay'.

"And a lyke difference is there betwene thcse two adverbes 'ye' and 'yes'. For if the questeion bee framed unto Tindall by thaffirmative in thys fashion: If an heretique falsely translate the Newe Testament into Englishe, to make hys false heresyes seeme the Worde of Godde, be hys bookes worthy to be burned? To this question, asked in thys wyse, yf he will aunswere true Englishe, he must aunswere 'ye' and not 'yes'. But nowe if the question be asked hym thus, lo, by the negative: If an heretike falsely translate the Newe Testament in to Englishe, to make hys false heresyes seme the Word of God, be not his bokes well worthy to be burned? To thys question, in thys fashion framed, if he wyll aunswere trew Englyshe, he maye not aunswere 'ye,' but he must aunswere 'yes,' and say: 'Yes, mary be they, bothe the translation and the translatour, and al that wyll holde wyth them'.

"And thys thing, lo, though it be no great matter, yet I have thought good to give Tindall warning of, because I would have him write true one way or other, that, though I can not make him by no meane to write true matter, I would have him yet at the lestwise write true Englishe." *

In this passage we have "God" and "Godde," "Tyndal" and "Tindall," "heretike" and "heretyque," "true" and "trew," "aunswer," "aunswere," "answereth," "answerring," and *i* interchanged with *y, ad libitum.* What would be gained by reproducing this medley, to the confusion of the modern reader?—not even More's own spelling, if my theory of the type-setter's discretion or licence is correct. Yet the passage shows that More's words may not be tampered with. He wrote the purest English of his day, notwithstanding "the tone and the tother," which was no vulgarism.

14. STATE PAPERS. I now come to my principal reason for composing a new Life of the great chancellor, rather than translating or annotating Stapleton. It is, that we have access to many important documents unknown to him or to any former biographer. *The Calendars of Letters and Papers,* illustrating the reign of Henry VIII., have been carried through and beyond the life of Sir Thomas. The diligence of the accomplished editors, Dr. Brewer and Mr. James Gairdner, has left almost nothing unprinted, or at least unindicated, that concerns either Henry or those brought into relations with him. With these great volumes as my help and guide, I had already become pretty familiar with all that bears on the life of More when composing my Life of his fellow-martyr, Blessed John Fisher; but I

---

* *English Works,* p. 448. This passage is followed by very interesting remarks on the force of the Greek article, and how its force may be rendered in English.

have gone through all the volumes a second time, and
sought out the originals in the Record Office or British
Museum, wherever there seemed to remain anything to
be cleared up.

Such, then, are the materials of this Memoir. Of the
use made of them the writer is no competent judge.
His self-love suggests to him no higher merits than that
he has been industrious, and has worked with a sympathy for his subject. Sympathy, however, does not
mean either blindness or partiality. I could have no
real sympathy with such a man as Sir Thomas More if
I did not appreciate the freedom of his judgment, and
freely use my own with due proportion. Mr. Gairdner,
in a very kind notice of my *Life of Blessed John Fisher*
in the *Academy*, remarks that, "for the great majority
of Christians, the recent 'Beatification' of Fisher,
More, and others, has raised them beyond the reach of
criticism by a distinct act of authority. Rome has declared her judgment; and no fine, discriminating
touches, no delicate lights and shades, can be permitted
to interfere with the uniform brightness of one of her
saintly martyrs." Mr. Gairdner somewhat guards these
words by adding: "This, we suspect, is what an ordinary Protestant will think, and an ordinary Romanist
will really think the same, with this difference merely,
that the latter is submissive and humble before an
authority that the former does not feel himself in any
way bound to respect ".* Mr. Gairdner is, however,
here not quite accurate. Though he seems to allow
that a few exceptional "Romanists" will exercise a

* *Academy*, August 4, 1888, p. 64.

freer judgment, he is not authorised to suppose that
even the most solemn judgment of canonisation places
the object of it beyond a fair, candid, and intelligent
criticism, even for the most docile and ordinary
Catholics. But the life, character, and writings of
Sir Thomas More have been subjected to no authoritative scrutiny by the Holy See, and no judgment
whatever has been passed upon them. It is only as
martyrs of the faith that he and those included in the
decree of the 29th December, 1886, are declared Blessed.
But neither by this first decree, permitting their public
cultus, nor by any further and more precise judgment,
will the Church wish to convert the biographer into a
writer of legend or a mere panegyrist. Canonisation
surrounds the saintly head with a halo, but does not
transform the features so that we cannot steadily fix
our gaze upon them. If I have been sparing in criticism, it is because the longer and more minutely I
have studied those features, the more I have admired
and loved them.

A word in conclusion regarding the frontispiece.
Several beautiful engravings of More's portrait have
been published, which I might have reproduced. The
portrait that I have chosen is somewhat worn and
blurred, but then it is absolutely authentic. It has been
photographed from the original crayon sketch by Holbein
in the Windsor Collection. The copies have been made,
with Her Majesty's gracious permission, by Messrs.
Braun & Co., of Paris, and the Autotype Co., London.

NOTICE TO SECOND EDITION.

IN this second edition I have corrected some misprints and slight inaccuracies, and added a few notes and appendices, and a new index. No charge of serious error has been made by my reviewers, and I have found nothing to retract or defend. Professor J. A. Froude's *The Divorce of Catherine of Aragon* has appeared, in which he treats once more of the deaths of Fisher and of More. This is not the place to discuss his defence of the execution of the Bishop of Rochester. Of Sir Thomas More he says : " His execution has been uniformly condemned by historians as an act of wanton tyranny. It was not wanton, and it was not an act of tyranny. It was an inevitable and painful incident of an infinitely blessed revolution." Mr. Froude's sole argument is this : Fisher, though not accused thereof at his trial, *may* have been known to Henry to have been guilty of treason. More was his intimate friend. Therefore there was no injustice in suspecting him of being Fisher's accomplice, and beheading him on this suspicion, though under another pretext. The public press has rightly received these as " astounding statements ". (*The Speaker*, Nov. 21, 1891.)

It will be enough for me to quote the words of Professor Palgrave in his exquisite poem on Sir Thomas More :—

> Base days, that win the plaudits of the base,
> Writ to their own disgrace,
> With casuist sneer o'erglossing works of blood,
> Miscalling evil, good ;
> Before some despot-hero falsely named
> Grovelling in shameful worship unashamed.*

* *Visions of England*, by Francis T. Palgrave.

PREFACE TO THIRD EDITION.

THE present edition is identical with the second, with the exception of additions in the Appendix. On Nov. 19, 1898, F. Bridgett communicated the following paper to the *Tablet* newspaper. He wished that it should form a Preface to a new edition.   THE EDITOR.

"As sickness warns me that I cannot live to clear up, in a new edition of the *Life of Blessed T. More*, an important question which might, if misunderstood, even affect his canonisation, I ask leave to place on record in your paper some remarks on two statements that have appeared since my second edition.

"Mr. Wilfrid Ward's words:

"On the other hand Catholics have perhaps, at all events until recently, shown an inadequate appreciation of the peculiar state of things which made men like Sir Thomas More *for years uncertain* that, to remain within the English Church, after the breach with Rome, was to part company with the Church Catholic. [*Nineteenth Century* (November 1895), Art. "The Rigidity of Rome," p. 802.]

"Mr. Hutton's words:

"He was placed suddenly in face of a critical question. He answered it as his successors in the English Church would not now answer. But it would be difficult to find in his writings any formal statement of doctrine which the English Church since his day has ever formally abandoned. It would be idle indeed to dispute with Roman Hagiologists their right to revere him as a martyr of their own, but no true theological estimate would deny that he belongs to the historic and continuous Church of England (p. 282). He laid down his life rather than surrender, for fear of death, what he again and again admitted to be but an opinion. He would lay no burden on the souls of other men and he would not speak against the new laws, the divorce, the King's marriage, the measures by which the Church was freed from foreign subjection. These were matters upon which his own views had changed, and upon which he could not feel that his judgment need be final or binding for other men. He condemned no man ; but he would not yield an inch himself. To him, almost alone among his contemporaries, the conclusions of the intellect seemed no less sacred than the chastity of the body. He died rather than tarnish the whiteness of his soul. (*Life of Sir Thomas More*, p. 277.)

"As I understand these two writers, they take different, though not necessarily contradictory views. Mr. Ward affirms that More was for years uncertain as to the necessity of communion with Rome; he contends however that More's case was anomalous and cannot fairly be made a precedent. Mr. Hutton concedes that More died for the Roman supremacy, but only as for a probable opinion, which he was too conscientious to reject. To me it seems that both these writers have mistaken the subject matter of More's uncertainties, and the state of his conscience.

"I must ask the reader to refer back to the pages indicated in my *Life of Blessed More* (first or second edition).

"More once thought that Papal supremacy was of ecclesiastical origin. Did it take him several years to correct this opinion after his attention was given to the matter? He nowhere says this; he says that he thus thought: 'until I read in that matter those things that the King's highness had written' (p. 343). After he read the King's book, and by all that he had read for ten years on the subject, he was so convinced that the Roman See had supremacy by divine institution, that 'his conscience would be in right great peril, if I should follow the other side, and deny the primacy to be provided of God' (p. 343–344). This he wrote in 1534. In his Latin book against Luther, written in 1523, he had declared his entire agreement with Fisher on this subject (see p. 219). He merely says that his ten years' subsequent studies had confirmed this conclusion. I have given my interpretation of More's early error at p. 346.

"More was so far from thinking that it might be lawful to live in separation from the Roman See, that he says this would be unlawful, whether the supremacy were divine or merely ecclesiastical (p. 344). He professes no *uncertainty* on the matter.

"Nor did he think, as Mr. Hutton says, that the Divine Institution of the Papal Supremacy was within the limits of mere theological opinion, as to which men might take one side or the other, according to private convictions. Whatever a general council has decided must be held as undoubted, and private opinion must yield to it (pp. 344, 372). Now on this subject, he says, general councils have spoken (pp. 219, 344).

" He had collected much material on this subject, but had thought it best to suppress it at that time (p. 345). In this is the answer to Mr. Hutton's remark about the absence of dogmatical propositions or 'formal statements.'

" What then was the meaning of the phrase so often used by More, that he followed his own conscience, but did not blame others who followed theirs ? I reply that he does not use this phrase regarding the Papal supremacy. He uses it of the oath of succession (pp. 353, 380) as proposed to him. Cranmer took up the word, and said that if More did not blame others, he could not be very sure himself, and that, therefore, since the King was in possession, and More his subject, he was bound to obey in a doubt (p. 355). More at first was puzzled, but soon saw that the conclusion was too wide (p. 356). In fact even a monastic superior could not have obliged his subject to swear that the doctrine of the 'Immaculate Conception' was false, when he was convinced of its truth.

" To the argument of the Abbot of Westminster, that he might yield to the authority of numbers, he replied that the authority was on his own side (p. 356). He referred, of course, not to England, but to the continent, and to the principles laid down in the preamble of the Act of succession. Now, as to this oath, it must be remarked that he could have taken it, if otherwise framed—that Fisher would have taken it in a form that More could not have accepted (p. 371); that More suggests several ways in which he supposes people might have taken it (p. 371), which he does not approve, but it was not for him to censure—also that he had, besides the reasons suggested by Cranmer (p. 358), other private reasons that he never had disclosed and never would disclose (pp. 375, 381-382); yet he was very strongly convinced. He was sure he could never change his mind (p. 380).

"Another question was the *king's supremacy*. This question must not be confounded with that of the Pope's supremacy, as if the one was the direct contradictory of the other. A man might deny the Pope's supremacy, yet not admit the king's—and he might admit the king's *in certain matters*, and yet not deny the Pope's. Yet More does not use the same language on this matter as on the oath of succession. He says he has a right to maintain silence (403), and would not even say until after his condemnation that his conscience went against the statute (406).

"Cromwell made a subtle objection—viz., that More had himself used inquisitorial power, and had not allowed people to be silent regarding the Pope's supremacy (407); why then might not the king demand an answer? More's answer is noteworthy. He says the Pope's supremacy is a matter *belonging to the common faith of the Church*—the king's is only an affair of this realm (p. 407).

"As regards the words about conscience (p. 408) it is clear that the members of the Council twitted him with his unsure conscience; but, as he had declared that he would not say how his conscience stood with regard to the king's supremacy, they must have been speaking

about the oath of succession.   If, however, they spoke of
the king's supremacy, his words must not be applied to
papal supremacy.   As to Rich's assertions, they are of
no value (pp. 418-419).

"At his trial he affirmed that he had never declared his
conscience as to the king's supremacy (p. 421), he had
told Fisher to inform his conscience on the matter
(p. 421), and had only put a hypothesis as regards his
own conscience (p. 421).

"After his sentence he declared that all doctors
and councils were against royal supremacy (p. 422),
and that he had studied this question for seven years
(p. 422).

"It should be clearly marked that already in 1534 he
had studied papal supremacy for ten years (p. 343), and
the question of royal supremacy for seven in 1535
(p. 422).   These two sayings have been constantly confused; yet they are utterly distinct.   He had been
aroused to the matter of the papal supremacy by Henry's
book in 1522; and to the royal supremacy by the divorce
proceedings of 1528.

"For what, then, did More die?   Directly, he died for
rejecting the king's supremacy.   This is the only matter
objected in the indictment, where there is not a word
about the Pope.   Yet, *indirectly*, he died for the
supremacy of the Holy See (pp. 422–424).

"I see then no grounds whatever for Mr. Ward's statement; and Mr. Hutton appears to me to have applied to
papal supremacy what More said only of the oath of
succession.   More did not hold the papal supremacy

as a merely probable theological conclusion, but as a matter of defined faith."

When the above paper appeared in the *Tablet*, F. Bridgett received the following letter from Mr. James Gairdner of the Record Office :—

"PINNEO, 23*rd Nov.* 1898.

"I really agree with you very much—indeed I might almost say completely—especially in your conclusion. More died 'directly' for rejecting the king's supremacy—that was why he was condemned. Indirectly, as you say, he suffered for his faith in the supremacy of the Holy See. But if we take cognisance of a cause for which he 'indirectly' suffered, he also died to uphold the sanctity of marriage, of which at that time there seemed apparently no other guarantee than papal jurisdiction. Nor did he and others die in vain, who protested against moral laws being twisted and turned upside down by royal authority to satisfy lust and self-will.—Yours very sincerely, JAMES GAIRDNER."

DECREE

[OF THE CONGREGATION OF SACRED RITES]

CONFIRMING THE HONOUR GIVEN TO THE
BLESSED MARTYRS,

JOHN CARDINAL FISHER, THOMAS MORE,

AND OTHERS,

PUT TO DEATH IN ENGLAND FOR THE FAITH
FROM THE YEAR 1535 TO 1583.

———————

ENGLAND, once called the Island of Saints and the Dowry of the Virgin Mother of God, as even from the first ages of the Church it had been renowned for the sufferings of many Martyrs, so also, when it was torn by the fearful schism of the sixteenth century from the obedience and communion of the Roman See, was not without the testimony of those who, *for the dignity of this See, and for the truth of the orthodox Faith, did not hesitate to lay down their lives by the shedding of their blood.**

In this most noble band of Martyrs nothing whatever is wanting to its completeness or its honour : neither the grandeur of the Roman purple, nor the venerable dignity of Bishops, nor the fortitude of the Clergy both secular and regular, nor the invincible firmness of the weaker sex. Eminent amongst them is JOHN FISHER, Bishop of Rochester and Cardinal of the Holy Roman Church, whom Paul III. speaks of in his Letters as *conspicuous for sanctity, celebrated for learning, venerable by age, an honour and an ornament to the kingdom, and to the Clergy of the whole world.* With him must be named the layman THOMAS MORE, Chancellor of England, whom the same Pontiff deservedly extols, as *excelling in sacred learning, and courageous in the defence of truth.*

* Gregory XIII. Constitution, *Quoniam divinae bonitati*, 1st May, 1579.

The most authoritative ecclesiastical historians, therefore, are unanimously of opinion that they all shed their blood for the defence, restoration, and preservation of the Catholic Faith. Gregory XIII. even granted in their honour several privileges appertaining to public and ecclesiastical worship; and chiefly that of using their relics in the consecration of altars, when relics of ancient Holy Martyrs could not be had. Moreover, after he had caused the sufferings of the Christian Martyrs to be painted in fresco by Nicholas Circiniana in the Church of St. Stephen on the Coelian Hill, he permitted also the Martyrs of the Church in England, both of ancient and of more recent times, to be represented in like manner by the same artist in the English Church of the Most Holy Trinity in Rome, including those who, from the year 1535 to 1583, had died under King Henry VIII. and Queen Elizabeth, for the Catholic Faith and for the Primacy of the Roman Pontiff. The representations of these martyrdoms painted in the said Church remained, with the knowledge and approbation of the Roman Pontiffs who succeeded Gregory XIII., for two centuries, until, about the end of the last century, they were destroyed by wicked men. But copies of them still remained; for in the year 1584, by privilege of the said Gregory XIII., they had been engraved at Rome on copper-plate with the title: *Sufferings of the Holy Martyrs who, in ancient and more recent times of persecution, have been put to death in England for Christ, and for professing the truth of the Catholic Faith.* From this record, either by inscriptions placed beneath them, or by other sure indications, many of these Martyrs are known by name; that is to say, fifty-four. They are:—

Those who suffered death under King Henry VIII.: *John Fisher*, Bishop of Rochester, Cardinal of the Holy Roman Church; *Thomas More*, Chancellor of England; *Margaret Pole*, Countess of Salisbury, mother of Cardinal Pole; *Richard Reynolds*, of the Order of St. Bridget; *John Haile*, Priest; eighteen Carthusians—namely, *John Houghton, Augustine Webster, Robert Laurence, William Exmew, Humphrey Middlemore, Sebastian Newdigate, John Rochester, James Walworth, William Greenwood, John Davy, Robert Salt, Walter Pierson, Thomas Green, Thomas Scryven, Thomas Redyng, Thomas Johnson, Richard Bere,* and *William Horne; John Forest,* Priest of the Order of St. Francis; *John Stone,* of the Order of St. Augustine; four Secular Priests—*Thomas Abel, Edward Powel, Richard Fetherston, John Larke;* and *German Gardiner,* a layman.

Those who suffered under Elizabeth: Priests—*Cuthbert Mayne, John Nelson, Everard Hanse, Rodolph Sherwin, John Payne, Thomas Ford, John Shert, Robert Johnson, William Fylby, Luke Kirby, Laurence*

Richardson, William Lacy, Richard Kirkman, James Hudson or *Tompson, William Hart, Richard Thirkeld, Thomas Woodhouse,* and —— *Plumtree.* Also three Priests of the Society of Jesus—*Edmund Campion, Alexander Briant,* and *Thomas Cottam.* Lastly, *John Storey,* Doctor of Laws ; *John Felton* and *Thomas Sherwood,* laymen.

Until lately, the Cause of these Martyrs had never been officially treated. Some time ago, in the year 1860, Cardinal Nicholas Wiseman, of illustrious memory, Archbishop of Westminster, and the other Bishops of England, petitioned the Sovereign Pontiff Pius IX., of sacred memory, to institute for the whole of England a Festival in honour of all Holy Martyrs, that is to say, even of those *who, though not yet declared to be such, have in latter times, for their defence of the Catholic Religion, and especially for asserting the authority of the Apostolic See, fallen by the hands of wicked men and resisted unto blood.* But as, according to the prevailing practice of the Congregation of Sacred Rites, a Festival can be instituted in regard only to those Servants of God to whom ecclesiastical honour (*cultus*) has been already given and rightly sanctioned by the Apostolic See, the said petition was not granted. Wherefore, in these last years, a new petition was presented to Our Holy Father the Sovereign Pontiff Leo XIII., by His Eminence Cardinal Henry Edward Manning, the present Archbishop of Westminster, and the other Bishops of England, together with the Ordinary Process which had been there completed, and other authentic documents, in which were contained the proofs of Martyrdom as to those who suffered from the year 1535 to 1583, and also the aforesaid concessions of the Roman Pontiffs in regard to those above-mentioned.

Our Holy Father was pleased to commit the examination of the whole matter to a Special Congregation, consisting of several Cardinals of the Holy Roman Church and of Officials of the Congregation of Sacred Rites—the examination to be preceded by a Disquisition, to be drawn up by the Right Reverend Augustine Caprara, Promoter of the Holy Faith. In this Special Congregation, assembled at the Vatican on the 4th day of December of the present year, the undersigned Cardinal Dominic Bartolini, Prefect of the said Sacred Congregation, who had charge of the Cause, proposed the following question : "*Whether, by reason of the special concessions of the Roman Pontiffs, in regard to the earlier Martyrs of England—who, from the year 1535 to 1583, suffered death for the Catholic Faith, and for the Primacy of the Roman Pontiff in the Church, and whose Martyrdoms were formerly painted, by authority of the Sovereign Pontiff Gregory XIII., in the English Church of the Most Holy Trinity in Rome, and in the year 1584 were engraved at Rome on copper-plate by privilege of the same Pontiff—there is evidence of the con-*

cession of public ecclesiastical honour, or of this being a case excepted by the Decrees of Pope Urban VIII., of Sacred Memory, in the matter and to the effect under consideration ".   The Most Eminent and Most Reverend Fathers, and the Official Prelates, after hearing the written and oral report of the aforesaid Promoter of the Holy Faith, and after the matter in regard to the fifty-four Martyrs above-named had been fully discussed, were of opinion that the answer to be given was : "*Affirmatively, or That it is proved to be a case excepted* ".

The undersigned Secretary having made a faithful report of all that precedes to Our Holy Father POPE LEO XIII., His Holiness vouchsafed to approve the decision of the Sacred Special Congregation, on the 9th day of December, 1886.

The present Decree was issued on this 29th day of December, sacred to the Martyr Thomas Archbishop of Canterbury, whose faith and constancy these Blessed Martyrs so strenuously imitated.

     D. CARDINAL BARTOLINI,
            PREFECT OF THE CONGREGATION OF SACRED RITES.
               LAURENCE SALVATI,
                     Secretary.

L. ✠ S.

TABLE OF CONTENTS.

c

SIR THOMAS MORE

LIFE OF SIR THOMAS MORE.

CHAPTER I.

CHILDHOOD.

BLESSED Thomas More, hitherto known as Sir Thomas More, Lord Chancellor of England, was the eldest son of John More, Gentleman, afterwards Sir John More, Knight, puisne judge of the King's Bench in the time of Henry VIII.

The early lives of Sir Thomas More place his birth in the year 1480, thus making him about fifty-five years old at the time of his martyrdom.* A recent discovery has proved that

---

* His son-in-law, Roper, says nothing of his age, nor does Harpsfield. Cresacre More says he was born in 1480. He seems to have taken this date from the family picture, commonly called the Burford Picture, painted in 1593. On this picture is an inscription stating that in 1505 Sir Thomas was in the twenty-sixth year of his age, and that he was in his fifty-fifth year at his death—6th July, 1535. The error arose from supposing that the more famous Holbein family picture, on which the ages are noted, was painted in 1530; for on this Sir Thomas is declared to be in his fiftieth year. The picture, however, was painted not later than January, 1528. This will be shown later on. Stapleton errs still more widely. In Chapter IV. he says that More wrote the *Utopia* in 1516, being then in his thirty-fourth year, and died in 1535, in his fifty-second year. This would place his birth in the latter part of 1482. Again, in Chapter VI., he says that at his death he was not yet fully fifty-two years old. The same mistake occurs in Chapter I. Though Stapleton was intimate with members of More's household, they apparently only guessed at his age, and it would seem from their mistake that he looked younger than he really was. Blessed John Fisher's looks, on the contrary, caused his age to be greatly exaggerated.

he was in reality two years older. The same document makes known to us the maiden name of his mother, and the correct number of his brothers and sisters. Stapleton could not discover the mother's name. Cresacre More gives it as Handcomb of Holiwell, in Bedfordshire. This, however, w is possibly the name—not of Sir Thomas's mother, but of his father's second wife.* The ignorance and mistakes are easily accounted for by the seizure of all family papers by the king at the at tainder of Sir Thomas.

In 1868, Mr. William Aldis Wright discovered, on the last leaves of a MS. in the Library of Trinity College, Cambridge, a series of family records, which supply names and dates till then unknown.† From these it appears that John More married on 24th April, 1474, Agnes, daughter of Thomas Graunger, in the parish of St. Giles in Cripplegate Without, London. They had issue, three sons and three daughters. The eldest child, Jane, was born on 11th March, 1475. The second child was Thomas, the future chancellor and martyr. The entry says : " On the Friday next after the Feast of the Purification of the Blessed Virgin Mary, viz., the seventh day of February, between the second and third hours of the morning, was born Thomas More, son of John More, Gentleman, in the 17th year of the reign of Edward IV." ‡ In the year 1478, 7th February was Saturday ; but by a natural confusion it has been set down as Friday, since the birth took place soon after midnight.

* According, however, to Mr. Foss, John More's second wife was Mrs. Bowes, a widow, whose maiden name was Barton (*Lives of Judges*, vi. 198). The third wife's name was More.

† See *Notes and Queries*, 17th October, 1868 ; also 31st October and 5th November ; republished also in Mr. Seebohm's *Oxford Reformers*, 2nd edition (1869). App. C.

‡ Md quod die veneris proximo post Festum purificacionis beate Marie virginis videlicet septimo die Februarii inter horam secundam et horam tertiam in mane natus fuit Thomas More filius Joannis More Gent. anno regni Regis Edwardi quarti post conquestum Angliæ decimo septimo.

Agatha, a third child, was born 31st January, 1479 ; John, the fourth, on 6th June, 1480 ; Edward, the fifth, on 3rd September, 1481 : and Elizabeth, the sixth and last, on 22nd September, 1482. Stapleton says Thomas had no brothers, and only two sisters, Jane and Elizabeth. This is repeated by Cresacre More, who adds another error in making Elizabeth older than Thomas. It is probable that John, Edward, and Agatha all died in their infancy.

In the epitaph which Sir Thomas prepared for himself, he says that he was born of "a family, not illustrious, yet honour-able ".* He was not noble, says his great-grandson, "as we here in England take nobility ; for none under a baron (except he be of the Privy Council) doth challenge it ; but as the word is taken in other countries for gentry, it was otherwise. For Judge More, " (the father of Sir Thomas), bare arms from his birth, having his coat quartered, which doth argue that he came to his inheritance by descent, and therefore, although by reason of King Henry's seizure of all our evidences, we cannot certainly tell who were Sir John's ancestors, yet must they needs be gentlemen ; and, as I have heard, they either came out of the Mores of Ireland, or they of Ireland came out of us ".†

Mr. Edward Foss, who has gone into the question of More's origin with much detail, differs entirely in his view as to the nobility of his family. His researches have led him to discover three men of the name of John More, connected with the Inns of Court. There was one in the Middle Temple who was reader in that society in 1505, and again in 1512. Mr. Foss gives convincing reasons that this gentleman cannot have been the future judge, who belonged to Lincoln's Inn, not to the Temple. Now, two John Mores were members of the society

---

* Familia non celebri sed honesta natus.

† *Life of More*, chap. i.

of Lincoln's Inn.   One had been butler * and steward, and was
admitted a student in 1470.   He was subsequently called to the
bar and became a bencher, and was appointed reader in 1489.
As he had been already a long time (*diu*) butler in 1470, we
must suppose him to have been forty, or at least thirty-five,
years old when he became a student.   He cannot then have
been the John More who was appointed judge in 1517, and
who died in 1530, aged seventy-eight.

   There is, however, a second John More in that society, who,
in 1482, is called Junior.   He also was butler, and Mr. Foss
takes him to have been a son of the one just mentioned, and
the father of Sir Thomas ; and he thinks he was raised from
the position he occupied to become a member of the society
by his father's influence.   Whatever may be the truth with
regard to this matter, the father of the future chancellor
received the coif of sergeant-at-law in November, 1503.   He
became a judge in the Court of Common Pleas in November,
1517, and was transferred to the King's Bench probably in
April, 1520.†

   A few years before his death, Sir Thomas composed his
own epitaph, in which he thus speaks of his father, who was
lately deceased : " His father, John More, Knight, appointed
by his king to the order of judges called the King's Bench,
was a man courteous, affable, innocent, gentle, merciful, just,
and uncorrupted ".   The crayon sketch made by Holbein of
this venerable man in 1527, when he was in his seventy-sixth
year, is still in existence in the Windsor collection.   It is a
charming face, full of life and kindly mirth.   He seems to be
uttering one of the pleasant sayings for which he is said to
have been famous, though eclipsed by his more brilliant son.
Two of these, which Sir Thomas has preserved for us, are

   * We need not think of this office as a mere menial function.   We find
noblemen bearing the title, and receiving a salary as " butler " to a
corporation.

   † On the pedigree and arms of Sir Thomas, see Appendix A.

somewhat satirical upon women, although the son quotes them only as amusing illustrations for other purposes : "I would that we were all in the case with our own faults, as my father saith that we be with our wives. For when he heareth folk blame wives, and say that there be so many of them shrews, he saith that they defame them falsely. For he saith plainly that there is but one shrew-wife in the world, but he saith indeed that every man weeneth he hath her, and that that one is his own. So would I fain that every man would ween there were but one man naught [good-for-nothing] in all the whole world, and that that one were himself." * And in another place, speaking about a man's choosing his religion among the various sects : "But now, if ye were in the case that I have heard my father merrily say every man is at the choice of his wife, that ye should put your hand into a blind bag full of snakes and eels together, seven snakes for one eel, ye would, I ween, reckon it a perilous choice to take up one at adventure, though ye had made your special prayer to speed well".† As Sir John More was three times married, it would be interesting to know the date of these sayings, and whether they embody the fruits of his experience, or were a kind of humorous philosophy, which formed no guide of his life. One of his son's epigrams alludes to this class of sharp sayings about wives :-

Hoc quisque dicit ; dicit, at ducit tamen,
Quin sex sepultis septimam ducit tamen.

John Clements heard Sir Thomas repeat what he had heard from his father, Sir John : that his first wife in a dream saw engraved on her marriage ring, as in a series of cameos, the names and likenesses of the children she should bear. One of these was so obscure that she could not recognise it, and this referred to a child of untimely birth ; another shone far brighter than the rest. It is to be supposed that it was after

* *English Works*, p. 233. † *Ib.*, p. 165.

his son's elevation to the chancellorship, which the old man lived to witness, that he remembered and related this story of his young wife's dream.*

A tradition was handed down in the family that when Thomas was an infant, his nurse was carrying him in her arms as she forded a river on horseback. The horse stumbled in ascending the bank; the nurse, in fear of falling into the water, threw the child over the neighbouring hedge. When she got safe to land she found the babe lying unhurt, and laughing as she stooped to pick him up.†

John More, at the time of his son's birth and long after, lived in Milk Street, in the city of London. Thomas was born in the heat of the civil wars of the Roses, and, being five years old at the death of Edward IV., overheard a neighbour relate to his father a prediction made by one of the followers of the Duke of York, afterwards Richard III., that his master would be king. This prediction, so soon followed by its fulfilment, made so deep an impression on the child that he never forgot it.‡

Roper, and after him Harpsfield and Stapleton, mention that the school in which young Thomas learned the rudiments of Latin was St. Anthony's, a free school belonging to the Hospital of St. Anthony in Threadneedle Street, London, at that time taught by an excellent master, Nicolas Holt.§ It had

* When a dream passes through five mouths—the mother, Sir John, Sir Thomas, Clements, Stapleton—and is at last written down 100 years after its occurrence, we cannot be sure of its original form. At all events it was not Sander's invention, as Burnet affirms. Stapleton says: Thomam Morum ex patre suo referentem audivit Joannes Clemens (*Vita Mori*, cap. 1).

† Stapleton may have learnt this from Mrs. Clements or from Dorothy Harris.

‡ Quem ego sermonem ab eo memini patri meo renuntiatum. The words are not in the English version of the *History of Richard III.*

§ Holt was author of a Latin grammar called *Lac Puerorum* (Foss, vi. 203).

been founded by Henry VI. in 1445. Thence he was transferred to the household of Cardinal Morton, Archbishop of Canterbury. The households of great ecclesiastics were schools both of learning and good breeding for the sons of the gentry, and even of the higher nobility. Many years later, and long after the Cardinal's death, More put the following description of his patron in the mouth of Hythloday, the supposed traveller to Utopia :—

" The Cardinal was of a middle stature, retaining his strength even in advanced age ; his looks begot reverence rather than fear ; his conversation was easy, but serious and grave ; he sometimes took pleasure to try the force of those that came as suitors to him upon business by speaking sharply, though decently, to them, and by that he discovered their spirit and presence of mind ; with which he was much delighted when it did not grow up to impudence, as bearing a great resemblance to his own temper, and he looked on such persons as the fittest men for affairs. He spoke both gracefully and weightily ; he was eminently skilled in the law, had a vast understanding, and a prodigious memory ; and those excellent talents with which nature had furnished him were improved by study and experience. When I was in England the king depended much on his counsels, and the Government seemed to be chiefly supported by him : for from his youth he had been all along practised in affairs ; and, having passed through many traverses of fortune, he had, with great cost, acquired a vast stock of wisdom, which is not soon lost when it is purchased so dear." *

It must certainly be counted among the special graces of More that his mind, so shrewd and inclined to satire, formed its first impressions of the Church from the frequentation of so excellent a prelate as Morton, rather than in the household of a Bainbridge or a Wolsey ; for, though the Church of

* *Utopia* (Burnet's translation).

Jesus Christ, as a Divine institution, is independent of its earthly representatives, yet a mind early prejudiced acquires with difficulty that well-balanced judgment that is able to consider calmly good and evil, and to assign each to its proper source.*

It was also very fortunate for More that Cardinal Morton formed a favourable opinion of the youth who had been committed to him. Roper writes as follows : "Though More were young of years, yet would he at Christmas suddenly sometimes step in among the players, and, never studying for the matter, make a part of his own there presently among them, which made the lookers-on more sport than the players beside.† In whose wit and towardness the Cardinal much delighting, would often say of him to the nobles that divers times dined with him : 'This child here waiting at the table, whoever shall live to see it, will prove a marvellous man'. Whereupon, for his better furtherance in learning, he placed him at Oxford."

---

* A Catholic writer, in the *Dublin Review* for June, 1858, says that "a tone of cold and sneering disrespect towards the Holy See pervades More's *Utopia* ; and that it is impossible not to see that More had imbibed these ideas from Cardinal Morton's conversation". As I can find no such tone in More's *Utopia*, it is impossible for me to attribute it to Morton's influence.

† These Christmas plays were, no doubt, in English ; Sir Thomas, however, in his *Utopia*, alludes to the plays of Plautus as if they were not unknown to the English stage, probably in the schools or universities. or inns of court.

CHAPTER II.

YOUTH.

IT was probably in the year 1492, when he was fourteen years old, that More was sent to the university. Of his Oxford career our information is very scanty. Roper merely says that Cardinal Morton "placed him at Oxford, where, when he was in the Greek and Latin tongues sufficiently instructed, he was then for the study of the law put to an Inn of Chancery". Harpsfield, an Oxford man, was able to add the length of his stay at the university: "For the short time of his abode," he writes, "being not fully two years, and for his age, he wonderfully profited in the Latin and Greek tongues; where if he had settled and fixed himself, and run his full race in the study of the liberal sciences and divinity, I trow he would have been the singular and only spectacle of this our time for learning". Cresacre adds that he was placed at Canterbury Hall.* This hall had been founded by Archbishop Islip in 1363, and was intended principally for the study of the canon and civil law. At the suppression it was transferred by Henry to his (or rather Wolsey's) great foundation of Christ Church. Its site is now occupied by Canterbury Quadrangle of that college.

It was easy for the Cardinal to find him an entrance in this hall. We are not told how far he contributed to his maintenance there. The life of a scholar, as provided by the foundation, was a hard one. More placed it at the lowest

---

* St. Mary's Hall has been mentioned by others as his residence.

degree of his experiences.   In his address to his family after
resigning the chancellorship, he said : " I have been brought
up at Oxford, at an Inn of the Chancery, at Lincoln's Inn, and
also in the King's Court, and so from the least degree to the
highest ".   If it is true that More's father was the quondam
butler of Lincoln's Inn, he would be only a young and struggling
barrister, burdened with a large family, at the period of his
son's Oxford residence.

Certain it is that More's allowance from his father did not
in any way mitigate the penury of his life, which is thus
described by Stapleton : " Grocyn had recently returned from
Italy, and was the first who brought Greek letters into England,
and publicly taught them at Oxford.   From his companion,
Thomas Linacre, More learnt Greek at Oxford, as he himself
mentions in his epistle to Dorpius.*   His father, however,
while desirous to give his son a liberal education, wished that
he should learn from his earliest years to be frugal and sober,
and to love nothing but his studies and literature.   For this
reason he gave him the bare necessaries, and would not allow
him a farthing to spend freely.   This he carried out so strictly
that he had not money to mend his worn-out shoes, without
asking it from his father.   More used often to relate this conduct of his father, and greatly extolled it.   ' It was thus ' (he
would say) ' that I indulged in no vice or pleasure, and spent
my time in no vain or hurtful amusements ; I did not know
what luxury meant, and never learnt to use money badly ; in a
word, I loved and thought of nothing but my studies.' "   These
words are the more remarkable that More was not defending
his treatment of his own children by the example of his father,
for we shall see that he could be very generous.

Erasmus declares that More's father, both while his son was
at Oxford and afterwards, treated him thus severely because he

---

* Quum ipse jam olim Aristotelis opus audirem Græce, perlegente
mihi atque interpretante Linacro.

saw him too much addicted to literature,* and feared that he might neglect his legal studies. Such a testimony cannot be lightly set aside, since Erasmus became intimate with More in his early manhood; but it is pushing the words of Erasmus beyond their necessary reach to suppose, as some have done, that John More was unwilling that his son should learn Greek, or that Thomas gave himself to this study in distinct opposition to his father's will. For, according to his biographers, his filial piety and deference to his father's wishes knew no bounds, and he seems to have complied with them fully by vigorously prosecuting his legal studies, and giving to literature those hours only which he could save from sleep or recreation.

Stapleton on this head writes : " Throughout his whole life he was most reverent towards his father, so that he neither offended him in anything, nor took offence at anything said or done by him. When he was chancellor he did not hesitate, publicly in the palace of Westminster, to kneel down and ask his father's blessing, according to the excellent custom of our country. For with us children are wont both morning and evening to kneel and ask the blessing of both parents, though, when grown up and married, especially in the higher classes, they discontinue the practice, whereas More continued it."

Besides Greek and Latin, he learned, in his youth, French, music, arithmetic, and geometry, and read every book of history he could procure. He was fond of music, and learned to play on the viol,† as well as on the flute.

If More's study of Greek was for the sake of the treasures of literature and philosophy embodied in that language, he studied Latin no less for its practical utility. Latin was still in a sense a

---

* Bonas literas a primis statim annis hauserat. Juvenis ad Græcas literas ac philosophiæ studium sese applicuit, adeo non opitulante patre, viro alioqui prudenti proboque, ut ea conantem omni subsidio destitueret ac pene pro abdicato haberet, quod a patriis studiis desciscere videretur (*Epist.* 605, to be given in full later on).

† Stapleton, cap. 2.

living language.   It was the means of communication not only in
the Church, but between statesmen, ambassadors, and the learned
and cultured of every country.   It was necessary to write and
to speak it with facility and elegance as well as to read it.
Probably not many days passed in More's life in which he was
not called on to converse in Latin.   His style was greatly
admired by his critical contemporaries.   It was not formed
without much labour.   Erasmus, in saying that More strove long
to render it easy and harmonious,* seems to imply that at first
it was somewhat involved or harsh.   It has been called
Erasmian, yet no one who has a moderate acquaintance with
the two writers could mistake one for the other, any more than
an Englishman at all familiar with our literature could attribute
a page of Johnson to Addison.

Richard Pace, secretary of Latin letters to Henry VIII. and
Dean of St. Paul's, himself an elegant scholar, and a very intimate friend of More's, published in 1517 a short Latin treatise
on "The Fruit to be derived from Learning".   In it he has some
interesting remarks on More's genius and scholarship.   I translate a few passages : " Here I will remark that no one ever lived
who did not first ascertain the meaning of words, and from
them gather the meaning of the sentences which they compose—
no one, I say, with one single exception, and that is our own
Thomas More.   For he is wont to gather the force of the words
from the sentences in which they occur, especially in his study
and translation of Greek.   This is not contrary to grammar,
but above it, and an instinct of genius.   Indeed, his genius is
more than human, and his learning not only eminent, but so
various, that there is nothing of which he seems to be ignorant.
His eloquence is incomparable and twofold, for he speaks with
the same facility in Latin as in his own language.   His sense
of fun is joined with perfect refinement—you may call humour

---

* **Diu luctatus est ut prosam orationem redderet molliorem, per omne
scripti genus stylum exercens** (*Ep.* 447).

his father, and wit his mother.* When the matter requires it, he can imitate a good cook, and serve up the meat in sharp sauce. . . . He has declared open war against such as give utterance to things that are neither true nor probable, and beyond the capacity or knowledge of the speaker. Thus he once heard two Scotist theologians, men of a certain importance, and preachers, seriously affirm that King Arthur—whom some deny ever to have been born, and others ever to have died— had made himself a cloak of the beards of the giants whom he had killed in battle. When More asked them how that could be, the elder of the two, putting on a grave countenance, re- plied : ' The reason, my youth, is clear, for the skin of a dead man is elastic '. The other, hearing this, not only assented, but admired the answer as subtle and Scotistic. More was but a boy, but he answered : ' What you say was hitherto quite as unknown to me as it was perfectly well known that one of you milks a he-goat while the other holds a sieve '.† When he saw that they did not understand his meaning, he laughed to him- self, and went his way.

"I regret to say that More has frequently the ill-luck that when- ever he says something very learned or acute among such digni- fied ‡ fathers in reference to their science, which is also quite as much his own, they always oppose him, and call his words puerile. It is not that they really think him wrong, or that he says anything puerile, but that they are jealous of his mar- vellous talent, and of his knowledge of so many other things of which they are ignorant." §

* Iam adeo non vulgariter facetus et urbanus, ut leporem ipsum ei patrem et facetiam matrem fuisse judices. Perhaps Pace had in his mind the words of Job: " I have said to rottenness : Thou art my father ; to worms, my mother and my sister " (*Job* xvii. 14).

† An allusion to an epigram of Martial.

‡ Leucomitratos—"white-mitred," or more probably "white-girdled," in allusion to the white cord of the Minorites ; for there does not seem to be any reference to bishops. Perhaps merely "white-haired".

§ *De Fructu qui ex doctrina percipitur*, p. 82 (ed. 1517).

Of More's Latin writings much will be said later on. This may be a fit place to mention some of his first efforts in English literature. William Rastell, in the time of Queen Mary, gathered together and reprinted whatever he could find of his Uncle More's boyish essays; amongst them are some English verses that More would gladly have let pass into oblivion. "A merry tale how a serjeant would learn to play the frere." I cannot say that there is much merriment in this piece. A line or two will be enough as a specimen of his rhyming powers :—

> A man of law that never saw
>   The ways to buy and sell,
> Weening to rise by merchandise—
>   I pray God speed him well.
> A merchant eke that will go seek,
>   By all the means he may,
> To fall in suit, till he dispute
>   His living clean away,
> Pleading the law for every straw,
>   Shall prove a thrifty man,
> With hate and strife; but, by my life,
>   I cannot tell you when. *

He printed at the beginning of a "Book of Fortune" a large number of verses in the seven-line stanzas then so popular. Though they are only the commonplaces of a clever boy's theme, yet they curiously represent the philosophy of his life, and the "Dialogue" which he wrote in the Tower when preparing for death is in many points only a development of this essay of his youth. He never at any time of his life lost sight of what he had written as a boy about Fortune's Wheel :—

> Alas! the foolish people cannot cease
> Ne void her train, till they the harm do feel—
> About her always busily they press;
> But, Lord! how he doth think himself full well
> That may set once his hand upon her wheel;
> He holdeth fast, but upward as he flieth,
> She whippeth her wheel about, and there he lieth.

* Always written by More "whan," and doubtless so pronounced

The following stanza is very striking and harmonious, and might have been written by Spenser or by Gray:—

> Fast by her side doth weary Labour stand,
> Pale Fear also, and Sorrow all bewept,
> Disdain and Hatred on that other hand
> Eke restless watch, from sleep with travail kept
> His eyes drowsy, and looking as he slept,
> Before her standeth Danger and Envy,
> Flattery, Deceit, Mischief and Tyranny.

Among the freaks of Fortune was one with which the preceding reigns had made the minds of men in England but too familiar:—

> She suddenly enhanceth them aloft,
>   And suddenly mischieveth all the flock;
> The head that late lay easily and full soft,
>   Instead of pillows lieth after on the block.

The Block! It is a popular superstition that when a cold shiver goes suddenly over a man, without any apparent cause, it is because someone has stepped over his future grave. Did any shadow pass over the bright and handsome face of young More when he wrote that terrible word—the Block? Or was it rather a halo that played for a moment around his brow?

There is another effort of his English Muse which gives greater promise than the preceding that he might, had he given himself to this species of composition, have anticipated something of the beauties of the Elizabethan poets. It is "A Rueful Lamentation" on the death of Queen Elizabeth—commonly called the Good—the wife of Henry VII. She died on 11th February, 1503. More was just twenty-five years old. On such occasions it was customary for scholars to make an offering of verse at Court. The poet represents the queen on her death-bed, taking her last farewell. Each stanza ends with the words, "and lo! now here I lie". The following lines remind us that the name of Shene had lately been exchanged for that of Richmond, in honour of the king's mother—Lady Margaret, Countess of Richmond—and that the king was building the beautiful chapel in Westminster Abbey that still bears his name :—

> Where are our castles, now where are our towers ?
> Goodly Richmond, soon art thou gone from me;
> At Westminster that costly work of yours,
> Mine own dear lord, now shall I never see.
> Almighty God vouchsafe to grant that ye
> For you and your children well may edify.
> My palace builded is, and lo! now here I lie.

After taking leave of her husband, she thus addresses her children. To understand the allusions, it must be remembered that Arthur, the eldest son, had been dead nearly a year; Margaret, the eldest daughter, had been lately married by proxy to the King of Scotland, but had not yet left England :—

> Farewell, my daughter, Lady Margaret,
> God wot full oft it grieved hath my mind
> That ye should go where we should seldom meet ;
> Now am I gone, and have left you behind.
> O mortal folk, that we be very blind !
> That we least fear, full oft it is most nigh.
> From you depart I first, and lo! now here I lie.

> Adieu, Lord Henry, my loving son, adieu!
> Our Lord increase your honour and estate.
> Adieu, my daughter Mary, bright of hue!
> God make you virtuous wife and fortunate.*
> Adieu, sweetheart, my little daughter Kate!
> Thou shalt, sweet babe—such is thy destiny—
> Thy mother never know, for lo! now here I lie. †

She then addresses her sisters, the youngest of whom, Bridget, was a Dominican nun at Dartford :—

---

* She was married to Louis XII., King of France and afterwards to Charles Brandon, Duke of Suffolk.

† This princess died in her infancy.

Lady Cecily, Anne and Katharine,
Farewell, my well-beloved sisters three;
O Lady Bridget! other sister mine,
Lo! here the end of worldly vanity;
Now well are ye that earthly folly flee,
And heavenly thingës love and magnify.
Farewell, and pray for me, for lo! now here I lie.

But More was neither destined to rival Skelton as poet-laureate nor to become illustrious among our English poets. His fame in literature rests rather on his Latin epigrams, and, still more, on his *Utopia*, which must be treated of when we come to the time of their publication. But gifts and qualities far higher than learning, wit or polished style have made the name of More illustrious; and we must now consider how the foundations of his noble life were laid in early manhood. When More was a youth in his father's house he conceived a plan for nine pageants to be executed in painting or tapestry, to represent the history of a human soul, and for these pageants he wrote appropriate mottoes. These have been printed, but there is a harshness in some of the lines that suggests the thought that they may have been inaccurately worked on the tapestry or inaccurately copied. They are full of interest, as bearing on the history of the young writer. Long before Shakspere wrote his *Seven Ages of Man* the same line of thought had been pursued both in verse and delineation.* More does not confine himself to this world. His pageants comprise both the present life and the next. They are Childhood, Manhood, Love (or Venus and Cupid), Age, Death, Fame, Time, and Eternity, and, lastly, the Poet summing up the whole and drawing the moral. In the first pageant Childhood says :—

In play is all my mind:
To cast a coit, a cokstele and a ball;

* See a treatise on the division of man's life into ages, by J. W. Jones, in *The Archæologia*, xxxv. 167, with illustrations.

> A top can I set, and drive it in its kind.
> But would to God these hateful books all
> Were in a fire brent to powder small.

If these words do not well represent More's boyhood, still less do the next give a picture of his youth :—

> To hunt and hawk, to nourish up and feed
> The greyhound to the course, the hawk to the flight,
> And to bestride a good and lusty steed—
> These things become a very man indeed.

It is easy to guess what Love and Age and Death have to say for themselves. In the sixth pageant Fame rebukes Death's proud boast :—

> O cruel Death! thy power I confound;
> When thou a noble man hast brought to ground,
> Maugre thy teeth to live cause him shall I,
> Of people in perpetual memory.

In the seventh, Time scoffs at this promise, since in his progress he will destroy the world itself, and then Fame will be mute. But Eternity rebukes Time, which is but the revolution of sun and moon. In the last pageant the poet writes in Latin. Evidently God only is the everlasting Good; let us distrust what is fleeting and love God alone :—

> Qui dabit æternam nobis pro munere vitam
> In permansuro ponite vota Deo.

In these verses the youth expressed what proved to be the philosophy of his whole life.

CHAPTER III.

CHOICE OF A STATE OF LIFE.

ON leaving Oxford, More was placed by his father at New Inn, an Inn of Chancery dependent on Lincoln's Inn. Here he was to acquire the learning of writs and procedure before studying the more abstruse branches of legal science at Lincoln's Inn.*

In the universities of Oxford and Cambridge Canon Law as well as Roman Civil Law were studied, while little attention was given to English (or Municipal) Law. This is divided into Common Law and Equity, the former of which guides and governs the Common Law Courts, and the latter the Court of Chancery. Hence, since the Law Courts sat principally at Westminster, the lawyers who there pleaded set up at an early period hostels or inns (*hospitia*) in London, not only as chambers and residences, but as places of study and training. In the middle of the fourteenth century, after the suppression of the Knights Templars, a more convenient site was procured, nearer to Westminster, and away from the noise of the city of London. This is still the lawyers' quarter. In the time of Sir Thomas More there were four Inns of Court—the Inner Temple, Middle Temple, Lincoln's Inn, and Gray's Inn, and ten Inns of Chancery dependent on the Inns of Court.†

The reader may be interested to know that the great hall of

* Lord Campbell.

† The Inns of Chancery are now only used as chambers, and are principally inhabited by solicitors and attorneys.

Lincoln's Inn was built in 1506. Over the gateway in Chancery
Lane is the date 1518. These, therefore, were seen by More,
though built when he had ceased to reside. Lord Campbell
writes: "With us a sufficient knowledge of jurisprudence is
supposed to be gained by eating a certain number of dinners in
the hall of one of the Inns of Court whereby men are often
called to the bar wholly ignorant of their profession; and being
pushed on by favour or accident, or native vigour of mind, they
are sometimes placed in high judicial situations, having no
acquaintance with law beyond what they may have picked up
as practitioners at the bar.* Then, the Inns of Court and
Chancery presented the discipline of a well constituted university; and, through professors, under the name of 'readers,'
and exercises under the name of 'mootings,' law was syste-
matically taught, and efficient tests of proficiency were applied
before the degree of barrister was conferred, entitling the
aspirant to practise as an advocate."†

These inns were not endowed like the colleges of the
universities. The students in the Inns of Chancery, called
apprenticii simply, were often poor enough, but those of the
Inns of Courts, called *apprenticii nobiliores*, were expected to
be able to spend 20 marks a year (about £13), a considerable
sum in those days. Roper (himself a lawyer) tells us that his
uncle "was admitted to Lincoln's Inn with very small allowance,
continuing there his study until he was made and accounted
a worthy 'utter barrister'". He was admitted into the Society
of Lincoln's Inn as a student on the 12th February, 1496,
being then just eighteen years old, and received certain dispen-
sations at the instance of his father.‡ The constitution and
mode of procedure of the Inns in former times is thus described

* Examinations have been instituted since Lord Campbell wrote.
† *Life of More.*
‡ Thomas More admissus est in Societ. 12 die Feb. aº supra dicto
[1496] et pardonat. est quatuor vacaciones ad instantiam Johis More
patris sui (Entry in the Register copied by Mr. Foss).

by our legal antiquarians : " In England it is said that the word
" barrister " arose from the arrangement of the halls of the
different Inns of Court.* The benchers and readers, being
the superiors of each house, occupied on public occasions of
assembly the upper end of the hall, which was raised on a dais,
and separated from the rest of the building by a bar. The next
in degree were the utter barristers, who, after they had attained
a certain standing, were called from the body of the hall to the
bar (*i.e.*, to the first place outside the bar), for the purpose of
taking a principal part in the *mootings* or exercises of the house.
The other members of the inn took their places nearer to the
centre of the hall, and from this manner of distribution appear
to have been called inner barristers.† The degree of utter
barrister did not originally communicate any authority to plead
in courts of justice.

"The benchers annually chose from their own body two
readers, whose duty it was to read openly to the Society in their
public hall, at least twice in the year. On these occasions,
which were observed with great solemnity, the reader selected
some statute, which he made the subject of formal examination
and discussion. Questions were then debated by the utter
barristers with the reader, after which the judges and serjeants,
several of whom were usually present, pronounced their opinions
separately upon the point that had been raised. The process
of *mooting* in the Inns of Courts differed considerably from
reading. On these occasions the reader of the inn for the
time being, with two or more benchers, presided in the open
hall. On each side of the bench table were two inner
barristers, who declared in law French some kind of action,
previously devised by them, and which always contained some

---

* In France the word " barreau " has a different origin. The pleader in
the court of justice was protected by a bar of wood or iron from the press
of the crowd ; so also we speak of our " prisoner at the bar ".

† The distinction no longer exists.

nice and doubtful points of law, the one stating the case or the plaintiff and the other the case for the defendant. The points of law arising in this fictitious case were then argued by two utter barristers, after which the reader and the benchers closed the proceedings by declaring their opinions separately." *

It seemed necessary to transcribe thus much for the intelligence of what is said about More's legal career by his biographers. We do not know the date of his call to the outer bar, nor when he was made a bencher. His legal education, however, lasted several years. Harpsfield says: "Utter barristers were not commonly made then but after many years' study. But this man's speedy and yet substantial profiting was such, that he enjoyed some prerogative of time."

He acquired so great a reputation, that the governors of the Society of Lincoln's Inn appointed him "reader" or lecturer on the science of law at Furnivall's Inn, one of the Inns of Chancery dependent on their house; and his lectures were so highly esteemed that his appointment was renewed three successive years.†

Another course of lectures mentioned by his biographers seems to have had no connection with his profession. He gave lectures (no doubt in Latin) on the great work of St. Augustine called *The City of God*. These lectures were delivered in the Church of St. Lawrence, in the Old Jewry in London, and they were attended by the most learned men, among whom is especially mentioned his old Greek preceptor Grocyn.‡   It

---

* Bohn's *Standard Library Cyclopædia of Political Knowledge*, Art. *Barrister*. In one of his latest works, *The Debellacion of Salem* v. *Bysance*, written in 1533, More writes: "I was waxen with the reading of his answer very merry, and waxen methought a young man again, and seemed set at a vacation mote with him in some Inn of Chancery, because of his proper cases of law" (*English Works*, p. 945).

† Roper says, "Three years and more".

‡ Grocyn had been lecturing about that time in St. Paul's (see Seebohm, p. 90). But Roper specially mentions him among More's auditors and admirers. Had Stapleton authority for saying that Grocyn's lectures were almost deserted for those of More?

is probable, indeed, that they were delivered at his desire, as he was then the rector of that church. Though there are many examples of lay-preaching in the history of the Church, More's lectures had in no sense the character of sermons, nor were they lectures in theology, but in history and the Divine philosophy of history. They must have been elaborated with great care to be read before such an audience. Alas! a beautiful and almost unique work has utterly perished. Not a fragment of these lectures has come down to us.

The subject he had chosen confirms what Erasmus says: that More's legal studies did not prevent him from following his bent for literature; nor did either law or letters turn his thoughts from heavenly things. He read the fathers and ecclesiastical writers carefully, and they made so deep an impression on him, that he hesitated for a considerable time about pursuing the career on which he had entered, and debated whether he should not rather become a priest or a religious.

No part of More's life has been so much misunderstood as this. It will be necessary to disentangle modern comments from the original statements of those who had means of knowing the truth. The words of Erasmus, his intimate friend and confidant, are these: "Meanwhile he applied his whole mind to exercises of piety, looking to and pondering on the priesthood in vigils, fasts, and prayers, and similar austerities. In which matter he proved himself far more prudent than most candidates, who thrust themselves rashly into that arduous profession, without any previous trial of their powers. The one thing that prevented him from giving himself to that kind of life was that he could not shake off the desire of the married state. He chose, therefore, to be a chaste husband rather than an impure priest." *

Mr. Seebohm's commentary on this last phrase is as follows: "That he did turn *in disgust from the impurity of the cloister*

* Erasm., *Ep.* 447.

to the better chances which he thought the world offered of living a chaste and useful life, we know from Erasmus".* Where does Erasmus say or hint any such thing? His words do not imply that in those days most priests were impure, any more than that most husbands were chaste. He merely says that Thomas More feared for himself, lest, perhaps, he might become an impure priest, not having the gift of perfect chastity, whereas he had good hope of living as a chaste husband. Erasmus has not a word of More's turning *with disgust* from anything, but, on the contrary, he implies that he turned with regret from a state which he loved and reverenced, but to which he feared to aspire.

Among the Jews "the fearful and faint-hearted" were exempt from military service.† Suppose, then, that someone, after due deliberation, had claimed this exemption; and that his biographer, wishing to extol his prudence, in contrast with the vainglorious rashness of others, had recorded that "he preferred to remain a respectable citizen rather than to become a cowardly soldier". What should we think of some modern Jew-hating writer, who should interpret this to mean, that "he turned with disgust from the cowardice of the army to the better chance presented to him of living an honourable life under his own vine and fig-tree," and on such grounds should go on to declaim against the poltroonery of the army of the Hebrews?

Further on Mr. Seebohm says: "More married . . . and gave up for ever all longings for monastic life".‡ This is, of course, true as regards effectual longings, or injudicious and unseasonable longings; but, taken in what is apparently Mr. Seebohm's meaning—that More looked on himself as having escaped from a delusion and chosen the nobler part—the words are in curious contradiction with More's own words to his

---

* *Oxford Reformers*, p. 151.   † *Deut.* xx. 8.
‡ *Oxford Reformers*, p. 160.

daughter, from which we find that, to the end of his life, he never lost his longing for that state which he had sorrowfully renounced in youth. When Margaret visited him in the Tower, he said to her : " I believe, Meg, that they that have put me here ween they have done me a high displeasure, but I assure thee on my faith, mine own good daughter, if it had not been for my wife and ye that be my children, I would not have failed long ere this to have closed myself in as strait a room, and straiter, too.* Methinketh God maketh me a wanton, and setteth me on His lap, and dandleth me ; " so delighted was he to realise in his prison his old ideal of an austere and contemplative life.†

Mr. Seebohm, recurring to the same idea elsewhere, says : " What would have happened to More had he been left alone with misadvising friends—whether the cloister would have received him, as it did his friend, Whitford, afterwards, to be another 'wretch of Sion'—none can tell. Happily for him, it was at this critical moment that Colet came up to London." ‡ These words seem to imply that Whitford, a Brigittine monk of Sion, near Isleworth, who, in his many ascetical books, called himself " The Wretch," implied thereby that he was disappointed and wretched in the modern sense of the word. Nothing can be farther from fact. His religious life was most happy : he was one of the few faithful against all Henry's menaces, and after the suppression, he persevered for many years, and till the end, in a mortified, prayerful, and solitary, but cheerful life.§ If, then, we are to conjecture what would

---

* I may mention it, as among the curiosities of literature, that Dr. Warner thinks More is here speaking of the grave, and that he meant that he would have *committed suicide* but for his wife and children !

† Margaret related this conversation to her husband, Roper, who has recorded it.

‡ *Oxford Reformers*, p. 147.

§ See his biography in Dom Raynal's ed. of Whitford's translation of the *Following of Christ*.

have been the fate of More had he entered the cloister, it is
not rash to think that he might have become a worthy colleague
of his friend, Whitford, as a defender of the faith by his pen,
and a confessor of it by his holy life ; or he might have been
associated in martyrdom with another monk of the same house,
Blessed Reginald or Reynolds, a man of the deepest learning
and of incomparable sanctity, who was also one of his friends,
and whose glorious death More looked on as the crown of his
monastic virtues.*   And, had he joined the Carthusians, we
should probably be now honouring his name with the glorious
band of Carthusians, victims of Henry's tyranny.   With the
Franciscans he would have stood with Peto and Elstow, or
died with Forest.   His name. however, was to stand apart in
a glory quite distinct.

Another of More's modern biographers, Lord Campbell,
after relating his penances and deliberations as to becoming a
Franciscan or Carthusian, says : " He found these (the penances) after a time not edifying to his piety, and he, a rigid
Roman Catholic, doubted the advantages supposed to be conferred on religion by the monastic orders, which a certain sec-
tion of professing Protestants are now so eager to re-establish ".

It was unworthy of Lord Chancellor Campbell, in writing
the life of another Lord Chancellor, to pen a sentence, with a
controversial purpose, for which there is not, either in the
works of More or in any of his early biographers, the very
slightest authority, and which may be refuted by innumerable
passages in his printed books.   The very first published by

---

* Blessed Reynolds of St. John's College, Cambridge, was distinguished
as a scholar in Latin, Greek, and Hebrew.   He shed his blood for the
faith with the Carthusians on 4th May, 1535, at Tyburn.   Erasmus, who
knew him, says he was *vir angelico vultu et angelico spiritu, sanique
judicii* (Letter on deaths of More and Fisher).   Cardinal Pole learnt
from an eye-witness that such was the joy of his countenance when he
placed his head in the fatal noose, that you would think it was the golden
chain of knighthood (*De Unit. Eccl.*).

him after his marriage was the *Life of Pico, Count of Mirandola*. In many respects, More took this extraordinary man as his model, and reproduced his virtues as well as his talents. Of Pico's austerities he writes : "We know many men which (as St. Jerome saith) put forth their hand to poor folk, but with the pleasures of the flesh they be overcome ; but he many days, and, namely, those days which represent unto us the passion and death that Christ suffered for our sake, beat and scourged his own flesh in the contemplation of that great benefit, and for cleansing of his old offences. He was of cheer always merry, of so benign a nature that he was never troubled with anger," etc. Surely the man who wrote this, and imitated it to the letter, had not discovered that austerity was superfluous.

Of Pico's love of God More wrote : "Of outward observances he gave no very great force. We speak not of those observances which the Church commandeth, for in those he was diligent ; but we speak of those ceremonies which folk bring up, setting the very service of God aside, who is (as Christ saith) to be worshipped in spirit and in truth. But in the inward affections of the mind he cleaved to God with very fervent love and devotion. . . . 'Nephew,' said he (on one occasion), 'this will I show thee ; I warn thee keep it secret. The substance that I have left, after certain books of mine finished, I intend to give out to poor people, and fencing myself with the crucifix, barefoot walking about the world, in every town and castle I purpose to preach of Christ.' Afterwards, as I understand, by the special commandment of God, he changed that purpose and appointed to profess himself in the Order of Friars Preachers." Could More have written thus or chosen these words for translation, had he himself turned in disgust from the impurity of the cloister, as Mr. Seebohm assures us; or come to doubt the advantages conferred on religion by the monastic orders, as Lord Campbell affirms?

It would be easy to quote much stronger testimonies to

More's esteem and love of religious orders from his later writings. But as it is thought by some that there was a re-action in his soul in favour of the Church on account of the violence of the Lutherans, I have preferred the above passages, taken from a work published by More in 1510, and probably composed or translated by him several years before. In the same book More gives an account of Savonarola's sermon at the death of Pico. More speaks of Jerome Savonarola as "a Friar-Preacher of Ferrara, a man as well in cunning [*i.e.*, learning] as holiness of living most famous". This Friar Jerome, after great eulogy of Pico, had told the people that it had been revealed to him that his friend was in purgatory for his delay in entering a religious order. "Howbeit, not being kind [*i.e.*, grateful] enough for so great benefices of God, or called back by the tenderness of his flesh (as he was a man of delicate complexion), he shrank from the labour; or, thinking, happily, that the religion had no need of him,* deferred it for a time. Howbeit this I speak only by conjecture. But for this delay I threatened him two years together that he would be punished if he forslothed that purpose which Our Lord had put in his mind."

It is almost incredible that Mr. Seebohm could, after reading the above, have written the following lines: "Pico's Works in More's translation present to the mind a type of Christianity so opposite to the ceremonial and external religion of the monks, that one may well cease to wonder that More, having caught the spirit of Pico's religion, could no longer entertain any notion of becoming a Carthusian brother". † With the writings of Dionysius, the Carthusian, accessible to him, of Thomas à Kempis, or even of Whitford, the wretch of Sion, Mr. See-

---

* The Latin has *arbitratus ejus opera religionem indigere*—" that re-ligion required his services," *i.e.*, the welfare of religion in the world. More puts in a negative, and takes the word religion technically, *i.e.*, the state of religion, or the Dominican Order.

† *Oxford Reformers*, p. 153.

bohm must be indeed mastered by prejudice to sneer at the external religion of the monks, and contrast it with solid piety. In any case, according to More's views of the Gospel, the worship of God in spirit and in truth was drawing on Pico to the religious state when he died.

How was it, then, it will be asked, that, with all More's admiration for the religious state, and attraction towards it, he still resolved finally not to embrace it? It was because he had not that indication of God's vocation which he supposes Pico to have received. Erasmus told the truth somewhat bluntly, as he heard it from More himself: he feared to become an impure priest, and determined to become a chaste husband. This was a matter for More himself and his confessor, and is one that scarcely admits of our discussion. It would seem, however, from Stapleton's words, that More would often say in later life that he had exaggerated the difficulties of a life of celibacy. His decision was at least guided by perfect humility, and not by the insane pride and contempt of others with which some of his modern biographers would burden him.*

Even Sir James Mackintosh, whose biography of More is distinguished both by candour and insight, has not disentangled himself from Protestant prejudices in writing on this episode of

---

* Those who wish to weigh this matter may find the materials in the following passages: Cum ætas ferret non abhorruit (Morus) a puellarum amoribus, sed citra infamiam, et sic ut oblatis magis frueretur quam captatis, et animo mutuo caperetur potius quam coitu (*Erasmus ad Ulrichum.*)

Meditabatur adolescens sacerdotium cum suo Lilio. Religionis etiam propositum ardenter desiderans, Minoritarum institutum arripere cogitabat. Sed quum exercitiis illis prædictis adhibitis, motus carnis qui in juventutis flore et ardore accidere solent, evincere non posse sibi videretur, uxorem ducere instituit. Solebat hæc ille postea narrare non sine magna animi tristitia et mœrore; dicebatque multo esse facilius legem carnis in cœlibatu vincere quam in matrimonio. Quod sane Apostolicis illis verbis conforme est: Tribulationem tamen carnis habebunt hujusmodi (Stapleton, *T. Mori Vita*, cap. 2).

his life. "The same affectionate disposition," he says,
"which had driven More towards the visions and, strange
as it may seem, to the austerities of the monks, now sought a
more natural element." What word of More's, what word of
any of his biographers, can have suggested that More was
either driven or drawn towards visions? There are doubtless
visions sent by God, as every reader of the Old or the New
Testament must know—St. Peter, on the day of Pentecost,
explained that a new era had begun, one of the characteristics of which should be that "young men should see visions".*
Yet the desire to see visions has never been counted among
the gifts of the Holy Ghost, and Sir Thomas More was the
last to covet them. His passion for austerities, on the other
hand, was a real one, and survived his marriage, though it was
controlled by discretion.

Sir James also writes: "He soon learnt, by self-examina-
tion, his unfitness for the priesthood, and relinquished his
project of taking orders, in words which should have warned
his church against the imposition of unnatural self-denial on
vast multitudes and successive generations of men". The
words alluded to are no doubt those of Erasmus, but even if
they express More's view, that certainly involved no condemnation of the discipline of celibacy, which More has warmly
defended in more than one treatise. His prudent conduct is
a warning to bishops "not to impose hands lightly," and to
candidates "to consider again and again the work they
undertake and the burden laid upon them". †

Perhaps on the subject of More's austerities and vocation,
some will be better disposed to listen to the words of a
married man. I will, therefore, let his great-grandson, Cresacre
More, relate with his own reflections the facts that he had
gathered from Stapleton: "When he was about eighteen or
twenty years old, finding his body, by reason of his years, most

* *Acts* ii. 17.   † Words of the Pontifical.

rebellious, he sought diligently to tame his unbridled con-
cupiscence by wonderful works of mortification. He used
oftentimes to wear a sharp shirt of hair next his skin, which
he never left off wholly—no, not when he was Lord Chancellor
of England. . . . He used also much fasting and watching,
lying often either upon the bare ground or upon some bench,
or laying some log under his head, allotting himself but four or
five hours in a night at the most for his sleep, imagining, with
the holy saints of Christ's Church, that his body was to be
used like an ass, with strokes and hard fare, lest provender
might prick it, and so bring his soul like a headlong jade into
the bottomless pit of hell. For chastity, especially in youth,
is a lingering martyrdom, and these are the best means to
preserve her from the dangerous gulf of evil custom. But he
is the best soldier in this fight that can run fastest away from
himself, this victory being hardly gotten with striving.

"He had inured himself to straightness that he might the
better enter the narrow gate of heaven, which is not got with
ease ; *sed violenti rapiunt illud*—that is to say, they that are
boisterous against themselves bear it away by force. For
this cause he lived for four years amongst the Carthusians,
dwelling near the Charterhouse, frequenting daily their spiritual
exercises, but without any vow. He had an earnest desire
also to be a Franciscan friar, that he might serve God in a
state of perfection ; but, finding that at that time religious men
in England had somewhat degenerated from their ancient
strictness and fervour of spirit, he altered his mind. *

* The relaxation, not the immorality, of the religious orders is here
assigned by Cresacre as the reason of his ancestor's decision ; but
Erasmus says that his one and only obstacle was in himself. In fact,
there was no such paucity of fervent religious among the Carthusians
and the Observant Franciscans—the two orders to which he had been
attracted—as to give rise to any difficulty on that score. Cresacre has
put down as a fact what Stapleton merely advanced as a conjecture. In
this he has been imitated by Mr. Walter. But Mr. Seebohm is not justified

" He had also after that, together with his faithful companion, Lilly, a purpose to be a priest, yet God had allotted him for another estate, not to live solitary, but that he might be a pattern to married men : how they should carefully bring up their children, how dearly they should love their wives, how they should employ their endeavour wholly for the good of their country, yet excellently perform the virtues of religious men, as piety, charity, humility, obedience and conjugal chastity."

The subject that has been under discussion in this chapter makes it opportune to ask what was the attitude of More towards the priesthood during the rest of his life.   One who has been disenchanted in his ideal, or disappointed in his aspirations, often looks with disgust on his shattered idol, and with anger on his wasted enthusiasm.   We find nothing whatever of this in More.   He forms a perfectly calm and equable judgment. " As for any partial favour that I bear to the clergy," writes More, " I never said that they were all faultless, nor I never excused their faults.   As I loved and honoured the good, so was I not slack in providing for the correction of those that were bad and slanderous to their own order.   Which sort had at my hand so little favour, that there was no man into whose hands they were more loth to come."*

In another place he writes on the subject as follows : " I wot well, the whole world is so wretched that spiritual and temporal everywhere all be bad enough ; God make us all better !   But yet, for that I have myself seen, and by credible folk have heard, like as ye say by our temporality (*i.e., of the laity*) that we be as good and honest as anywhere else, so dare I boldly

in saying that " More's Catholic biographers have acknowledged that he turned in disgust from the impurity of the cloister to the better chances which he thought the world offered of living a chaste and useful life ".   Neither Erasmus nor Stapleton, nor Cresacre More, nor Walter, nor any other Catholic writer, has acknowledged or suggeste any such thing.

* *English Works*, p. 868 (*Apology*, chap. x.).

say that the spirituality of England, and specially that part in which ye find most fault—that is, to wit, that part which we commonly call the secular clergy—is, in learning and honest living, well able to match, and (saving the comparisons be odious) I would say further, far able to overmatch, number for number, the spirituality of any nation Christian. I wot well there be therein many very lewd and naught ; and surely, wheresoever there is a multitude, it is not without miracle well possible to be otherwise. But now, if the bishops would once take unto priesthood better laymen and fewer, for of us be they made, all the matter were more than half amended.

" Now, where ye say that ye see more vice in them than in ourselves, truth it is that everything in them is greater, because they be more bounden to be better. But else the things that they missdo be the selfsame that we sin in ourselves, which vices that, as ye say, we see more in them than in ourselves, the cause is (I suppose), for we look more upon theirs than on our own, and fare, as Æsop saith in a fable, that every man carrieth a double wallet on his shoulder, and into the one that hangeth at his breast he putteth other folk's faults, and therein he looketh and poreth often. In the other he layeth up all his own and swingeth it at his back, which himself never listeth to look in, but other that come after him cast an eye into it among (i.e., sometimes).

" Would God we were all of the mind that every man thought no man so bad as himself, for that were the way to mend both them and us. Now they blame us and we blame them, and both blameworthy, and either part more ready to find other's faults than to mend their own. For in reproach of them we be so studious that neither good nor bad passeth unreproved. If they be familiar we call them light ; if they be solitary we call them fantastic ; if they be sad (i.e., serious) we call them solemn ; if they be merry we call them mad ; if they be holy we call them hypocrites ; if they keep few servants we call them niggards ; if they keep many we call them pompous ;

if a lewd priest do a lewd deed, then we say : 'Lo, see what
example the clergy giveth us !' as though that priest were the
clergy. But then forget we to look what good men be therein,
and what good counsel they give us, and what good ensample
they show us.   But we fare as do the ravens and the carrion
crows, that never meddle with any quick (*i.e.*, live) flesh ; but
where they may find a dead dog in a ditch thereto they flee,
and thereon they feed apace."

" Undoubtedly," he concludes, " if the clergy be nought, we
must needs be worse, as I heard once Master Colet, the good
dean of Paul's, preach.   For he said that it can be none other,
but that we (*i.e.*, the laity) must ever be one degree under
them.   For surely (as he said) it can be no lie that Our Saviour
saith Himself, which saith of them that they be the salt of the
earth ; and if the salt once appall, the world must need wax
unsavoury.   And He saith that they be the light of the world ;
and then if the light, saith He, be darked, how dark will then
the darkness be—that is, to wit, all the world beside, whereof He
called the clergy only the light ? " *

More, however, spoke out very strongly on that which was
the principal abuse of the Church in England in those days—
indiscriminate ordination.   His friend and director, Colet, had
made this the main subject of his *concio ad clerum* before the
Convocation in 1512.   In Barclay's poetical translation of the
" Ship of Fools," which appeared about the same time, the
matter was thus sturdily handled :—

> The cause why so many priestis lacketh wit
>   Is in you bishops, if I durst truth express,
> Which not consider what men that ye admit
>   Of living, cunning, person, and godliness.
> But who so ever himself thereto will dress
>   If an angel † be his broker to the scribe,
> He is admitted, howbeit he be witless ;
>   Thus sold is priesthood for an unhappy bribe. ‡

* *English Works*, p. 225.   (*Dialogue*, Bk. iii. ch. 11.)
† A coin worth 10s. bearing the effigy of an angel.
‡ Of the abusion of the Spirituality.

Following in the track of these authors, Sir Thomas wrote in his *Dialogue*, published in 1528 : " ' Verily, were all the bishops of my mind, as I know some that be, ye should not of priests have the plenty that ye have. . . . Gold would we not set by if it were as common as chalk or clay. And whereof is there now such plenty as of priests ? . . . The time was when few men durst presume to take upon them the high office of priest, not even when they were chosen and called there unto. Now runneth every rascal and boldly offereth himself for able. And where the dignity passeth all princes, and they that lewd be desire it for worldly winning, yet cometh that sort thereto with such a mad mind that they reckon almost God much bounden to them that they vouchsafe to take it. But were I Pope ——' ' By my soul,' quoth he, ' I would ye were, and my lady, your wife, Popess too ! ' ' Well,' quoth I, ' then should she devise for nuns. And as for me, touching the choice of priests, I could not well devise better provisions than are by the laws of the Church provided already, *if they were as well kept as they be well made.'*

" ' But for the number, I would surely see such a way therein that we should not have such a rabble ; that every mean man must have a priest in his house to wait upon his wife, which no man almost lacketh now, to the contempt of priesthood in as vile office as his horse keeper ! ' * ' That is,' quoth he, ' truth indeed, and worse too, for they keep† hawks and dogs, and yet me seemeth surely a more honest service to wait on a horse than on a dog.' ' And yet I suppose,' quoth I, ' if the laws of the Church, which Luther and Tindall would have all broken, were all well observed and kept, this gear should not be thus, but the number of priests would be much minished, and the remnant much the better. For it is by the laws of the Church provided, to the intent no priest should (unto the slander of priesthood) be driven to live in such lewd manner

---

* *i.e.*, till he looks on the priest's office as no better than an ostler's.
† *i.e.*, tend, take care of.

or worse, there should none be admitted unto priesthood until he have a title of a sufficient yearly living, either of his own patrimony or otherwise. Nor at this day they be none otherwise accepted.' 'Why,' quoth he, 'wherefore go there then so many of them a-begging?' 'Marry,' quoth I, 'for they delude the law and themselves also. For they never have grant of a living that may serve them in sight for that purpose, but they secretly discharge it ere they have it, or else they could not get it. And thus the bishop is blinded by the sight of the writing, and the priest goeth a-begging, for all his grant of a good living and the law is deluded, and the order is rebuked, by the priest's begging and lewd living, which either is fain to walk at rovers and live upon trentals * or worse, or else to serve in a secular man's house, which should not need if this gap were stopped.'" †

* To become a tramp, and to get a trental (or 30 days' masses) here and there.

† *English Works*, 227, 8.

CHAPTER IV.

EARLY MANHOOD.

THE question of vocation appears to have been debated by More during several years, before it was finally closed by his marriage. Before speaking of that event, I must go back and try to arrange what has been recorded of his early manhood. Unfortunately his first biographers give us very few dates; and while we are able to determine some events from known history, there are a few of which the exact time must be left to conjecture. He must, then, have left Oxford at the early age of sixteen.* After having spent some time, probably two years, at New Inn, he was entered as a student at Lincoln's Inn in February, 1496, being just eighteen. We know that in the spring of 1504, when he was twenty-six, he became a member of Parliament, and he married some time in the year 1505. His biographers tell us that he resided for four years near the Charter-House. These were almost certainly the years that immediately preceded his marriage. A letter of Erasmus, dated 12th April, mentions that More is in Lincoln's Inn. The year to which this letter belongs is fixed by a reference to his work called the *Adagia* being then in the press and to appear after Easter. The work came out in 1501.†

---

* He did not remain to take any degree, and it was no very unusual thing for youths of fourteen or fifteen to proceed to the universities. I cannot see any likelihood, however, that a youth of that age would have been admitted to the society of Colet or of Grocyn, as Mr. Seebohm has conjectured.

† *Letter* 29. The Leyden editor has affixed the year 1498 erroneously.

So much will have to be said of Erasmus in connection with
More, that it is worth while to investigate here the beginnings
of their acquaintance.   A ridiculous tale has got into circulation,
which places the earliest interview between More and Erasmus
when the former was chancellor.*   It is enough to say that
they had been the dearest of friends for more than thirty years.
Erasmus first came to England in 1497 on a visit to William
Blount, Lord Mountjoy, who had been his pupil in Paris.   It
was probably at his house that he met young More.   After a
short stay in London he went to Oxford.   From a letter written
by Erasmus from Oxford on 28th October, 1499 (or 1498), we
find that they were already corresponding as dear friends.   " I
have poured curses on the letter-carrier, by whose laziness or
treachery I fancy it must be that I have been disappointed of
the most eagerly expected letters of my dear More (*Mori mei*).

* *A Book of Pleasant Tales and Stories* relates the matter as
follows: " Sir T. More being at my Lord Mayor's table, word was
brought him that a foreigner inquired for his Lordship (he being then
Lord Chancellor).   They having well-nigh dined, the Lord Mayor
ordered one of his officers to take the gent into his care and give him
what he best liked.   The officer took Erasmus into the Lord Mayor's
cellar, where he chose to eat oysters, and drank wine drawn into a
leathern jack and poured into a silver cup.   As soon as Erasmus had
well refreshed himself he was introduced to Sir T. More.   At his first
coming in he saluted Sir Thomas in Latin.   Sir Thomas, having never
seen him before, asked him, *Unde venis ?* (Whence do you come ?).   Erasmus answered, *Ex inferis* (from the lower regions), which has three
meanings—the Netherlands, the cellar, and hell.   Sir Thomas : *Quid
ibi agitur ?* (What is done there ?).   Erasmus : *Vivis vescuntur et bibunt
ex ocreis* (They feed on the living and drink out of boots).   Sir Thomas :
An me noscis ? (Do you know me ?).   Erasmus : *Aut tu es Morus aut
nullus* (You are More or no one).   Sir Thomas : *Et tu es aut Deus
aut demon aut meus Erasmus* (You are either God or the devil or
my own Erasmus).   In another story they first met at table without
introduction and got into debate about the Real Presence.   Erasmus put
forward sceptical arguments, and More defended the Catholic Faith.   At
last Erasmus exclaimed : *Aut tu es Morus aut nullus* ; and More retorted :
Aut tu es Erasmus aut diabolus.

For that you have failed on your part I neither want nor ought to suspect, though I expostulated with you most vehemently in my last letter. . . . Adieu, my most delightful More (*Vale, jucundissime More*)." More was then twenty-one, Erasmus about ten years older. In a letter (to be quoted later) Erasmus describes the beauty, or rather the charm, of his person, only surpassed by the grace of his manners and disposition. Jacobus Battus tells how Erasmus, returning to the Continent in January, 1500, from his first visit to England, spoke with enthusiasm of the kindness of Prior Richard Charnock, the erudition of Colet, and the sweetness of More (*suavitatem*).* In another letter Erasmus says : *Thomæ Mori ingenio quid unquam finxit natura vel mollius vel dulcius vel felicius ?* (*Ep.* 14). " Did Nature ever frame a sweeter, happier character than that of More ? " † It speaks much for both More and Erasmus that these terms of admiration and endearment continue to the end. In the interests of truth, I must declare at the outset that I cannot find the very slightest foundation for the assertion of Stapleton, copied by Cresacre More and many others, that in the course of time their friendship cooled. Abundant proofs of the contrary will appear as we proceed.

In giving an account of his various writings, Erasmus has related an event that illustrates the life of More at this epoch : " I composed a heroic poem on the praise of Henry VII. and of his children, and of Britain. It was only a three days' task, yet it was a task, for it was some years since I had written or even read a poem. It was partly shame and partly pain that drew this from me. Thomas More, who, while I was staying in the country house of Mountjoy, had paid me a visit, took me out for a walk, to a neighbouring village. There all the king's children, except Arthur, the eldest, were being educated. When we reached the Hall the attendants (*tota pompa*) both of that house and of Lord Mountjoy's were assembled. In the midst

* *Ep.* 62.   † *Ep.* 14.   Dec. 5, 1497 (or rather 1498).

stood Henry, then nine years old, yet already with a royal bearing, betokening a certain loftiness of mind joined with singular condescension. At his right was Margaret, about eleven years old. She afterwards married James, King of the Scots. At his left in play was Mary, four years old. Edmund, an infant, was carried by the nurse. More with his friend Arnold,* after saluting Prince Henry, presented him with I know not what writing. As I was entirely taken by surprise I had nothing to offer, and I was obliged to make a promise that I would write something to show my respect. I was somewhat vexed with More for not warning me, and especially so since the prince while we were dining sent me a note asking some fruit of my pen. I went home and in spite of the Muses, from whom I had long been separated, I finished my poem within three days." †

The date of this incident is fixed by the mention of Prince Edmund, who was born on Feb. 21, 1499. Erasmus, therefore, previous to leaving England in January, 1500, had gone to take leave of his former pupil, Lord Mountjoy. That nobleman had studied under the direction of the Dutch scholar in Paris ; he was now beginning his political career and had lately married. Erasmus relates that at the desire of Mountjoy he had undertaken to write a "declamation" for and against the desirability of taking a wife. When he had finished the first part he showed it to his young patron, who read it carefully. "How do you like it ?" said the author. "So much that you have thoroughly persuaded me to marry," replied Mountjoy. "Stay," said Erasmus, "till you see what I have to say on the other side." "No," replied the young man, "that part will do for you ; what you have written suits me exactly." When Erasmus wrote this in 1524, Mountjoy had buried his third wife, and is sure, says Erasmus, to take a fourth if he lives.‡

---

* Another young lawyer.
† *Epist. ad Botzhemum*, written in Feb. 1524, 5. ‡ *Ib.*

When Erasmus heard that the merciless tyrant Henry had placed on a pole on London Bridge the parboiled head of his "most sweet," "most delightful," his "darling" More, how must the horror as well as the pathos of the thought have been increased by the memory of that pretty scene in the Royal nursery, where he had the first glimpse of Henry and took note of his princely affability! (*humanitas*). Whether this was More's first acquaintance with Prince Henry we are not told. It may have been such, and it seems likely that the little plot was arranged by Lord Mountjoy, not to get Erasmus into a scrape, but to bring about an introduction that might be useful to him in later years, when Henry should have become a prince of the Church, which before his brother's death was considered his probable destiny. As it was, the young prince, by having seen Erasmus, came to take a natural interest in his writings, by the aid of which he tried, not altogether unsuccessfully, to form for himself a good Latin style. At a later period Henry sought to attach him to his court and bestowed some not very royal largesse.

At that court More was to spend the best part of his life, but, as we have already seen, he was as yet undecided, and was by no means eager to lay hold of the wheel of fortune. Indeed his first step in public life was more calculated to ruin himself and others, than to lead to wealth or honour. The matter is thus related by Roper: "In the time of King Henry the Seventh, More was made a burgess of the Parliament wherein was demanded by the king (as I have heard reported) about three-fifteenths, for the marriage of his eldest daughter, that then should be Scottish Queen; at the last debating whereof he made such arguments and reasons against, that the king's demands were thereby overthrown. So that one of the king's privy chamber, named M. Tyler, being present thereat, brought word to the king out of the Parliament house that a beardless boy had disappointed all his purpose. Whereupon the king, conceiving great indignation towards him, could not be satisfied until he had some way revenged it. And forasmuch as he, nothing having, nothing could lose, his Grace devised a cause- less quarrel against his father, keeping him in the Tower till he had made him pay a hundred pounds' fine.

"Shortly hereupon it fortuned that this Sir Thomas More,* coming in a suit to Dr. Fox, Bishop of Winchester, one of the king's privy council, the bishop called him aside, and pre- tended great favour towards him, and promised that if he would be ruled by him he would not fail but bring him into the king's favour again, meaning, as it afterwards appeared, to cause him thereby to confess his offence against the king, whereby his Highness might with the better colour have occasion to revenge his displeasure against him. But when he came from the bishop, he fell in communication with one Mr. Whitford, his familiar friend, then chaplain to that bishop, and afterwards a father of Sion, and showed him what the bishop had said to him, desiring to hear his advice therein ; who, for the Passion of God, prayed him in no wise to follow his counsel : 'for my lord,' quoth he, 'to serve the king's turn, will not stick to agree to his own father's death '. So Sir Thomas More returned to the bishop no more ; and had not the king soon after died, he was determined to have gone over sea, thinking that being in the king's indignation, he could not live in England without great danger."

The Parliament in which the events thus related occurred was that called in the spring of 1504. No returns can now be found to tell us what borough More represented,† nor has any of his biographers supplied the name. There was nothing

---

* Called *Sir* by anticipation.

† There were seven parliaments in the reign of Henry VII., but for none of them have returns been found (see Parliamentary Blue Book, called " Parliaments of England," 1879, being a Return to Order of House of Lords of 1877). Bishop Stubbs, in his *Lectures on Mediæval and Modern History*, discusses the financial matters of the reign of Henry VII. p. 356, *sqq.*

factious or unreasonable in More's character, and he must have felt strongly on the subject of the king's avarice, to lead the opposition as he did. It will be remembered that under the advice of Sir Richard Empson and Edmund Dudley, Barons of the Exchequer, the king was at that time rousing the whole nation to so great a pitch of exasperation by his exactions and the unjust expedients to which he resorted, that his advisers both suffered the penalty of death at the beginning of the next reign. Several of the citizens of London had suffered in their goods or liberty; and it is probable that More was their parliamentary representative. The treatment of John More is a specimen of what was happening to hundreds. There was never wanting a pretext to throw into prison, at the accusation of an informer, any official or prominent person; and, as the accused felt sure of condemnation by a packed jury if he came to trial, he was glad to purchase freedom by payment of a fine. The very preachers in the pulpits were admonishing Henry, and protesting against what was going on.* As More could not remedy these evils, he thought it at least his duty to make a stand against excessive generosity to such a king. By his influence the grant was reduced from £113,000, which would have been the product of the three-fifteenths demanded, to £30,000.† Dudley had been Speaker in this Parliament. Stapleton relates that, when some years later he was condemned to death, More visited him in prison, and asked him whether he had not acted well in resisting the exaction. "Yes!" replied Dudley, "and God was with you that you confessed no fault against the king. Had you done so, you would have paid the penalty with your head."

* Hall's *Chronicle.*

† See Seebohm, p. 145, and Lingard's account of the last years of Henry VII. Lingard, however, only mentions this parliamentary grant in a note, and has no reference to More, or to the demand of the three-fifteenths.

Roper has mentioned More's project of seeking security on the Continent. We know from his own statement that he did in fact cross the sea, whether to make a tour, as was the custom with young gentlemen, as Stapleton supposes, or to choose a place of retirement, is uncertain. In 1515 he wrote a letter to Martin Dorpius, in which he thus mentions this visit :—

"What esteem you have for our English universities I do not know. You seem to set so much by Louvain and Paris, that, as regards dialectics at least, you think they are banished from the rest of the world. Now, seven years ago I was in both those universities, and though not for a very long time, yet I took pains to ascertain what was taught there and what methods were followed. Though I respect both of them, yet neither from what I then saw, nor from what I have since heard, have I found any reason why, even in dialectics, I should wish any sons of mine (for whom I desire the very best education) to be taught there rather than at Oxford or Cambridge."

This letter is dated October, 1515. The visit, therefore, to France and Flanders must have been in 1508, before the death of Henry VII., but subsequent to his own marriage.

Before we come to that turning-point of his life something must be said of a few of his other friends. One of these was William Lilly, a young man who, after his course at Oxford, had gone to Rhodes, and resided there some years for the study of Greek.* Similarity of taste drew him and More closely to-gether. More perfected himself in Greek by Lilly's deeper knowledge, and in his turn imparted to Lilly some of his own ardent piety. They exercised and amused themselves by translating into Latin verse epigrams from the Greek Antho-logia. Their respective translations were printed in juxtaposi-tion in the *Progymnastica Thomæ Mori et Gulielmi Lilii Sodalium.*† A few years later Lilly became head master of St.

---

* Rhodes was then in the possession of the Knights of St. John.

† They will be noticed in Chapter VII.

Paul's School, and his name was long known to every educated youth in England by the Latin grammar which he composed.

In the last chapter mention was twice made of Dr. Colet, Dean of St. Paul's—by Mr. Seebohm, as of one who appeared opportunely to rescue More from the fate into which his ill-advised enthusiasm for the priesthood was hurrying him, and by More himself, as of one who inspired him with the veneration for the priesthood which he had just explained and defended. Colet, like More, was a Londoner by birth, and an Oxford student. He was a man of considerable learning, of great zeal, especially as a preacher, but he was pre-eminently a man of character fitted to influence others. His determination may sometimes have been pushed into obstinacy and contentiousness. More, who loved and admired him greatly, notes this foible in a letter to Erasmus : "Colet is busy at Greek, using the occasional help of my Clements. I believe he will persevere and succeed, especially if you urge him from Louvain. Yet, perhaps you had better leave him to his own impulse. You know how, out of a certain disputatiousness, he resists those who urge him, even though they are only persuading him to that on which he was already bent." *

It is possible, though not certain, that Colet had made the acquaintance of More when they were both at Oxford, though Colet was ten or eleven years older, and a lecturer in Holy Scripture when More was merely a student in arts. At a later period Colet used to say that More was the one genius of whom Britain could then boast, and Erasmus, who quotes the words, remarks that Colet was a man of keen and accurate judgment. This eminent man More had chosen as his confessor. At what period he placed himself under his spiritual guidance we are not told. Erasmus, who knew Colet's life and opinions thoroughly, mentions his sentiments regarding the confessional : "He had the utmost esteem for secret confession, and used to say that from no practice did he derive so much

* Inter Epist. Erasm. App. 25 (25th Feb., 1516).

consolation and spiritual profit; but he was equally opposed to scrupulous confessions and constant repetitions ".*

If he loved a delicate but disliked a timid and feeble conscience, in More he would find one after his own heart, and from their spiritual intercourse there grew up an intimate and lasting friendship.

Stapleton has preserved a letter written by More to Dr. Colet. The Latin is evidently the original work of More, and not due to Stapleton. It is probable that a rough copy came into the hands of one of More's secretaries, who communicated it to More's biographer:—

"I was walking up and down the law courts when your servant met me. I was delighted at seeing him, both because I have always been fond of him, and still more because I thought he had not come [to London] without you. But when I learnt, not only that you had not returned, but were not to return for a considerable time, I was as greatly dejected. What can be more distressing to me than to be deprived of your most dear society, after being guided by your wise counsels, cheered by your charming familiarity, assured by your earnest sermons, and helped forward by your example, so that I used to obey your very look or nod? With these helps I felt myself strengthened, but without them I seem to languish. Following your guidance, I had escaped almost from the jaws of hell; now, like Euridice, I know not by what force I am being drawn back into darkness. Euridice, however, suffered this violence because of the presence of Orpheus; I, because of your absence. What is there in the city to incite to virtue? On the contrary, when one wishes to live well, by a thousand devices and seductions the life of a city drags one down. False love and flattery

---

* Ut confessionem secretam vehementer probabat, negans se ulla ex re capere tantumdem consolationis ac boni spiritus, ita anxiam ac subinde repetitam vehementer damnabat (*Epist.* 435). Though Erasmus in this is probably speaking of Colet's principles as a penitent, they would of course guide him also as a confessor.

on the one side : on the other, hatreds and quarrels and legal wranglings. One sees nothing but butchers, fishmongers, cooks, confectioners, fishermen, fowlers, ministering to the appetites of the body, and to the world and its prince, the devil. Why, the very houses intercept a great part of the light, and prevent one from seeing the heavens. It is not the horizon * that bounds the prospects, but the roofs of the houses. So I do not blame you that you are not yet tired of the country, where you see the simple country folk, ignorant of city tricks ; and, wherever you turn your eyes, the beautiful landscape refreshes, the fresh air exhilarates, and the sight of heaven delights you. You see nothing but the kind gifts of nature, and the holy impressions of innocence. Still, I would not have you so captivated by these charms as not to hasten back to us as soon as possible. For if you dislike the town, yet your country parish of Stepney, for which also you must be solicitous, will afford you as many attractions as the place where you now are ; and from thence you can now and then pass into the city, where you will find a great field of merit. In the country, men are, of their own nature, harmless—or, at least, not involved in such enormous crimes—so that the hand of an ordinary physician will suffice for them ; whereas, in the city, both on account of the multitude of the diseases and their inveteracy, no physician but the most skilled can do any good.

"There come sometimes into the pulpit of St. Paul's some who promise health ; yet, when they seem to have preached beautifully, their life is so contrary to their words that they irritate our wounds rather than cure them. For they cannot persuade us to believe them fit to have the cure of other men's diseases entrusted to them when they are themselves more sick than any. No ; we get angry, and refuse to allow our wounds to be touched by those whose own wounds are ulcers. But if, as naturalists affirm. the physician in whom the patient has

* ὁρίζωνος ille circulus.

perfect confidence is the one likely to cure, there is no doubt
that there is no one more fit than yourself to undertake the
cure of this whole city.   How ready all are to put themselves
in your hands—to trust and obey you—you have already found
by experience, and at the present time their longing and eager
desire proves.

"Come, then, my dear Colet, even for the sake of your
Stepney, which laments your long absence as an infant does
its mother's ; come for the sake of [London] your native place,
which merits your care no less than do your parents.   Lastly,
though this is but a feeble motive, let your regard for me move
you, since I have given myself entirely to you, and am awaiting
your return full of solicitude.   Meanwhile I shall pass my time
with Grocyn, Linacre and our friend Lilly : the first of whom
is, as you know, the only director of my life in your absence ;
the second, the master of my studies ; the third, my most dear
companion.   Farewell, and continue to love me as you do.—
From London, the 10th November."

As Colet resigned the cure of Stepney on 21st September,
1505, this letter could not have been written later than 1504,
nor can it have an earlier date, since only in that year had he
begun to preach in St. Paul's.   More, therefore, was twenty-six
years old.   If the letter has a little of the tone of a boy's
theme, it must be remembered that it was written in Latin, which
suggested a literary exercise with its classical allusions, rather
than the familiar language of the heart.   This was a natural
reaction after the vernacular barbarisms of the last century, as
seen in the Paston letters.   At a more advanced age More did
not disdain to write in English when addressing an Englishman,
though he wrote occasionally in Latin to his own daughters as
an exercise or encouragement to them.

The rhetorical style of the letter just quoted seems to justify
a suspicion of exaggeration in the picture of the great preachers
who had the coveted honour of appearing in the pulpit of St.
Paul's.   They can scarcely have been all mere sounding brass

or tinkling cymbals. In any case too much has been sometimes made of More's expressions, which imply pride and ostentation rather than immorality.*

Having seen in this letter More's practice of frequent confession, a practice to which he was faithful to the end of his life, it will help us to estimate a peculiarity of More's character if I place here a specimen of his epigrams, probably composed about this time. The following translation is very literal:—†

> A squall arose; the vessel's tossed;
> The sailors fear their lives are lost.
> "Our sins, our sins," dismayed they cry,
> "Have wrought this fatal destiny!"
> A monk, it chanced, was of the crew,
> And round him to confess they drew.
> Yet still the restless ship is tossed,
> And still they fear their lives are lost.
> One sailor, keener than the rest,
> Cries, "With our sins she's still oppressed;
> Heave out that monk who bears them all,
> And then full well she'll ride the squall".
> So said, so done; with one accord
> They threw the caitiff overboard;
> And now the bark before the gale
> Scuds with light hull and easy sail.
> > Learn hence the weight of sin to know,
> > With which a ship could scarcely go.

These good-humoured and innocent lines Mr. Seebohm gives as "a sample of the epigrams in which the pent-up bitter thoughts of the past year or two were making their escape.

* The criticism strikes one as not too charitable, and exemplifies what More himself says about readiness to find fault (see *supra*, p. 33). Men *openly* immoral could hardly be invited to occupy that pulpit, and to accuse them of secret immoralities would be grave slander. Perhaps, after all, this letter may be simply a first draft from which Stapleton printed.

† It is by Archdeacon Wrangham, and was printed in Cayley's *Life of More*.

Some were on priests and monks—sharp biting satires on their evil side, and by no means showing abject faith in monkhood."*

Another writer, with equally portentous gravity, observes : "Among the Epigrammata we find one upon the subject of auricular confession which no strict adherent to the Church of Rome would have ventured to circulate among his friends, and much less to print".†

No doubt these writers are sincere in their criticism. The anonymous author of *Philomorus*, though very friendly to More, perhaps I should rather say, *because* very friendly, thinks he was at least half sceptical as regards certain Catholic doctrines and practices, and that if he had lived till now he would have been a good Anglican. Mr. Seebohm first imagines More a disgusted and disappointed man, and then takes a bit of simple fun for "biting satire on the monks". But surely, if there is any biting satire here, it is on the sailors, not on the monk. The monk, in presence of death, calmly and courageously performs a difficult duty, and shows his entire conviction of what he had always taught. There is no more satire on the monks than in the old lines :—

> When the devil was sick, the devil a monk would be,
> When the devil got well, the devil a monk was he.

I draw attention, however, to this epigram and the comments of modern Protestant writers, not to defend or explain these lines, but because More so frequently indulged in such jokes and tales that to some he appears sceptical, and to others superstitious. "It is indeed most wonderful," exclaims one biographer, "that at no period of his life did a ray of that light that was now breaking upon the world penetrate his mind. With talents, learning, and wit far beyond his contemporaries, he was also far beyond them in religious bigotry and superstition."‡ Yet this blind bigot is claimed by others as a forerunner of the

---

* *Oxford Reformers*, p. 181.   † *Philomorus*, p. 127.
‡ Writer in Chalmer's *Dictionary of Biography*.

Reformation, or the teacher of a deeper and more fundamental Reformation than that which has usurped the name.* Neither party seems to understand that a man can believe earnestly, even so as to be willing to die for his faith, and yet talk and write easily and merrily about it. "Protestants," says Cardinal Newman, "keep the exhibition of their faith for high days and great occasions, when it comes forth with sufficient pomp and gravity of language, and ceremonial of manner. Truths slowly totter out with Scripture texts at their elbow, as unable to walk alone. . . . Protestants condemn Catholics, because, however religious they may be, they are natural, unaffected, easy and cheerful in their mention of sacred things; and they think *themselves* never so real as when they are especially solemn." †

It will be necessary to say more on this subject when we consider how the *Encomium Moriæ* was written by Erasmus in More's house, and with his approbation and encouragement, and when we consider More's style of controversy. Enough has been said for my present purpose, which is not to defend More, who needs no defence, much less to defend anything Catholic, but to utter a protest against the sincere but most groundless and unreasonable deductions made from More's acts or words at this crisis of his life. We may now study him as a married man and a lawyer.

* This is Mr. Seebohm's thesis.
† Lectures on Difficulties felt by Anglicans (*Lect.* ix. n. 7).

CHAPTER V.

PERSONAL.

MORE had sought earnestly to discover the will of God regarding the disposition of his life. He had a thorough determination to serve God with his whole heart, whatever might be his state. He had felt himself drawn in two opposite directions: to the married life, which involved the profession of the law to which his father had dedicated him, but for which he felt no attraction; and to the life of a priest, or, perhaps, of a monk. His literary education and his taste for letters fitted him for either life. Learning was no longer confined to ecclesiastics, though they still formed by far the majority of studious and cultured men. He had a profound piety; but piety befits the laity no less than the clergy. At length, after many counsels and much prayer, his decision was taken. Having seen that he was called to the married state, it remained for him to seek for a lady who should be a suitable partner of his life, for no previous inclination of the heart had led him to set aside the state of celibacy.

It seems probable, indeed, that there had been some transient attachment in early youth, but it was altogether past and could never have been very serious. In a Latin poem among his *Epigrams* he tells us his little romance :—

Scarce had I bid my sixteenth summer hail,
And two in thine were wanting to the tale,

> When thy soft mien—ah, mien for ever fled !—
> On my tranced heart its guiltless influence shed.

The premature passion caused some amusement among his companions and indignation in the young lady's relatives, for More at that time was but a poor law student at New Inn.

> Then the duenna and the guarded door
> Baffled the stars, and bade us meet no more.

They did not meet again until five-and-twenty years had past. More was then married for the second time, and the lady's charms had passed away ; but the poet elegantly described the impression made by the meeting :—

> Crimeless, my heart you stole in life's soft prime,
> And still possess that heart without a crime ;
> Pure was the love which in my youth prevailed,
> And age would keep it pure if honour failed.*

There was very little romance connected with either his first or second marriage. Both wives were rather short in stature, and when More was asked why he had not selected taller women he replied, rather in the spirit of his father : " Of two evils you should choose the less ".† This, of course, was a mere joke, and Roper has given the true history of his first courtship, as he heard it from More's own lips, after the death of the lady : " He resorted to the house of one Mr. Colt, a gentleman of Essex,‡ that had often invited him thither, having three daughters, whose honest conversation and virtuous education provoked him there specially to set his affection. And, albeit his mind most served him to the second daughter, for

* Wrangham's translation. The poem is not in the first edition of the *Epigrams* of 1518, but in the second of 1520. It was written in 1519, when twenty-five years (*quinque lustra*) had passed since he was sixteen ; another proof that he was born in 1478.

† Stapleton, ch. xiii.

‡ Cresacre says, of Newhall in Essex.

that he thought her the fairest and best favoured, yet when he considered that it would be both great grief and some shame to the eldest to see her younger sister preferred before her in marriage, he then of a certain pity* framed his fancy to her, and soon after married her." The young lady's Christian name was Joan or Jane.

"She was very young," says Erasmus, "of good family, with a mind somewhat uncultivated, having always resided in the country with her parents and sisters; but she was all the more apt to be moulded according to his habits. He took care to have her instructed in learning, and especially in all musical accomplishments, and had made her such that he could have willingly passed his whole life with her, but a premature death separated them." His affection is shown by one little word in his own epitaph, composed more than twenty years after her death. He calls her More's dear little wife (*uxorcula Mori*). It is curious that love of books and love of music, on the part of a wife, are two of the components of conjugal happiness mentioned by More in his poem to Candidus, of which the title is, "What sort of wife to choose". She must neither be too talkative nor too taciturn, but she must sing and she must read.

> Far from her lips' soft door
>   Be noise, be silence stern,
> And her's be learning's store,
>   Or her's the power to learn;
> While still thy raptured gaze
>   Is on her features hung,
> As words of honied grace
>   Steal from her honied tongue.

---

* Sir James Mackintosh defends the use of the word "pity" from the charge of being ungallant. It signifies, he says, "the natural refinement, which shrinks from humbling the harmless self-complacency of an innocent girl". (*See* Appendix B.)

Such Orpheus' wife, whose fate
    With tears old fables tell,
Or never would her mate
    Have fetched her back from hell.*

After his marriage More went to live in Bucklesbury, in the parish of St. Stephen, Wallbrook.† From this marriage sprang four children : Margaret, Elizabeth, Cecily, and John. Margaret, the eldest, was born towards the end of 1505 or early in 1506 ; John, the youngest, in 1509.‡ After about six years of happy married life his wife died, seemingly in childbirth.§ Within two or three years, according to Cresacre, or as Erasmus, better informed, says : " within a few months of the death of his wife " he married again.

Of this second marriage and of the education of his family I shall speak later on. This seems the place to give some account of the man himself : his appearance, his habits, and his general character. Fortunately his portrait has been drawn by a master hand, and by one who drew from the life and not from the report of others. It is in a letter of Erasmus to Von

* Proculque stulta sit   Talem olim ego putem
  Parvis labellulis   Et vatis Orphei
  Semper loquacitas ;   Fuisse conjugem ;
  Proculque rusticum   Nec unquam ab inferis
  Semper silentium.   Curasset improbo
  Sit illa vel modo   Labore fœminam
  Instructa literis   Referre rusticam.
  Vel talis ut modo
  Sit apta literis
          *   *   *   *

† " In the paryshe of St. Stephen's, Wallbroke, in London, where I dwelled before I come to Chelsith " (*English Works*, p. 131). Bucklesbury is just south of the Poultry, Cheapside.

‡ The precise dates are unknown, but the calculation is made from their ages marked on the Basle picture.

§ Erasmus hints at a dead child : " liberos aliquot, quorum adhuc super-sunt puellæ tres, puer unus ".

Hutten. Erasmus, as we have seen, had known and loved More as a youth. After about six years' absence from England he returned to find More married. They renewed their friendship and pursued their Greek studies together. The letter that I am about to translate was not written until 1519, by which time, from several years' residence in England, and much intercourse with More, Erasmus had ample opportunity to strengthen or to correct his first impressions. Of these visits and this intercourse much will be said. The picture which we are about to contemplate does not belong to one year more than another, but is that of More's manhood before he had risen to high dignity at court.

Ulrich von Hutten, a German noble, who subsequently proved himself to have little resemblance with More,[*] had been so charmed by his *Epigrams*, his translations from Lucian, and his *Utopia*, that he wrote to their common friend Erasmus, begging him to tell him all he knew concerning the brilliant Englishman. I will give his answer without modifying a syllable, but omitting a few sentences that are unimportant or quoted by me elsewhere :—

"You ask me to paint you a full-length portrait of More as in a picture. Would that I could do it as perfectly as you eagerly desire it. At least I will try to give a sketch of the man, as well as from my long familiarity with him I have either observed or can now recall. To begin, then, with what is least known to you, in stature he is not tall, though not remarkably short. His limbs are formed with such perfect symmetry as to leave nothing to be desired. His complexion is white, his face fair rather than pale, and though by no means ruddy, a faint flush of pink appears beneath the whiteness of his skin. His hair is dark brown, or brownish black. The eyes are grayish

---

[*] In quadam epistola confero illum (Huttenum) cum Thoma Moro, quo viro multis jam sæculis nihil vidit sol integrius, candidius, amicius, cordatius. Hujus se vehementer dissimilem probavit Huttenus, meque vanum præconem fecit (Erasm. *Ep. ad Botzhemum*).

blue, with some spots, a kind which betokens singular talent, and among the English is considered attractive, whereas Germans generally prefer black. It is said that none are so free from vice.

"His countenance is in harmony with his character, being always expressive of an amiable joyousness, and even an incipient laughter, and, to speak candidly, it is better framed for gladness than for gravity and dignity, though without any approach to folly or buffoonery. The right shoulder is a little higher than the left, especially when he walks. This is not a defect of birth, but the result of habit, such as we often con- tract.* In the rest of his person there is nothing to offend. His hands are the least refined part of his body.

"He was from his boyhood always most careless about what- ever concerned his body. His youthful beauty may be guessed from what still remains, though I knew him when he was not more than three-and-twenty.† Even now he is not much over forty. He has good health, though not robust ; able to endure all honourable toil, and subject to very few diseases. He seems to promise a long life, as his father still survives in a wonderfully green old age.

"I never saw anyone so indifferent about food. Until he was a young man he delighted in drinking water, but that was natural to him (*id illi patrium fuit*). Yet not to seem singular or morose, he would hide his temperance from his guests by drinking out of a pewter vessel beer almost as light as water, or often pure water. It is the custom in England to pledge each other in drinking wine. In doing so he will merely touch it

---

* "Such men be even like followers of Chaucer and Petrarch as one here in England did follow Sir Thomas More ; who, being most unlike unto him in wit and learning, nevertheless in wearing his gown awry upon the one shoulder, as Sir Thomas was wont to do, would needs be counted like unto him " (Roger Ascham, *The Schoolmaster*, p. 216 ; ed. 1884).

† More was not yet twenty when Erasmus first made his acquaintance.

with his lips, not to seem to dislike it, or to fall in with the custom. He likes to eat corned beef and coarse bread much leavened, rather than what most people count delicacies. Otherwise he has no aversion to what gives harmless pleasure to the body. He prefers milk diet and fruits, and is especially fond of eggs.

" His voice is neither loud nor very weak, but penetrating ; not resounding or soft, but that of a clear speaker. Though he delights in every kind of music he has no vocal talents.* He speaks with great clearness and perfect articulation, without rapidity or hesitation. He likes a simple dress, using neither silk nor purple nor gold chain, except when it may not be omitted. It is wonderful how negligent he is as regards all the ceremonious forms in which most men make politeness to consist. He does not require them from others, nor is he anxious to use them himself, at interviews or banquets, though he is not unacquainted with them when necessary. But he thinks it unmanly to spend much time in such trifles. Formerly he was most averse to the frequentation of the court, for he has a great hatred of constraint (*tyrannis*) and loves equality. Not without much trouble he was drawn into the court of Henry VIII., though nothing more gentle and modest than that prince can be desired. By nature More is chary of his liberty and of ease, yet, though he enjoys ease, no one is more alert or patient when duty requires it.

" He seems born and framed for friendship, and is a most faithful and enduring friend. He is easy of access to all ; but if he chances to get familiar with one whose vices admit no correction, he manages to loosen and let go the intimacy rather than to break it off suddenly. When he finds any sincere and according to his heart, he so delights in their society and conversation as to place in it the principal charm of life. He abhors games of tennis, dice, cards, and the like, by which

---

* He could, however, sing with the choir in the church.

most gentlemen kill time. Though he is rather too negligent of his own interests, no one is more diligent in those of his friends.* In a word, if you want a perfect model of friendship, you will find it in no one better than in More. In society he is so polite, so sweet-mannered, that no one is of so melancholy a disposition as not to be cheered by him, and there is no misfortune that he does not alleviate. Since his boyhood he has so delighted in merriment, that it seems to be part of his nature ; yet he does not carry it to buffoonery, nor did he ever like biting pleasantries. When a youth he both wrote and acted some small comedies. If a retort is made against himself, even without ground, he likes it from the pleasure he finds in witty repartees. Hence he amused himself with composing epigrams when a young man, and enjoyed Lucian above all writers. Indeed, it was he who pushed me to write the "Praise of Folly," that is to say, he made a camel frisk.

"In human affairs there is nothing from which he does not extract enjoyment, even from things that are most serious. If he converses with the learned and judicious, he delights in their talent; if with the ignorant and foolish, he enjoys their stupidity. He is not even offended by professional jesters. With a wonderful dexterity he accommodates himself to every disposition. As a rule, in talking with women, even with his own wife, he is full of jokes and banter.

"No one is less led by the opinions of the crowd, yet no one departs less from common sense. One of his great delights is to consider the forms, the habits, and the instincts of different kinds of animals. There is hardly a species of bird that he does not keep in his house, and rare animals such as monkeys, foxes, ferrets, weasels and the like. If he meets with anything foreign, or in any way remarkable, he eagerly buys it, so that his house is full of such things, and at every turn they attract

---

* Several of the letters of Erasmus show that More acted as his banker and postmaster.

the eye of visitors, and his own pleasure is renewed whenever he sees others pleased."

The letter goes on to describe More's literary pursuits and his care and education of his family. For these passages a more convenient place will be found. To complete what Erasmus has said of his personal habits, I will add some extracts from Stapleton, whose testimony in these matters is almost as authentic as that of Erasmus, being derived from members of More's family. He enters into details concerning More's practices of piety, which it would have been an impertinence in Erasmus to relate during his friend's lifetime, especially in writing to a man like Ulrich von Hutten, who had little sympathy with such things.

But let us first hear More himself describe the division of his day, and his view of the duties of a man of the world. His words in the Preface to his *Utopia* are as follows : "While I do daily bestow my time about law matters—some to plead, some to hear, some as an arbitrator with mine award to determine, some as an umpire or a judge with my sentence finally to discuss ; while I go one way to see and visit my friend ; another way about mine own private affairs; while I spend almost all the day abroad amongst other, and the residue at home amongst my own ; I leave to myself, I mean to my book, no time. For when I am come home I must commune with my wife, chat with my children, and talk with my servants. All the which things I reckon and account among business, forasmuch as they must of necessity be done ; and done must they needs be, unless a man will be a stranger in his own house. And in any wise a man must so fashion and order his conditions, and so appoint and dispose himself, that he be merry, jocund, and pleasant among them, whom either nature has provided, or chance hath made, or he himself hath chosen to be the fellows and companions of his life. . . . When do I write, then ? and all this while have I spoken no word of sleep, neither yet of meat, which among a great number doth waste no less time than doth sleep—wherein almost half the lifetime of man creepeth away. I, therefore, do win and get only that time which I steal from sleep and meat." *

From this we might conjecture that Thomas More kept late hours, that he remained studying when others had retired to rest. He adopted a much wiser course. Those were indeed days of early rising and early sleeping according to our notions. But More's hours were extraordinary even then. Stapleton says : " His custom was not to give more than four, or at most five, hours to sleep. He used to rise at two o'clock in the morning, and until seven to give himself to study and devotion. †

" Every day before any other business—his very early studies alone excepted—he used to hear Mass. This duty he so strictly observed, that when summoned once by the king at a time when he was assisting at Mass, and sent for a second and third time, he would not go until the whole Mass was ended ; and to those who called him and urged him to go at once to the king and leave the Mass, he replied that he was paying his court to a greater and better Lord, and must first perform that duty. Henry was then pious and God-fearing, and did not take in bad part this piety of More.

" He used," continues Stapleton, " daily to recite morning and evening prayers, to which he would add the seven peni- tential psalms and the litanies.‡ He would often add to these the gradual psalms and the psalm *Beati Immaculati*.§ He had also a collection of private prayers, some in Latin, some in

* Letter to Peter Giles (translation of Ralph Robinson).

† *Vita*, cap. 4.

‡ The litanies referred to by Stapleton are those now called the Litany of the Saints. As found in the Sarum Breviaries of the time of More, they varied for each day of the week, though with some features in com- mon. The number of saints explicitly named was much greater than at present.

§ There are fifteen psalms called Gradual, formerly recited by all priests on the Wednesdays in Lent, now only by monks. The psalm *Beati* is the very long 118th psalm, which is daily recited in the morning hours.

English, as may be seen in his English works. He had made up also, imitating in this St. Jerome and others, a small psaltery consisting of selected psalms, which he often used. He would also make pilgrimages to holy places, sometimes seven miles from his house, and always on foot, which even the common people scarcely do in England." * Among these holy places near London would be, no doubt, Our Lady of the Pew, at Westminster ; Our Lady of Barking, near the Tower ; Our Lady of Willesden, then much frequented ; and Our Lady of Grace, near the Tower.† Besides Our Lady's shrines there were many others then much venerated in London—as the Rood at the north door of St. Paul's, the Rood called St. Saviour in Southwark, St. Dominick at the Black Friars, St. Francis at the Grey Friars, etc. At a later period Sir Thomas earnestly defended the practice of making pilgrimages.

"Whenever he entered on a new office, or undertook a difficult business, he strengthened himself by the Holy Communion." So far Stapleton.‡

Some other details will be given of his private devotion when we come to his life at Chelsea, to which period may be reserved what has been handed down regarding his family devotions and his co-operation in the public worship in his parish church, as well as his alms-giving.

As I began this chapter with an account of More's earthly love, and have come now to speak of his heavenly love, I may conclude by a few words from his translation of the works of Pico, Count of Mirandula, which was made just before, or at an early period of, his married life, in which these two kinds of love are compared. I would beg the reader who wishes seriously to study the life of one of the world's best and greatest men not to skip the following passage as if it were a bit of laborious

* *Vita*, cap. 6.
† The abbey near the Tower called Eastminster was destroyed by Henry.
‡ *Vita*, cap. 6.

trifling of clever men, like the "conceits" of Donne or Cowley. We have More's ideal of human and Christian life—an ideal which he never changed, and which he strove hard, and not unsuccessfully, to realise. "The twelve properties or conditions of a lover" given by Pico are these :—

1. To love one alone.
2. To think him unhappy that is not with his love.
3. To adorn himself for the pleasure of his love.
4. To suffer all things, even death, to be with his love.
5. To desire to suffer shame and harm for his love.
6. To be ever with his love, at least in thought.
7. To love all things that pertain to his love.
8. To covet the praise of his love.
9. To believe of his love all things excellent.
10. To weep often with his love for joy or sorrow.
11. To languish and burn in the desire of his love.
12. To serve his love, nothing thinking of reward.

Each of these properties is developed by More in verse, or, as he calls it, in ballad—the lover of God taking lessons for himself from the conduct, and even fantasies, of earthly lovers. I must be content here with one specimen. In the following stanzas are developed the second "property" of the twelve :—

> Of his love, lo ! the sight and company
> To the lover so glad and pleasant is,
> That whoso hath the grace to come thereby
> He judgeth him in perfect joy and bliss ;
> And whoso of that company doth miss,
> Live he in never so prosperous estate,
> He thinketh him wretched—unfortunate.
>
> So should the lover of God esteem, that he
> Which all the pleasure hath, mirth and disport
> That in this world is possible to be,
> Yet till the time that he may once resort
> Unto that blessed, joyful, heavenly port,
> Where he of God may have the glorious sight
> Is void of perfect joy and sure delight.

We have seen how joyous was the character of More ; we shall see that his whole life, until the last great catastrophe (in a worldly sense), was continuous happiness and prosperity. Yet it is no exaggeration to say that a man more detached from this world never lived, for the reason that his mind was entirely set upon the joy that can never fail. In the letter to Ulrich, Erasmus gives the following emphatic testimony: "Although in so many respects he is one of the happiest of men (and vainglory generally accompanies happiness), I never yet met mortal man so perfectly free from this vice. . . . Without the least taint of superstition, he is earnest in all true piety. He has his hours set apart for prayer—prayer not of routine, but from the heart. With his friends he so converses on the life that will follow this, that you cannot doubt that he speaks from the heart with a most earnest hope." *

* Cum amicis sic fabulatur de vita futuri sæculi ut agnoscas illum ex animo loqui, neque sine optima spe.

CHAPTER VI.

PROFESSIONAL.

WE have seen More promoted to the rank of utter barrister, and chosen for the honourable office of reader in an Inn of Chancery. This is not to be confounded with reader at an Inn of Court. The latter office demanded much higher learning and ability, and was reserved for the benchers. The Chancery reader had for his audience young students, clerks, and attornies: the reader at the Inn of Court, his brother barristers, and even the judges. After his marriage, says Roper, More applied himself diligently to the study of the law, "until he was called to the bench,* and had read there twice, which is as often as any judge of the law doth ordinarily read". "This office of reader," adds Stapleton, writing for the information of foreigners, "is most illustrious in England, and only given to seniors, and never exercised except by the most skilful, the rest who feel them selves unfit purchasing their liberty at a great expense." †

It was not until after the accession of Henry VIII. that More became a bencher. His first reading took place in the autumn of 1511, his second in Lent, 1516. ‡ On 3rd September, 1510, he was made under-sheriff of London. This office was in many respects different from that which is now known by the same name. He was the sheriff's judicial representative, and a great number of cases came under his jurisdiction. Hence it was the custom for the Common Council to select

---

* Made bencher, not judge.　　† *Vita*, cap. 2.　　‡ Foss.

for the office some learned lawyer, who continued to hold it
year after year by renomination. "I conjecture," writes
Lord Campbell, "that the under-sheriff, besides his other
duties, sat in the court of the Lord Mayor and the sheriffs,
in which causes of importance were then determined, and the
jurisdiction of which, by the process of foreign attachment,
was very extensive." * Erasmus, who resided with More
while he was under-sheriff, gives the following account :
"In London he has held for some years the office of judge
in civil causes. The office is noways onerous, for the judge
sits only on Thursdays, and during the forenoon, but it is
considered very honourable. No one ever concluded more
cases, or decided them with greater integrity. He often
remits the fees which it is customary for the suitors to pay.
Before the opening of the case each party pays in three
groats, † nor is it allowed to demand anything further. By
his way of acting he has become very popular with the citizens
of London." ‡

By his private practice as barrister, and by his official position,
he made, as Roper learnt from himself, an income of about
£400 a year, equal to about £5000 in our own time. Yet
Erasmus says : "No one was ever more free from avarice.
He would set aside from his income for his children what he
thought sufficient, and the remainder he used bountifully.
While he was still dependent on his fees, he gave to all true
and friendly counsel, considering their interests rather than
his own ; he persuaded many to settle with their opponents as
the cheaper course. If he could not induce them to act in
that manner—for some men deught in litigation—he would
still indicate the method that was least expensive." § Stapleton

* *Lives of Chancellors (More).*

† *Tres drachmas*—Harpsfield translated groats. A groat = 4d.

‡ Letter to Ulrich. The office of under-sheriff had been held by
Dudley, Henry VII.'s evil adviser (Seebohm, p. 192).

§ *Ib.*

adds details that he may easily have gathered from Harris, who had been More's clerk : "He would never defend a cause until he had thoroughly examined it, and discovered the whole truth. He used to advise his clients, whether they were relations, friends, or strangers—for he made no distinction —that above all things they should not misrepresent in the very least the facts of the case. After he had listened to them, he would say : 'If the case is as you report, I think you will gain your suit'. But if their cause was unjust, he told them so plainly, and exhorted them to desist. If they would not listen to him, he told them to seek their advocate elsewhere." *

He became the most popular barrister of the day, according to both Erasmus and Roper, and the king, who liked to have clever men in his service, instructed Wolsey to do his best to attract him. His efforts were at first unsuccessful, for More loved his liberty, and was perfectly contented with his position. By degrees, however, circumstances forced him to yield. The London merchants had controversies with those of the Still-yard, or the foreign merchants resident in London, and as these claimed treaties in their favour, it was necessary to send an embassy to Flanders to the Archduke Charles (afterwards emperor), to settle the questions amicably. The Londoners had so much trust in More that they asked the king to allow him to represent their interests. "Young More," as he is called by Wolsey,† no doubt in distinction from his father, was put in the commission with Cuthbert Tunstall (then arch-deacon of Chester), Richard Sampson (another ecclesiastic), Sir Thomas Spinelly and John Clyfford. ‡ He left England on 12th May, 1515,§ and was absent for more than six months,

* *Vita*, cap. 3.

† *Letters and Papers of Henry VIII.*, vol. ii. n. 534.

‡ Rymer, xiii. 497.

§ Sir James Mackintosh says that "an entry in the city records states that on 8th May, 1514, it was agreed by the Common Council that Thomas More, gentleman, one of the under-sheriffs of London, should occupy

residing principally in Bruges, Brussels, and Antwerp. The
diets of the ambassadors were twenty shillings a day, those of
More (as the junior member), only 13s. 4d.* Payment was
made in advance for two months, but as the embassy was
prolonged, Tunstall wrote to Wolsey in July : "Master More,
as being at a low ebb, desires by Your Grace to be set on float
again ". † For us, the interest of this embassy is not in the
questions debated, but in the friendships made by More on
the Continent, and his famous *Utopia*, which was begun during
his stay in Flanders. Postponing for a time the consideration
of this book, let us first follow More a little further in his
external life.

Soon after his return he wrote to Erasmus a long letter, of
which I omit only some business matters which regarded his
friend :—

"Since you left us ‡ I have received in all three letters from
you. If I were to say that I had written to you as often,
however hard I should lie, you would probably not believe me,
since you know how indolent I am in letter-writing, and that I
am not so superstitious about truth as to hate a fib in all respects like murder. Our friend, Pace, is engaged on an embassy in your parts ; at least, if he is not exactly with you, he
is away from here. I seem to have lost half myself by his
absence, and the other half by yours. . . .

"The Archbishop of Canterbury [Warham] has at last got
free from his office of chancellor. You know how many years

his office and chamber by a sufficient deputy, during his absence as the
king's ambassador in Flanders ". If so, the embassy was postponed to
1515. I can find no mention in the State Papers of any embassy in the
preceding year, whereas More did leave England early in May, 1515.
Sir James, however, says that both years are mentioned in the City
Records (*Life*, p. 68).

* *Letters and Papers*, ii. part ii, p. 1467, p. 1468-1470, also n. 678.
† *Ib.* n. 670.
‡ Erasmus had made one of his short visits to England early in 1515.

he sought this freedom. The king has appointed the Cardinal of York [Wolsey] as his successor, who is conducting himself so as to surpass even the great hopes that his virtues had excited.*

"You will be glad to hear that our legation was pretty successful, except that it dragged on much longer than I expected or wished. When I left home I thought I should be away for a couple of months, whereas I spent more than six in the legation. However, if the delay was long, the result was satisfactory. So when I saw the business for which I had come concluded, and that other affairs were likely to arise, I wrote to the cardinal and obtained leave to return home. I managed this by the help of my friends, and especially of Pace, who had not then left England. While I was returning I met him unexpectedly at Gravelines, but he was hurrying on so fast that we had barely time to salute each other. Tunstall has lately returned to England, but after scarcely ten days' interval not spent in rest, but most tediously and anxiously, in giving a report of his legation, he is now forced upon another embassy, to his great regret. But he might not decline it. The office of ambassador never much pleased me. It does not seem so suitable to us laymen as to you priests, who have no wives and children to leave at home, or who find them wherever you go. When we have been a short time away, our hearts are drawn back by the longing for our families. Besides, when a priest is sent out, he can take his whole household with him, and maintain them at the king's expense, though, when at home, he had to provide for them at his own; but, when I am away, I must provide for a double household, one at home, the other abroad. A liberal allowance was granted me by the king for the servants I took with me, but no account was taken of those whom I was obliged to leave at home. And yet, though

* He became chancellor on December 22, 1515. He had been made cardinal on September 10.

you know what a fond husband I am, what an indulgent father,
and gentle master, I was unable to prevail on them for my
sake to remain fasting even during the short time till my return
home.   Lastly, it is an easy matter for princes to reward priests
for their labours and expenses by ecclesiastical promotions,
without any cost to themselves.   There is no such rich or easy
provision for us.   On my return, an annual pension was, indeed, apppointed for me by the king, and one by no means
contemptible, either as regards the honour or the fruits, yet
hitherto I have refused it, and I think I shall continue to do
so, because, if I accepted it, my present office in the city, which
I prefer even to a better one, would either have to be resigned,
or else retained not without some offence to the citizens ; which
I should be most loth to give.   For, should any question arise
between them and the king about their privileges (as sometimes
happens), they might look on me as less sincere and trustworthy, being bound to the king by an annual pension.*

   " However, in my legation, some things greatly delighted me.
First, the living so long and continually with Tunstall, a man
who, while he is surpassed by none in culture, nor in strictness
of life, is also unequalled in sweetness of manners.   Next I acquired the friendship of Busleyden,† who received me with a
magnificence in proportion to his great riches, and a cordiality
in harmony with his goodness of soul.   He showed me his
house so marvellously built and splendidly furnished, and so
many antiquities in which you know my curiosity and delight, ‡

   * It seems, however, that he accepted the pension (see *infra*, p. 76).

   † Jerome Busleyden (Buslidius), a native of Luxembourg, was canon
of Liège, Cambrai, Malines, and Brussels, provost of St. Peter at Aire,
maitre des requêtes and counsellor, ambassador to Julius II., Francis I.,
and Henry VIII.   He died in 1517.   He was founder of the College of
the Three Languages at Louvain.   A letter of his is prefixed to the
Utopia.

   ‡ Ad haec tot vetustatis monumenta, quorum me scis esse percupidum.
Among More's epigrams are verses on Busleyden's coins, and on his
house at Mechlin.

and, above all, his library so well filled, and his breast more richly stocked than any library, so that he fairly bewildered me. I hear that he is about to undertake an embassy to our king.

"But in all my travels nothing was more to my wishes than my intercourse with your host, Peter Œgidius [Giles] of Antwerp, a man so learned, witty, modest, and so true a friend, that I would willingly purchase my intimacy with him at the cost of a great part of my fortune. He sent to me your *Apology*, and your commentary on the Psalm *Beatus Vir*. Dorpius has had your letter printed and prefixed to your *Apology*. I should have liked to meet him, but as I could not, I sent him a short letter ; for I could not leave without some salutation a man who is dear to me, both for his singular erudition, and for many other reasons, and not least, that by his criticisms of your *Moria*, he gave you the occasion to write your *Apology*. I rejoice that your *St. Jerome* and your *New Testament* are advancing so well ; they are most eagerly expected by all. Linacre has the greatest esteem for you, and everywhere talks of you. This I have heard from some who were present, when, at supper with the king, he spoke of you most profusely and affectionately ; and the king answered in such a way that my informers were of opinion that some eminent fortune would soon be bestowed on you. I pray God it may be so. Farewell, my dear Erasmus. My wife salutes you,* and Clements, who makes such daily progress in Latin and Greek literature, that I entertain no slight hope that he will be an ornament to his country and to letters. Farewell again, and be contented with this one letter for many months ; for in it I have imitated misers, who rarely give entertainments, and if they do chance to give a dinner, make it a long one, so as to avoid the expense of frequent invitations. London, 1516."†

* This is his second wife.

† There is no date of the month, but the letter must have been written very early in the year 1516.

More remained in England throughout the year 1516. He was busy in the preparation of his *Utopia* for the press, and in other literary work, which will be mentioned in the next chapter. In this Lent he was giving his second course of legal lectures in Lincoln's Inn. Wolsey was endeavouring to bring him to court. His friend Ammonio writes, on 17th February, 1516, to Erasmus : "More, having honourably accomplished his embassy in Flanders has returned home, and frequents the court with us. No one is earlier in the chancellor's ante-chamber." * And Erasmus replies, 10th March : "I am vexed that your occupations prevent the Muses having full possession of you. I see that More, till now unconquered, is being carried away into the same whirlwinds." † And in a letter to More himself : "I foresee that the favourable wind will carry you away from us ; but I resign myself, since it will be for your happiness ".‡ In his letter to Hutten, Erasmus reiterates that More was altogether unwilling to have honouis thrust upon him. "The king," he says, "really dragged him to his court. No one ever strove more eagerly to gain ad-mission there than More did to avoid it."

The favour with which he was regarded both by the king and the citizens of London is proved by his having been appointed by the Privy Council to appease the mob, in the great riot which gained for the 1st May, 1517, the name of Evil May Day. The jealousy with which the foreign merchants were regarded by the English merchants and apprentices in London, led to a very serious outbreak during the night of the 30th April. The aldermen and their guards had fled for their lives ; prisons were being broken open and houses plundered. In the midst of the tumult, however, when More addressed

* Nemo temperius eo matutinum Eboracensi portat Ave (Inter Epist. Erasm. 236).

† *Letter* 21. Erasmus writes from Antwerp. I am not sure that he had returned so soon from Basle. Perhaps the letter should be dated 1517.

‡ *Letter* 17, in App. dated 1st January, 1515 (probably 1517).

the rioters near St. Martin's Gate, he was listened to with respect, and had almost persuaded them to disperse, when stones thrown from a neighbouring house injured some who were with him and provoked retaliations, which caused the angry fires to blaze more fiercely than before. The result of this riot belongs to general history. More's name only occurs in it as a peacemaker.*

There is, however, a very interesting allusion to this riot in one of his latest works. He is showing how much mischief might arise from spreading about the rumour that heretics were very numerous in the country: "I remember that here in London, after the great business that was there on a May-day in the morning, by a rising made against strangers, for which divers of the 'prentices and journeymen suffered execution of treason, by an old statute made long before, against all such as would violate the king's safe-conduct. I was appointed, among others, to inquire by diligent examination, in what wise, and by what persons, that fiery conspiracy began. And in good faith, after much diligence used therein, we perfectly tried out at last, that all that business began only by the conspiracy of two young lads that were 'prentices in Cheap. Which, after the thing devised first between them twain, perused prior by the journeymen first, and after the 'prentices of many of the mean crafts in the city, bearing the first that they spake with in hand, that they had secretly spoken with many other occupations already, and that they were all agreed thereunto : and that, besides them, there were two or three hundred of serving men of divers lords' houses, and some of the king's too, which would not be named or known, that would yet in the night be at hand, and when they were once up, would not fail to fall in with them and take their part. And with this ungracious invention of those two lewd lads,

* See Hall and Stow ; also Brewer's Introduction to *Letters and Papers*, ii. 214.

which yet in the business fled away themselves," the riot and
disaster had their origin.* Sir Thomas goes on to show that
he did not forget this his first lesson as to the mischief of
secret societies.

The summer of 1517 brought a greater calamity to London
than a riot. A deadly disease called "the Sweating Sickness'
spread its ravages far and wide. As we shall meet this several
times in the life of More, it may be well to form some general
notion of what it was. Dr. Caius, a contemporary physician,
gives the following account of the origin and nature of this
dreadful sickness : "In the year of our Lord God 1485,
shortly after the 7th day of August, at which time King Henry
VII. arrived at Milford in Wales out of France, and in the
first year of his reign, there chanced a disease among the
people, lasting the rest of that month and all September, which
for the sudden sharpness and unwont cruellness passed the
pestilence. For this [the pestilence] commonly giveth in four,
often seven, sometime nine, sometime eleven, and sometime
fourteen days' respite to whom it vexeth. But that [the
Sweating Sickness] immediately killed some in opening their
windows, some in playing with children in their street doors,
some in one hour, many in two, it destroyed ; and at the
longest to them who merrily dined it gave a sorrowful supper.
As it found them, so it took them : some in sleep, some in
wake, some in mirth, some in care, some busy, and some idle ;
and in one house sometime three, sometime five, sometime
more, sometime all ; of the which, if the half in every town
escaped, it was thought great favour. This disease, because it
most did stand in sweating from the beginning until the ending,
was called here 'the Sweating Sickness' ; and because it first
began in England, it was named in other countries 'the
English Sweat'." †

* *Apology*, ch. xlvii. *English Works*, p. 920.
† Quoted by Mr. Brewer. Introduction to *Letters and Papers*, ii. 207.

More thus writes to Erasmus in August, 1517 : "We are in the greatest sorrow and danger. Multitudes are dying all round us : almost everyone in Oxford, Cambridge and London has been ill lately, and we have lost many of our best and most honoured friends ; among them—I grieve at the grief I shall cause you in relating it—our dear Andrew Ammonio, in whose death both letters and all good men suffer a great loss. He thought himself well fortified against the contagion by his moderation in diet. He attributed it to this, that, whereas he met hardly anyone whose whole family had not been attacked, the evil had touched none of his household. He was boasting of this to me and many others not many hours before his death, for in this ' Sweating Sickness' no one dies except on the first day of attack. I myself and my wife and children are as yet untouched, and the rest of my household have recovered. I assure you there is less danger on the battlefield than in the city. Now, as I hear, the plague has begun to rage in Calais, just when we are being forced to land there on our embassy, as if it was not enough to have lived in the midst of the contagion, but we must follow it also. But what would you have ! We must bear our lot. I have prepared myself for any event. Farewell, in haste. London, 19th August." *

In this letter More refers to an embassy to Calais. During the wars with France, wrongs had been perpetrated on both sides, and it was resolved to settle the disputes in conference. The commissioners were to meet at Calais, then English territory. After long delays, a commission was issued to Sir Richard Wingfield, the deputy of Calais, to Dr. Knight and Thomas More, on 26th August.† The negotiations were still further delayed because it was found that the French commissioners'

---

* Inter Epist. Erasm. 522. The Leyden editor has dated this 1520. As Ammonio died in the summer of 1517, it must have been written that year.

† *Letters and Papers*, ii. 3624.

faculties were not sufficiently extended. Thus the negotiations dragged on into November.* On the 15th of that month Erasmus wrote to Peter Giles from Louvain: "More is still at Calais, utterly wearied and at great expense, and engaged in hateful negotiations. Thus it is that kings beatify their friends. This it is to be beloved of cardinals." † This was an echo of More's letter of 25th October to Erasmus: "I quite approve of your resolution not to meddle with the laborious triflings of princes; and you show your love for me in wishing that I may extricate myself from them. You can scarcely believe how unwillingly I am engaged in them. Nothing can be more odious than this legation. I am relegated to this little maritime town, ‡ of which both the surroundings and the climate are unpleasant; and if litigation even at home, where it brings gain, is so abhorrent to my nature, how tedious must it be here, where it only brings loss!" § The allowance or diets made to ambassadors in those days were scanty enough, and it must have been indeed a serious loss to More to forego his professional income. A successful embassy was, however, generally rewarded by some ecclesiastical promotion to a clergyman, or by an annuity to a layman. ‖ Thus, among the fees and gratuities paid by the king in 1516 is mentioned, "Thomas More, councillor, for life £100".¶ On 21st June, 1518, when this payment recurs, it is recorded as paid out of the little customs of London. **

Roper relates an event which caused the king to draw More

---

* *Ib.*, 3750, 3766, 3772.

† *Epist.* 344. Wrongly dated by the editor 1518.

‡ His only relaxation seems to have been a two days' visit to the Abbot of St. Bertin's, an old friend of Erasmus. Letter of 7th October (Inter Ep. Erasm. 192, in App.).

§ Misdated by editor 1520.

‖ In the king's book of payments is an entry of £26 13s. 4d. each to Knight and More for this embassy.

¶ *Letters and Papers*, ii. part i. 2736, or p. 875.

** *Ib.*, part ii. 4247.

enti ely from his profession and place him at court. A great ship belonging to the Pope had been obliged to put in at Southampton, and was claimed by the king as a forfeiture. The papal nuncio asked that the matter should be publicly discussed before the king or his commissioners. More not only acted as interpreter, explaining to the ambassador, in Latin, the arguments made use of on either side, but argued so learnedly himself on the Pope's side that the matter was decided in his favour. The king, hearing how greatly he had distinguished himself, called him to his service. But, before we follow his career at court, we must go back to consider him in his literary and in his domestic life.*

---

* In 1879 Mr. E. W. Brabrook, F.S.A., read a paper before the Royal Society of Literature, showing that in 1514 a T. Morus was admitted into the Society of Advocates, or Professors of Civil Law, commonly called Doctors' Commons. The following entry occurs in the register, now in Lambeth :—

"Ego T. Morus, 3° die decembris a° a Christo nato 1514to, admissus sum in hanc societatem et polliceor me soluturum in annos singulos, s. 6. d. 8."

Mr. Brabrook seems to have good reason to take this T. Morus to be the future chancellor. The writing, of which Mr. Brabrook prints a facsimile in the Transactions of Royal Society of Literature (xii. pt. i., 1879), bears a close resemblance to Sir Thomas's later writing in Latin, which in several respects differed from English writing ; nor is any other T. More known to whom it can be attributed. That a common law lawyer should be associated with the professors of civil (or Roman) law may be explained both by More's wide culture, and by his desire to qualify himself better for foreign embassies. Bishop Stubbs writes : "In the infancy of international law and the administration of both admiralty and martial law, the English jurists had to go beyond their insular practice, and to no other source could they apply themselves [than the civil law]; hence the association, which to the present day has subsisted, between the curiously unconnected departments of maritime and matrimonial jurisdiction". (*Lectures on Mediæval and Medern History*, p. 309.) It seems very probable that the question regarding the Pope's ship was argued before the Admiralty Court, and that More's admission into the Society of Advocates entitled him to plead, though the fact is not mentioned by his biographers.

CHAPTER VII.

LITERARY.

I. LIFE OF JOHN PICUS.

IN 1510, More published his "Life of John Picus, Earl of Mirandula, a great Lord of Italy, an excellent cunning man in all sciences, and virtuous of living, with divers *Epistles* and other works of the said John Picus". He had probably made this translation some years before, during the time of his retirement from the displeasure of Henry VII.

Giovanni Pico della Mirandola, Count of Concordia, had died in 1494, at the age of thirty-two, leaving a name famous for his great talents and erudition, his first vainglorious appearance before the world and then his thorough conversion to God.* His complete works had been printed in Bologna in 1496, and again in Venice in 1498. The latter edition, which is much superior to the former, was the one used by More. Out of it he selected the life prefixed by Pico's nephew, four letters, and a commentary on the sixteenth psalm.

Pico had appended to one of his letters twelve rules of spiritual warfare, twelve weapons, and twelve properties or conditions of a lover. Taking these for his theme, More

---

* His epitaph is felicitous :—

"Joannes jacet hic Mirandula ; cætera norunt
Et Tagus et Ganges, forsan et Antipodes ".

This was written before Vasco de Gama had rounded the Cape of Good Hope.

developed them in his favourite seven-line stanzas. The poetry is entirely his own, there are no corresponding Latin verses in the works of Pico. But Pico wrote a beautiful prayer in Latin elegiac verse, of which More has given a translation or rather paraphrase in the same stanzas as the rest. More's verses cannot be called poetical. They served, however, to put spiritual maxims in a form that would arrest the attention and cling to the memory. A specimen was given in Chapter V.

The translation of Pico's Life and Letters was dedicated by More to " his right entirely beloved sister in Christ, Joyeuse Leigh," as a new year's present. This lady seems to have been a nun.*

In the year 1513, while More was under-sheriff, he managed to find time to compose his *History of Richard III.*, both in English and Latin. It was, however, never completed, nor was it published during More's life. It appeared, "corrupted" by omissions and additions, in Harding's and Hall's *Chronicles ;* but was reprinted correctly by Rastell from a copy in More's handwriting. Some have doubted whether this work is by More or merely translated by him. The intrinsic evidence is in favour of its being his composition. The English is beautiful, and More paid no less attention to his English prose than to his Latin style. The book is full of pithy sayings. The speeches introduced (though not to be taken as really spoken) are the work of an orator like More, who had carefully trained himself on ancient models. A most competent critic has said : " As if it had been the lot of More to open all the paths through the wilds of our old English speech, he is to be considered as our earliest prose writer, and as the first Englishman who wrote the history of his country in its present language. . . . The composition has an ease and rotundity which gratify

* Since the above was written More's translation has been republished with notes and a very interesting Introduction on the writings of Pico, by J. M. Rigg, Esq. (Nutt, 1890).

the ear without awakening the suspicion of art, of which there
was no model in any preceding writer of English prose." *

II. Translation of Lucian.

We have seen the friendship that sprang up between More
and Erasmus during the visit made by the latter to England in
1498 and 1499. Erasmus did not return to England until the
end of 1505, when More was married and had taken up in
earnest his profession of the law. He found the young
barrister surrounded by literary friends; Colet, vicar of
Stepney, and then or soon after dean of St. Paul's; Grocyn,
formerly professor of Greek at Oxford, and then rector of St.
Lawrence, in the Jewry; Linacre, a most learned priest, and
physician to Henry VII. (as he was afterwards to Henry VIII.);
Lilly, a younger man than the others, yet not less cultivated.
In fact, from a still earlier date and to the end of his life,
More's company was eagerly sought by every man of the new
culture, whether English or foreign, who came to London.

Erasmus was invited to stay with More, and the two scholars
found a most congenial occupation in the translation from
Greek into Latin of several of Lucian's dialogues. More
selected three of these for his own share — the Cynicus,
Menippus or Necromantia, and Philopseudes, as the most
witty. In his dedication of these to Thomas Ruthal, secretary
to Henry VIII., and afterwards Bishop of Durham, More
extols the truth and wisdom, as well as the wit, of these
dialogues. That Lucian was incredulous even of man's immortality does not much trouble him. "What do I care for
the opinions of a heathen on such matters?" Lucian may

---

* Sir James Mackintosh (*Life of Sir T. More* (1844), p. 41). The
objection made by Sir H. Ellis that the writer remembered something
said to his father at the death of Edward IV. in 1483, and that More was
then only three years old, is of no force, since he was really five ; and it
is not unusual to remember isolated facts which made an impression at
the age of four or five.

help us to laugh at superstition without touching our religious faith, which has no foundation in human dreams and fictions, but rests on solid historical proofs, which are only contaminated and weakened when mixed up with fables.*

In addition to these translations More composed a Declamation in imitation of Lucian. Mr. Seebohm says : "At More's suggestion both (he and Erasmus) wrote a full answer to Lucian's arguments in favour of tyrannicide ".† This account might lead those unacquainted with More's writings to think that, while Lucian defended the slaying of tyrants, More rejected and reprobated it. What may have been More's serious judgment on such a subject we can only gather indirectly, from his submission to the Church's teaching both in faith and morals. In his *Life of Pico* he had said that Pico "committed (like a good Christian man) both his defence and all other things that he should write to the most holy judgment of our mother Holy Church".‡ But on the subject of tyrannicide in general More has written nothing. Like Lucian, he presupposes the lawfulness and excellent merit of slaying a tyrant; yet if he does this, it is merely in a literary exercise. Lucian had supposed a Greek city, of a republican constitution, of which one of the chief magistrates had made himself the oppressor and tyrant. There was a constitutional law in the republic authorising any citizen to take the life of such a usurper, and entitling him to a great reward in case of success. A man, intent on freeing his city from the tyrant, manages to get secretly into his citadel, in order to assassinate him. He does not find the tyrant, but kills his son and leaves his sword in the

---

* After the above he continues: Quas scriptura nobis historias divinitus inspirita commendat, eis indubitata fides habenda est. Cæteras vero ad Christi doctrinam, tanquam ad Critolai regulam, applicantes caute et cum judicio, aut recipiamus aut respuamus si carere volumus et inani fiducia et superstitiosa formidine (*Epist. Dedic.*).

† *Oxford Reformers*, p. 182.

‡ *English Works*, p. 4.

body. The tyrant, finding his son slain, kills himself with the sword. The assassin then claims the reward of tyrannicide from his fellow-citizens. The supposed pleading of this man is Lucian's Declamation, and the Declamation of More is an answer to the assassin's pleadings. He supposes himself to be a citizen in this Greek republic, and he proves that, though accidentally the city has been freed, the assassin can claim no merit or reward, but rather deserves punishment, since his ill-planned attempt and the murder of the son were more likely to have enraged the tyrant, and to have confirmed his tyranny, than to have overthrown it. More's imaginary speech is well worthy to be both read and studied. It is a masterpiece of oratory, and gives us a specimen of that skill in arranging argument, and expressing it in powerful and dignified language, which placed More the first (in order of time) on the list of great English orators.

Erasmus also published his Declamation on the same subject. In the dedication to Richard Whitford, chaplain to the Bishop of Winchester,* he says that he has written this essay in oratory at the instigation of More, whose eloquence is so great that he could obtain anything even from an enemy, and whom Erasmus loves so dearly that if he asked him to dance on the tight-rope he would obey without a murmur. "Unless my ardent love blinds me, nature never made any one so ready of wit, so keen sighted, so shrewd. His intellect is equalled by his power of speech ; and his suavity is so great, his humour so keen yet so innocuous, that he has every quality of a perfect advocate." †

Elsewhere he says : " The style of his oratory approaches more the structure and dialectic subtlety of Isocrates than the limpid stream of Cicero, although in urbanity he is in no way inferior to Tully. He paid so much attention in his youth to

* The same Whitford, afterwards named The Wretch of Sion, and the author of the well-known *Psalter of Jesus.*

† *Eras. Opera*, t. i. 266.

writing poetry, that you may now discern the poet in his prose compositions."

III. The Moria of Erasmus.

In 1508 Erasmus was again in England, and again the guest of More. In his house, and with his encouragement, he composed his famous *Praise of Folly*, *Encomium Moriæ*, so called with a little intentional joke on the name More. It does not belong to my subject to notice in any detail the writings of Erasmus, but More is so closely connected with this work that I must enter into some explanations. We have, then, two facts to consider—that More is honoured by the Church, and that this book, written under his roof and with his applause, was placed on the index of prohibited books. To say that More is honoured merely as a martyr, *i.e.*, for his heroic death, and that this implies no approval of the details of his previous life, may be a sufficient vindication of the consistency of the Holy Church, but it does not clear the character of More. To admire and extol that character it is not indeed necessary to clear it from every stain. No one insisted on this more frequently than More himself, when speaking of our veneration for the fathers and saints of the Church. Shall it then be said, in all candour, that as Erasmus was led astray by his satirical spirit in this work, so More too was somewhat blinded by his partiality for Erasmus and his own love of fun? Some may be inclined to take this view. Stapleton says that the friendship which existed between these two eminent men was honourable to Erasmus rather than useful to More ; that in later life More exhorted Erasmus to imitate St. Augustine in publishing a book of Retractations, but that Erasmus was so far from this humility that in his collection of letters he even suppressed this request of More's.* Candour, however, compels me to take a different

* *Vita*, cap. 4. Is not Stapleton mistaken? In a letter to Edward Lee in 1519 More writes : Neque enim unquam me pro tanto viro gessi a quo vel in aliquo literarum genere, vel in rerum perpensione communium Erasmus admonendus esse videretur (Apud Jortin, ii. 652).

view, for I do not find that More ever repented his share in the *Praise of Folly*. This book is satirical on all classes, from popes and kings to pilgrims and beggars; yet its satire is moderate compared with that of many previous writers whose faith and loyalty to the Church have never been called in question. Satire on ecclesiastical persons—whatever opinion we may form of it—must not be confounded with the ridicule cast by heretics on Divine dogmas, or institutions, or practices approved by the Church. There was never one day in his life when More would have applauded or tolerated an attack or a sneer at anything which he knew the Church to have countenanced. A work, however, like that of Erasmus, written in Latin, and intended merely for the learned, might easily seem to him quite inoffensive.* Some years earlier a German named Sebastian Brant had written in German verse a book called the *Ship of Fools*. There had been no outcry against it. It had been at once translated into Latin, Dutch, French, and English. A recent Scotch editor of this book, Mr. Jamieson, writes : " Brant can scarcely be classed in the great army of Protestant reformers. He was a reformer from within, a biting and unsparing exposer of every priestly abuse, but a loyal son of the Church." Of the English translator, or rather adapter, of this book, Alexander Barclay, a priest, Mr. Jamieson also says : " Barclay applies the cudgel as vigorously to the priest's pate as to the Lollard's back. But he disliked modern innovation as much as ancient abuses, in this also faithfully reflecting the mind of the people."† This seems to me a perfectly just estimate, and explains why More saw no harm or danger in

---

* Erasmus in his letter to Bozthem says that the book was received with great applause—præsertim apud magnates—those who were most caustically attacked. It began to give offence especially when Lystrius (while defending it) added commentaries to explain its allusions. It was thus brought to the level of men for whom it had not been intended.

† *Ship of Fools*, translated in verse by Alex. Barclay. Ed. by F. H. Jamieson (Edinburgh : Paterson, 1874, 2 vols.).

the somewhat similar book of Erasmus when it first appeared. The *Ship of Fools* had been received with applause throughout Europe. It had even been taken as a text-book for sermons in Germany.* In England it was translated into both prose and verse, without reclamation or protest.† Why should a deeper book, written in Latin for more learned men, be pernicious or perilous? That it was judged and declared to be so by the Church more than fifty years later, proves what it had become, not what it was at its first appearance. Circumstances had totally changed, and it is often the circumstances in which a book is read that determine its weight. There was a time when the Pagan classics were dangerous reading, not only from a moral, but a dogmatic point of view. That time is long since past for those who are brought up Christians. There was a time when the speculations of the Manichees could entangle a clever rationalising youth like Augustine. At the present day, not only could a clever youth read them without danger, but he would read them with wonder that they could ever have had attractions for a reasonable man. And as a book may cease to be dangerous, so also it may become dangerous by change of times.

When Erasmus wrote his *Praise of Folly*, the whole of Europe was Catholic; Luther's name was yet unknown except in Wittenburg, where he bore the character of a good Catholic. There was no prospect of heresy on any large scale, but among all good men there were hopes of Catholic Reformation. Whether the satire of Erasmus was likely to hasten it might well be doubted. More thought it would, and welcomed the book. In later years, long before it was officially condemned, he regretted its appearance, not because he had changed his opinion of the book itself, but because he saw that it had been inopportune, and was abused by heretics and injurious to

---

* *Navicula sive speculum fatuorum* of Dr. John Geiler, printed in 1510. Each sermon has for text: "The number of fools is infinite".
† By Henry Watson, in 1509. It was printed by Wynkyn de Worde.

feeble-minded Catholics. It will be better, however, to hear his own words on the subject.

In 1532, he wrote thus to Erasmus: "Your adversaries cannot be ignorant how candidly you confess that, before these pestilent heresies arose, which have since spread everywhere and upset everything, you treated certain matters in a way you would not have treated them had you been able to guess that such enemies of religion and such traitors would ever arise. You would then have put what you had to say more mildly and with more limitations.* You wrote strongly then because you were indignant at seeing how some cherished their vices as if they were virtues."†

Again, writing against Tindale in 1532, More says that Erasmus in his *Moria* had in a dramatic spirit put the objections against certain matters in a caustic and whimsical way, just as he had himself done in his *Dialogue*, "Quoth he and Quoth I," where he makes the "messenger" speak strongly and sarcastically against many things, which More then, in his own person, either allows to be abuses, or defends with a distinction, or explains and altogether approves. "But," continues More, "in these days in which Tindale hath with the

---

* Mitius ac dilutius.

† Inter Epist. Erasm. 1123. Among the words of Erasmus referred to by More I may mention these: Moriam scripsi tranquillis rebus, quum mundus altum indormiret cæremoniis ac præscriptis hominum, haudquaquam scripturus, si horum tempestatem exorituram præscissem (*ad Botzhem*). "Si præscissem hujusmodi sæculum exoriturum, aut non scripsissem quædam, quæ scripsi, aut aliter scripsissem" (*Ep.* 572 anno 1521). In another letter of 1524 he says in general that what he was accused of having written about the origin of the Pope's supremacy, about confession, marriage, etc., he wrote when there was no thought as yet of Luther's errors; that he merely wrote doubting, not asserting; and that he was always ready to submit to the Church; lastly, that he had modified what might give offence or handle to the new errors (*Ep.* 667). This is but a poor apology for sowing doubts in matters of faith; but as regards the form of his satire in things not of faith (and in such only is the character of More concerned), the excuse is a valid one.

infection of his contagious heresies so sore poisoned malicious
and new-fangled folk . . . in these days in which men, by their
own default, misconstrue and take harm out of the very Scripture of God, until men better amend, if any man would now
translate *Moria* into English, or some works either that I have
myself written ere this, albeit there be none harm therein, folk
yet being given to take harm of that which is good, I would not
only 'my darling's' [*i.e.*, Erasmus's *] books, but mine own also,
help to burn them both with mine own hands, rather than folk
should (though through their own fault) take any harm of them,
seeing that I see them likely in these days so to do." †

IV. PRIVATE LETTERS.

More speaks here of works of his own, *in which there was no
harm*, yet which might be made hurtful. In spite of a recent
attempt by Mr. Seebohm to draw from the writings of Blessed
Thomas More, and from those of his friends, Colet and
Erasmus, those very conclusions which More protests should
not be drawn from them, I do not think there is much danger
at the present day that the fun, or the satire, or the serious
reproofs of any of these writers can do any injury to any
Catholic doctrine, practice, or sentiment. I speak, indeed,
with great reserve of the works of Erasmus, which require a
prudent reader. But I have been unable to find in the writings
of More any pages that I could wish unwritten or burnt for fear of
scandal to the weak or simple ; nor do I fear his blame if I
now print in English what he would certainly not *then* have
written in English, or what he never intended for publication
in any way, but wrote for the eye of Erasmus only.

In 1516, Erasmus had published his translation and notes on
the New Testament, which, though dedicated to the Pope, and
honoured with a letter from him, and cordially approved by men
like Warham and Fisher, had caused a commotion among

---

* Tindale had thus named him.　　　† *English Works*, p. 422.

certain theologians and in certain religious orders. On 31st October, 1516, More writes to Erasmus that there is a great conspiracy brewing against him. "Who are the conspirators? I fear to tell you lest you should quail before such terrible and powerful enemies. Well, if I must say it, one is that renowned Franciscan theologian whom you know, and of whom you make honourable mention in your edition of *St. Jerome.* He has entered into a plot with other chosen men of the same order and the same kidney, to write against your errors. To do this more easily and efficaciously, they have conspired to divide your works among them, to scrutinise everything and understand nothing. Do you see the danger impending over you? The resolution was made in a nocturnal assembly, when they were well soaked. Next day, as I hear, when they had slept off the dregs, having forgotten their resolution and cancelled their decree, since it had been written in wine, they relinquished the undertaking, and from reading betook themselves again to begging, which long experience had taught them to be more useful. *

"It is worth while to see how the *Epistolæ Obscurorum Virorum* pleases all, the learned as a joke, the unlearned seriously.† When we laugh, these latter think we are only amused by the style, which they don't defend; but they say it is compensated by the gravity of the matter, and that a most beautiful sword is hidden in a rude scabbard. What a pity a better title was not found! But for that in a hundred years they would never have discovered that the author was making a nose at them longer than the horn of a rhinoceros."‡

It is clear that, when More wrote this, he was a little infected with the spirit of the book he had been just reading, which is

---

* Notwithstanding this passage, More writes: Ordo Minoritarum, quo, nisi me fallit opinio, nullus est ordo sanctior (Letter to a monk, in Jortin ii. 695).

† The first volume of this satirical book had just appeared.

‡ Inter Epist. Erasm. 87.

a merciless parody on the writings and ways of the monks and friars.   Let it however be remembered that he did not write this letter for publication, and that it was first published without his leave.   Of such letters, Erasmus himself says : " I was try- ing my hand, killing time, amusing myself with intimate friends, getting rid of my bile, jesting at most, and expecting nothing less than that my friends would copy out and preserve such absurdities ".*

At first MS. collections of such private letters were made and sold by booksellers, then unauthorised editions published, until the author was obliged in self-defence to print an accurate edition.   Erasmus complains that in this way everything was perverted and misunderstood, " no attention being paid to the time in which a man wrote, but what was written at first most appropriately is afterwards applied most inopportunely.   Besides this, men sometimes write their letters after their wine, or when sleepy, or tired, or half-sick, or when pre-occupied with other affairs, or against their will—and very often they accommodate their style to the capacity or the tact of their correspondent." What mischief will arise when such letters get into the hands of those for whom they were never intended !

V. Letter to Dorpius.

No such explanation or apology is applicable to letters written in order to be spread about or published.   There are two such pamphlets, as we should call them, written by More in defence of Erasmus, and of the critical studies in which Erasmus was engaged on the New Testament and on the Fathers, between the years 1516 and 1520.   Of these I shall now speak.

A theologian of Louvain, named Martin Dorpius, a man of

* *Letter* 507, to Beatus Rhenanus, prefixed to an edition of his *Epistles* in 1520, which he was obliged to reprint because the letters had been already printed surreptitiously.

much reputation in polite letters and a personal friend of Erasmus, had written to him some rather sharp expostulations, both on his *Encomium Moriæ*, and on his pretension to set aside the authority of the Vulgate by a new Latin version. When More was in Flanders in the autumn of 1515, he saw copies of these letters. He had wished to make the personal acquaintance of Dorpius, but not having the opportunity of meeting him, he wrote to him a long Latin letter in defence of Erasmus. He complains especially that Dorpius treats Erasmus as if he were a mere grammarian, a master of words and form, without theological learning, and also that Erasmus is accused of attacking theologians in general, whereas he had merely satirised the excesses or follies of a few. More then goes on to assert that there are theologians who neither study the Holy Scriptures nor esteem the Fathers, but give themselves entirely to scholastic subtleties and trifling—men as far removed from true theology as from common sense. Here More's humour makes him illustrate his subject by a racy anecdote: "I was dining," he says, "with an Italian merchant as learned as he was rich.* There was present at table a monk who was a theologian and a notable disputant, lately arrived from the Continent, for the very purpose of ventilating some questions that he had got up, to see what kind of debaters he could find in England, and to make his name as famous in England as in his own country. At the dinner nothing was said by anyone, however well weighed and guarded, that this man did not, before it was well uttered, seek to refute with a syllogism, though the matter belonged neither to theology nor philosophy and was altogether foreign to his profession. I am wrong. His profession was to dispute. He had stated at the beginning of dinner that he was ready to take either side on any question. By degrees our host, the Italian merchant, turned the conversation to theological topics, such as usury, tithes, or confession

* Probably Antonio Bonvisi, a great friend of More's and a learned man.

to friars outside the penitent's parish, and the like. Whatever
was said the theologian took at once the opposite view. . . .
The merchant soon perceived that the monk was not so well
up in his Bible as he was ready with his syllogisms; so he
began to draw his arguments from authority rather than from
reason. He invented, *ex tempore*, certain quotations in favour
of his own side of the question, taking one from a supposed
Epistle of St. Paul, another from St. Peter, a third from the
Gospel, and affecting to do this with the greatest exactness,
naming the chapter, but in such a way that, if a book was
divided into sixteen chapters, he would quote from the
twentieth. What did our theologian do now? Hitherto he
had rolled himself up in his spikes like a hedgehog. Now he
has to dodge from side to side to escape these supposed texts.
He managed it, however. He had no notion that the passages
quoted were spurious, while, of course, he could not refuse the
authority of Scripture; but, as, on the other hand, it would be
a base thing to own himself beaten, he had his answer ready at
once. 'Yes, sir,' he said, 'your quotation is good, but I
understand the text in this way,' and then made a distinction
of senses, one of which might be in favour of his adversary, the
other of himself; and when the merchant insisted that his was
the only possible sense, the theologian swore till you would
almost believe him, that the sense which he had selected was
that given by Nicolas of Lyra." Now how, concludes More,
can anyone help laughing at theologians like this? And such
are the only men ridiculed by Erasmus.

The passage I have quoted is but a page in a long letter full
of erudition, of theological as well as classical learning, and of
very earnest and eloquent pleading. Dorpius had seemed to
underrate the difficulties of the study of Holy Scripture in
order to exalt scholastic theology. No professor of sacred
exegesis could dwell more warmly on the depths of God's word
than does the witty lawyer; and then turning to scholasticism,
he says: "But let us suppose that Scripture is easy, and your

questions difficult, yet the knowledge of the former may be far
more fruitful than the guessing at the latter.   To dance or to
bend double like an acrobat is more difficult than to walk, and
it is easier to masticate bread than to grind pot-sherds between
the teeth, but what man would not prefer the common processes
of nature to such empty feats ?   Which, then, of these disciplines is the easier I will not ask, but I cannot hear it said that
these minute questionings are more useful than the knowledge
of the sacred writings to the flock for which Christ died.   If
you merely maintain that they are things worth studying, I will
not contest it ; if you put them on a level with the dissertations
of the ancient Fathers, I cannot listen to you ; but when you
not only compare but prefer these kitchen-maids to the most
holy Bible, the Queen of all books, forgive me, Dorpius, but I
cannot refrain from saying to them with Terence : Abite hinc
in malam rem cum istac magnificentia fugitiva : adeo putatis
vos aut vestra facta ignorarier ? . . .

" I do not think you will contest this with me, that whatever
is necessary for salvation is communicated to us in the first
place from the sacred Scriptures, then from the ancient interpreters, and by traditional customs handed down from the
ancient Fathers from hand to hand, and in fine by the sacred
definitions of the Church.   If, in addition to all this, these
acute disputants have curiously discovered anything, though I
grant it may be convenient and useful, yet I think it belongs
to the class of things without which it is possible to live.   Perhaps you will say that in the ancient writers everything is not
so ready at hand and easy to find, not sorted so well as in
modern writers, who have arranged whatever is known under
certain heads, and enrolled each individual in its proper family.
Well, I grant all this ; and I allow that there is some convenience in putting literary matters in their right places, just as we
arrange our domestic furniture, so that without mistake we may
lay our hand at once on what we want.   This is a convenience,
yet it is used so inconveniently by some, that it would be

almost better to be without it. The reason why the ancient interpreters are so much neglected, is because certain unhappy geniuses have first persuaded themselves, and then led others to believe, that there is nowhere any honey besides what has already been stored up in the hives of the Summists. . . . Theologians of this kind, who read nothing of the Fathers or of the Scriptures except in the Sentences, and the commentators on the Sentences, seem to me to act as if one were to set aside all the authors who have written in Latin, and, gathering the rules of grammar from Alexander, try to learn all else from the *Cornucopia* of Perottus and from Calepinus, being convinced that all Latin words will be found there. Well, most words will be found there, and the choicest words, and the sentences from ancient poets and orators, some of whom are no longer extant elsewhere. Yet such a method will never make a good Latinist. And so also, though in your Summists and Masters of Sentences you will find many sayings of the ancients quoted as authorities, yet the study of these things alone will never make a good theologian, even though he is conversant with ten thousand thorny questions. . . .

"And what purpose does this kind of theology serve? To convert or refute heretics? Certainly not. If these are unlearned you might as well try to bring a Turk to the faith by a French sermon. If they are learned, these very questions supply them with weapons. It becomes like a fight between two naked men among a heap of sharp stones; each of them has the means of injuring the other, and neither of them can defend himself. Heretics are versed in all these tricks, and would never be overcome by such theologians, if they were not more afraid of one faggot than of whole bundles of these syllogisms. Can such a theologian make a preacher? Why, as the people understand nothing of this kind of language, he must lay it aside and learn by heart a sermon from his *Veni mecum* or his *Dormi secure*,* foolish in itself, and when it is declaimed

* The names of popular sermon manuals.

by a man more foolish still, how dull and stupid the whole affair will be."

The above passages must suffice as specimens both of the style and matter of More's first public essay in theology. We know that even before his death an immense movement had begun in the Church, both in scriptural and patristic studies, while scholastic theology was purified and developed. It can scarcely be denied that an English layman may claim some influence in this movement. Of More's knowledge in theology a further account will be given when we come to his English controversial works.

The letter which More wrote to Dorpius was well received by him, and he publicly retracted what he had written against Erasmus. Nothing can be prettier than the letter in which More congratulates him on this magnanimity. " It is well-nigh impossible," he says, "to extort a retractation even from the most modest. Almost all are so stupid with false shame that they would rather show themselves always fools, than acknowledge that they were such once ; while you, who have so much cleverness, learning and eloquence, that even if you were to defend something quite improbable or purely paradoxical, you would be able to convince your readers ; you, I say, caring more for truth than for appearances, prefer to tell all the world that you were once deceived, rather than to go on deceiving. Such an act will bring you eternal glory." *   More himself did his best to suppress the letter that had gained this victory. †

VI. LETTER TO A MONK.

There is another letter or pamphlet, written a few years later, also in defence of Erasmus, but in a much severer tone.

* Letter in Jortin ii. 668.

† See his letter to Lee, *Ib.*, 653. It was, however, reprinted in 1525. *Thomae Mori Dissertatio Epistolica de aliquot sui temporis theologastrorum ineptiis, etc., Ad Martinum Dorpium. Lugduni Batavorum,* 1525. It is now in his collected works.

A monk of a contemplative order, whom More had known as a youth before his entrance into religion, had taken on himself to write a letter of very solemn warning against the errors of Erasmus, and the danger to More's eternal welfare of associating with such a man. There was a tone of assumed sanctity in the letter, united with calumnies so atrocious, that More thought it his duty, not only to defend Erasmus, but to strip the mask of false zeal from his assailant, to show him how rash were his judgments, how grossly unjust his words ; and, to bring home the matter, he pointed out how hypocrisy and superstition, and even gross immorality, sometimes get into the cloister, so that it was more befitting for a contemplative monk to watch against spiritual pride, than to meddle with things out of his sphere, to criticise one far more learned than himself, and to blame where the Sovereign Pontiff approved. Out of this letter I will merely select a few passages, which may show Blessed Thomas More in his graver mood, when his indignation had been stirred by an unjust attack, not on himself, but on his esteemed and beloved friend.

"I wonder," he says, "at the unbounded leisure, which you find to devote to schismatical and heretical books. Or have you so few good books that you are obliged to consume your short leisure on bad ones? If the books (of Erasmus) are good, why do you condemn them? If they are bad, why do you read them? As you gave up the care of the world, when you shut yourself up in the cloister, you are not one of those to whom leave is given to read bad books for the sake of refuting them. Hence by reading what is perverse you are merely learning it. Not only do you spend good hours on bad books, but you consume much time, as it appears, in talk and gossip worse than bad books; so that I notice there is no kind of rumour or calumny which does not find its way straight to your cell. We read that formerly monks so hid themselves from the world, that they would not even read the letters sent to them by their friends, nor glance back at the

Sodom they had left.   Now, I see, they read schismatical and heretical books, and immense volumes filled with mere trifles. Now, what they formerly dreaded to hear in the world, and fled to the cloister lest they should hear it, the cunning enemy has found a means of carrying into their very cells. Their solemn religious surroundings only serve to impose on the unwary, their leisure serves to elaborate their calumnies, their retirement from the eyes of men to prevent them from being abashed, and their closed cells to injure the reputation of those outside.   Whoever enters their cells must say an *Our Father* that the conversation may be holy.   But where is the use of beginning slanderous gossip with the Lord's Prayer? If that is not taking the Name of God in vain, what is?" *

More's rebukes are severe.   From the same letter I give one specimen of a lighter style, because it brings before us an incident of his life.

"There was at Coventry a Franciscan of the unreformed sort.   This man preached in the city, the suburbs, the neighbourhood, and villages about, that whosoever should say daily the Psalter of the Blessed Virgin [*i.e.*, the fifteen decades of the Rosary] could never be lost.   The people listened greedily to this easy way of getting to heaven.   The pastor there, an excellent and learned man, though he thought the saying very foolish, said nothing for a time, thinking that no harm would come from it, since the people would become the more devout to God from greater devotion to the Blessed Virgin.   But at last he found his flock infected with such a disease that the very worst were especially addicted to the Rosary for no other reason than that they promised themselves impunity in everything; for how could they doubt of heaven, when it was promised to them with such assurance by so grave a man, a friar direct from heaven?   The pastor then began to warn his flock not to trust too much in the Rosary, even though they said it ten

* Apud Jortin, ii. 687.

times a day ; that those who would say it well would do an
excellent thing, provided they did not say it with presumption,
otherwise they would do better to omit the prayers altogether,
on condition that they omitted also the crimes which they were
committing more easily under the shelter of these prayers.

"When he said this from the pulpit he was heard with
indignation, and everywhere spoken of as an enemy of Our
Lady. Another day the friar mounts the pulpit, and to hit the
parish priest harder takes for his text the words, *Dignare me
laudare te, Virgo sacrata ; da mihi virtutem contra hostes tuos.*
For they say that Scotus used this text at Paris when disputing
on the Immaculate Conception, having been transported there,
as they falsely allege, in a moment, from a distance of 300
miles, as the Virgin otherwise would have been in danger. Of
course our friar easily convinces men so willing to listen to him
that the pastor was as foolish as he was impious.

"While the matter was at its hottest, it happened that I
arrived at Coventry on a visit to my sister.* I had scarcely
got off my horse when the question was proposed also to me,
whether anyone could be damned who should daily recite the
Rosary ? I laughed at the foolish question, but was at once
warned that I was doing a dangerous thing ; that a most holy
and most learned father had preached against those who did
so. I pooh-poohed the whole matter as no affair of mine. I
was immediately invited to a dinner, and accepted the invitation
and went. There enters also an old friar with head bent, grave
and grim ; a boy follows him with books. I saw that I was in
for a quarrel. We sat down, and no time was lost ; the question was at once proposed by the host. The friar answered
just as he had preached. I said nothing ; I do not like to
meddle in odious and fruitless disputes. At last they asked my
opinion. As I was obliged to speak, I told them what I thought,

* It will be remembered that More had two sisters, both married. As
Rastell's wife lived in London, this must have been his eldest sister, Jane,
married to Richard Stafferton.

but only in a few words and without emphasis. Then the friar pours out a long prepared speech which might have made two sermons. His whole argument hung on certain miracles which he read from a *Mariale* and from other books of that kind, which he had brought to table for greater authority. When at last he had come to an end, I modestly replied that he had said nothing in his whole discourse capable of convincing those who should not admit the truth of those miracles, which they might perhaps deny without abjuring the Christian faith ; and that even if they were perfectly true, they did not prove his point. For though you may easily find a king ready to pardon something in an enemy at the prayers of his mother, yet there is nowhere one so great a fool as to promulgate a law by which to encourage the audacity of his subjects against himself, by a promise of impunity to traitors, on condition of their paying a certain homage to his mother. Much was said on both sides, but I only succeeded in getting laughed at while he was extolled. The matter reached at last such a height through the depraved dispositions of men who, under colour of piety, favoured their own vices, that it could hardly be calmed down, though the bishop strove to do so with all his strength.

"I have not related this in order to impute crime to any body of religious, since the same ground produces herbs both wholesome and poisonous ; nor do I wish to find fault with the custom of those who salute Our Lady, than which nothing can be more beneficial ; but because some trust so much in their devotions that they draw from them boldness to sin. It is such things as these that Erasmus censures ; if anyone is indignant against him for it, why is he not also indignant with St. Jerome ? " *

---

* *Ib.*, p. 693. This letter was first printed at Basle by Froben in 1520, amongst a number of letters against Edward Lee, though there is no reference in it to Lee. On the above passage Mr. Seebohm finds nothing more appropriate to say, than that, although More had not set aside

From passages like those here quoted, some writers have drawn the conclusion that More's early veneration for religious orders had been shaken, when he discovered how much the reality differed from his ideal. They should have marked more carefully what he says in the same letter : "I have no doubt that there is no good man to be found anywhere, to whom all religious orders are not extremely dear and cherished. Not only have I ever loved them, but intensely venerated them ; for I have been wont to honour the poorest person commended by his virtue, more than one who is merely ennobled by his riches or illustrious by his birth. I desire, indeed, all mortals to honour you and your orders, and to regard you with the deepest charity, for your merits deserve it ; and I know that by your prayers the misery of the world itself is somewhat diminished. If the assiduous prayer of the just man is of much value, what must be the efficacy of the un- wearied prayers of so many thousands? Yet, on the other hand, I would wish that you should not with a false zeal be so partial to yourselves, that if anyone ventures to touch on what regards you, you should try, by your way of relating it, to give an evil turn to what he has said well, or that what he at least intended well you should misinterpret and pervert."

In going to the root of this touchiness, More remarks both wisely and wittily : " Everyone loves what is his own—his own farm, his own money, his own nation, his own guild or associa- tion. We prefer our own private fasts to the public fasts of the Church. If we have chosen a patron saint, we make more of him than of ten more excellent, because he is our own, and the rest of the saints belong to all. Now, if anyone finds

---

mariolatry he was travelling in that direction. That Luther had not then (in 1519) travelled so far, though in after years he travelled faster ! (*Oxford Reformers*, p. 476.) Surely More was a man acute enough to know in what direction he had been travelling. When we come to his controversies with the Lutherans we shall hear his own account of the matter.

fault with this partiality, he is not carping at the piety of the people, but warning them lest, under pretext of piety, impiety find an entrance. No one will blame a nation for honouring a certain saint by name, for good reasons ; yet, it may occur to some that such partiality is carried too far, when the patron saint of a hostile country is torn down and thrown out of a church into the mud. *

" Now, just as this kind of veneration and private ceremonial does not always turn out well with us laymen, neither does partisanship always thrive with you who are religious. Many esteem their own devotions and practices more than those of their monastery; those of their own monastery more than those of their order ; those of their own order more than what belongs to all religious ; and those which are peculiar to religious they set more value on than the lowly, humble things which belong specially to no one, but are common to the whole Christian people—such as the plebeian virtues of faith, hope and charity, the fear of God, humility, and such like. This is no new thing. It is a long time since Christ reproved the chosen race : 'Why do you transgress the commandments of God for your traditions?' Of course, those who do so will deny it. Who is so senseless as to confess to himself that he makes more account of ceremonies than of precepts, since he knows that, unless he obeys the latter, the former are useless? Doubtless all will answer well in words if they are questioned ; but by their doings they belie their words. May I be held a liar if there are not religious in certain places who observe silence so obstinately that at no price could you get them even to whisper in their corridors ; but, draw them one foot outside, and they will not hesitate to storm at whoever offends them. There are some who would fear lest the devil should carry them off alive if they made any change in their dress, and who have no fear of heap-

---

* Perhaps St. Denis had been thus treated at the cry of " St. George for England," during the French wars.

ing up money, of opposing and deposing their abbot. Are there not many who, if they omitted a verse of their office, would think it a crime to be expiated with many tears, and who have not the least scruple to take part in calumnious gossip longer than their longest prayers? Thus they crush a gnat and swallow an elephant whole." *

I have given these long quotations that the reader may know the good and evil of More's times, and may see him in his many-sided character, and not be led to believe, by a short sentence taken here or there from his writings, that he was either an incipient rationalist or a narrow-minded bigot.

VII. Utopia.

I now come to his *Utopia*. This is the work by which More is best known. He wrote it in Latin, and, though it was soon translated into French and other European languages, it was not translated into English until long after his death. He certainly had no wish that it should be read by the people of England in the days of Henry VIII. Neither its serious wisdom nor its peculiar irony, nor its subtle mixture of philosophy and banter, were on the level of the half-educated men and women who could only read English. Probably More was not loth that his free speculations should be unknown to some of the great lords, like the Dukes of Norfolk and Suffolk, who ruled in the king's council.

The second book of the *Utopia* was written first, probably during the leisure hours of his first embassy in Flanders. He there showed it to some of his learned friends, such as Giles and Busleyden. He was urged by them so earnestly to complete and publish it that he set about writing the Introduction, or first part, on his return to England in 1516. It was printed in Louvain by Thierry Martins in December, 1516, under the editorship of Erasmus, Peter Giles, and others. The reprints have been innumerable.

* *Ib.*, 691.

The book is so well known that it need scarcely be said that an imaginary Portuguese traveller, named Raphael Hythloday, a companion of Amerigo Vespucci, is supposed to have met More and Peter Giles at Antwerp, and to have described to them the institutions of a wonderful people he had found in an island called Utopia or Nowhere.* I will not here analyse his book, nor mention the various social, political, philosophical and religious questions on which he treats. Every educated man should read *Utopia* for himself; but, in doing so, he must bear in mind the peculiarity of More's character and the circumstances in which the book was published.

As regards More himself, Erasmus has remarked that his countenance was often a mystery, so that even members of his own family would be puzzled to gather from his look or tone whether he was speaking in jest or in earnest.† So it was his

---

* Philomorus quotes an epigram by John Heywood, a contemporary of More's, to the effect that More wrote his *Utopia* at North Mimms, in Hertfordshire, where he had a house:

> "There famous More did his *Utopia* write,
> And there came Heywood's epigrams to light".
>   —*Philomorus*, p. 9.

But this is doubtful. Sir *John* More had a residence at North Mimms, but probably at a later date. *Utopia* (Οὐτόπος) or *Nusquama* (as More sometimes calls it in his letters), "Nowhere". Revised and reprinted by Froben at Basle, November, 1518; reprinted in Paris and Vienna during the author's life, but not in England. An English translation, by Ralph Robinson, appeared in 1551; it has been reprinted by Dibdin, by Arber, and Lumley. Dibdin's edition, with his notes, was beautifully reprinted by Roberts in 1878. Another translation was made by Burnet in 1684; it has been edited by Mr. Morley in Cassell's National Library (price 3d.). The introduction and notes to Mr. Lumley's edition will be found very useful to those who wish to study the book. He has joined with it Roper's *Life of More*.

† More himself refers to this. In his *Dialogue* his companion says: "Ye use (my master saith) to look so sadly when ye mean merrily, that many times man doubt whether ye speak in sport when ye mean good earnest" (*English Works*, p. 127).

peculiar humour to mystify his readers. "He hovers," says Mr. Brewer, "so perpetually on the confines of jest and earnest, passes so naturally from one to the other, that the reader is in constant suspense whether his jest be serious or his seriousness a jest." * There was policy in adopting this style in the *Utopia*. He had some rude truths to tell the king, as will be seen in a future chapter; he had many burning questions to discuss; it was necessary therefore to mix with them some matters which could not be taken seriously or attributed to him as his own opinions. Thus he says of the Utopians that they have no lawyers among them, and consider them as a sort of people whose profession it is to disguise matters and to wrest the laws aside. Who can say whether this does or does not express his real opinion? The Utopians use no money, and have no private property. Such a supposition gave him scope to show the evils that come from avarice and attend property; but no one can argue that More seriously taught communism or the injustice of private property. There is a voluntary communism which the Church has ever approved in her religious orders, and which, in Apostolic days, was practised even by families. More merely supposes this to be adopted by a whole nation. He attributes to his islanders most repulsive principles on treachery in war. Under cover of this he writes many things concerning European military tactics and diplomatic treaties that it would have been dangerous to state without a mixture of absurdity.

Mr. Seebohm, nevertheless, seems to think that whatever More writes on the subject of religion, on toleration, on divorce, and the rest, must have represented his serious views at that time of his life. His analysis is as follows: "Their priests were very few in number, of either sex, and, like all other magistrates, elected by ballot; and it was a point of dispute even with the Utopian *Christians* whether *they* could not elect

* Introduction to *Letters and Papers*, ii. p. 268.

their own Christian priests in like manner, and qualify them to perform all priestly offices, without any Apostolic succession or authority from the Pope. Their priests were, in fact, rather conductors of the public worship, inspectors of the public morals, and ministers of education, than "priests' in any sacerdotal sense of the word. . . . The hatred of the Oxford Reformers for the endless dissensions of European Christians . . . pointed to a mode of worship in which all of every shade of sentiment could unite."* What are we to think of all this? Was Thomas More in 1516 really an advanced Protestant of the type here described? If not, why are these things in his *Utopia*? The simple answer seems to be that More is describing purely natural and unrevealed religion. He admits that in Utopia there were many opinions and divisions in religion, and even some idolatry. To the better class, however, he attributes a kind of beautiful deism, not as something which he would substitute for Christianity, but which might be an excellent preparation for Christianity, could it be supposed to exist, and in the description of which he could reprove some vices of professing Christians. Thus, for example, in the eagerness of the Utopians to die, in order to see and possess the God whom they worshipped, he indirectly satirises the reluctance of Christians to go and enjoy the Beatific Vision.

But if he so extols the natural piety of his Utopians as to put Christians to the blush, surely it by no means follows that the Christian revelation, in More's view, contained nothing regarding the sacrifice of the Mass or the sacrament of Holy Orders. We know that More, from his boyhood, had the tenderest devotion to Our Lord's Passion, and the firmest belief in the redemption of the world by the Precious Blood. Yet he writes of his Utopians : "They offer up no living creature in sacrifice, nor do they think it suitable to the Divine Being, from whose bounty it is that those creatures had derived their lives, to take

* *Oxford Reformers*, p. 363.

pleasure in their deaths or the offering up of their blood ". It
would be as reasonable to conclude from these words that
More was a Socinian at heart as that he was sceptical regarding
the constitution and discipline of the Catholic Church because
of his pictures of Utopian modes of worship. This would be a
perfectly legitimate answer to Mr. Seebohm's conclusions had
More died, like his friend Colet, before the Lutheran and
Zwinglian heresies had arisen. But what can be the purpose
of arguing by induction from a work which was put out as a
jeu d'esprit when the writer has left hundreds of pages in
which his real belief is expressed without ambiguity?

Among the various points of Utopian discipline let us take
the first in Mr. Seebohm's enumeration as a specimen. More
says that the female sex was not excluded from the priesthood,
though female priests were few, and only widows advanced in
age were elected. What is there in this contrary to natural
religion, which More is describing? And considering the kind
of functions which alone he assigns to priests, what is there in
this contrary even to Catholic discipline, which has ever given
a high and honourable part to women, especially in religious
orders? But the question is whether More held that in
Christ's Church there is no Apostolical succession, no sacrament
of Holy Orders, no Divinely communicated jurisdiction, no
Divinely appointed distinction between the sexes as regards the
priesthood. Well, it so happens that Tindall, an English
Lutheran, put out a theory that in case of need—as, for example,
if a woman were cast by shipwreck on an island where there
were no Christians—she might preach and consecrate the Holy
Eucharist. More replied : "Tindall may make himself sure,
that since there falleth not a sparrow upon the ground without
Our Father that is in heaven, there shall no woman fall aland
in any so far an island, where God will have His name preached
and His sacraments ministered, but that God can, and will,
well enough provide a man or twain to come to land with her ;
whereof we have had already meetly good experience, and that

within few years.　For I am sure there hath been more islands
and more part of the firm land and continent discovered and
founden out, within these forty years last past, than was new
founden, as far as any man may perceive, this three thousand
years afore.　And in many of these places the name of Christ,
now new known too, and preachings had, and sacraments ministered, without any woman fallen aland alone.　But God hath
provided that His name is preached by such good Christian
folk as Tindall now most raileth upon, that is good religious
friars, and specially the Friar Observants, honest, godly, chaste,
virtuous people ; not by such as Friar Luther is, that is run out
of religion, nor by casting to land alone any such holy nun as
his harlot is."*　And in another place : " His heresy reckoneth
every woman a priest, and as able to say Mass as ever was St.
Peter.　And in good faith, as for such Masses as he would have
said, without the canon, without the secrets, without oblation,
without sacrifice, without the Body or Blood of Christ, with
bare signs and tokens instead of the Blessed Sacrament, I ween
a woman were indeed a more meet priest than St. Peter." †

As early as 1523, that is, seven years after the publication of
the *Utopia*, those very points which Mr. Seebohm would persuade the world were the advanced liberal creed of Colet, More,
and Erasmus, More had selected as the *insanissima dogmata*,
the " most mad doctrines " of Luther.‡　Nor did it once occur

---

* *English Works*, p. 428.

† *Ib.*, p. 623.

‡ Luther rejected the visible Catholic Church and appealed to the true
invisible Church of Christ.　More takes him at his word and answers
him as follows : " Profer tu gentem aliquam, ubi unquam in tot ætatibus,
ante natum te, tuæ probatæ sunt hæreses.　Ostende apud quos Christianos sacerdos nil distarit a laico, apud quos Christianos mulieres admissæ
sint ad audiendas confessiones, ubi creditæ sint fœminæ sacerdotes esse
et idoneæ quæ conficerent Eucharistiam.　Quæcumque tot ætatibus vera
fuit ecclesia, sive illa fuit bonorum malorumque multitudo promiscua, sive

to him, or to his opponents, that these were the very doctrines that he and his friends Colet and Erasmus had secretly held, or endeavoured covertly to insinuate.

As regards the *Utopia*, Harpsfield assures us that the zeal of many good priests was so stirred in reading More's account of this admirable people, so near to the kingdom of God, that they wished to set out at once to convert them to the faith of Christ. Their innocent error in taking Utopia for a real country was not so ridiculous as that of Mr. Seebohm, in taking More's description of their religion for More's own profession of Christianity.*

VIII. Epigrams.

Together with the Basle edition of the *Utopia* there appeared in March, 1518, a collection of Latin Epigrams, by Thomas More and William Lilly, and a further series by Erasmus. A second edition came out in November of the same year, and a more complete collection in 1520. Prefixed is a letter of Erasmus to Froben, the publisher, in which he says : " What might have been expected had Italy given birth to so happy a genius, if he had given himself entirely to the Muses, and if his talent had ripened to its autumnal fruit? For he was but a

numerus duntaxat bonorum, sive in his regionibus quæ parent Romano Pontifici, sive alibi ubicumque terrarum, semper contra te sensit illa, et tua damnavit insanissima dogmata " (*Responsio ad Lutherum*, cap. x. p. 62, ed. Francofurt).

* "The true notion of *Utopia* is, that it intimates a variety of doctrines, and exhibits a multiplicity of projects, which the writer regards with almost every possible degree of approbation and shade of assent ; from the frontiers of serious and entire belief, through gradations of descending plausibility, where the lowest are scarcely more than the exercises of ingenuity, and to which some wild paradoxes are appended, either as a vehicle or as an easy means (if necessary) of disavowing the serious intention of the whole of the Platonic fiction."—Sir James Mackintosh (*Life of More*, p. 61).

youth when he amused himself with these Epigrams, and no more than a boy when he wrote many of them. He has never left his native Britain but once or twice, when he was an envoy of his prince in Flanders." *

The epigrams appeared with the title of "Progymnasmata" or exercises, because several of them were efforts of skill in translation from Greek into Latin. These, however, make only a fourth part of the whole collection.

A writer, who has illustrated More's epigrams in a very scholarly and interesting book, remarks that "the term Epigramma, as used in the time of Erasmus, was of a more comprehensive character than our modern word Epigram. Like the Epigram, it was a fugitive composition springing out of the more salient topics of every-day life, terse in diction, and steady in its pursuit of one subject. But it was frequently of greater length than our modern Epigram. Many of the Epigrammata might be classed under the modern designation of *vers de société*." I do not think it necessary to offer any criticism or further account of More's verses. Those who are interested will find all they can wish in the *Philomorus*.†

One short piece, however, may be here mentioned, as being connected with some pictures painted at the period we have been reviewing, and which are said still to exist.

When More was at Calais in 1517, he received a present which caused him singular pleasure. His two friends, Erasmus and Peter Giles (Egidius), had their portraits painted by Quentin Matsys on two panels united as a diptych. Erasmus was represented as writing the first lines of his Paraphrase on the Epistle of St. Paul to the Romans. Giles was holding in his hand a letter to which More's name was legibly subscribed. Erasmus sent the diptych by a messenger with a short letter :—

" I send you these portraits that we may be in some way pre-

* *Epist. Erasm.* 167, in App.

† *Philomorus.* Second edition. Longmans, 1878.

sent with you, even if by chance we should be taken away. Peter pays one-half of the cost, and I the other. Either of us would gladly have paid the whole, but we wished the gift to be from both. . . . I am sorry you are shut up in Calais. If nothing else can be done, write frequently, though it be only a few words. Farewell, dearest of mortals. From Antwerp, 8th September, 1517." *

Giles, while the portraits were being painted, had been very ill. More writes to him on 6th October : " My dearest Peter, I am longing to hear about your health ; no matter of my own gives me more anxiety. Some give me good hope, either well founded, as I trust, or else to comfort me. I have written a letter to Erasmus, but I send it open to you ; you will seal it yourself. There is no need to close against you whatever I write to him. I have written for you a few verses about the picture, though they are as unskilful as that is skilful. If you think them deserving of it, send them to Erasmus ; if not, throw them in the fire." † The Latin verses were very happy, both in matter and form. In his letter to Erasmus, More says : " You cannot believe, my Erasmus, my darling Erasmus, ‡ how this eagerness of yours to bind me still more closely to you, has heightened my love for you, though I thought nothing could be added to it ; and how triumphant I am in the glory of being so much esteemed by you, as that you should make it known by a monument like this, that there is no one whose love you prefer to mine. It may be a proud thought, but most certainly I esteem your gift to mean that you would wish the memory of you to be renewed in my mind, not daily only, but every hour. You know me so well that I

* *Epist. Erasm.* 179, in App. Egidius wrote to Erasmus on 27th September : " Si Morus Caleti est jam habet spectacula nostra" (*Ib.*, 193).

† *Ib.*, 192.

‡ *Erasmiotatos*, the superlative of *Erasmios*, which had been incorrectly turned into *Erasmus*. It means " beloved ".

need not labour to prove to you that, with all my faults, I am
no great boaster. Yet, to tell the truth, there is one craving
for glory I cannot shake off, and it is wonderful how sweetly
I am elated when the thought occurs to me that I shall be
commended to the most distant ages by the friendship, the
letters, the books, the pictures of Erasmus." *

In another letter More reverts to the subject with one of his
characteristic jokes. In his verses he had likened Erasmus
and Egidius to the twin brothers, Castor and Pollux. A friar
had criticised the similitude. Erasmus and Egidius, he said,
were friends, not brothers. They would, therefore, have been
more aptly compared to Pylades and Orestes, or to Theseus
and Pirithous, who were fast friends, though not brothers.
This criticism drew from More the following epigram :—

> Duos amicos versibus paucis modo
>   Magnos volens ostendere,
> Tantos amicos dixeram, quanti olim erant
>   Castorque Polluxque invicem.
> " Fratres amicis," ait, " inepte comparas,"
>   Ineptiens fraterculus.
> " Quidni ? " inquam ; " an alteri esse quisquam amicior.
>   " Quam frater est fratri, potest ? "
> Irrisit ille inscitiam tantam meam,
>   Qui rem tam apertam nesciam.
> " Est ampla nobis," inquit, " ac frequens domus,
>   " Plus quam ducentis fratribus,
> " Sex ex ducentis, pereo, si reperis duos
>   " Fratres amicos invicem." †

The man would deserve a far severer epigram who should take

---

* *Ib.*, 193.

† Inter. Epist. Erasm., 204, in App. For those who do not know
Latin I may state the substance of the lines in the text :—

> " All brothers are not friends, you truly say ;
>   For friars are brothers, yet what friends are they ? "

these verses seriously, as if More thought ill of the friars, or as if the friars would not have laughed heartily at the epigram.*

* The reader will be interested to know that at least one of the two portraits is still in existence. According to Mr. J. G. Nichols, the portrait of Egidius in the collection of Lord Radnor, at Longford Castle, which was long attributed to Holbein, is undoubtedly the work of Quentin Matsys mentioned in these letters. It has been detached from its companion. Quentin's companion picture of Erasmus, or, according to Mr. Nichols, a copy of it, is in Hampton Court, and was also wrongly attributed to Holbein (see in *Archæologia*, vol. xliv. p. 435, an article written in 1873, thoroughly discussing the subject). There exists also in the British Museum the small illuminated book of Latin verses by More presented to Henry VIII. soon after his marriage. The red rose of Lancaster has an interior circle of white petals, in allusion to the white rose of York of Henry's mother. (Cotton MSS. *Titus D*. iv., at the beginning.) Among More's epigrams are one or two that his admirers would wish he had not written. Of these he says in a letter to Erasmus : " You know that, when my epigrams were being printed, I did all I could to suppress those that might be personal, as well as a few that did not seem to me severe enough, though they are very far from that obscenity for which alone I see some epigrams commended ". (*T. Mori Lucubrationes*, p. 435. Ed. 1563.)

CHAPTER VIII.

DOMESTIC.

THE strange fascination exerted by More, which has made even the foes of his religion speak of him both reverently and affectionately, is probably due to the beautiful details of his domestic life that have been handed down to us, rather than to his wit or literary excellence. Had he been all that he was in life and death, with one only exception—an ecclesiastic, instead of a father of a family—he would have been still great, amiable, and holy, but Macaulay would probably not have selected him as "a choice specimen of human wisdom and virtue," in stating his paradoxes about transubstantiation. Thus the very circumstances, by which in his own eyes More was placed on a lower level than his unmarried and consecrated fellow-martyrs, have raised him to a higher estimation in the minds of modern Englishmen; the "worldly wretch," as he called himself, who had twice gone to earthly nuptials, is preferred to the "blessed fathers" of the Charterhouse, whom More admired "going like bridegrooms to their (heavenly) marriage". Yet, while holding with the Church of all ages, that it is a more blessed state to remain unmarried for the kingdom of heaven's sake, we may nevertheless, and for that very reason, admire all the more a married man and a father, to whom family ties were no impediment, whose heart remained undivided and altogether God's, and who equalled on the scaffold both the constancy and the joy of his venerable fellow-sufferers; and we may thank God for giving to us in both states of life, examples, variously attractive yet equally admirable, of the power of His grace.

SECTION I. THE FAMILY.

We owe to Erasmus more than one beautiful picture of More's domestic life, and I will translate his words without abridgment or interruption, reserving the details that have come to us from other sources until we have looked carefully at his masterly sketch. The letter to Ulrich von Hutten, which has been frequently quoted, was written on the 23rd July, 1519. At that time More had been eight or nine years married to his second wife, who had given him no children, but had been as a mother to his four children by his first wife. He was forty-one years old, his eldest child thirteen.

A few months after the death of Jane Colt he had married, against the advice of his friends, a widow named Alice Middleton, neither young nor handsome—*nec bella nec puella*, as More would sometimes say laughingly to Erasmus; "but an active and vigilant housewife, with whom," continues his friend, " he lives as pleasantly and sweetly as if she had all the charms of youth. You will scarcely find a husband who, by authority or severity, has gained such ready compliance as More by playful flattery. What, indeed, would he not obtain, when he has prevailed on a woman already getting old, by no means of a pliable disposition, and intent on domestic affairs, to learn to play the harp, the lute, the monochord, and the flute (*cithara, testudine, monochordo, tibiis*), and by the appointment of her husband to devote to this task a fixed time every day? * With the same address he guides his whole household, in which there are no disturbances or strife. If such arise he immediately appeases it and sets all right again, never conceiving enmity

* More's friend Pace tells us that More played duets with his wife: Sicut Morus meus didicit pulsare tibias cum conjuge (*De Fructu*, etc., p. 35).

8

himself nor making an enemy. Indeed, there seems to be a kind of fateful happiness in this house, so that no one has lived in it without rising to higher fortune ; no member of it has ever incurred any stain on his reputation. You will scarcely find any who live in such harmony with a mother as does Thomas More with his step-mother, for his father had married again, and the son was as affectionate towards her as to his own mother. Quite recently he has married a third wife, and More swears he never knew a better woman. Towards his parents and his children and his sisters his love is never intrusive or exacting, while he omits nothing that can show his sincere attachment."

Two years later, towards the end of the year 1521, Erasmus returns to the same subject in a letter to Budée, a very learned French statesman, and a married man like More.

"If More had the means he would be a great Mæcenas of learning. He has helped the learned even when he himself was in debt. Nor does he adorn letters merely by his own learning or his partiality for learned men, for he has reared his whole family in excellent studies—a new example, but one which is likely to be much imitated, unless I am mistaken, so successful has it been. He has three daughters, of whom the eldest, Margaret, is married to a young man who is wealthy (*beato*), of excellent and modest character, and not unacquainted with literature. More has been careful to have all his children, from their earliest years, thoroughly imbued, first with chaste and holy morals, and then with polite letters. He has taken into his family another girl, and adopted her as companion to his daughters. He has a step-daughter of rare beauty and talent, who has been some years married to a young man not unlearned, and of a most amiable character. He has a son by his first wife, the youngest of his children, about thirteen years old.*

* Here the memory of Erasmus is defective, though he says "plus minus". Young John More could not be over eleven in the autumn of 1521.

" A year ago it occurred to More to send me a specimen of their progress in study. He bade them all write to me, each one without any help, neither the subject being suggested nor the language corrected ; for when they offered their papers to their father for correction, he affected to be displeased with the bad writing, and made them copy out their letters more neatly and accurately. When they had done so, he closed the letters and sent them to me without changing a syllable. Believe me, dear Budée, I never was more surprised ; there was nothing whatever either silly or girlish in what was said, and the style was such that you could feel they were making daily progress. This amiable circle, with the two husbands,* all live in his house. In that house you will find no one idle, no one busied in feminine trifles. Titus Livius is ever in their hands. They have advanced so far that they can read such authors and understand them without a translation, unless there occurs some such word as would perhaps perplex myself. His wife, who excels in good sense and experience rather than in learning, governs the little company with wonderful tact, assigning to each a task, and requiring its performance, allowing no one to be idle or to be occupied in trifles.

"You complain occasionally in your letters to me that philology † has got a bad name through you, since it has both injured your health and made you poorer. But More manages to be well spoken of by all and in all respects ; and he avers that he is indebted to literature both for better health, for the favour and affection he meets with from his excellent prince, as well as from his own countrymen and foreigners, for an increase of wealth, for becoming more agreeable both to himself and his friends, more useful to his country and his relatives, more fitted for the life at court, and intercourse with nobles, as well as for all society and social life, and lastly, more dear to

* *Duobus sponsis* ; I will discuss the meaning of this word presently.

† Budée was a scholar and antiquarian. His great work, *De Asse*, had already been published.

heaven.   Formerly learning had a bad name, since it seemed
to deprive its votaries of common sense.   Well, no journey, no
business, however prolonged or arduous, makes More lay aside
his books ; yet you will find no one who is so companionable
a man at all times, and to every class,* so ready to render
service, so affable, so lively in conversation, or who knows so
well how to unite solid prudence with sweetness of manners.
Hence it has come to pass that, whereas a short time since,
love of literature was held to be useless either for practical or
ornamental purposes, now there is scarcely a nobleman who
considers his children worthy of his ancestors unless they are
educated in good letters.   Even in kings a great part of their
royal splendour is seen to be wanting where there is little
acquaintance with literature." †

We may now go back and consider the various personages
mentioned in these letters.   And first his wife, the step-mother
of his children.   Cresacre More writes : " I have heard it reported he wooed her for a friend of his, not once thinking to
have her himself, but she wisely answering him ' that he might
speed if he would speak in his own behalf,' telling his friend
what she had said unto him, with his good liking he married
her, and did that which otherwise he would never have thought
to have done ".   None of More's contemporaries mentions this
story, and though I cannot disprove it, it seems to me to have
been invented to match the second courtship with the first, and
to explain what might seem a somewhat ill-assorted marriage.
Yet, if More sought the benefit of his children rather than himself, he appears to have made an excellent choice, and so
philosophical was his mind and happy his disposition that he
lived with her as pleasantly, if not as affectionately, as if they
had been drawn together by similarity of tastes and character.
She was seven years his senior, as we know from the inscrip-

* Omnibus omnium horarum homo.

† *Epist.* 605.

tion on the family picture. The character of this good lady seems to me to have been most gratuitously blackened. "Any heart but More's," writes Mr. Dibdin, "would have been broken by this match, for Mrs. Alice Middleton appears to have been one of the most loquacious, ignorant, and narrow-minded of women. Like another Socrates, More endeavoured to laugh away his conjugal miseries; always replying to the sarcastic remarks of his wife with complacency and poignant good humour." * Let us be just. There is nothing in the letters of Erasmus or More to authorise such a censure as this. It is said that Erasmus found the lady rude and inhospitable. It is true that in 1516 he mentions in one of his letters that he is growing weary of England, and finds that he has outstayed his welcome with More's wife.† Yet although a lady should make her husband's guest and dear friend feel at home, let it be remembered that Erasmus had never taken the trouble to learn a word of English. ‡ It would surely be a trial to the meekest or most genial of wives to hear all the conversation and the laughter-moving jokes carried on daily, for weeks together, in a language of which she could not understand a word.

Perhaps she was somewhat worldly, "but so," as Sir Thomas would say of her, "that she was often penny-wise and pound-foolish, saving a candle's end and spoiling a velvet gown".§ More, however, had chosen her that her economical habits might counterbalance his own rather excessive carelessness, and we do not find that she complained of his generous alms. We may sometimes know a person's character better by the letters he receives than by those he writes, since the former indicate

* Biographical Introduction to More's *Utopia.*

† Ni jam me tæderet Britanniæ, et sentirem me vetulum jam hospitem uxori Moricæ suppetere (*Epist.* 133). The editor has dated the letter 1511. From the allusions in it, it should be 1516.

‡ Erasmus confesses his entire ignorance of English in *Letter* 165, written after he had spent years in England.

§ Cresacre's *Life.*

the judgment entertained regarding him.   Judged by this rule Lady More must have been a Christian and generous-hearted woman, to whom her husband could write the following letter :—

"Mistress Alice, in my most hearty wise I recommend me to you.   And whereas I am informed by my son Heron of the loss of our barns and our neighbours' also [by fire] with all the corn that was therein ; albeit, saving God's pleasure, it is great pity of so much good corn lost, yet since it hath liked Him to send us such a chance, we must and are bounden, not only to be content, but also to be glad of His visitation.   He sent us all that we have lost, and since He hath by such a chance taken it away again, His pleasure be fulfilled.   Let us never grieve thereat, but take it in good worth and heartily thank Him as well for adversity as for prosperity.   And peradventure we have more cause to thank Him for our loss than for our winning.   For His wisdom better seeth what is good for us than we do ourselves.   Therefore, I pray you be of good cheer, and take all the household with you to Church, and there thank God both for that He hath given us, and for that He hath taken away from us, and for that He hath left us, which, if it please Him, He can increase when He will.   And if it please Him to leave us less yet, at His pleasure be it.

"I pray you to make some good ensearch what my poor neighbours have lost, and bid them take no thought therefor ; for, and I should not leave myself a spoon, there shall no poor neighbour of mine bear no loss happened by any chance in my house.   I pray you be with my children and your household merry in God.   And devise somewhat with your friends what way were best to take for provision to be made for corn for our household, and for seed this year coming, if ye think it good that we keep the ground still in our hands.   And whether ye think it good that we shall do so or not, yet I think it were not best suddenly thus to leave it all up and to put away our folk off our farm, till we have somewhat advised us thereon.

Howbeit if we have more now than ye shall need, and which can get them other masters, ye may then discharge us of them. But I would not that any man were suddenly sent away he wot ne'er whither.

"At my coming hither I perceived none other but that I should tarry still with the king's grace. But now I shall (I think) because of this chance, get leave this next week to come home and see you ; and then shall we further devise together upon all things what order shall be best to take. And thus as heartily fare you well, with all our children, as ye can wish. At Woodstock the third day of September, by the hand of your loving husband, THOMAS MORE, Knight." *

If this letter proves that Sir Thomas More had the detach-ment, the love of justice and care of inferiors that we admire in Job, it equally proves that Lady More was not like Job's wife, but like the "valiant woman" of whom it is written : " The heart of her husband trusteth in her ".

Again, if the widow of Mr. Middleton had occasionally a sharp tongue, she was no termagant. In a letter to Erasmus of 15th December, 1517, More writes : "My wife desires a million of compliments, especially for your careful wish that she may live many years. She says she is the more anxious for this as she will live the longer to plague me." † This kind of playful banter does not belong to a Xantippe. Harpsfield writes as follows : " This wife on a time after shrift bade Sir Thomas More be merry, 'for I have,' saith she, 'this day left all my shrewdness, and to-morrow I will begin afresh,' with merry-conceited talk, though now and then it proved very true. Indeed, Sir Thomas More could well digest and like it in her and

---

* *English Works*, p. 1419. The editor adds that the fire occurred through the negligence of a neighbour's carter, not through the fault of any of More's servants, which makes his generosity all the more striking. The letter was written in August, 1529, just after his return from his embassy at Cambrai. A few months later he was made chancellor.

† Inter Epist. Erasm., 221, in App.

others; neither was he in her debt for repaying home again oftentimes such kind of talk. Among other things, when he divers times beheld his wife what pains she took in straight binding up her hair to make her a fair large forehead, and with strait bracing in her body to make her middle small, both twain to her great pain, for the pride of a little foolish praise, he said to her : ' Forsooth, madam, if God give you not hell he shall do you great wrong, for it must needs be your own of very right, for you buy it very dear, and take very great pains therefor '.*

"This wife, when she saw that Sir Thomas had no great list greatly to get upward in the world, neither would labour for office of authority, and besides that he forsook a right worship-ful room when it was offered him, she fell in hand with him and asked: 'What will you do that ye list not to put forth yourself as other folks do ? Will you sit still by the fire, and make goslings in the ashes with a stick, as children do ? Would God I were a man, and look what I would do.' 'Why, wife,' quoth her husband, 'what would you do?' 'What ? by God, go forward with the best. For, as my mother was wont to say (God have mercy on her soul), it is ever better to rule than to be ruled. And, therefore, by God, I would not, I warrant you, be so foolish to be ruled when I might rule.' 'By my troth, wife,' quoth her husband, 'in this I daresay you say truth, for I never found you willing to be ruled as yet.'"†

We have now seen all the evil that can be alleged against

---

* This saying is attributed by More to " a good worshipful man ". It is by no means certain that the saying was his own, or the lady his wife (*English Works*, 1205).

† This last paragraph is taken by Harpsfield from More's dialogue, written in the Tower, called " Comfort in Tribulation " (*English Works*, p. 1224), where the lady is called "a stout master-woman ". It is not said to be More's wife, but the allusion is evident. I have corrected Harpsfield by More himself.

this lady, and it certainly does not justify our classing Blessed More amongst the ill-matched great men. * To say that when his time of suffering came she did not rise to the height of his soul, is merely to class her with nearly all her contemporaries, including almost every abbess, abbot and bishop in the country.

We may pass now to the other members of More's household. Erasmus mentions two *sponsi*. The word is ambiguous. It may mean one engaged merely, or a husband, especially one recently married. Here it must stand for husbands. Erasmus had mentioned that More's eldest daughter was recently married. Her husband was William Roper. The second sponsus must have been the husband of Alice Middleton, More's step-daughter. This young lady had been educated with great care in More's house. She married young, and I do not find the name of her husband. After his death, and during More's lifetime, she took for her second husband, Giles (afterwards Sir Giles) Alington. † She will be mentioned at the time of More's imprisonment in the Tower as interesting herself much for her "father". She appears to have lived on very affectionate terms with the family. It is not recorded at what period she and her husband ceased to be inmates of More's house.

Of William Roper, a strange story is related by Harpsfield, Stapleton and Cresacre More. As Harpsfield's narrative was written under Roper's own eye, and dedicated to him, I will give it in his words: "Mr. William Roper, at what time he

---

* I cannot claim in favour of Mistress Alice the following letter of Ammonius, because though the Leyden editor has dated it 19th May, 1515, the year should be 1511, and it refers to the first wife, who died shortly after it was written : *Morus noster mellitissimus, cum sua facillima conjuge, quæ nunquam tui meminit, quin tibi bene precetur, et liberis ac universa familia, pulcherrime valet* (Inter. Epist. Erasm., 175).

† See More's *English Works*, p. 1435, where he speaks of her present and her late husband.

married with Mistress Margaret More, was a marvellous, zealous Protestant, and so fervent and withal so well and properly liked of himself and his divine learning, that he took the bridle into the teeth, and ran forward like a headstrong horse hard to be plucked back again. Neither was he contented to whisper it in hugger-mugger, but thirsted very sore to publish his new doctrine and divulge it, and thought himself very able so to do, and it were even at St. Paul's Cross. Yea, for the burning zeal that he bare to the furtherance of Luther's new broached religion, and for the pretty liking of himself, he longed so sore to be pulpited, that to have satisfied his mind he could have been contented to have foregone a good portion of his lands. . . . This fall into heresy, Mr. Roper (as he can conjecture) first did grow of a scruple of his own conscience, for lack of grace and better knowledge, as some do upon other occasions. He daily did use immoderate fasting and many prayers, which, with good discretion well-used, had not been to be misliked; but using them without order and good consideration, thinking God thereby never to be pleased, did weary himself *usque ad tædium.* Then did he understand of Luther's works brought into this realm, and as Eve of a curious mind, desirous to know both good and evil, so did he, for the strangeness and delectation of that doctrine, fall into great desire to read his works. Amongst other his works he read a book of Luther's *De Libertate Christiana,* and another *De Captivitate Babylonica,* and was in affection so with them bewitched, that he did then believe every matter set forth by Luther to be true.

"And with these books' ignorance, pride, false allegations, sophistical reasons and arguments, and with his own corrupt affections, he was deceived, and fully persuaded that faith only did justify; that the works of man did nothing profit; and that, if man could once believe that our Saviour, Christ, shed His Precious Blood and died on the Cross for our sins, the same only belief should be sufficient for our salvation. Then thought he that all the ceremonies and sacraments in Christ's Church were very vain ; and was at length so far waded into heresy, and puffed up with pride, that he wished that he might be suffered publicly to preach. . . . Who, for his open talk and companying with divers of his own sect of the Stillyard and other merchants, was, with them, before Cardinal Wolsey, convented of heresy : which merchants, for their opinions, were openly, for heresy, at Paul's Cross abjured. Yet he, for love borne by the cardinal to Sir Thomas More, his father-in-law, was, with a friendly warning, discharged. And albeit he had married the eldest daughter of Sir Thomas More, whom then of all the world he did during that time most abhor, though he was a man of most mildness and notable patience. . . . And these lessons he did so well like as he soon after gave over his fasting, prayer, his primer, and got to him a Lutheran Bible,* wherein upon the holy days, instead of his prayers, he spent his whole time.

"And so after continued he in his heresies until upon a time that Sir Thomas More privately in his garden talked with his daughter Margaret, and said : ' Meg, I have borne a long time with thy husband ; I have reasoned and argued with him in these points of religion, and still given to him my poor fatherly counsel, but I perceive none of all this able to call him home; and therefore, Meg, I will no longer dispute with him, but will clean give him over and get me to God and pray for him '. And soon after, as Roper verily believed, through the great mercy of God, at the devout prayers of Sir Thomas More, he perceived his own ignorance, oversight, malice and folly, and turned him again to the Catholic faith, wherein (God be thanked) he hath hitherto continued."

Notwithstanding what Harpsfield and others tell us of More's arguments and prayers on this occasion, some have concluded

---

* Luther translated the New Testament into German in 1521.

that More could not at that period have been a very staunch
Catholic, when he allowed his daughter to marry a heretic. It
seems to me to be pushing too far Harpsfield's expression "at
what time he married" to force it to mean "before he married".
If he became "a Protestant" (the word is used by Harpsfield
by anticipation, for it was not then invented) shortly after his
marriage, all is easily explained. The books of Luther that
made so much impression on him—*The Babylonian Captivity*
and *Christian Liberty*—only appeared in Germany at the end
of 1520. When Erasmus, at the end of 1521, wrote his eulogy
of Margaret's husband, the news had not reached him of his fall
into the new opinions of Luther. It is likely that this happened
after his marriage, either in 1521 or 1522. Besides this : as
obstinate Lutheranism at that time in England meant death, it
is impossible that Sir Thomas could have allowed his favourite
daughter to marry one already fallen into that heresy. Roper
tells us that he resided with his father-in-law for sixteen years
and more. If this is correct, he must have been taken into the
family at the beginning of 1519, when he was about twenty-three
years old and Margaret about thirteen. She would be in her
sixteenth year when she married him in 1521.* Margaret
Roper will frequently appear in this history. I pass on to the
others.

Elizabeth, a year younger than Margaret, married the son and
heir of Sir John Daunsey (or Dancy). Among the sketches by
Holbein in Her Majesty's collection is one which a former
keeper has supposed to represent Lady Barkley. It is really a
portrait of Elizabeth Dancy.

Cecily, the third daughter, married Mr. Giles Heron of
Shakelwell, or Spedwell in Hackney, son of Sir John Heron.
Sir Thomas More received from the king, in March, 1523, a

* In *Utopia* it is said : " Their women are not married before eighteen ".
We do not know why Sir Thomas departed from this rule. He probably
thought an early marriage better than a long courtship.

grant of the wardship of this young gentleman.* He was foreman of the jury that tried Anne Boleyn ; and he was martyred at Tyburn, 4th August, 1540.

John, the youngest child and only son of Sir Thomas, is but little known to us. Dibdin says : "It seems that More's wife wished very much for a boy ; at last she brought him this son, who proved to be but of slender capacity, upon which Sir Thomas is reported to have said to his wife that she had prayed so long for a boy that she had now one who would be a boy as long as he lived ".† If Mr. Dibdin had remarked that John's mother died before he was a year old, he would have seen that More could not have made such a remark to her—at least, with the sense indicated. Contemporary writers, on the contrary, all speak of the son as a studious youth of good abilities. Erasmus dedicated to him his edition of *Aristotle*, with a very complimentary letter, and Grynæus his *Plato* and other works. Cresacre More writes : " Sir Thomas's son, my grandfather, married Anne Cresacre, sole daughter and heir of Edward Cresacre (deceased) of Baronborough, in the county of York, esquire, whom Sir Thomas bought of the king, being his ward, upon error for another body's land lying in the same town, as was afterwards proved ".

Margaret Gigey, or Gigs, appears to have been an orphan girl and a relative of the family. ‡ She was treated in every way as one of his own children. She became singularly learned, and married Dr. Clements, who was also an inmate of More's

---

* *Letters and Papers*, iii. 2900; iv. 314. Such grants were profitable, and were one of the means at the king's disposal of rewarding his servants or his favourites. On 23rd January, 1527, More received the custody of John Morton, an idiot (*Letters and Papers*, iv. 2758).

† Dibdin quotes *Old Biog. Brit.* v. 3168.

‡ "Cognata," in the family picture. In the Holbein crayons in Her Majesty's collection is a portrait of Margaret Gigs, or Clements. It is erroneously inscribed (not by Holbein) " Mother Jak," by which name Mrs. Jackson, nurse of Edward VI., was known.

house.   She had all the affection of a daughter towards her
benefactor, and loved to relate to Stapleton, in her old age,
little traits of More's piety and other virtues.   Amongst other
things she said she would now and then commit some slight
fault for the pleasure of drawing down on herself his gentle and
sweet correction.   Twice only throughout his life did she see
him really angry.*   The husband of this lady, John Clements,
had been taken into More's family from St. Paul's School,
probably at the recommendation of Dean Colet, its founder.
He fulfilled the high expectation that had been formed of his
virtue and ability.   He seems to have acted as tutor in his
patron's family while he pursued his own Latin and Greek
studies.   He became professor of Greek at Oxford, † but forsook his chair for the study of medicine.   He suffered exile
for the faith, both under Edward VI. and Elizabeth. ‡

Another inmate was John Harris, who acted partly as More's
secretary, partly as tutor.   He also is said to have been learned
in Greek and Latin.   He married Dorothy Colley, who was
lady's maid to Mrs. Roper, and altogether worthy of such a
mistress.

Nor must Henry Patenson, the "fool," be forgotten in the
account of More's household, since More himself has rendered
him famous, both by introducing him into the family picture
and by several stories about him in his various works.   In the
entertainment of a domestic fool, More not on'y conformed to
a fashion, but followed his own judgment, for he thus writes of
the Utopians : "They have singular delight and pleasure in

* Stapleton, *Vita*, cap. 9.

† More writes of him in the highest possible terms (see Stapleton, cap.
10.

‡ "John Clement and his wife Margaret," writes Sander, "had one son,
named Thomas, and four daughters, all Greek and Latin scholars, of
whom Dorothy is a Poor Clare at Louvain, and Margaret, at St. Ursula's
Convent there, though a young nun and an Englishwoman among Flemings, is superioress over eighty sisters by their pre-election " (*De Vis.
Monarch.*).

Fools. And as it is a great reproach to do any of them hurt or injury, so they prohibit not to take pleasure of foolishness, for that, they think, doth much good to the fools. And if any man be so sad and stern that he cannot laugh, neither at their words nor at their deeds, none of them be committed to his tuition, for fear lest he would not intreat them gently and favourably enough; to whom they should bring no delectation (for other goodness in them is there none), much less any profit should they yield him."*

However, when More became chancellor, he dispensed with his jester and gave him to Sir John More, his father.† At his father's death Sir Thomas gave him to the Lord Mayor, on condition that he should also serve his successors during their time of office. ‡

Section II. Education.

We may turn now to More's method of educating his children. We have a very full exposition both of his principles and practice in a Latin letter written to William Gunnell, a learned ecclesiastic of Cambridge, who held for a time the office of tutor in his family. The letter bears no date of year. "I have received, my dear Gunnell, your letter, elegant, as your letters always are, and full of affection. From your letter I perceive your devotion to my children; I argue their diligence from their own. Every one of their letters pleased me, but I was particularly pleased because I notice that Elizabeth shows a

* Robinson's translation.
† Stapleton *Vita*, cap. 9.
‡ Lord Herbert, *Life of Henry VIII.* He was of course a "servus" or bondsman, as he is marked on the family picture. More tells us of another fool or madman, named Cliff, who lived for many years in his house, and got into some trouble for breaking off the head of the Infant Jesus in the arms of Our Lady, on London Bridge; "for," says Sir Thomas, "he got the same kind of notions into his head in his madness, that the Lutherans have in their sadness" (*English Works*, p. 935).

gentleness and self-command in the absence of her mother, *
which some children would not show in her presence.   Let her
understand that such conduct delights me more than all possible
letters I could receive from anyone.   Though I prefer learning
joined with virtue, to all the treasures of kings, yet renown for
learning, when it is not united with a good life is nothing else
than splendid and notorious infamy : this would be specially the
case in a woman.   Since erudition in women is a new thing and
a reproach to the sloth of men, many will gladly assail it, and
impute to literature what is really the fault of nature, thinking
from the vices of the learned to get their own ignorance
esteemed as virtue.   On the other hand, if a woman (and this
I desire and hope with you as their teacher for all my daughters)
to eminent virtue should add an outwork of even moderate
skill in literature, I think she will have more real profit than if
she had obtained the riches of Crœsus and the beauty of Helen.
I do not say this because of the glory which will be hers, though
glory follows virtue as a shadow follows a body, but because the
reward of wisdom is too solid to be lost like riches or to decay
like beauty, since it depends on the intimate conscience of what
is right, not on the talk of men, than which nothing is more
foolish or mischievous.

"It belongs to a good man, no doubt, to avoid infamy, but
to lay himself out for renown is the conduct of a man who is
not only proud, but ridiculous and miserable.   A soul must be
without peace which is ever fluctuating between elation and dis-
appointment from the opinions of men.   Among all the benefits that learning bestows on men, there is none more excellent
than this, that by the study of books we are taught in that very
study to seek not praise, but utility.   Such has been the teach-

* The edition of Stapleton of 1689 has *patre*, that of 1588 *matre*.   I have
translated all the letters myself, instead of giving Cresacre's translation,
lest the old English should make the reader think he has More's own
words ; and because I find that Cresacre's translation, with all its charms,
is not always correct.

ing of the most learned men, especially of philosophers, who are the guides of human life, although some may have abused learning, like other good things, simply to court empty glory and popular renown.

"I have dwelt so much on this matter, my dear Gunnell, because of what you say in your letter, that Margaret's lofty character should not be abased. In this judgment I quite agree with you ; but to me, and, no doubt, to you also, that man would seem to abase a generous character who should accustom it to admire what is vain and low. He, on the con-trary, raises the character who rises to virtue and true goods, and who looks down with contempt from the contemplation of what is sublime, on those shadows of good things which almost all mortals,* through ignorance of truth, greedily snatch at as if they were true goods.

"Therefore, my dear Gunnell, since we must walk by this road, I have often begged not you only, who, out of your affec-tion for my children, would do it of your own accord, nor my wife, who is sufficiently urged by her maternal love for them, which has been proved to me in so many ways, but all my friends, to warn my children to avoid the precipices of pride and haughtiness, and to walk in the pleasant meadows of modesty ; not to be dazzled at the sight of gold ; not to lament that they do not possess what they erroneously admire in others ; not to think more of themselves for gaudy trappings, nor less for the want of them ; neither to deform the beauty that nature has given them by neglect, nor to try to heighten it by artifice ; to put virtue in the first place, learning in the second ; and in their studies to esteem most whatever may teach them piety towards God, charity to all, and modesty and Christian humility in themselves. By such means they will

---

* *Moniales* (nuns) is in the edition of Frankfort, 1689. There is nothing in the context to justify any allusion to nuns. It is clear that the word was *mortales*, as in edition 1588.

9

receive from God the reward of an innocent life, and in the assured expectation of it, will view death without horror, and meanwhile possessing solid joy, will neither be puffed up by the empty praise of men, nor dejected by evil tongues. These I consider the genuine fruits of learning, and, though I admit that all literary men do not possess them, I would maintain that those who give themselves to study with such views, wi l easily attain their end and become perfect.

"Nor do I think that the harvest will be much affected whether it is a man or a woman who sows the field. They both have the same human nature, which reason differentiates from that of beasts; both, therefore, are equally suited for those studies by which reason is perfectioned, and becomes fruitful like a ploughed land on which the seed of good lessons has been sown. If it be true that the soil of woman's brain be bad, and apter to bear bracken than corn, by which saying many keep women from study, I think, on the contrary, that a woman's wit is on that account all the more diligently to be cultivated, that nature's defect may be redressed by industry. This was the opinion of the ancients, of those who were most prudent as well as most holy. Not to speak of the rest, St. Jerome and St. Augustine not only exhorted excellent matrons and most noble virgins to study, but also, in order to assist them, diligently explained the abstruse meanings of Holy Scripture, and wrote for tender girls letters replete with so much erudition, that now-a-days old men, who call themselves professors of sacred science, can scarcely read them correctly, much less understand them. Do you, my learned Gunnell, have the kindness to see that my daughters thoroughly learn these works of those holy men. . . .

"I fancy I hear you object that these precepts, though true, are beyond the capacity of my young children, since you will scarcely find a man, however old and advanced, whose mind is so firmly set as not to be tickled sometimes with desire of glory. But, dear Gunnell, the more I see the difficulty of getting rid of this pest of pride, the more do I see the necessity of setting to work at it from childhood. For I find no other reason why this evil clings so to our hearts, than because almost as soon as we are born, it is sown in the tender minds of children by their nurses, it is cultivated by their teachers, and brought to its full growth by their parents ; no one teaching even what is good without, at the same time, awakening the expectation of praise, as of the proper reward of virtue. Thus we grow accustomed to make so much of praise, that while we study how to please the greater number (who will always be the worst), we grow ashamed of being good (with the few). That this plague of vainglory may be banished far from my children, I do desire that you, my dear Gunnell, and their mother and all their friends, would sing this song to them, and repeat it, and beat it into their heads, that vainglory is a thing despicable, and to be spit upon ; and that there is nothing more sublime than that humble modesty so often praised by Christ ; and this your prudent charity will so enforce as to teach virtue rather than reprove vice, and make them love good advice instead of hating it. To this purpose nothing will more conduce than to read to them the lessons of the ancient Fathers, who, they know, cannot be angry with them, and, as they honour them for their sanctity, they must needs be much moved by their authority. If you will teach something of this sort, in addition to their lesson in Sallust—to Margaret and Elizabeth, as being more advanced than John and Cecily —you will bind me and them still more to you. And thus you will bring about that my children, who are dear to me by nature, and still more dear by learning and virtue, will become most dear by that advance in knowledge and good conduct. Adieu. From the Court on the vigil of Pentecost."

It will be seen from this and his other letters that while More taught his children to hate vainglory and not to consider praise as the end for which knowledge or virtue should be cultivated, he was far from condemning in a child the desire of a virtuous father's approbation, and he bestowed it most liberally.   More will ever stand foremost in the rank of the defenders of female culture; but his example would be perhaps rashly quoted in proof that the education of women should be in all respects the same as that of men, or that familiarity with the ancient classic writers is essential to all true culture, for the field of both science and literature was so restricted in his days, that the woman who was not trained to read Plato and Sophocles, or at least Livy and Sallust, was limited to her needlework and her viol, or to Chaucer and Boccacio and the "Romaunt de la Rose"—works certainly less conducive to purity of life than the masterpieces of the old heathen world.

It is not likely that the above letter was intended merely for Gunnell.   It would be copied out by the children, translated, and perhaps learned by heart, and would be the subject of their Latin letters to their father.   For More never ceased to superintend the education of each one of them.   His letters to his children were preserved as precious treasures in the family, and several of them have come down to us by the care of Stapleton.

I would not willingly either omit or abridge these letters, which are among his most venerated relics.

"Thomas More to his whole school,—

"See what a compendious salutation I have found, to save both time and paper, which would otherwise have been wasted in reciting the names of each one of you, and my labour would have been to no purpose, since, though each of you is dear to me by some special title, of which I could have omitted none in a set and formal salutation, no one is dearer to me by any title than each one of you by that of scholar.   Your zeal for knowledge binds me to you almost more closely than the ties of blood.   I rejoice that Mr. Drew has returned safe, for I was anxious, as you know, about him.   If I did not love you so much I should be really envious of your happiness in having so many and such excellent tutors.   But I think you have no longer any need of Mr. Nicholas, since you have learnt whatever he had to teach you about astronomy. I hear you are so far advanced in that science that you can not only point out the polar-star or the dog-star, or any of the constellations, but are able also—which requires a skilful and profound astrologer—among all those leading heavenly bodies, to distinguish the sun from the moon! Go forward, then, in that new and admirable science by which you ascend to the stars. But while you gaze on them assiduously, consider that this holy time of Lent warns you, and that beautiful and holy poem of Boetius keeps singing in your ears, to raise your mind also to heaven, lest the soul look downwards to the earth, after the manner of brutes, while the body looks upwards. Farewell, my dearest. From Court, the 23rd March."

Another letter is on the subject of letter-writing. Stapleton says that the original, from which he printed, was almost worn to pieces, so frequently had it been read.

"Thomas More to his dearest children, and to Margaret Giggs, whom he numbers amongst his own,—

"The Bristol merchant brought me your letters the day after he left you, with which I was extremely delighted. Nothing can come from your workshop, however rude or unfinished, that will not give me more pleasure than the most accurate thing that another can write. So much does my affection for you recommend whatever you write to me. Indeed, without any recommendation, your letters are capable of pleasing by their own merits, their wit and pure Latinity. There was not one of your letters that did not please me extremely; but, to confess ingenuously what I feel, the letter of my son John pleased me best, both because it was longer than the others, and because he seems to have given to it more labour and study. For he not only put out his matter prettily and composed in fairly polished language, but he plays with me both pleasantly and cleverly, and turns my jokes on myself wittily enough. And this he does not only merrily, but with due moderation, showing that he does not forget that he is joking with his

father and that he is cautious not to give offence at the same
time that he is eager to give delight.

"Now I expect from each of you a letter almost every day.
I will not admit excuses—John makes none—such as want of
time, sudden departure of the letter-carrier, or, want of something to write about. No one hinders you from writing, but,
on the contrary, all are urging you to do it. And that you may
not keep the letter-carrier waiting, why not anticipate his coming, and have your letters written and sealed, ready for anyone
to take? How can a subject be wanting when you write to
me, since I am glad to hear of your studies or of your games,
and you will please me most if, when there is nothing to write
about, you write about that nothing at great length. Nothing
can be easier for you, since you are girls, loquacious by nature,
who have always a world to say about nothing at all. One
thing, however, I admonish you, whether you write serious
matters or the merest trifles, it is my wish that you write everything diligently and thoughtfully. It will be no harm, if you
first write the whole in English, for then you will have much
less trouble in turning it into Latin ; not having to look for the
matter, your mind will be intent only on the language. That,
however, I leave to your own choice, whereas I strictly enjoin
that whatever you have composed you carefully examine before
writing it out clean ; and in this examination, first scrutinise
the whole sentence and then every part of it. Thus, if any
solecisms have escaped you, you will easily detect them.
Correct these, write out the whole letter again, and even then
examine it once more, for sometimes, in rewriting, faults slip
in again that one had expunged. By this diligence your little
trifles will become serious matters ; for while there is nothing
so neat and witty that will not be made insipid by silly and
inconsiderate loquacity, so also there is nothing in itself so
insipid, that you cannot season with grace and wit if you give
a little thought to it. Farewell, my dear children. From the
Court, the 3rd September."

In one of his letters to his eldest daughter he writes: "I beg you, Margaret, tell me about the progress you are all making in your studies. For I assure you that, rather than allow my children to be idle and slothful, I would make a sacrifice of wealth, and bid adieu to other cares and business, to attend to my children and my family, amongst whom none is more dear to me than yourself, my beloved daughter."

We have seen that, when More was a boy, his father stinted him in money, and that he used to speak gratefully of this wise severity when he grew up. If filial love made him thus speak, his paternal love expressed itself differently: "You ask, my dear Margaret, for money with too much bashfulness and timidity, since you are asking from a father who is eager to give, and since you have written to me a letter such that I would not only repay each line of it with a golden philippine, as Alexander did the verses of Cherilos, but, if my means were as great as my desire, I would reward each syllable with two gold ounces. As it is, I send only what you have asked, but would have added more, only that as I am eager to give, so am I desirous to be asked and coaxed by my daughter, especially by you, whom virtue and learning have made so dear to my soul. So the sooner you spend this money well, as you are wont to do, and the sooner you ask for more, the more you will be sure of pleasing your father."

Among the few pieces added to the second edition of More's *Epigrams* in 1520 is an epistle in Latin elegiac verse to his children. It was composed on horseback, in the rain, while his beast was stumbling in the deep ruts or wading through a ford. It must be taken then, says the writer, as a proof of the affection that will not allow him to forget his children even amid such miseries to himself. He reminds them how, on returning from his journeys, he has ever brought back some cakes or fruit, or piece of silk to deck them; how he has always given them plenty of kisses and but very few strokes of the rod, the rod itself being only a bundle of peacock's feathers.

Though he has by nature a tender and loving heart towards his
children, their progress in virtue and learning has made it far
more loving, and he begs them to go on in the same way until
even his present love may seem nothing by comparison with
what he will then feel.

> Efficitote (potestis enim) virtutibus isdem
> Ut posthac videar vos nec amare modo.

Stapleton has preserved several letters written by More to his
favourite daughter, Margaret, most like to himself (says his biographer) in stature, face, voice, talent and general character.
He had also several pieces of her composition, both in prose
and verse, which he feared to print, as not bearing directly on
her father's life.   For the same reason I pass by some of the
letters, and conclude this account of More's education of his
children by one which shows that even marriage was considered no obstacle to the pursuit of knowledge and the study
of literature :—

"Thomas More to his most dear daughter Margaret,—

"There was no reason, my most sweet child, why you should
have put off writing for a day, because in your great self-distrust
you feared lest your letter should be such that I could not read
it without distaste.   Even had it not been perfect, yet the
honour of your sex would have gained you pardon from any,
while to a father even a blemish will seem beautiful in the face
of a child.   But, indeed, my dear Margaret, your letter was so
elegant and polished and gave so little cause for you to dread
the judgment of an indulgent parent, that you might have
despised the censorship even of an angry Momus.

"You tell me that Nicholas, who is so fond of you, and so
learned in astronomy, has begun again with you the system of
the heavenly bodies.   I am grateful to him and I congratulate
you in your good fortune ; for in the space of one month, with
only a slight labour, you will thus learn thoroughly these sublime wonders of the Eternal Workman, which so many men of

illustrious and almost superhuman intellect have only discovered with hot toil and study, or rather with cold shiverings and nightly vigils in the open air in the course of many ages.

"I am, therefore, delighted to read that you have made up your mind to give yourself diligently to philosophy, and to make up by your earnestness in future for what you have lost in the past by neglect. My darling Margaret, I indeed have never found you idling, and your unusual learning in almost every kind of literature shows that you have been making active progress. So I take your words as an example of the great modesty that makes you prefer to accuse yourself falsely of sloth, rather than to boast of your diligence ; unless your meaning is that you will give yourself so earnestly to study, that your past industry will seem like indolence by comparison. If this is your meaning nothing could be more delightful to me, or more fortunate, my sweetest daughter, for you.

"Though I earnestly hope that you will devote the rest of your life to medical science and sacred literature, so that you may be well furnished for the whole scope of human life, which is to have a healthy soul in a healthy body, and I know that you have already laid the foundations of these studies, and there will be always opportunity to continue the building ; yet I am of opinion that you may, with great advantage, give some years of your yet flourishing youth to humane letters and liberal studies. And this both because youth is more fitted for a struggle with difficulties ; and because it is uncertain whether you will ever in future have the benefit of so sedulous, affectionate and learned a teacher. I need not say that by such studies a good judgment is formed or perfected.

"It would be a delight, my dear Margaret, to me to converse long with you on these matters ; but I have just been interrupted and called away by the servants, who have brought in supper. I must have regard to others, else to sup is not so sweet as to talk with you. Farewell, my dearest child, and salute for me my most gentle son, your husband. I am extremely

glad that he is following the same course of study as yourself.
I am ever wont to persuade you to yield in everything to your
husband ; now, on the contrary, I give you full leave to strive
to get before him in the knowledge of the celestial system.*
Farewell again.   Salute your whole company, but especially
your tutor."

Such letters as these make the reader almost as much in love
with Margaret Roper as her father was ; and certainly whatever
little romance is wanting in the courtships of this singular man
is made up for in the intensity of affection poured out from the
father's heart on this gracious child from her cradle to his
scaffold.

It is clear that Sir Thomas had a little Utopia of his own in
his family.   He was making an experiment in education, and
he was delighted with its success.   The fame of his learned
daughters became European, through the praises of Erasmus ;
and was so great in England that in 1529, when they were all
married ladies, they were invited by the king to hold a kind of
philosophical tournament in his presence.   We learn this from a
letter of John Palsgrave, who was a prebendary of St. Paul's, and
tutor to the Duke of Richmond, Henry's son.   He writes to
More in July, 1529 : " when your daughters disputed on philosophy afore the King's Grace, I would it had been my fortune
to be present " ; † an ineffectual wish in which the writer of
this memoir heartily joins.‡

Section III. Home and Parish.

From Bucklesbury More had removed (it is said) to Crosby

* *In pernoscenda sphæra.*

† *Letters and Papers*, iv. 5806.

‡ The treatise *Of the Sphere* is referred to more than once in this chapter.   More was fond of astronomy, and we know that the king would
take him on the leads at night and discourse with him about the
heavenly bodies.   There is a rather amusing passage in one of his controversial works giving an account of the geocentric system then taught.
It will be found in App. C. of this work.

Place, in Bishopsgate Street (Within),* and in 1523 he purchased a piece of land in Chelsea, then more properly called Chels-hithe, a small village utterly separated from London, and even from Westminster. The approach was principally by the river Thames, a clear and pleasant stream bordered by gardens and palaces. Here More laid out a large garden stretching down to the river, and built himself a mansion about a hundred yards from the river side, "commodious rather than magnificent," says Erasmus. Every vestige of More's house has disappeared. After his attainder and death it passed through the hands of a long series of proprietors, until it was pulled down in 1740, by Sir Hans Sloane. Beaufort Row runs over or near its site. In course of time, when, besides his daughters and their husbands, his son and his son's wife, no less than eleven grandchildren resided with him, he erected another house, detached from the first, and called the New Building. In this was his domestic oratory, his library, and study.

In his *Utopia*, More complained of the great number of retainers living idle and vicious lives in the service of noblemen, and becoming the pest of the country as thieves and murderers when out of service, from being unfit or unwilling to work. Stapleton tells us how carefully he avoided this evil in the management of his own household. It was one of the necessities of his dignity at court that he should have several attendants when he went out. When they were not engaged in this service he would not allow them to remain idle. He divided his garden into portions, to each of which he assigned one of his men as its cultivator. Some learnt to sing, others to play on the organ; but he absolutely forbade games of cards or dice, even to the young gentlemen in his house. The maid-servants lived quite apart from the men, and they seldom met.

* A part of Crosby Place still stands, and is one of the most interesting relics of Old London. From More it passed to his rich friend Antonio Bonvisi, the merchant of Lucca, and from him to William Roper, and William Rastell.

When he was at home he had night prayers for his family, at which he presided, even when he was chancellor. He recited with them especially the three psalms, *Miserere*, *Ad Te Domine levavi*, and *Deus misereatur nostri* with the *Salve Regina* and *Collect*, and the *De Profundis* for the holy souls.

Writing in one of his controversial works against Luther's and Tindale's assertions as to Christian liberty, he says there is no man so mad as to doubt " that servants in a man's household are so bound to obey their master's lawful commandments that if they would refuse at his bidding to kneel down and say certain prayers with him to bedward, all the whole house together, till he should show them some such commandment in scripture, they were well worthy to go to the devil for their proud disobedience in the defence of their false evangelical freedom ". From this he argues as to the authority of the Church, and the " lewd lither losils that list not to rise, but lie still in bed and say that are not bound by men's traditions" when a general procession is ordered.*

Every year on Good Friday he called the whole of his family in to the New Building and there had the Passion read to to them, generally by his secretary, John Harris. More would sometimes interrupt the reading with a few words of pious meditation. At table one of his daughters intoned after the monastic fashion † some passage of Holy Scripture, after which a short commentary by Nicholas of Lyra or one of the Fathers was read. Then he would propose a question concerning the passage read, and there would be a friendly discussion. This was done especially if any learned guest was present, and it need scarcely be said all this was in Latin. Then he would begin in English a joyous recreation, in which his fool or jester, Henry Patenson, would take part. The task of reading at table

---

* *English Works*, p. 508.

† Intonando, more prorsus ecclesiastico vel potius monastico, nam et subjiciebatur in fine : *Tu autem*, et legebatur quousque daretur signum.

was taken by turns by the unmarried children; after their marriage by Margaret Giggs.

It has been said that he had his domestic chapel, with licence to have the holy sacrifice offered within it. This chapel was to him a favourite place of resort. There, according to Roper, he used to spend the greater part of every Friday, when at home, meditating on the Passion, his favourite subject, with prayers and sacred penitential exercises. When his daughter Margaret was at the very point of death with the sweating sickness, and the doctors had given up all hopes, Sir Thomas, "going up after his usual manner into his aforesaid New Building, there in his chapel on his knees with tears most devoutly besought Almighty God that it would like His goodness, unto whom nothing is impossible, if it were His blessed will to vouchsafe graciously to hear his petition". During his prayer, a remedy that the doctors had not tried came into his mind. It proved effectual, though "God's marks," or the signs of death, were already on his daughter's body; "by her father's most fervent prayers," says his grateful son-in-law, "as it was thought, was she miraculously recovered; whom if it had pleased God at that time to have taken to His mercy, her father said he would never have meddled in worldly matters more".

His love of his domestic oratory and family devotions did not in any way cause him to neglect his parish church. In defending the use and sanctity of churches against the false spirituality of the heretics of his own days More has written: "Albeit that some good men here and there, one among ten thousand, as St. Paul and St. Anthony, do live all heavenly, far out of all fleshly company—as far from all occasions of worldly wretchedness, as from the common temple or parish church—yet if churches and congregations of Christian people resorting together to God's service were once abolished and put away, we were like to have few good temples of God in men's souls, but all would within a while wear away clean and clearly fall to nought. And this prove we by experience, that

those which be the best temples of God in their souls they most
use to come to the temple of stone ; and those that least come
there be well known for very ribalds and unthrifts, and openly
perceived for the temples of the devil.   And this not in our
days only, but so hath been from Christ's days hither." *

"In the parish church of Chelsea," says Stapleton, "he had
built a chapel and furnished it copiously with everything
necessary for the worship of God.†   In this matter he was
very generous and gave many vessels of gold and silver to his
church, being wont to say : 'The good give and the bad steal'.
In his parish church he would put on a surplice and take his
part with the choir."‡   Once when he was chancellor of the
kingdom, the Duke of Norfolk found him wearing a surplice
and singing.   "To whom, after service," writes Roper, "as
they went homeward arm in arm, the duke said : 'God's body,
God's body, my Lord Chancellor !   What ! a parish clerk—a
parish clerk !   You dishonour the king and his office.'
'Nay,' quote Sir Thomas More, smiling on the duke, 'Your
Grace may not think that the king, your master and mine,
will with me for serving God his Master be offended, or thereby
account his office dishonoured.' "

"Sometimes," adds Stapleton, "he served the priest's Mass,
and sometimes in the public supplications he carried the
Cross before the priest, not refusing or blushing to perform
the office of a verger, rejoicing rather like David to become
still more vile and humble in his own eyes.   Though he did
not carry the Cross when chancellor, yet he followed in the

* *English Works*, p. 122.

† This was the south aisle.

‡ Sacerdoti canenti concinebat.   *Canere*, in old ecclesiastical language
does not always mean to sing the psalms and prayers in the Divine
Office, but " to say mass ".   Even a low Mass offered in a low voice was
said to be sung.   Hence a chapel for such a Mass was called a chantry.
Yet here Stapleton is speaking of the choir.   He mentions serving at
Mass subsequently.

rogation processions round the parish, and though the walk
was long and difficult, and he was asked by his friends to
ride, on account of his dignity, he always refused, saying:
'My Lord goes on foot, I will not follow Him on horseback'."

More was fortunate in his parish priest. John Larke, whom
he had appointed to the rectory of Chelsea in 1530, laid down
his life rather than defile his soul with the oath of the royal
supremacy, the pastor being no doubt strengthened to this
noble martyrdom by the example and prayers of this leader
of his flock. Both now are honoured as Blessed by the
Church, having been joined together in the Decree of 29th
December, 1886.

Stapleton writes as follows of More's charity and almsgiving:
"He used himself to go through the back lanes, and inquire
into the state of poor families; and he would relieve their
distress, not by scattering a few small coins as is the general
custom, but when he ascertained a real need, by two, three
or four gold pieces. When his official position and duties
prevented this personal attention, he would send some of his
family to dispense his alms, especially to the sick and the
aged. This office often fell to Margaret Gigs, and it was
especially at the time of the great feasts of the Church that
these visitations were made. He very often invited to his
table his poorer neighbours, receiving them (not condescend-
ingly but) familiarly and joyously; he rarely invited the rich,
and scarcely ever the nobility. In his parish of Chelsea he
hired a house, in which he gathered many infirm, poor and
old people, and maintained them at his own expense. When
More was away, his daughter, Margaret, had the care of this
house. He even went so far as to receive into his own family
and maintain, a poor gentlewoman, a widow named Paula,
who had expended all she had in an unsuccessful lawsuit.
To widows and orphans, when he practised at the bar, he
even gave his services gratuitously." *

* *Vita*, cap. 6.

SECTION IV. PORTRAITS.

To conclude these details of domestic and parochial life, before we follow More in his public career, I will give some account of the picture by which the family group is made familiar to us. Erasmus, while living in Basle, had made the acquaintance of Hans Holbein, the younger. Holbein had been accustomed to work for the corporation, and was also employed by Froben the publisher in illustrating some of his books. But when the heresy of Œcolampadius prevailed in that city in 1525 and 1526, so great was the iconoclastic fury of the mob, that the painter's business came to an end. At this time he heard of England, as a place where his art would be better appreciated and rewarded. Erasmus was living in Fribourg. From him Holbein obtained an introduction to Sir Thomas More, and with it arrived in England towards the end of 1526. In a letter, dated 18th December of that year, More replies to Erasmus : "Your painter is a wonderful artist, but I fear he may not find England so fertile a field as he expected. I will do my best that he may not find it barren." *

More was true to his promise, and it was owing in great measure to his friendship that Holbein attained both wealth and celebrity. Holbein brought with him two portraits of

---

* Inter Epist. Erasm., 334, in App. I have consulted with regard to the portraits of More, Dr. Alfred Woltmann's *Holbein and his times* (Eng. tr. 1872), *Wornum's Holbein* and *Hans Holbein*, by J. Cundall (1882). The letter quoted above, alluding to Holbein, is (as usual), misdated as to the year by the editor of *Erasmus*. He gives it as 18th Dec., 1525. Dr. Woltmann places it in 1524, and remarks that it is dated "from the Court at Greenwich," and that the court was at Greenwich in the Christmas of 1524, but not in 1525. The correct date, however, is 1526. In that year also the king was to arrive at Greenwich on the 19th Dec., and More had no doubt preceded him by a day (*Letters and Papers*, iv. 2712). That the letter belongs to 1526 is proved by the reference to the second part of the " Hyperaspistes of Erasmus," which only appeared that year. Dr. Woltmann admits that Holbein did not reach England until 1526. He therefore needlessly conjectured that the pictures spoken of by More had been sent in advance.

Erasmus, one of which is said to be in the possession of the Earl of Radnor at Longford Castle, near Salisbury. His work was a better recommendation than the letter of Erasmus, and through More's influence, though he did not as yet get known at court, several great ecclesiastics and noblemen sat for their portraits. It was on the occasion of this visit to England that he painted his exquisite portrait of Archbishop Warham, now owned by Lord Dillon. Fisher, also, the Bishop of Rochester, sat to him, and though no picture of the holy martyr by the hand of Holbein is now in existence, there are two sketches in crayon, one in the Queen's Windsor collection, the other in the British Museum.* It is asserted by Van Mander, the first biographer of Holbein, that during his stay in England he was a guest of More's. Though this is in accordance with More's well-known hospitality, the assertion rests on no historical grounds, and Van Mander makes so many mistakes about this period, that it is clear he had no authentic information; nor was Holbein altogether, either in faith or morals, a man in whose society More would have found pleasure, however much he admired his art. Of course, More himself gave him his first commission. The exquisite portrait, which was kindly exhibited by Mr. Henry Huth in the National Historical Portrait Exhibition of 1866, and again by Mr. Edward Huth in the Tudor Exhibition of 1890, bears on the table on which More is leaning the date 1527. More was not then Lord High Chancellor, but he was both Treasurer of the Household and Chancellor of the Duchy of Lancaster. A heavy gold chain round his neck indicates one or other of these dignities.† The portrait is a half-length

---

* It was Holbein's custom to make a rapid sketch on paper, from which he worked leisurely on canvas. His eye and his pencil were unerring.

† The Collar of S.S., instituted by Henry IV., was a Lancastrian badge. It was totally distinct from the collar of knighthood (see Cussan's *Handbook of Heraldry*, p. 240 (3rd ed.), and *Retrospective Review* (2nd series) ii. 500).

figure nearly life-size. The face is clean shaved, and turned to the right of the spectator. Beneath the lappets of the cap is shown some dark brown hair. The dress is handsome—a dark green coat, with deep fur collar and crimson sleeves. The hands, lightly joined, lean against a table—a ring is on the first finger of the left hand, the right holds a book.

Besides this portrait, Holbein painted a large family group, representing Sir John and Sir Thomas, Lady More, the three married daughters and the son; Anne Cresacre, young John More's *fiancée*; and Margaret Giggs, his adopted daughter, the wife of Dr. John Clements. The Rev. John Lewis of Maidstone, who edited Roper's *Life of More* in 1729, describes as follows the picture, which he saw in March, 1717, at Well Hall, the seat of the Roper family at Eltham, in Kent: "The room which is here represented seemed to me to be a large dining-room. At the upper end stands a chamber organ on a cup-board, with a curtain drawn before it. On each end of the cupboard, which is covered with a carpet of tapestry, stands a flowerpot of flowers, and on the cupboard are laid a lute, a base viol, a pint pot or ewer covered in part with a cloth folded several times, and *Boethius, De Consolatione Philosophiæ*, with two other books, upon it. By this cupboard stands a daughter of Sir Thomas More's, putting on her right-hand glove, and having under her arm a book bound in red turkey leather and gilt, with this inscription round the outside of the cover: *Epistolica Senecæ*. Over her head is written *Elizabetha Dancea Thomæ Mori filia, anno* 21. Behind her stands a woman hold-ing a book open with both hands, over whose head is written *Uxor Johannis Clements.** Next to Mrs. Dancy is Sir John More in his robes as one of the justices of the King's Bench, and by him Sir Thomas in his chancellor's robes † and collar

---

* On the Basle sketch it is *Margareta Giga Clementis uxor Thomæ, Mori filiabus condiscipula et cognata, anno* 22.

† When this picture was painted More was not yet Lord High Chan-cellor, nor does he wear any robe ↖ dignity, but the common furred gown.

of S.S., with a rose pendant before. They are both sitting on a sort of tressel or armed bench; one of the arms and legs and one of the tassels of the cushion appear on the left side of Sir Thomas. At the feet of Sir John lies a cur dog, and at Sir Thomas's a Bologna shock. Over Sir John's head is written *Johannes Morus pater, anno* 76 ; over Sir Thomas's, *Thomas Morus, anno* 50. Between them, behind, stands the wife* of John More (Sir Thomas's son), over whose head is written *Anna Crisacria Joannis Mori sponsa, anno* 15. Behind Sir Thomas, a little on his left, stands his only son, John More, pictured with a very foolish aspect,† and looking earnestly in a book which he holds open with both his hands. Over his head is written *Joannes Morus Thomæ filius, anno* 19. A little to the left of Sir Thomas are sitting on low stools his two other daughters, Cæcilia and Margaret. Next him is Cæcilia, who has a book in her hand clasped. By her sits her sister Margaret, who has likewise a book in her lap, but wide open, in which is written : *L. An. Senecæ Ædipus. Fata si liceat mihi fingere arbitrio meo, temperem zephyro levis.* On Cæcilia's pettycoat is written *Cæcilia Herond,‡ Thomæ Mori filia, anno* 20, and on Margaret's *Margareta Ropera Thomæ Mori filia, anno* 22. Just by Mrs. Roper sits Sir Thomas's lady in an elbow chair holding a book open in her hands. About her neck she has a gold chain with a cross hanging to it before. On her left hand is a monkey chained, and holding part of it with one paw and part of it with the other. Over her head is written *Uxor Thomæ Mori, anno* 57.§ Behind her is a large arched window in which is placed a flower-pot of flowers and a

---

* Not wife (*uxor*) but fiancée (*sponsa*).

† This is a mere foolish fancy of Lewis. Mr. Wornum says of the Basle sketch " he here makes the impression of a gentle, reflective, and sterling youth " (p. 320).

‡ *Herona* in the Basle sketch.

§ In the Basle sketch it is *Alicia Thomæ Mori uxor, anno* 57.

couple of oranges.   Behind the two ladies stands Sir Thomas's fool.   He has his cap on and in it are stuck a red and white rose, and on the brim of it is a shield with a red cross in it, and a sort of seal pendant.   About his neck he wears a black string with a cross hanging before him, and his left thumb is stuck in a broad leathern girdle clasped about him. Over his head is written *Henricus Pattison Thomæ servus.** At the entrance of the room where Sir Thomas and his family are stands a man in the portal who has in his left hand a roll of papers or parchments with two seals appendant, as if he was some way belonging to Sir Thomas [as Lord Chancellor].† Over his head is written *Joannes Heresius Thomæ Mori famulus.* ‡ In another room, at some distance, is seen through the door-case, a man standing at a large bow window with short black hair, in an open-sleeved gown of a sea-green colour, holding a book open in his hands, written or printed in the black letter, and reading very earnestly in it.   About the middle of the room over against Sir Thomas hangs a clock, with strings and leaden weights without any case." §

However minute, this is a very inartistic and unsatisfactory description of this famous picture.   Mr. Lewis says nothing about its size, nor whether it is painted on canvas or wood, nor with what pigments.   Had he not mentioned the colour of a book cover, the red and white rose, and the sea-green colour of a servant's gown in the background, we should have been left uncertain whether it was a painting at all, or a mere cartoon, or a pen and ink drawing like that at Basle.

In the Basle Museum is preserved the study made for this picture, a small pen and ink sketch, on which, besides the in-

---

* In the Basle sketch *Henricus Patensonus Thomæ Mori morio, anno* 40.

† See note at last page.

‡ He is not in the Basle sketch

§ Lewis Roper, App. xv.

scriptions of names and ages in Latin,* are notes in German by Holbein for his own direction. The Basle sketch corresponds in general with Lewis's account, but Lady More is kneeling on a prie-dieu instead of sitting in an arm-chair. But Holbein has written *Diese soll sitzen* (this one shall sit), and above Sir John's head, where a violin and clock are hanging on the wall, is a note "Clavicord and other instruments on a shelf". In the Basle sketch also the clerk or secretary John Harris is not seen, nor the two dogs.

The picture described by Lewis is now in the possession of Lord St. Oswald (formerly Rowland Winn, Esq.), at Nostel Priory, near Wakefield. The size of the canvas is 11 ft. 6 in. *w.* by 8 ft. 3 in. *h.* Whether this is the original by Holbein or an exceedingly able copy has been disputed.†

It is certain that Sir Thomas sent this or a similar family group as a present to Erasmus by Holbein's own hands, and it is certain that Holbein had reached Basle by August, 1528. Whether the group that he conveyed was the only picture finished by him, or whether it was a replica of one left in England, or whether it was merely the pen and ink sketch now in Basle, I do not find recorded. In the absence of evidence, I should conjecture that Holbein retained his own sketch or study now in the Basle Museum, and conveyed an oil painting to Erasmus. Karel van Mander, who wrote in 1608, mentions an original painting by Holbein of this family group being then in the possession of the art collector, Andries Van Loo. "From

---

* Mr. Seebohm says "in Sir Thomas's handwriting," Mr. Wornum, "perhaps by Erasmus himself"; which seems very improbable, for how should Erasmus know the ages of every member of the household, even the fool?

† A copy somewhat mutilated was in possession of Mr. Eyston of East Hendred in 1867, and another at Thorndon Hall, the seat of Lord Petre. They are described by Mr. Wornum in his *Life and Works of Holbein*, p. 237. Both these are coarsely painted, and are certainly not by Holbein. The genuineness of the Nostel Priory picture is discussed at length by Mr. Wornum. *Ib.*, p. 239.

him," writes Mr. Cundall, "it went back to a grandson of Sir
Thomas More; since then it has entirely disappeared." *

It is important to notice that the engravings of the Basle
sketch have an inscription "Joannes Holbein ad vivum delin.
Londini, 1530". But this date is not on the original, and is
incorrect. Holbein left England in 1528, and was in Basle in
1530. The same erroneous date 1530 having been marked on
other copies led to misdating the ages of Sir Thomas and all
his family. The ages marked by Sir Thomas refer to the latter
part of 1527 or early in 1528.

A letter was, no doubt, sent by Sir Thomas to Erasmus, with
the picture; but it no longer exists, nor the answer of Erasmus.
It would seem, however, that another letter was sent by the
young ladies, for there is a letter addressed by Erasmus :—

"To Margaret Roper, the ornament of Britain,—

"I cannot find words to express the joy I felt when Holbein's
picture showed me your whole family almost as faithfully as if
I had you before my eyes. Often do I form the wish that even
once before my last day I may look upon that most dear
society, to which I owe a great part of whatever little fortune or
glory I possess; and to none could I be indebted more willingly.
The painter's skill has given me no small portion of my wish.
I recognise you all, but no one better than yourself. I seem
to behold through all your beautiful household a soul shining
forth still more beautiful. I congratulate you all in that family
happiness, but most of all your excellent father." After a few
words on female culture and its advantages, he concludes: "I am
writing in bad health and in the midst of overwhelming work,
therefore I must leave it to your tact to convince all your sisters
that this is a fair and adequate letter; and written to each one
of them no less than to yourself. Convey my respectful and

---

* *Hans Holbein*, by Joseph Cundall (1882), p. 54. This of course
supposes that the Well Hall picture, now Lord St. Oswald's, is either a
copy, or a replica.

affectionate salutations to the honoured Lady Alice, your mother. I kiss her picture as I cannot kiss herself.* To my godson, John More, I wish every happiness, and you will give a special salutation on my part to your honourable husband, so justly dear to you. May God keep you all, and give you every prosperity by His almighty grace. From Fribourg, 6th September, 1529."†

Margaret Roper replied in a beautiful Latin letter. Quirinus had brought Erasmus's elegant and loving letter. She had never deserved or expected such an honour as to receive a letter from the hand of one who was the pride and ornament of the whole world (*totius orbis decus*). She does not know how to thank him worthily: "You say that the visit of the painter (Holbein) caused you great pleasure, because he brought the picture of both my parents and of us all. We are most thankful that you are pleased, and we desire nothing more ardently than to see once more our former tutor to whom we owe whatever culture we possess, and still more to converse with the old and faithful friend of our father. My mother cordially salutes you, also my husband and my brother, and both my sisters. London, 4th November, 1529."‡

Many portraits have been mistaken for Sir Thomas More's. A bearded picture of Sir Thomas Wyatt, by Holbein, in the Louvre, was called Sir Thomas More because of a gold chain. Even the burgomaster of Dresden and his family in Holbein's

---

* Erasmus mentions jokingly elsewhere the custom then universal in England of thus saluting ladies.

† *Letter* 1075.

‡ *Letter* 352, in App. With the words of Margaret Roper—*Utriusque mei parentis nostrumque omnium effigiem depictam*—I do not understand how Mr. Wornum can doubt whether Sir Thomas sent any picture to Erasmus, and imagine that Holbein either carried with him a mere sketch, or drew one from memory. Erasmus also makes mention of a *pictura*, and of its being perfectly life-like. How could such expressions be used of a small pen and ink sketch?

Meyer Madonna have been taken for More and his family, though there is not an English line in face or dress.

Another family group formerly at Burford Priory, the seat of Mr. Lenthall, now in the possession of Mr. Walter Strickland of Cokethorpe Park, Oxfordshire, is a composition. It contains Sir John and Sir Thomas, with four other male and four female figures, besides another female who appears in a framed portrait. Some of these were descendants of Sir Thomas of a much later date, for the picture was painted in 1593. The margin contains long inscriptions, not always accurate.

It is instructive and somewhat amusing to compare the descriptions of professed or professional art critics. There are two crayons of Sir Thomas More's head, unquestionably by Holbein, in Her Majesty's Windsor collection. In perfect agreement with these is the finished portrait in the possession of Mr. Huth. Mr. Wornum says, "the expression in this picture is harsh and even repulsive"; yet I have myself seen crowds around this picture so charmed as to be almost unable to draw themselves away, and all uttering exclamations on the beauty and sweetness of the expression. It would seem that Holbein's portrait shares the mysterious property of the face it copied; it was a riddle to each one who read it, or guessed at it as he felt disposed.*

---

* Dr. Oliver, in a notice of Thomas More, S.J., who died in 1795 in Bristol, quotes from a letter of F. Talbot, S.J., to Lord Arundel, 5th June, 1793: "Mr. More proposes taking up his residence with his sister at Bath for the rest of his days. In consequence I have sent down his effects, particularly his three famous pictures of Sir T. More, Bishop Fisher, and Card. Pole." What is the history of these pictures, and where are they?

CHAPTER IX

THE events of More's public life, from 1517 to 1529, when he became chancellor, are touched on, but very slightly, in his son-in-law's notes. Yet they were very important years, the years in which he forsook the profession of the law for the career of a statesman. That More's name does not appear much more prominently during those years in English history, is greatly due to his want of ambition. There is not a solitary example in his life of his seeking any advancement either in honours or in wealth. He discharged his various offices, not because he delighted in them—for several inspired him with repugnance—yet always cheerfully as acquitting himself of a duty to God and his country.

When he first perceived the likelihood of his being drawn into public life, he expressed his thoughts on it in such a manner in his *Utopia*, that his words might serve as a protest or declaration of principles, even if they did not prove to Wolsey and the king that he was a man unfit for statecraft. The long extracts I am about to give from his *Utopia* require no apology. They are an exposition by More himself of his views of the work in which he spent the years of his manhood. It is worth while to observe that, at the very time when More was satirising the diplomacy of his age, Machiavelli in Italy, whether satirically or not, was elaborating it into a perfect system. *

* Seebohm.

Peter Giles and More, it will be remembered, were discoursing with Raphael Hythloday, the traveller. Peter had expressed his surprise that Hythloday should not give the benefit of his great experience to some prince. "'I do not see any other way in which you can be so useful, both in private to your friends and to the public, and by which you can make your own condition happier.' 'Happier?' answered Raphael, 'is that to be compassed in a way so abhorrent to my genius? Now I live as I will, to which, I believe, few courtiers can pretend; and there are so many that court the favour of great men, that there will be no great loss if they are not troubled either with me or with others of my temper.' Upon this, said I, 'I perceive, Raphael, that you neither desire wealth nor greatness; and, indeed, I value and admire such a man much more than I do any of the great men in the world. Yet I think you would do what would well become so generous and philosophical a soul as yours is, if you would apply your time and thoughts to public affairs, even though you may happen to find it a little uneasy to yourself; and this you can never do with so much advantage as by being taken into the council of some great prince and putting him on noble and worthy actions, which I know you would do if you were in such a post; for the springs both of good and evil flow from the prince over a whole nation, as from a lasting fountain. So much learning as you have, even without practice in affairs, or so great a practice as you have had, without any other learning, would render you a very fit counsellor to any king whatsoever.' 'You are doubly mistaken,' said he, 'Mr. More, both in your opinion of me and in the judgment you make of things: for as I have not that capacity that you fancy I have, so if I had it, the public would not be one jot the better when I had sacrificed my quiet to it. For most princes apply themselves more to affairs of war than to the useful arts of peace; and in these I neither have any knowledge, nor do I much desire it; they are generally more set on acquiring new kingdoms right or wrong, than on governing

well those they possess : and, among the ministers of princes,
there are none that are not so wise as to need no assistance, or,
at least, that do not think themselves so wise that they
imagine they need none ; and if they court any, it is only those
for whom the prince has much personal favour, whom by
their fawnings and flatteries they endeavour to fix to their own
interests ; and, indeed, nature has so made us, that we all love
to be flattered and to please ourselves with our own notions :
the old crow loves his young, and the ape her cubs. Now, if
in such a court, made up of persons who envy all others and
only admire themselves, a person should but propose anything that he had either read in history or observed in
his travels, the rest would think that the reputation of
their wisdom would sink, and that their interests would be
much depressed if they could not run it down : and if all other
things failed, then they would fly to this, that such or such
things pleased our ancestors, and it were well for us if we could
but match them. They would set up their rest on such an
answer as a sufficient confutation of all that could be said, as
if it were a great misfortune that any should be found wiser
than his ancestors. But though they willingly let go all the
good things that were among those of former ages, yet, if better
things are proposed, they cover themselves obstinately with
this excuse of reverence to past times. I have met with these
proud, morose, and absurd judgments of things in many places,
particularly once in England.' "

Then, after a long story of a conversation at Cardinal
Morton's table, they return once more to the subject. " 'You
have done me a great kindness,' said I, ' in this relation ; you
have made me imagine that I was in my own country and
grown young again, by recalling that good cardinal to my
thoughts, in whose family I was bred from my childhood ; but
after all this I cannot change my opinion, for I still think that if
you could overcome that aversion which you have to the courts
of princes, you might, by the advice which it is in your power

to give, do a great deal of good to mankind, and this is the chief design that every good man ought to propose to himself in living ; for your friend Plato thinks that nations will be happy when either philosophers become kings or kings become philosophers. It is no wonder if we are so far from that happiness while philosophers will not think it their duty to assist kings with their counsels.' 'They are not so base-minded,' said he, 'but that they would willingly do it ; many of them have already done it by their books, if those that are in power would but hearken to their good advice. But Plato judged right, that except kings themselves became philosophers, they who from their childhood are corrupted with false notions would never fall in entirely with the counsels of philosophers, and this he himself found to be true in the person of Dionysius.

"'Do not you think that if I were about any king, propos-ing good laws to him, and endeavouring to root out all the cursed seeds of evil that I found in him, I should either be turned out of his court, or, at least, be laughed at for my pains ? For instance, what could I signify if I were about the King of France, and were called into his cabinet council, where several wise men, in his hearing, were proposing many expedients : as, by what arts and practices Milan may be kept, and Naples, that has so often slipped out of their hands, recovered ; how the Venetians, and after them the rest of Italy, may be subdued ; and then how Flanders, Brabant, and all Burgundy, and some other kingdoms which he has swallowed already in his designs, may be added to his empire ? One proposes a league with the Venetians, to be kept as long as he finds his account in it, and that he ought to communicate counsels with them, and give them some share of the spoil till his success makes him need or fear them less, and then it will be easily taken out of their hands ; another proposes the hiring the Germans and the securing the Switzers by pensions ; another proposes pro-pitiating the deity of the emperor by a sacrifice of gold ; another proposes a peace with the King of Arragon, and, in order to cement it, the yielding up the King of Navarre's pretensions; another thinks that the Prince of Castile is to be wrought on by the hope of an alliance, and that some of his courtiers are to be gained to the French faction by pensions. The hardest point of all is, what to do with England; a treaty of peace is to be set on foot, and, if their alliance is not to be depended on, yet it is to be made as firm as possible, and they are to be called friends, but suspected as enemies : therefore the Scots are to be kept in readiness to be let loose upon England on every occasion; and some banished nobleman is to be supported underhand (for by the league it cannot be done avowedly) who has a pretension to the crown, by which means that suspected prince may be kept in awe.

"'Now, when things are in so great a fermentation, and so many gallant men are joining counsels how to carry on the war, if so mean a man as I should stand up and wish them to change all their counsels—to let Italy alone and stay at home, since the kingdom of France was indeed greater than could be well governed by one man; that therefore he ought not to think of adding others to it; and if, after this, I should propose to them the resolutions of the Achorians, a people that lie on the south-east of Utopia, who long ago engaged in war in order to add to the dominions of their prince another kingdom, to which he had some pretensions by an ancient alliance; this they conquered, but found that the trouble of keeping it was equal to that by which it was gained; that the conquered people were always either in rebellion or exposed to foreign invasions, while they were obliged to be incessantly at war, either for or against them, and consequently could never disband their army; that in the meantime they were oppressed with taxes, their money went out of the kingdom, their blood was spilt for the glory of others without peace being secured; and that, their manners being corrupted by a long war, robbery and murders everywhere abounded, and their laws fell into contempt; while their king, distracted with the care of two kingdoms, was the less able to apply his mind to the interest of either. When they saw this, and that there would be no end to these evils, they by joint counsels made an humble address to their king, desiring him to choose which of the two kingdoms he had the greatest mind to keep, since he could not hold both; for they were too great a people to be governed by a divided king, since no man would willingly have a groom that should be in common between him and another. Upon which the good prince was forced to quit his new kingdom to one of his friends (who was not long after dethroned), and to be contented with his old one. To this I would add that, after all those warlike attempts, the vast confusions, and the consumption both of treasure and of people that must follow them, perhaps upon some misfortune they might be forced to throw up all at last; therefore, it seemed much more eligible that the king should improve his ancient kingdom all he could, and make it flourish as much as possible; that he should love his people, and be beloved of them; that he should live among them, govern them gently, and let other kingdoms alone, since that which had fallen to his share was big enough, if not too big, for him :— pray, how do you think would such a speech as this be heard?'

"'I confess,' said I, 'I think not very well.'

"'But what,' said he, 'if I should sort with another kind of ministers, whose chief contrivances and consultations were by what art the prince's treasures might be increased? where one proposes raising the value of specie when the king's debts are large, and lowering it when his revenues were to come in, that so he might both pay much with a little, and in a little receive a great deal. Another proposes a pretence of war, that money might be raised in order to carry it on, and that a peace be concluded as soon as that was done; and this with such appearances of religion as might work on the people, and make them impute it to the piety of their prince, and to his tenderness for the lives of his subjects. A third offers

some old musty laws that have been antiquated by a long
disuse (and which, as they had been forgotten by all the
subjects, so they had also been broken by them), and proposes
the levying the penalties of these laws, that, as it would bring
in a vast treasure, so there might be a very good pretence for
it, since it would look like the executing a law and the doing
of justice.   A fourth proposes the prohibiting of many things
under severe penalties, especially such as were against the
interest of the people, and then the dispensing with these pro-
hibitions, upon great compositions, to those who might find their
advantage in breaking them.   This would serve two ends, both
of them acceptable to many ; for as those whose avarice led
them to transgress would be severely fined, so the selling
licenses dear would look as if a prince were tender of his
people, and would not easily, or at low rates, dispense with
anything that might be against the public good.   Another
proposes that the judges must be made sure, that they may
declare always in favour of the prerogative ; that they must be
often sent for to court, that the king may hear them argue those
points in which he is concerned ; since, how unjust soever any
of his pretensions may be, yet still some one or other of them,
either out of contradiction to others, or the pride of singularity,
or to make their court, would find out some pretence or other
to give the king a fair colour to carry the point.   For if the
judges but differ in opinion, the clearest thing in the world is
made by that means disputable, and truth being once brought
in question, the king may then take advantage to expound the
law for his own profit ; while the judges that stand out will be
brought over, either through fear or modesty ; and they being
thus gained, all of them may be sent to the bench to give
sentence boldly as the king would have it ; for fair pretences
will never be wanting when sentence is to be given in the
prince's favour.   It will either be said that equity lies of his
side, or some words in the law will be found sounding that
way, or some forced sense will be put on them ; and, when all

other things fail, the king's undoubted prerogative will be pretended, as that which is above all law, and to which a religious
judge ought to have a special regard.   Thus all consent to that
maxim of Crassus, that a prince cannot have treasure enough,
since he must maintain his armies out of it; that a king, even
though he would, can do nothing unjustly; that all property is
in him, not excepting the very persons of his subjects; and
that no man has any other property but that which the king,
out of his goodness, thinks fit to leave him.   And they think
it is the prince's interest that there be as little of this left as
may be, as if it were his advantage that his people should have
neither riches nor liberty, since these things make them less
easy and willing to submit to a cruel and unjust government.
Whereas necessity and poverty blunts them, makes them
patient, beats them down, and breaks that height of spirit that
might otherwise dispose them to rebel.

"'Now, what if, after all these propositions were made, I should
rise up and assert that such counsels were both unbecoming a
king and mischievous to him; and that not only his honour,
but his safety, consisted more in his people's wealth than in his
own; if I should show that they choose a king for their own
sake, and not for his; that, by his care and endeavours, they
may be both easy and safe; and that, therefore, a prince ought
to take more care of his people's happiness than of his own, as
a shepherd is to take more care of his flock than of himself?
It is also certain that they are much mistaken that think the
poverty of a nation is a means of the public safety.   Who
quarrel more than beggars? who does more earnestly long for
a change than he that is uneasy in his present circumstances?
and who run to create confusions with so desperate a boldness
as those who, having nothing to lose, hope to gain by them?
If a king should fall under such contempt or envy that he could
not keep his subjects in their duty but by oppression and ill
usage, and by rendering them poor and miserable, it were
certainly better for him to quit his kingdom than to retain it by

such methods as make him, while he keeps the name of authority, lose the majesty due to it. Nor is it so becoming the dignity of a king to reign over beggars as over rich and happy subjects. And therefore Fabricius, a man of a noble and exalted temper, said "he would rather govern rich men than be rich himself; since for one man to abound in wealth and pleasure when all about him are mourning and groaning, is to be a gaoler and not a king". He is an unskilful physician that cannot cure one disease without casting his patient into another. So he that can find no other way for correcting the errors of his people but by taking from them the conveniences of life, shows that he knows not what it is to govern a free nation. He himself ought rather to shake off his sloth, or to lay down his pride, for the contempt or hatred that his people have for him takes its rise from the vices in himself. Let him live upon what belongs to him without wronging others, and accommodate his expense to his revenue. Let him punish crimes, and, by his wise conduct, let him endeavour to prevent them, rather than be severe when he has suffered them to be too common. Let him not rashly revive laws that are abrogated by disuse, especially if they have been long forgotten and never wanted. And let him never take any penalty for the breach of them to which a judge would not give way in a private man, but would look on him as a crafty and unjust person for pretending to it.

"'If I should talk of these or such-like things to men that had taken their bias another way, how deaf would they be to all I could say!'

"'No doubt, very deaf,' answered I; 'and no wonder, for one is never to offer propositions or advice that we are certain will not be entertained. Discourses so much out of the road could not avail anything nor have any effect on men whose minds were prepossessed with different sentiments. This philosophical way of speculating is not unpleasant among friends in a free conversation; but there is no room for it in the courts of princes, where great affairs are carried on by authority.'

"'That is what I was saying,' replied he, 'that there is no room for philosophy in the courts of princes.' 'Yes, there is,' said I, 'but not for this speculative philosophy, that makes everything to be alike fitting at all times; but there is another philosophy that is more pliable, that knows its proper scene, accommodates itself to it, and teaches a man with propriety and decency to act that part which has fallen to his share. If when one of Plautus' comedies is upon the stage, and a company of servants are acting their parts, you should come out in the garb of a philosopher, and repeat, out of *Octavia*, a discourse of Seneca's to Nero, would it not be better for you to say nothing than by mixing things of different natures to make an impertinent tragic-comedy? for you spoil and corrupt the play that is in hand when you mix with it things of an opposite nature, even though they are much better. Therefore, go through with the play that is acting the best you can, and do not confound it because another that is pleasanter comes into your thoughts. It is even so in a commonwealth and in the councils of princes; if ill opinions cannot be quite rooted out, and you cannot cure some received vice according to your wishes, you must not, therefore, abandon the commonwealth, for the same reasons as you should not forsake the ship in a storm because you cannot command the winds. You are not obliged to assault people with discourses that are out of their road, when you see that their received notions must prevent your making an impression upon them: you ought rather to cast about and to manage things with all the dexterity in your power, so that, if you are not able to make them go well, they may be as little ill as possible; for, except all men were good, everything cannot be right, and that is a blessing that I do not at present hope to see.'

"'According to your argument,' answered he, 'all that I could be able to do would be to preserve myself from being mad while I endeavour to cure the madness of others ; for, if I speak truth, I must repeat what I have said to you ; and as for lying, whether a philosopher can do it or not I cannot tell : I am sure I cannot do it. But though these discourses may be uneasy and ungrateful to them, I do not see why they should seem foolish or extravagant ; indeed, if I should either propose such things as Plato has contrived in his " Commonwealth," or as the Utopians practise in theirs, though they might seem better, as certainly they are, yet they are so different from our establishment, which is founded on property (there being no such thing among them), that I could not expect that it would have any effect on them. But such discourses as mine, which only call past evils to mind and give warning of what may follow, have nothing in them that is so absurd that they may not be used at any time, for they can only be unpleasant to those who are resolved to run headlong the contrary way ; and if we must let alone everything as absurd or extravagant, which, by reason of the wicked lives of many, may seem uncouth, we must, even among Christians, give over pressing the greatest part of those things that Christ hath taught us, though He has commanded us not to conceal them, but to proclaim on the housetops that which He taught in secret. The greatest parts of His precepts are more opposite to the lives of the men of this age than any part of my discourse has been, but the preachers seem to have learned that craft to which you advise me : for they, observing that the world would not willingly suit their lives to the rules that Christ has given, have fitted His doctrine, as if it had been a leaden rule, to their lives, that so, some way or other, they might agree with one another. But I see no other effect of this compliance except it be that men become more secure in their wickedness by it ; and this is all the success that I can have in a court, for either I must always differ from the rest, and then I shall signify nothing : or, if I agree with them, I shall then only help forward their madness. I do not comprehend what you mean by your "casting about," or by "the bending and handling things so dexterously that, if they go not well, they may go as little ill as may be"; for in courts they will not bear with a man's holding his peace or conniving at what others do : a man must barefacedly approve of the worst counsels and consent to the blackest designs, so that he would pass for a spy, or, possibly, for a traitor, that did but coldly approve of such wicked practices ; and, therefore, when a man is engaged in such a society, he will be so far from being able to mend matters by his " casting about," as you call it, that he will find no occasions of doing any good—the ill company will sooner corrupt him than be the better for him ; or if, notwithstanding all their ill company, he still remains steady and innocent, yet their follies and knavery will be imputed to him ; and, by mixing counsels with them, he must bear his share of all the blame that belongs wholly to others.' " *

No one can say that More had not spoken out. The simplest peasant in England would have known that, whatever truth there was in his invective against the insatiable ambition and crooked policy of the French kings, Louis XII. and Francis I., the discourse was aimed at the foolish vanity of the king of England, who was dreaming of the recovery of the possessions of his ancestors on the continent, and for that end had twice invaded France.† It is somewhat to the honour of Henry that, after reading this declaration of free and noble principles, he should have been so eager to secure the writer as his councillor. Years afterwards More respectfully declared to the king, that "he always bare in mind the most godly words that his Highness spoke unto him upon his first entry into his noble service—the most virtuous lesson that ever prince taught his servant—willing him first to look unto God, and after God, unto him ; so in good faith, he said, he did, or

* Burnet's translation, slightly corrected by the Latin.

† In 1512 and 1513.

else might His Grace well account him for his most unworthy servant". *

From this review of his principles let us now turn to his acts. Roper's memory was not quite accurate as to the sequence of events. He says that More "continued in the king's singular favour and trusty service twenty years and above". If we reckon from the spring of 1532, when he resigned the chancellorship, this would take us back to 1512, which is quite too early. On the other hand, Roper says that "before he came to the service of the king he had been twice ambassador" in the interests of the London merchants. Now, the second embassy brings us to the end of 1517, and this date is confirmed from other sources. But, again, his son-in-law is certainly mistaken when he says that the king summoned him to court, "made him Master of the Requests (having then no better room void), and within a month after knight, and one of his privy council".

When we control these assertions by authentic records, it appears that early in 1518 More became finally a courtier, or rather took office at court; † he was probably not made a privy councillor until the summer of that year, and not knighted until the summer of 1521.

A word or two about the Privy Council in the time of Henry VIII. will help the reader to realise More's position. The King's Great Court or Council had originally combined the legislative, judicial and administrative functions. A large portion of its judicial functions was separated from it, and constituted the three tribunals of the King's Bench, Common Pleas, and Exchequer. The king, however, still retained near him his chief ministers who formed his Privy Council— the Chancellor, Treasurer, Lord Steward, Lord Admiral, Lord

* Roper.

† He did not, however, resign his office of under-sheriff until 23rd July, 1519, according to Mr. Foss and Sir James Mackintosh.

Marshall, the Keeper of the Privy Seal, the Chamberlain, Treasurer and Comptroller of the Household, the Chancellor of the Exchequer, and Chancellor of the Duchy of Lancaster, the Master of the Wardrobe, the Judges, Attorney-General and Master of the Rolls. When the business was special those only to whose department it belonged were summoned : the chancellor and judges for matters of law ; the officers of state for what concerned the revenue or household. Whether unconstitutionally or not, the business of the Council under the Tudors was both deliberative and judicial ; they issued ordinances, and claimed and exercised the right to imprison without formal conviction of crime.

The first charge given to More was that of Master of Requests. As the king made his progresses from place to place, many petitions were presented to him. These were referred to certain members of his household, of whom at least two were to be always in attendance. More still retained this office after being promoted to high dignity, and it gave him many opportunities of exercising justice and charity. *

The records of the Privy Council are lost for the whole period of More's lifetime, so that we are left to glean our information from occasional mention in letters or documents of the time. His reputation for uprightness made his access to the king welcome news to all good men. Sebastian Justiniani, the Venetian ambassador, wrote on 18th February, 1518, that the cardinal had appointed Richard Pace and Thomas More as commissioners to negotiate the repeal of the wine duties. " They are," he says, " the most sage, most virtuous, and most linked with myself of any in England. I suspect, however, that this promise will not be performed, because Pace is known to be devoted to the Signory *and More to justice.*"† On 3rd

---

* In 1526, when the household was remodelled, he remained one of the examiners of petitions (*Letters and Papers*, iv. 1939).

† *Venetian State Papers*, ii. 1010.

September, 1517, More had written to Erasmus : "I gave your letters to the Venetian ambassador. We scratched each other with set speeches and lengthened compliments ; but, to tell the truth, he pleases me much. He seems a most honourable man, with great experience of the world, and now bent on the knowledge of things divine ; last, not least, very fond of you."

Erasmus rejoiced that literature had gained a new patron. "Many learned men," he writes, 26th July, 1518, "are now in the English Court: Linacre, the king's physician; Tunstall, master of the rolls; More, privy councillor; Pace, secretary; Mountjoy, chamberlain; Colet, preacher; Stokesley, confessor." * All, however, were not learned men in the Council, and More must have been often amused at the uncouth spelling of the king's brother-in-law, the Duke of Suffolk. A specimen from a letter just of this date will amuse the reader. He writes that it hath pleased God "to wyesset his wife (the ex-Queen of France) wyet a nague, the wyche has taken Her Grace hewarre third day 4 tyemes wyree sharpe"† (in modern spelling, "to visit her with an ague, the which has taken Her Grace every third day four times very sharp "). The dice and cards, hunting, masquerades, and feasting, of which More now saw so much, and for all of which, according to Erasmus, he had a great aversion, must have given him less amusement than ignorance in high places. The king was fond of theological discussions as well as of dice, and More had to take part in these ; but though His Majesty was willing to lose money at cards, he would not care to be refuted in argument. He was just then maintaining a thesis as to whether laymen are bound to vocal prayer, and had put his arguments on paper. Wolsey had taken the opposite side to the king, but when he saw the royal logic in writing, he declared himself convinced, which much

---

* This is the earliest mention I have found of More as privy councillor.   The date of his appointment is unknown. Sir James Mackintosh says the beginning of 1516.   This seems too early.

† *Letters and Papers*, ii. 4134.

pleased the conqueror, and probably encouraged him a few
years later to measure theological swords with Luther.*

Henry VIII. at this period of his life was a most amiable
prince. In a letter to the Bishop of Rochester he is thus described by More : "He is so affable and courteous to all men, that
each one thinks himself his favourite, even as the citizens' wives
imagine that Our Lady's picture at the tower smiles upon them
as they pray before it ".† It is not strange that such a prince,
the evil parts of whose character were as yet but little developed,
should have been attracted strongly by a man like More—a
scholar, an orator, an accomplished gentleman—whom he
would prize, moreover, as his conquest.

Writing in 1519, Erasmus draws a beautiful picture of More
as a courtier: "In serious matters no man's advice is more
prized, while if the king wishes to recreate himself, no man's
conversation is gayer. Often there are deep and intricate
matters that demand a grave and prudent judge. More un-
ravels them in such a way that he satisfies both sides. No one,
however, has ever prevailed on him to receive a gift for his
decision. Happy the commonwealth where kings appoint such
officials ! His elevation has brought with it no pride. Amidst
all the weight of state affairs he remembers the humble friends
of old, and from time to time returns to his beloved literature.
Whatever influence he has acquired by his dignity, whatever
favour he enjoys with his opulent king, he uses for the good
of the state and for the assistance of his friends. He was ever
desirous of conferring benefits, and wonderfully prone to com-

* Letter of Pace to Wolsey, 22nd June, 1518. It is strange that
Mr. Brewer should imagine that this letter can refer to a first sketch of the
king's book against Luther. Erasmus tells us the subject of this first
book of Henry (*Epist.* 418). Luther's book on the Babylonian
captivity, to which Henry replied, did not appear till two years after
this letter of Pace's.

† A " picture " in the language of those days often meant a painted
statue or image.

passion.   This disposition has grown with his power of indul-
ging it.   Some he assists with money, others he protects by his
authority, others he advances by his recommendation.   If he
can help in no other way, he does it by his counsels; he sends
no one away dejected.   You would say that he had been appointed the public guardian of all those in need." *

Several casual illustrations occur here and there in state
papers of the truth of this beautiful picture drawn by a devoted
friend.   One of the first duties of a councillor is secrecy.   On
the 18th September, 1518, the Venetian ambassador writes to
the Doge that, in a visit he had made to the king at Eltham
he had " contrived a conference with Thomas More, newly
made councillor, who was a great friend of his, but he could
learn nothing from him, as the Cardinal of York, according to
him, alone transacted the business with the French ambassador," etc. †   So also three years later a great ecclesiastic,
who had thought by acts of courtesy to draw some secret
intelligence from More, writes that he failed to get "the
slightest hint ". ‡

Of his disposition to act as peace-maker, we have an
instance in a letter of Sir Arthur Poole.   That gentleman
says that when he complained to the king how unjustly he
had been handled by the Earl of Arundel, he was greatly mis-
content, and told him to speak to Mr. More, and by his aid

---

* Letter to Hutten.   After describing More's piety and other virtues,
Erasmus exclaims : " Ac talis Morus est etiam in aula, et postea sunt qui
putent Christianos non inveniri nisi in monasteriis," which was a sop to
Hutten, who hated monks.   Then of Henry : " Hos habet arbitros ac
testes perpetuos vitæ suæ ".   As the Duke of Richmond, Henry's natural
son, was already born, and acknowledged by his father, it was rather
bold to prove the king immaculate because of the presence of men like
More in his court.   As yet, however, the court was comparatively
decent.

† *Venetian State Papers*, ii. 1072.

‡ See *infra*, p. 190.

to devise a sharp letter to him; but More thought it better
to send him a loving letter first. *

To form some conception of the variety of duties that now
fell to More's lot, it will be best to follow him in the first years
of his court life. He travelled with the king, who was fond
of moving from place to place, especially when flying from the
terrible sweating sickness. In the spring of 1518 the court
was at Abingdon, near Oxford. More soon found that to live
under a monarch's roof did not exempt him from the petty
troubles of life. His friend, Chief Secretary Pace, writes to
Wolsey on 1st April: "Dr. Clark and Mr. More desire your
Grace to write to my Lord Steward that they may have their
daily allowance of meat which has been granted them by the
king. Here is such bribery that they be compelled to buy
meat in the town for their servants, which is to them intolerable, and to the king's grace dishonourable." †

The under-sheriff now found himself suddenly transformed
into a sanitary official. The court had moved to Woodstock
on 17th April, but More remained at Oxford to take measures
against the plague. He shut up infected houses, and had
them marked by wisps of hay; those serving the sick, if
obliged to go out, had to carry white rods.‡

Proximity to Oxford involved him in another plague, though
somewhat more congenial, for a controversy was raging there
about the study of his favourite Greek, and he had to
intervene. Erasmus has related some incidents in his amusing
style. His letter is no doubt an echo of one from More or
from Pace, which has not been preserved. " England,"

* *Letters and Papers*, iii. 2636 (24th Oct., 1522).

† *Ib.*, ii. 4055. There is frequent mention of More's liveries, as
they are called, *i.e.*, breakfasts, dinners, etc., in the *Royal Accounts*.
At the beginning of 1526 an attempt was made to remedy abuses, and
minute regulations were drawn up (*Ib.*, iv. 1939). *Sed quis custodiet
ipsos custodes ?*

‡ *Ib.*, 4125.

writes Erasmus, "has two universities, Cambridge and
Oxford, both of good renown. Greek literature is taught
in both, but in Cambridge quietly, because its chancellor
is John Fisher, Bishop of Rochester, a man as theological
in life as in erudition. At Oxford, where there is a young
professor of Greek of no ordinary learning,* a barbarous
preacher furiously attacked the study of Greek in a public
sermon. But the king, who was in the neighbourhood,
and who is both well instructed, and a patron of letters,
having heard of the affair from Pace and More, gave orders
that the study should be encouraged. Again, a theologian
who had to preach in the presence of the king, began
stupidly and impudently to attack Greek studies, and the
new interpreters (of scripture). Pace looked at the king
to see how he took it. The king replied by a smile. When
the sermon was ended the theologian was called. More
was appointed to defend Greek, and the king was himself
present at the discussion. After More, with much eloquence,
had made a long defence, and the reply of the theologian
was expected, instead of speaking he suddenly went on his
knees before the king and asked pardon, affirming, however,
in his excuse, that while preaching he had felt himself inspired
to say what he did against Greek. 'The spirit which inspired
you,' replied the king, 'was certainly not that of Christ, but
rather the spirit of folly.' Then he asked him whether he had
read any of the writings of Erasmus, since the king perceived
that he had been girding at me. He said that he had not.
'Then you clearly prove your folly,' said the king, 'since
you condemn what you have not read.' 'Well, I have read
one thing, called *Moria*,' replied the theologian. 'May t
please Your Highness,' interposed Pace, 'his argument well
befits that book.' Meanwhile the theologian hits on a train
of reasoning to mitigate his blunder. 'I am not altogether

* This was John Clements, More's protégé.

opposed to Greek,' he says, 'since it is derived from the Hebrew.' The king, astonished at the man's folly, dismissed him, but forbade him ever again to preach at court." *

In this letter Erasmus mentions two sermons and two preachers. To the sermon delivered at Oxford he merely alludes, perhaps he did not know the details of the affair. The sermon was the occasion of a very important Latin letter addressed by More to the university. A fragment of it is given by Stapleton, who calls it *luculenta oratio*, a brilliant address. He tells us also that it was translated by one of More's daughters into English, and the English version again turned into Latin by another daughter.† That English translation has not been preserved, but I will give the reader the substance of the original, which has been printed in Latin more than once. ‡

The letter, as will be seen, contains some very severe rebuke, addressed not to the university (except indirectly) but to the preacher, and would doubtless have raised some clamour at a layman taking on himself the office of a bishop, had it not been known that More was really writing in the name of the king, not in his own.

"He begins by apologising for his insufficiency and boldness in addressing so illustrious an academy. Whatever learning he has he owes to Oxford, and he would rather incur the reproach of arrogance, than of ingratitude in keeping silence when the interests of the university are at stake. When in London he

---

* *Epist. Erasm.* 380. The letter is, as usual, wrongly dated by the editor, viz., 1519 instead of 1518.

† *Vita Mori*, cap. 4 et cap. 10.

‡ At Oxford by John Lichfield in 1633, and in the appendix to Jortin's *Erasmus* in 1760. The title, in which More is called *Eques auratus*, does not belong to the original, and the date is wrongly given as 1519. It should be 1518. Most unaccountably Sir James Mackintosh supposes More's letter to have been written by him in 1497, in which year he places him as a student in Oxford.

had heard of a faction at Oxford calling themselves Trojans, either out of hatred of Greek studies or from love of fun. The leader was said to be called Priam, another was Hector, a third Paris, and so on. These Trojans were accustomed to jeer at and otherwise molest all the students of Greek. He had thought these were merely the regrettable follies of young men ; but since he had accompanied the king to Abingdon, he has found that the folly is growing into madness, and that one of these Trojans, a man, wise in his own esteem and merry in the judgment of others, but who must be counted insane by all who consider his conduct, has in a public sermon, in the sacred time of Lent, raved not only against Greek literature and Latin culture, but most liberally against all liberal arts. And, that all might be of a piece, he did not comment on a complete passage of Holy Scripture, after the manner of the ancients, nor take a Scripture text after the modern custom, but took for his texts some old women's proverbs in English.   He is sure the hearers must have been deeply offended, since who could have a spark of Christian feeling in his breast, and not lament to see the majesty of the preacher's office, which had gained the world to Christ, degraded by one whose duty it was to adorn and guard it ?   What greater infamy could be offered to the function of the preacher, than that the preacher himself, in the holiest time of the year, before a great assembly of Christian men, in the very temple of God, from a lofty pulpit as from the throne of Christ, in the presence of the venerable Body of Christ, should turn a Lenten sermon into a Bacchanalian farce ?   As to his attack on all secular studies, if the good man had long withdrawn from the world and spent years in the desert, and suddenly coming from his solitude had urged his hearers to give themselves to watching, prayer and fasting, saying that by such means only could they gain heaven, and that all the rest was but trifling; that the study of literature was the forging of fetters, and that the rude and unlearned fly to heaven unhindered; from

such a preacher such a sermon might have been endured. His
simplicity might have gained him pardon, some kind hearers
might have called it sanctity, and even those who liked it least
might have excused it as piety and devotion.   But here they
see a man ascend the pulpit elegantly dressed with a furred
mantle, and the insignia of a man of learning, and there, in the
midst of a university to which no one comes except for the sake
of learning, openly rail against almost every kind of literature.
Who can deem this anything but mere malice and envy ?   How
came it into his head to preach about the Latin tongue, of
which he knows but little ; or the liberal sciences, of which he
knows still less; or about Greek, of which he does not understand an iota ?   Had he not matter enough in the seven capital
sins—matter, too, in which he is better skilled ?   Since he is
so disposed that he prefers to blame what he is ignorant of
rather than to learn, is not this sloth ?   Since he calumniates
those who happen to know what he is prevented from knowing
either by his indolence or his incapacity, is not this envy ?
Since he would have no science esteemed except what he
falsely fancies himself to possess, and vaunts his ignorance
rather than his science, is not this the height of pride ?   We
all know, forsooth, that without secular literature a man can
save his soul ; yet even secular learning, as he calls it, prepares
the mind for virtue.   In any case it is for learning, and for
learning alone, men come to Oxford ; for every good woman
could teach her child at home rude and unlettered virtue.   Nor
do all come to the university to learn theology ; some study
law, and others seek the knowledge of human affairs, a matter
so useful even to a theologian, that without it he may perhaps
sing pleasantly to himself, but will certainly not sing agreeably
to the people.   And this knowledge can nowhere be drawn so
abundantly as from the poets, orators, and historians.   There
are even some who make the knowledge of things natural a
road to heavenly contemplation, and so pass from philosophy
and the liberal arts—which this man condemns under the

general name of secular literature—to theology, despoiling the
women of Egypt to adorn the queen.   And as regards theology
itself, which alone he seems to approve, if indeed he approves
even that, I do not see how he can attain it without
the knowledge of language, either Hebrew, Greek, or Latin,
unless, indeed, in his fondness for English tales he has persuaded himself that he will find it in such collections.   Or
perhaps he thinks that the whole of theology is comprised in
the limits of those questions on which such as he are always
disputing, for the knowledge of which it must be admitted that
little enough Latin is wanted.

"Will it be pretended that what he condemns is not literature,
but the immoderate study of it ?   Surely that sin is not so common, or the rush of men so headlong towards study, that they
need to be held back by a public sermon.   We do not hear of
many who have advanced so far, but that, even when they go
still further, they will be yet not half-way to the goal.   But the
good man had no such moderate designs, for he openly called
the students of Greek heretics, the professors he nicknamed big
devils, and the disciples the devil's imps.   And with this insane
fury he pointed at a man by the name of a devil whom all knew
to be such that the real devil would be most loth to see him
made a preacher.   He did not name him, but all who listened
were as sure whom he meant as they were of the madness of
the preacher."

Of course the Greek scholar thus indicated was no other than
More's friend Erasmus.   The writer then addresses the university, and points out some of the advantages of the study of
Greek, as he had done in his letter to Dorpius.   He stimulates
the authorities by the example of Cambridge, "to which you
have hitherto always served as model (*cui vos prælucere semper con-
suevistis*), where there is now such zeal for Greek, that even
those who do not study it themselves, generously contribute to
maintain its professors".

" In conclusion," he says " that he has written, not to instruct the learned authorities in their duties, which they understand far better than he, but to warn them not to let those factions grow and bring disgrace on the university, lest their chancellor, the Archbishop of Canterbury (Warham), or the Cardinal of York the great patron of letters, should be forced to intervene; and, lastly—and here is the point of the whole letter, indicating from whom it really emanated—the learned and most Christian king will certainly not tolerate that good learning should decay in a place so favoured by himself and his ancestors. By re-pressing the factions of which he has spoken, the authorities will gain the favour of those most reverend fathers, and of their illustrious prince. Thomas More, from Abingdon, the 29th March (1518)."

This letter was written in Holy Week. On the very same day Pace wrote from Abingdon to Wolsey that "carding and dicing were turned into picking of arrows over the screen in the hall".* We may imagine the smile of More at this change of amusements. Though he was doubtless excused from feats of archery he was certainly throwing arrows, very sharp ones, and with no little effect, among some of the old-fashioned and self-satisfied "dons" of Oxford.

By way of contrast with the above, I am glad to mention his relations with the sister university. Scarcely had he been made knight, when his friend and fellow-martyr, the Bishop of Rochester, sent to him a young theologian, whom he wished to be presented to the king. In the letter of introduction Fisher says : " Let some ray of favour shine from the throne by your means upon our Cantabrigians, in order to quicken and spur on our youth to the love of good letters, by the hope of sharing in the liberalities of so flourishing a prince. We have but few friends at court, who are both able and willing to recommend our affairs to the king's Highness, and of these few we reckon you the first, who hitherto and while in a lower orb have ever

* *Letters and Papers*, ii. 4043.

proved yourself our kind protector.   Now that you are assumed
to the equestrian order, and are so near the king (on which we
both congratulate you and rejoice for ourselves) show how
much you favour us."   To this Sir Thomas replied that whatever influence he had, though it was but little, should be at
their service.   He thanked them for the kind letters they had
written to him.   No man's house opens more freely to its
master than his service and influence to them.*

There were others besides More to write the king's letters
both in Latin and in English, but More was a practised orator
in both languages, and whenever an important or a ceremonial
speech had to be made, it was allotted to him.   In July, 1518,
Cardinal Laurence Campeggio arrived as legate *a latere*, in
which commission Wolsey had been joined with him, to treat
of resistance to the Turk. †   The pomp with which he was
received at Deal and brought to London was no doubt of
Wolsey's contrivance.   From Blackheath he was accompanied
to London by the Duke of Norfolk, the ambassadors of other
powers, bishops, lords, and gentlemen in a cavalcade of 2000
horses.   As they drew near London Bridge the street was
lined on both sides by the clergy in copes of gold, with no less
than 60 gold and silver crosses and censers.   At London
Bridge two bishops presented him with the relics to kiss amid
salvos of artillery.   The crafts began their order at Gracechurch
Street, and in Cheapside he was welcomed by the mayor and
alderman and a brief Latin oration was delivered by Master
More.   Thence he proceeded to St. Paul's, and after another
address by the Bishop of London was led to the altar.

At the beginning of June, 1525, Lorenzo Orio, knight,
arrived in England as Venetian ambassador.   The king sent
Lord Dacre and Sir John Dauncy with a great number of
horsemen to conduct the envoy to Windsor.   On the 6th of

* Stapleton, cap. 5.
† Ten years later they were again united in the matter of the divorce.

June, the king received him in state with the cardinal, the
Dukes of Norfolk and Suffolk, the Marquis of Dorset, and
nearly all the knights of the garter.   After he had presented
his credentials and made his speech, " Sir Thomas More, a
man of singular and rare learning, and in great favour with the
king and cardinal"—such is Orio's report to the Doge and
Signory—" returned thanks to the State ".   The public cere-
mony being ended, they went to Mass, no doubt in St. George's
Chapel, after which the envoy dined with the cardinal, who
afterwards took him to the queen's chamber, where he was
received so graciously as to surprise all the bystanders ; so
reports the gratified ambassador. *

The year following he had again to address the ambassador
of Venice.   The matter is thus related to Francis I., by his
own envoys who were present: " Last Sunday the Venetian
ambassador had his first audience at Greenwich.   He made a
fair oration full of thanks to the king and Wolsey, to which
Master More made a premeditated reply, a draft of the speech
having been given by the ambassador to Wolsey three days
before, at the request of the latter." †   From these examples
it is clear that More was the Latin orator, who had to do
honour to the court of Henry, as well as to second the
diplomacy of Wolsey.   We shall trace presently More's own
action in the treaties and embassies of Europe.   He had
joined the court in the hope of urging the king to the better
government of his own country, and it is pleasant to find that
he was not so disappointed as Hythloday predicted.   Stowe
gives an account of a work in which we may trace the influence
of the new councillor.   " About this time," he says, speaking
of the year 1521, "the king being moved by such of his
council as had regard to the commonwealth of this realm,
considering how for the space of fifty years past and more,

the nobles and gentlemen of England had been given to grazing of cattle, and keeping of sheep, to the great decay of husbandry and tillage," caused the statutes to be put in force against unauthorised inclosures, and the houses from which husbandmen had been evicted to be rebuilt. More had written strongly on this subject in his *Utopia*, and there is no doubt that these measures were taken at his suggestion.*

* More does not appear at any time to have been official secretary. He is indeed called secretary by Spinelli (see *infra*, p. 200, note), but either he mistakes, or he uses the word in a loose sense, as I have done, because More was well known to write many of the king's letters. The chief secretary at that period was Pace, another was John Millet, who was also clerk of the signet. John Meautis was French, and Andreas Ammonius Latin secretary. Some of these were mere clerks, writing letters fair for the king to sign. Pace (like More) wrote at the king's command, but in his own name. I am indebted for the above information to the kindness of Mr. Gairdner. [Note to 2nd Edition.]

CHAPTER X.

DIPLOMATIST AND STATESMAN.

WHEN More first entered into court life, and on the career of diplomacy, he compared himself, in a letter to Fisher, to a man, who not being trained to ride, sits awkwardly in his saddle. Yet, if there is one quality which shines conspicuously in More, it is his exquisite tact. This enabled him not merely to acquit himself well of his duties, or to ingratiate himself with all whom he met, but above all to keep his conscience upright and his soul unsullied.

In following him through the remainder of the twelve years spent in the " king's service " previous to the chancellorship, the *State Papers* recently arranged and edited will be our principal guide, since the information to be derived from his biographers is scanty and confused. Throughout the whole of that period, when not absent on legations or duties belonging to his various offices, he acted as one of the royal secretaries. Wolsey, on account of his functions as chancellor had often to remain in Westminster, when the king was either amusing himself or seeking purer air in one of his country houses ; thus many letters passed between the great minister and the monarch. Wolsey's letters were addressed to More and by him read to the king, who gave to More the substance of his answer. The first volume of the large collection of *State Papers of Henry VIII.** contains a considerable number of

---

* In eleven volumes, printed between 1830 and 1852. These are not to be confounded with the *Letters and Papers of Henry VIII.*, still in course of publication. The latter cover a much wider field, but give in many cases a mere precis or abridgment of documents, especially of those already printed in full in the *State Papers.*

such letters, and others have been printed by Sir Henry Ellis ; but as in these More is merely a secretary, his personal action and character are but slightly and indirectly illustrated by them.

The addresses of these letters show the restlessness of the king. They are dated from Greenwich, Hampton Court, Woodstock, Abingdon, Wallingford, "The More" (in Hertfordshire), Oking (or Woking) in Surrey, New Hall (in Essex), Windsor and East Hampstead (near Windsor), Guildford, etc. This change of residence of course involved More's frequent absence from his home, and led to that correspondence with his children, some of which we have seen.

It was his duty also to accompany the king on more solemn progresses. His name appears in the list of gentlemen from the county of Middlesex who were appointed to wait on the king and queen at the famous meeting with Francis I. between Calais and Boulogne in June, 1520, which from its gorgeous preparations was called the meeting of the Field of the Cloth of Gold.* There was little sincerity in this great show, unless the rivalry in magnificence betrayed its real character. At the same time counter negotiations were being carried on with the young emperor Charles V. More was one of the commissioners for the renewal of a treaty of commerce with the emperor, which was solemnly sworn to and subscribed on 12th April in the chapel at Greenwich; at which time also a meeting was arranged between Henry and Charles.† This was to have taken place at Gravelines and Calais, after the interview with Francis; but, taking advantage of a favourable wind, the emperor sailed for England in May, and managed to anticipate his rival. On 26th May, 1520, the vigil of Pentecost, More writes to Erasmus from Canterbury : "The emperor is expected to-day ; the king will set out to meet him early in the morning, perhaps to-night. It is impossible to describe the delight of the king, the nobles and

* *Letters and Papers*, iii. part ii. p. 243 (March 1520).
† Rymer, xiii. 714. *Letters and Papers*, iii. 798, 804.

even the people, when the message arrived that the emperor
was on his way to England." *   Charles landed at Hithe with
the Queen of Aragon and many noblemen and ladies.   They
were met by Wolsey and conducted to Dover Castle, which
they reached at 10 p.m.   At 2 a.m. on the morning of Whit-
sunday the king arrived at Dover, and the emperor arose to meet
him.   Early in the morning they rode to Canterbury to keep
the feast, and were received in great state by Cardinal Wolsey
and the Archbishop (Warham).   The emperor and king
walked together, under one canopy, to the shrine of St.
Thomas (which Henry was one day to plunder), and thence to
the palace, where the emperor embraced his aunt, Queen
Catharine (whom the king was one day to repudiate).   At the
High Mass the emperor offered first, then the king.   Of course
there was great banqueting.   On Tuesday the sovereigns rode
towards Dover, and Charles re-embarked at Sandwich.

This was only the beginning of the pageants in which More
had to play his part.   On Thursday the king and queen, with
their immense train of 4334 persons and 1637 horses, passed
over to Calais.   The great festivities lasted from the 4th to
the 25th June, but need not be here described.   Have they
not been made famous by Shakespeare ?

> To-day, the French
> All clinquant, all in gold, like heathen gods,
> Shone down the English : and to-morrow, they
> Made Britain, India : every man that stood
> Show'd like a mine.

What followed is less known.   The emperor was waiting for
the king of England at Gravelines, and after taking leave of
Francis, Henry made his return visit to his imperial nephew
on the 10th July.   When the emperor next day rode with the
king to Calais, all the lords and estates of England vacated
their lodgings to give hospitality to the Spaniards and Flemings.

---

* Inter. Epist. Erasm. 433.   The date is wrongly given by the editor.

A marvellous banqueting house had been prepared; on the ceiling were painted the heavens, with sun, moon, stars, and clouds, and images of wickerwork, covered with painted canvas, represented men of every nation, with "reasons" or inscriptions in various languages. It is probable enough that the learning of More had been enlisted in this pageantry. But, alas! when all the preparations were complete for the most splendid banquet ever given since the days of the Cæsars, "the wind began to rise," says Stowe, "and increasing to the evening, it then on a sudden blew off the canvas heavens with the planets, and blew out more than 1000 torches of wax". However, on the 12th, amid new festivities, were solemnly read "all the articles of the league tripartite," between the emperor and the kings of France and England; the emperor returned to Gravelines, and Henry to Dover.

We may safely gather the thoughts of More, during the silly and wasteful extravagance of those months from what he had written, four years previously, in his *Utopia*, where he had quaintly jested on the use of the precious metals and of jewels, as follows:—

"The folly of men has enhanced the value of gold and silver because of their scarcity; whereas, on the contrary, it is the opinion of the Utopians that nature, as an indulgent parent, has freely given us all the best things in great abundance, such as air, water, and earth, but has laid up and hid from us the things that are vain and useless.

"To teach disdain for gold they have fallen upon an expedient which, as it agrees with their other policy, so is it very different from ours, and will scarce gain belief among us who value gold so much, and lay it up so carefully. They eat and drink out of vessels of earth and glass, which makes an agreeable appearance, though formed of brittle materials; while they make their vilest utensils of gold and silver, and that not only in their public halls but in their private houses. Of the same metals they likewise make chains and fetters for their slaves, to some of whom, as a badge of infamy, they hang an ear-ring of gold, and make others wear a ring, a chain, or a coronet of the same metal ; and thus they take care by all possible means to render gold and silver of no esteem. They find pearls on their coasts, and diamonds and carbuncles on their rocks ; they do not look after them, but, if they find them by chance, they polish them, and with them they adorn their children, who are delighted with them, and glory in them during their childhood ; but when they grow to years, and see that none but children use such baubles, they of their own accord, without being bid by their parents, lay them aside, and would be as much ashamed to use them afterwards as children among us, when they come to years, are of their puppets and other toys."

There is also a clear reminiscence of the Field of Cloth of Gold in the answer which More made to Luther's declaration, that he would like to throw all the relics of the true Cross where the sun would never shine on them, and give their golden reliquaries to the poor. Among other things More answers : "How small a portion were the gold about all the pieces of Christ's Cross, if it were compared with the gold that is quite cast away about the gilding of knives, swords, spurs, arras and painted cloths ; and as though these things could not consume gold fast enough, the gilding of posts and whole roses, not only in the palaces of princes and great prelates, but also many right mean men's houses ! And yet among all these things could Luther spy no gold that grievously glittered in his bleared eyes, but only about the Cross of Christ." *

It is amusing that the writer of all this should have been made a knight, or as he was then called, *Eques auratus,* "a gilded knight," because this dignity both entitled him and required of him to wear golden insignia, and to deck with gold the trappings of his horse,† and that he should generally

* *English Works,* p. 119.
† Selden's *Titles of Honour,* p. 437.

be represented as wearing round his neck one of those massive gold chains, which he made the badge of notorious malefactors among his Utopians.

While at Calais More had the great pleasure of meeting again his dear Erasmus,* and of being introduced by him to other learned men, among others to William Budée, the French king's secretary, and to Francis Cranefeld, councillor of the empire. To Budée, More wrote some weeks after: "I know not, my dear Budée, whether it is not better never to possess what becomes very near to our hearts, unless we can afterwards retain it. The reading of your works had created a beautiful image of you in my mind before we met, and I counted myself happy if I should ever behold you in reality. When my wish was at last fulfilled, I was happier than happiness itself. But alas! our duties prevented us from meeting often enough to satisfy my desire of conversing with you, and in a few days, as our kings were obliged to separate, our intercourse was broken off when it had scarce begun, and we were torn away perhaps never to meet again." He trusts that they may continue their friendship by frequent correspondence. In another letter he tells him that, among various things that rendered him so dear, one was that erudition, formerly the prerogative of the clergy, was now seen in the highest degree in a married man.† It is to be regretted that the whole correspondence between these two learned statesmen is not extant. When Budée was collecting his own letters for publication, he wished to include those received from More, but the latter demurred, as he had not written with the thought of publicity, and wished to re-examine them. Thus they were not printed. Budée mentions presents

* *Letters of Erasmus*, 496, 509.

† Tam incomparabilis eruditio, quæ peculiaris olim cleri gloria fuerat, tibi feliciter obtigit uxorato ; nam λαικὸν appellare non sustineo, tam multis, tam egregiis dotibus, tam alte subvectum supra λαόν (Apud Stapleton, cap. 5).

received from More of English dogs, of which he seems to have been glad to dispose very quickly to others. *

Francis Cranefeld wrote to Erasmus from Bruges, thanking him for having introduced him to More. After Erasmus's departure they had conceived a great friendship for each other, and Cranefeld had been delighted with More's urbanity. More had given his wife a gold ring with an English inscription, and to himself some ancient coins, one of gold, and another of silver, one having the effigy of Tiberius, the other of Augustus. More also wrote to Erasmus, to tell the pleasure he had found in Cranefeld's company.†

There was one jarring note in all this harmony—a literary controversy, the details of which occupy a considerable space in More's Latin works and the letters of Erasmus ; but, while it cannot be altogether passed over in a *Life of More*, it will be sufficient to give it in mere outline. During the war between France and England in 1512, there had been a great naval contest, in which a large French ship, named the " Cordelier " (Chordigera), being already on fire, had borne down on a great English ship, grappled with it, and involved it in its own fate. A Frenchman, named Germain De Brie (Brixius), wrote some verses in glorification of this feat. Against the " Chordigera" of De Brie More composed some sharp epigrams, which had been circulated in MS. When it was proposed to publish a collection of his epigrams in 1517, More had suggested to Erasmus and the friends who were superintending this publication on the continent, the propriety of omitting these anti-French verses, now that peace was established. ‡ They, however, decided to print them. The anger of De Brie was aroused, and he composed a satirical poem, which he called "Antimorus," in which he did his best to turn all More's epigrams

---

* Letters given by Brewer. *Letters and Papers*, iii. 413.
† Inter. Epist. Erasm., 532, 550.
‡ *Ib.*, 174 (in App.) (3rd Sept. 1517).

into ridicule.   Erasmus, who was a friend of both, intervened to prevent the publication of De Brie's poem, and when his efforts were unsuccessful, to prevent More from retaliating.

To De Brie, Erasmus complains of his acerbities, and tells him that More stands too high in general estimation for him to injure—that if More wrote somewhat against France, it was during the war.   Why, then, make quarrels now in time of peace? More has not published but merely allowed the publication of his epigrams, if others would superintend it.*   To More he wrote a soothing letter, telling him De Brie could do him no real harm, and that it was more dignified to remain silent. † More replied that he had heard two years ago that De Brie was preparing his attack, and he had intended writing to him a most friendly letter, but he had heard so much about him from Paris that he saw it would be in vain.   Berald, Lascar, Budée, and Deloin, had all sought to no purpose to prevent him from publishing his book.   In the meantime More had hoped that, from so long a preparation, something learned and witty would come, which he should have enjoyed, even though the laugh was against himself.   He found it, however, full of folly and venom, and had resolved not to answer it ; but he was overpersuaded by friends to whom he was wont to defer. Still, Erasmus's wish has so much force with him, that, though his answer is already printed, he has bought it all up.   Five copies only had been sold, when the letter of Erasmus came to hand, and he at once stopped the sale.   He had sent a copy to Erasmus and another to Peter Giles, the rest he would keep until he heard further from Erasmus.   He left himself in his hands as to the publication or non-publication of the book. "When we come to Calais," he writes, "for which the king is about to start, we will talk over the matter more at length. In t' is meeting of the kings I expect you and De Brie also ;

* *Letter* 511, of 25th June, 1520, a letter very honourable to More as well as to the writer.

† *Letter* 503.

since the French queen will be there, and he, as her secretary, can hardly be absent. So far as I am concerned you can easily arrange the matter; for though without any reason he has so treated me, as to show that the only thing wanting to him for my destruction is ability, yet since you, Erasmus, are more than half of myself, the fact that De Brie is your friend will weigh more with me than that he is my enemy." *

For some reason not known to us, More finally published his book. Erasmus wrote to Budée, 16th February, 1521 : "I fear the quarrel between De Brie and More will grow hot, for the letter of More, which I think you saw before More showed it me at Calais already printed, is so sharp, that I who am thought by some pretty mordant, am toothless compared with him; and yet he almost promised me that he would suppress it, if De Brie would keep quiet ".† There is little to interest us at present in More's pamphlet, except perhaps his defence of what he had written against the avarice which disfigured the last years of Henry VII. On the whole, the temper of More appears less to advantage in this piece than in any other of his writings. The thought is forced on us, as we read the Latin letters, and dedications and controversies of the literates of the sixteenth century, that their mutual praises are somewhat boyish, and that they show themselves over sensitive of their reputation as scholars.

More was not knighted at the time he accompanied the king to Calais. This dignity seems to have been conferred on him in the summer of 1521, about the time he was made sub-treasurer. Erasmus wrote to Pace on 11th June, 1521 : "I hear that More has been made treasurer, and that the office is as profitable as it is honourable. He succeeds so well at court that I pity him. But I am rejoiced by the hope he gives me that I may see him again in August;"‡ and a few

* Inter. Epist. Erasm., 553.   † Ib., 565.
‡ Ib., 577.

months later he writes to Budée: "More has been made treasurer. That office in England is most honourable, and at the same time neither very troublesome in itself, nor exposed to odium. He had a rival candidate, a man who was in good favour, who was willing to take the office, and to live at his own expense. But the excellent king gave an undoubted proof of his partiality for More, when, rather than accept his rival's offer, he preferred to give the office to More without his seeking it, and with a salary besides. And not satisfied with this, he has raised him to the dignity of a knight."*

Erasmus calls More treasurer. This office, however, was always reserved for one of the great lords; and at that time was held by the Duke of Norfolk. More was under-treasurer, an office which corresponds in some respects with that of chancellor of the exchequer at the present day, who is also technically under-treasurer.†

Not a year had passed since the tripartite Treaty was read at Calais, before the emperor and the king of France were again at war, and Wolsey again crossed the Channel to make peace, or to affect to do so, while intriguing in his own king's interest. The Imperial and French ambassadors met him at Calais, with the Papal Nuncio, the ambassadors of Naples and Hungary, and the Venetian envoy to England. The last mentioned, Antonio Suriano, wrote to the Signory on July 25, 1521, from London: "A diet is being held about certain disputes concerning the merchants. This morning the Government sends thither Sir Thomas More, Dr. Sampson, etc."‡ He was to join the cardinal at Calais when his own work at Bruges was completed. On 24th July, Pace, the king's secretary, wrote to Wolsey: "The king signifieth to Your Grace that,

* *Epist. Erasm.* 605, Equitis aurati dignitatem adjecit.
† Sir James Mackintosh (*Life of More*, p. 73).
‡ *Venetian State Papers*, iii. 272.

whereas old men do now decay greatly within this his realm, his mind is to acquaint other young men with his great affairs, and, therefore, he desireth Your Grace to make Sir William Sandys and Sir Thomas More privy to all such matters as Your Grace shall treat at Calais ".*

Wolsey, with his great following, had arrived at Calais on 2nd August; but as the papal ambassador had not received the necessary commission to sign the league between the Pope, the emperor, and the two kings, while a messenger was being despatched to Rome, Wolsey took advantage of the delay to visit the emperor at Bruges, where he remained a fortnight. We have a glimpse of Sir Thomas in a letter of Gasparo Contarini, patriarch of Venice, and at that time ambassador of his republic with Charles V. : "On coming away from solemn Mass of the Holy Ghost in St. James's Church (celebrated in the presence of the emperor, the cardinal, and the resident ambassadors), I invited an English gentleman, by name Master Thomas More, a very learned man, to dine with me. He had accompanied Wolsey to Bruges. During dinner we discussed the business negotiated with the emperor, but More did not drop the slightest hint of any other treaty than that of peace between the king of France and His Imperial Majesty."† More was probably aware of what we know now, that the real subject of the conferences was the betrothal of the emperor to his cousin, the Princess Mary of England.

Stapleton tells us ‡ that during their stay in Bruges some vain-glorious disputant put up a public challenge to dispute on any question in civil or canon law, or matter of science or literature. More could not let slip an opportunity for a joke. By way of answer he affixed this question from English law : *An averia capta in withernamia sunt irreplegiabilia ?* which is said to mean : "Whether cattle taken in withernam be irrepleviable?" (Wither-

---

* *State Papers of Henry VIII.* i. 19.

† *Venetian State Papers*, iii. 302.

‡ *Vita Mori*, cap. 13.

nam was a writ to make reprisals on one who had wrongfully
distrained another man's cattle, and driven them out of the
county.) The document stated that there was a gentleman in
the English ambassador's suite who was willing to discuss this
point of law with the challenger. It is unnecessary to say that
the doctor *utriusque juris* could not understand even the terms
of the question, and got well laughed at for his vanity.

More returned with Wolsey to Calais, where negotiations
were protracted until November ; but in October he was sent as
special messenger to the king. Wolsey wrote to the king that,
with regard to certain matters, he had sent Sir Thomas More,
the under-treasurer, and Sir William Fitzwilliam : "to the which,
your councillors, it may like your Grace not only to give firm
credence in, but also to give unto them your gracious thanks
for such their laudable acquittal and diligent attendance as they
have done and taken in this journey for the advancement of
your honour and contentation of your pleasure".*

The spring of 1522 renewed the splendours of 1521, though
on a different field. The emperor again visited England, and
this time advanced not only to Canterbury but to London and
Windsor. Full descriptions of the festivities are found in the
chroniclers, but the mere fact that More was present would not
justify any detail here.

In April, 1523, a parliament was summoned, and by the
influence of Wolsey, Sir Thomas was chosen speaker. He
according to custom " disabled " himself, *i.e.*, declared his
unfitness for such an office ; and when his excuses were rejected

---

* *State Papers*, i. 74. Also, *Letters and Papers*, iii. App. 31. In
the royal expenses for 1521 we find £80 to Sir T. More, of which £5 was
a loan, and £75 for his "diets" when absent from England with the
" Easterlings," at the rate of 20s. a day (*Letters*, etc., iii. 1775). On
8th May, 1522, he had a grant of the manor of South, in Kent, with advowson, which had come into the king's hands by the attainder of the
Duke of Buckingham (*Ib.*, iii. 2239).

† *Letters and Papers*, iii. 2288.

by the king, he went on in a speech which Roper has given at
length and probably transcribed from the draft left of it by
More, to demand the usual privileges of the speaker and of
the commons, especially for the latter freedom of deliberation.
Roper proceeds to tell how Cardinal Wolsey came down to the
House of Commons in order to urge them to grant the subsidy,
to which they had shown reluctance.   The commons debated
whether it were better to receive him with a few only of his
lords, or with his whole train.   The opinion of the majority
was that his attendants should be very few, but Sir Thomas
thus addressed them : " Masters, forasmuch as my Lord
Cardinal lately laid to our charges the lightness of our tongues
for things uttered out of this house, it shall not in my mind be
amiss to receive him with all his pomp, with his maces, his
pillars, poleaxes, his crosses, his hat, and the great seal too, to
the intent that if he find the like fault with us hereafter, we may
be bolder from ourselves to lay the blame on those that his Grace
brought here with him ".*   This advice prevailed, the cardinal
addressed the house, but in vain tried to get a word of answer
from anyone, though he appealed to some by name.   Sir
Thomas on his knees excused this silence, saying that it was
the ancient privilege to speak only by the speaker's mouth, but
that he could not do this until he had heard their debates.

" Whereupon," says Roper, " the cardinal, displeased with
Sir Thomas More that had not in this parliament in all things
satisfied his desire,† suddenly arose and departed, and, after
the parliament ended, in his gallery at Whitehall said to him :
' Would God you had been at Rome, Mr. More, when I made
you speaker '.   ' Your Grace not offended, so would I too,'

* He can scarcely have made so sarcastic a speech publicly ; the terms
are such as he might have used in private conversation when asked his
opinion.

† " The speaker of the Tudor reigns," writes Bishop Stubbs, " is the
manager of business on the part of the crown " (*Lectures on Medieval
and Modern History*, p. 272).

quoth Sir Thomas. And to wind such quarrels out of the cardinal's head he began to talk of the gallery, saying, 'I like this gallery of yours much better than your gallery of Hampton Court'. Wherewith so wisely broke he off the cardinal's displeasant talk, that the cardinal at that present, as it seemed, wist not what more to say to him. But for the revengement of his displeasure counselled the king to send him ambassador to Spain, commending to his Highness his wisdom, fitness and learning for that voyage. And the difficulty of the cause considered, none was there, he said, so fit so serve his Grace therein. Which when the king had broken to Sir Thomas More, and that he had declared unto his Grace how unfit a journey it was for him, the nature of the country, and the disposition of his complexion so disagreeing together, that he should never be able to do his Grace acceptable service there, knowing right well that if his Grace sent him thither he should send him to his grave ; but showing himself nevertheless ready according to his duty, were it with the loss of his life, to fulfil his Grace's pleasure in that behalf. The king, allowing well his answer, said unto him : ' It is not our pleasure, Mr. More, to do you hurt, but to do you good would we be glad. We will, therefore, for this purpose devise some other, and employ your service otherwise.' "

These things must have been related to Roper by More when they occurred, and their substantial truth can, therefore, scarcely be called in question.* Yet if any part of More's conduct as speaker really caused Wolsey to say some hasty words, the following letter of Wolsey to the king was certainly not written under any feeling of displeasure :—

"Sir,—After my most humble recommendations. It may like your Grace to understand, I have showed unto this bearer, Sir Thomas More, divers matters to be by him on my behalf declared unto your Highness. And, sire, whereas it hath been accustomed that the speakers of the parliaments, in considera-

* Unfortunately there are no Journals of the *Commons* before 1547

tion of their diligence and pains taken, have had, though the parliament hath been right soon finished, above the £100 ordinary, a reward of £100, for the better maintenance of their household, and other charges sustained in the same; I suppose, sir, that the faithful diligence of the said Sir Thomas in all your causes treated in this your late parliament, as well for your subsidy right honourably passed, as otherwise, considered, no man could better deserve the same than he hath done; wherefore, your pleasure known therein, I shall cause the same to be advanced to him accordingly—ascertaining your Grace that I am the rather moved to put your Highness in remembrance thereof, because he is not the most ready to speak and solicit his own cause.   At your Manor of Hampton Court, the 24th day of August [1523], by your most humble chaplain.   T. CARD., *Ebor*." *

If this letter shows a very kind feeling on the cardinal's part towards Sir Thomas, a letter of More's to Wolsey, written a few days later, proves that the feeling was mutual.   He was acting as the king's secretary at Woking.   He tells the cardinal how pleased the king had been with a certain letter which Wolsey had drafted, to be sent to the Queen of Scots, the king's sister :—

"Among which, the letter which your Grace devised in the name of his Highness to the queen, his sister, his Grace so well liked that I never saw him like anything better, and, so help me God, in my poor phantasy, not causeless, for it is for the quantity one of the best made letters for words, matter, sentences, and couching that ever I read in my life". †

No one will suspect More of flattering with an interested motive, or even of insincerity in these words.   He liked to praise when he could, as we have seen in his letters to his children, and if such language shows that he knew that the great minister was somewhat childish in his love of admiration, yet he humoured him out of native kindliness and gratitude.

---

* *State Papers*, . 124.   † *State Papers*, i. 128.

Stapleton relates that, when More had been but a short time privy councillor, Wolsey proposed that a new office should be created—that of Supreme Constable of the Kingdom, to represent the king everywhere, a thing unknown to the constitution, the cardinal having, of course, an ambitious motive in such a proposal. The whole Council was easily won over to his view; but when More's turn came to speak, he disapproved the plan, and defended his opinion with so many solid reasons that the Council declared that the matter required further deliberation. The cardinal, in his anger, exclaimed: "Are you not ashamed, Mr. More, being the last in place and dignity, to dissent from so many noble and prudent men? You show yourself a foolish councillor." "Thanks be to God," replied More at once, "that his royal Highness has but one fool in his Council." However, the question was postponed, and Wolsey's plan finally rejected.*

On the whole, the relations between Wolsey and More seem to have been cordial. It is probable that the cardinal rather feared than loved him,† since he could not doubt that More was quite unawed by his grandeur, and read his character thoroughly. Yet he knew that More was no rival, and he admired his disinterestedness and integrity. To propose for him an embassy in Spain, might be an honourable way of removing one whom he could not make his tool, yet there was surely nothing in the Spanish climate so deadly as to justify us in attributing to him the revengeful and murderous motive hinted at by Roper. All seems to be explained, if we suppose that More saw in the cardinal's proposal a plan to get him away from England, and that More also saw (what the cardinal did not see) that for him the climate would be perilous. The Catholics of the days of Mary and Elizabeth bore a very resentful feeling towards Cardinal Wolsey. They were convinced

---

* Stapleton, cap 13.

† *Ib.*, cap. 3. Erasmus says the same thing.

that his pride, ambition, and worldly policy had been the principal cause of the degeneracy of Henry VIII. and of the schism into which the country had been cast; and they were inclined to wrest all his words and deeds *in sinistram partem.*

The records of the next few years contain nothing on which we need delay. Sir Thomas More's name is among those of the gentlemen in the royal army beyond the sea, under the Duke of Suffolk, when war broke out again between England and France, in August, 1523; yet other documents show that he did not leave England. Either then the arrangements were cancelled, or the document refers to another Sir Thomas More, a gentlemen of Dorset.* In August, 1523, Sir Thomas, the subject of this memoir, was appointed one of the collectors of the subsidy in Middlesex.† In July, 1525, without ceasing to be sub-treasurer, he was made Chancellor of the Duchy of Lancaster, an office of dignity and importance; while the king still kept him near his person to act as his secretary and his master of requests.‡ Indeed, the king seems to have been impatient of his absence even in the necessary discharge of his duties. On 26th November, 1523, the cardinal writes to the king: "For such great matters, as at the knitting up of this term be requisite to be ordered in your exchequer, Sir Thomas More may in no wise be spared from thence for four or five

---

* For Sir Thomas More's name, see *Letters and Papers*, iii. 3288. The presence of Sir Thomas More, the councillor and treasurer, in England throughout August and September, 1523, from many letters in *State Papers*, vol. i. Sir Thomas More, of "Mylplesshe," Dorset, *Letters and Papers*, iv. 6721, v. 1598, 1694, vii. 508, etc. To this latter probably belongs the £733 6s. 8d., a debt due to the king by Sir Thomas More, among the debts "whereof the days of payment be past, and the money not paid". This particular debt had been contracted *tempore Henrici VII.* It could not be by *our* More. A licence to export 1000 woollen cloths (*Ib.*, iv. 2248) to Sir Thomas More may also belong to the Dorsetshire knight.

† *Letters*, etc., iii. 3282.

‡ *Ib.*, iv. 1939.

days; for which time it may like your Highness to forbear his coming ".*

Of the king's fondness for More, Roper has given us details, of some of which he was eye-witness, while the rest he could learn from his intimate familiarity with his father-in-law. "The king," he says, "upon holidays, when he had done his own devotions, used to send for him into his traverse, and there, sometimes in matters of astronomy, geometry, divinity, and such other faculties, and sometimes of his worldly affairs, to sit and converse with him.   And otherwhile in the night would he have him up into his leads, there to consider with him the diversities, courses, motions and operations of the stars and planets.   And because he was of a pleasant disposition, it pleased the king and queen after the council had supped, yea at the time of their supper, to send for him to be merry with them.   Who, when he perceived so much in his talk to delight that he could not in a month get leave to go home to his wife and children (whose company he most desired), and to be absent from the court two days together, but that he should be thither sent for again; he, much misliking this restraint of liberty, began thereupon somewhat to dissemble his nature, and so by little and little from his accustomed mirth to disuse himself, that he was of them thenceforth no more so ordinarily sent for at such seasons."

Elsewhere, however, the same writer tells us that if More escaped for some time by this artifice, the king's desire of his company was not appeased: "Such entire favour did the king bear him that he made him Chancellor of the Duchy of Lancaster; and for the pleasure he took in his company would His Grace suddenly sometimes come home to his house at Chelsea, to be merry with him.   Whither, on a time unlooked for, he came to dinner with him, and after dinner, in a fair garden of his, walked with him by the space of an hour,

* *State Papers*, i. 146.

holding his arm about his neck.* As soon as his Grace was
gone, I, rejoicing thereat, said to Sir Thomas More, how
happy he was whom the king had so familiarly entertained, as
I never had seen him do to any other, except Cardinal Wolsey,
whom I saw His Grace walk once with arm in arm. ' I thank
our Lord, son,' quoth he, ' I find His Grace my very good
lord indeed, and I believe he doth as singularly favour me as
any subject within this realm. Howbeit, son Roper, I may
tell thee, I have no cause to be proud thereof, for if my head
would win him a castle in France (for then was there war
betwixt us), it should not fail to go.' " †

This saying is a remarkable evidence of More's insight into
character, and, it may be said, of his prescience. It also reminds us that to understand More's life and character we must
not lose sight of the fact that, while he was yearly progressing
in wisdom and virtue, the king was fast declining. On this
subject I may quote the words of Dr. Brewer, as one best
qualified to speak :—

"Until the close of the year 1524," says this writer, "the
superabundant activity of the king himself and his young
courtiers, wasting itself mainly in muscular amusements, or ex-
changing them for the less justifiable excitement of dice and
card-playing, found more wholesome occupation in the war with
France, or the expectation of war. But the defeat of Francis
at the battle of Pavia left them in utter idleness, without the
hope of employment. Men of education, sagacity and experience—generally ecclesiastics—were at that time engaged
in all diplomatic posts requiring more than usual tact and
ability. For such employment the nobility and gentry who
frequented the new court were either disqualified by ignorance
of their own, and still more of the Latin tongue—the common

* The king was tall, More somewhat short.
† Though Roper had mentioned the appointment to the chancellorship of the duchy, this conversation must have been earlier, for there
was no war with France after that date.

vehicle of communication—or declined to qualify themselves by the necessary sacrifices of their time and amusements.

"In 1525 the king, then thirty-six years old, was beginning to pay less attention to business. He hated the drudgery of looking over files of despatches, from which the most exciting topic was absent; withdrew himself more and more from the metropolis, and spent his days in hunting. Removed more than ever from the personal influence of Wolsey, Henry was surrounded by favourites, who recommended themselves to his notice by ministering to his pleasures, and fostering his love of profusion. With them, or some of them, Henry spent the day in hunting and the night in gambling, losing occasionally large sums of money. In 1525 he had attempted to make a favourite of Sir Thomas More, professing to be delighted with his society, his wit, his modesty, and his learning. At the death of Sir Richard Wingfield, in July, 1525, the king had advanced More to the Chancellorship of the Duchy of Lancaster.

"That More, combining the religious fervour and devotion of the recluse with the urbanity, grace, and ready wit of the most cultivated man of the world, a considerate and patient master, a pattern of conjugal purity and fidelity, should not seek to push his fortune among the unscrupulous candidates for royal favour, is no more than might be expected. He knew well what were the king's intentions at that time (1527),* and did not approve of them. He knew, also, how hard it was to contend with one whose arguments he could not admit without peril of his conscience, or contradict without peril of his life. His learning, his reputation, his legal acquirements, were sure to point him out to the king as the one man above all others whose judgment on the question none would venture to impugn, and few would be inclined to dispute. That judgment he had avoided giving with all the tact and dexterity of which he was master. But the pursuits of the court and the individuals

* The allusion is to the divorce.

of which its innermost circle was composed were scarcely
such as could command his sympathy and approbation. There
was hardly one of them whose character was not seriously
tainted with that vice against which the unsullied purity of
More's mind revolted ; not one who looked upon the trans-
gression of the marriage vow as deserving reprobation or
censure, or at least as worse than a jest." *

This passage, in its review of More's position at court, has
brought us to the date of the great divorce question. I will
postpone this for awhile, and conclude the chapter by mentioning some of the diplomatic labours in which More was engaged
previous to his receiving the great seal as chancellor of the
kingdom.

In August, 1525, he was appointed, together with Nicolas
West, Bishop of Ely, to arrange with the French envoys the
conditions of a truce between France and England.† A treaty
was enacted the next year at Hampton Court, and again More
was one of the Commission.‡ Similar negotiations were concluded at Westminster in May, 1527. On this occasion More's
colleague was Stephen Gardiner. § These various treaties were
only preliminaries to a solemn embassy sent into France in
1527. Wolsey went in person, with almost more than royal
state, to meet the French king. Sir Thomas More was one
of those who accompanied the cardinal, not simply to swell his
pomp, but to act as his councillor. They left London on
Wednesday, the 3rd July. Thursday night was spent in the
Bishop of Rochester's palace. We know of the long interview
in which Wolsey tried to over-reach the holy bishop with regard

---

* Brewer, Introduction to *Letters and Papers*, vol. iv. p. 216, *sq.*

† Rymer, xiv. 48.

‡ Rymer, xiv. 185.   On 14th July, 1526, Spinelli writes that " Sir
Thomas More, his Majesty's secretary, has returned from France, with
the articles of the " mutual obligation " (*Venetian State Papers*, iii.
1351).

§ *Letters and Papers*, iv. 3080, 3105, 3138.

to the question of the king's marriage, which had just then been
secretly mooted before the two archbishops, but we have no
record of the cordial embraces between Fisher and More, the
two loving friends so soon to be brother-martyrs.   Their conversation would have been about the captivity and danger of
the Holy Father Clement VII., then besieged in his castle of
St. Angelo, while Rome was given up to the most cruel and
brutal outrages ever recorded in history.   Before leaving home,
More had gone with his family to take part in the solemn supplications for the Pope in his parish church.   On leaving
Rochester he joined Wolsey and Warham in the Cathedral
Church of Canterbury in similar devotions.   Passing over to
Calais on the 11th, they remained there some days, and then
went by Boulogne to Abbeville, where they were detained by
the diplomacy of Francis.   On Sunday, the 3rd August, they
were met outside Amiens by the French king, the king of
Navarre, cardinals, bishops and nobles.   After saluting the
cardinal, Francis (says Wolsey, in his report to the king),
"saluted my Lord of London (Tunstall), my Lord Chamberlain
(Lord Sandys), Master Controller (Sir Henry Guildford), the
Chancellor of the Duchy (Sir T. More), and such other servants and gentlemen as accompanied me ".   After preparing
himself in the magnificent lodging to which the king conducted
him in person, Wolsey went with his great gentlemen, among
whom was More, to visit the queen-mother.   On Sunday, 17th
August, the treaty of peace was solemnly sworn in the cathedral
church of Amiens.   They remained at Amiens honoured by
splendid festivities till the end of August, and the king accompanied them for some distance on their journey home.   It was
nearly the end of September when they reached the shores of
England.*

More crossed the English Channel many times, but not once
the Irish Sea.   On 15th June, 1529, John Du Bellay, the

* Various letters in *State Papers*, vol. i., and Cavendish's *Life of
Wolsey*.

French ambassador in London, wrote to Montmorency : " In Ireland there were some practices going on by those of the country, to which a stop has been put in good time. I think they are going to send Master More thither to treat with them." [*] Another employment was however found. He was joined with the Bishop of London (Tunstall), Knight and Hacket, in an embassy to Cambray, in which the English ambassadors were to meet those of the emperor, of the Pope, and of the king of France. Campeggio, who had come to England as legate on the affair of the divorce, wrote on the 29th June to Salviati : " I hear the king has had much discussion with the Cardinal of York, proposing, as the cardinal is unable to go to Cambray, to send thither the Bishop of London, a man of sense and merit, and More, a learned layman". [†] The next day the Bishop of Bayonne wrote to the king of France that the king of England begged him to defer his proceedings at Cambray till his ambassadors, the Bishop of London and Master More, should arrive ; for considering their age and quality, they could not be expected to travel post. [‡]

In another letter Cardinal Campeggio writes : " The Bishop of London and More departed on the 1st (July) to attend the congress. They had particular instructions to promote the interests of the Pope and the Holy See. I believe they will use their good offices in this respect, because I did my utmost both with the king and with them." [§]   These words are full of interest. Had the three men thus brought together died in that year, 1529, history would have classed them together, as equally loyal and zealous for the honour and welfare of the Sovereign Pontiff. In a few years, however, they had been

---

[*] *Letters and Papers*, iv. 5679.

[†] *Ib.*, iv. 5733.

[‡] *Ib.*, iv. 5741. In the treasurer's account is an entry of £66 13s. 4d. advanced to Sir Thomas More for his diets at 26s. 8d. per day (*Ib.*, v. 312).

[§] *Ib.*, 5775.

"sifted like wheat". Henry's pride and sensuality had driven him into hatred of the Pope and obstinate schism, in which he died. Tunstall had followed him into schism, but recovered and died at last in the unity of the Church. More had won the martyr's crown in defence of the supremacy.

The Treaty of Cambray was signed by Margaret of Savoy on the part of Charles V.: by Tunstall, More, and Hacket, on the part of Henry: and by Francis, on 8th August, 1529, in the Cathedral Church of Cambray;* the ambassadors returned to England, and More visited Wolsey on 23rd August. But the days of that minister's glory were nearly numbered, and More was to be his successor.

In mentioning in this and preceding chapters the numerous treaties of which Sir Thomas More was a negotiator, I have said very little as to their causes, their provisions, or their result. To have done so, it would have been necessary to enter more deeply into public history than befits a biography. It may have been noticed, however, that his legal and practical skill was chiefly employed in commercial treaties. As regards the purely political diplomacy of those days, he had spoken with ruthless satire in his *Utopia*. The whole passage will be the best commentary on this chapter:—

"The Utopians call those nations that come and ask magistrates from them Neighbours; but those to whom they have been of more particular service, Friends; and as all other nations are perpetually either making leagues or breaking them, they never enter into an alliance with any state. They think leagues are useless things, and believe that if the common ties of humanity do not knit men together, the faith of promises will have no great effect; and they are the more confirmed in this by what they see among the nations round about them, who are no strict observers of leagues and treaties. We know how religiously they are observed in Europe, more particularly where the Christian doctrine is received, among whom they are

* Rymer, xiv. 326.

sacred and inviolable ! which is partly owing to the justice and goodness of the princes themselves, and partly to the reverence they pay to the Popes, who, as they are the most religious observers of their own promises, so they exhort all other princes to perform theirs ; and, when fainter methods do not prevail, they compel them to it by the severity of the pastoral censure, and think that it would be the most indecent thing possible if men who are particularly distinguished by the title of 'The Faithful' should not religiously keep the faith of their treaties. But in that new-found world, which is not more distant from us in situation than the people are in their manners and course of life, there is no trusting to leagues, even though they were made with all the pomp of the most sacred ceremonies ; on the contrary, they are on this account the sooner broken, some slight pretence being found in the words of the treaties, which are purposely couched in such ambiguous terms that they can never be so strictly bound but they will always find some loop-hole to escape at ; and thus they break both their leagues and their faith ; and this is done with such impudence, that those very men who value themselves on having suggested these expedients to their princes would, with a haughty scorn, declaim against such craft, or, to speak plainer, such fraud and deceit, if they found private men make use of it in their bargains, and would readily say that they deserved to be hanged.

" By this means it is that every sort of justice passes with them for a low-spirited and vulgar virtue, far below the dignity of royal greatness—or at least there are set up two sorts of justice : the one is mean and creeps on the ground, and, there-fore, becomes none but the lower part of mankind, and, being kept in severely by many restraints, is not able to break out be-yond the bounds that are set to it ; the other is the peculiar virtue of princes, which, as it is more majestic than that which becomes the rabble, so takes a freer compass, and thus nothing is unlawful except what is unpleasant. These practices of the princes that lie about Utopia, who make so little account of their faith, seem to be the reasons that determine them to engage in no confederacy. Perhaps they would change their mind if they lived among us."

If this biting irony had been deserved by the diplomacy of Europe in 1515, when More thus wrote, it had not ceased to be merited in 1529, when Machiavelli's principles had practically become the code of princes, and Charles V., Francis I., and Henry VIII. were ceaselessly intent on outwitting each other. Sir Thomas More's part, however, was confined to the making of the promises and engagements; he left the responsibility of breaking them to others.

After this review of More's public life and period of prosperity, the reader will be interested to know what was his interior life before God. In addition to what has been said of this by his biographers, especially Roper and Stapleton, as related in previous chapters, we have a picture of a holy statesman drawn by his own pen, in which he has unconsciously described himself; or rather we have an account given of a method of sanctification, which we know from other sources to have been the one so successfully adopted by himself. In the *Dialogue of Comfort against Tribulation*, written in the Tower, Sir Thomas gives the following advice as to the means by which a man may keep himself humble in a state of honour and prosperity: "To the intent that he may think of such things (as death and judgment) the better, let him use often to resort to confession, and there open his heart, and by the mouth of some good, virtuous, ghostly father, have such things oft renewed in his remembrance. Let him also choose himself some secret solitary place, as far from noise and company as he conveniently can, and thither let him sometimes secretly resort alone, imagining himself as one going out of the world, even straight unto the giving up of his reckoning unto God of his sinful life. Then let him there before an altar, or some pitiful image of Christ's bitter Passion, kneel down or fall prostrate, as at the feet of Almighty God, verily believing Him to be there invisibly present, as without any doubt He is. There let him open his heart to God, and confess his faults, such as he can call to mind, and pray God of forgiveness. Let him also call to remembrance the benefits that God hath given him, either in general among other men, or privately to himself, and give Him humble, hearty thanks therefor. There let him declare unto God the temptations of the devil, the suggestions of the flesh, the occasions of the world and of his worldly friends—much worse many times in drawing a man from God than are his most mortal enemies. There let him lament and bewail unto God his own fraility, negligence, and sloth in resisting and with-standing of temptations, his readiness and pronity to fall there-unto. Then let him beseech God of His gracious aid and help to strengthen his infirmity withal, both in keeping him from falling, and when he by his own fault misfortuneth to fall, then with the helping hand of His merciful grace to lift him up and set him on his feet in the state of grace again. And let this man not doubt that God heareth him and granteth him gladly this boon; and so, dwelling in the faithful trust of God's help, he shall well use his prosperity and persevere in his good, profitable business, and shall have therein the truth of God to compass him about with a pavice [a shield] of His heavenly defence, that of the devil's arrow flying in the day* of worldly wealth he shall not need to dread." †

* " Scuto circumdabit te veritas ejus . . . a sagitta volante in die " (*Ps.* xc. 5, 6).

† Book ii. ch. xvii., *English Works.* p. 1201.

CHAPTER XI.

THE GERMAN REFORMATION.

WE come now to a new phase in the life we are studying. Among many writers it has become a theory that there were two Thomas Mores, as there were two Henries called the Eighth; that as the king degenerated, under the influence of baffled lust and wounded pride, from a pious and affable prince to a sensual and cruel despot, so too his minister degenerated, under the influence of political and social fears, from a liberal and somewhat sceptical philosopher, to a bigoted persecutor. Horace Walpole, describing the portrait of Sir Thomas, painted by Holbein in 1527, writes: "It is Sir Thomas More in the rigour of his sense, not in the sweetness of his pleasantry. Here is rather that single, cruel judge, whom one knows not how to hate, and who, in the vigour of abilities, of knowledge and good humour, persecuted others in defence of superstitions that he himself had exposed; and who, capable of disdaining life at the price of his sincerity, yet thought that God was to be served by promoting an imposture; who triumphed over Henry and death, and sunk to be an accomplice, at least the dupe, of the Holy Maid of Kent!" *

There is no doubt much coxcombry in all this balanced antithesis, yet it expresses the perplexity which the apparent contrast between the earlier and later life of More has excited in deeper minds than Walpole's. The perplexity, however, is

* *Anecdotes of Painting*, vol. i. 70 (ed. Wornum).

self-created by those who, turning over the pages of the *Utopia* or the *Praise of Folly*, dream of a sceptical, rationalistic, Utopian More; and contrast him with the More who has depicted himself in his epitaph as the sworn enemy of malefactors and heretics—words most true, yet easily misunderstood at the present day. Postponing for future consideration the charge of persecution, I will here confine my remarks to his Latin controversial writings, and especially to the book against Luther. Tindale hinted at some such contrast as that described above, and Sir Thomas replied as follows : " Of Erasmus' book on the *Praise of Folly*, Tindale saith, that if it were in English every man should then well see that I was then far otherwise minded than I now write. If this be true, then the more cause have I to thank God of amendment.　But surely this is not true ; for, God be thanked, I never had that mind in myself to have holy saints' images or their holy relics out of reverence.　Nor if there were any such thing in *Moria*, that thing could not yet make any man see that I were myself of that mind, the book being made by another man, though he were ' my darling ' never so dear. Howbeit, that book of *Moria* doth indeed but jest upon the abuses of such things, after the manner of the disour's* part in a play, and yet not so far neither by a great deal as the 'Messenger' doth in my *Dialogue*, which I have yet suffered to stand still in my *Dialogue*, and that rather yet by the counsel of other men than myself." †

Nor did Erasmus ever hint that any revolution had taken place in the mind of his candid, his darling More, any otherwise than he admits a change in his own view of things.　The world had changed, and new opponents had arisen, who aroused new feelings and required a new language ; but neither More nor Erasmus defended what they had before ridiculed, nor attacked what they had before encouraged.

---

* Disour, *i.e.*, clown, jester.　　　　† *English Works*, p. 422.

More, it is said, was in his early days a zealous reformer ; in his later days he was a conservative and resisted the reformers. But Reform is an ambiguous word. More had lamented the prevalence of *evil* works among professing Catholics. It surely does not follow that he should have welcomed the reform of Luther, whose principal outcry was against the importance attached by Catholics to *good* works.* More declared war, as Pace tells us, against certain scholastic theologians, who affirmed too dogmatically things that were obscure and altogether outside the faith. Was he, on that account, to accept Luther contradicting the first principles of Catholic faith ?

But if the consistency of More is admitted, what is to be said on the charge of asperity and scurrility brought against his controversial writings ? This question cannot be shirked by a biographer of More. To begin with the accusation of scurrility. Of More's book against Luther, published in 1523, Bishop Atterbury has said : "It is throughout nothing but downright ribaldry, without a grain of reasoning to support it; so that it gave the author no other reputation but that of having the best knack of any man in Europe at calling bad names in good Latin".† It is difficult to suppose that Atterbury had ever read the book of which he could thus write. It is replete with keen irony and powerful reasoning, as well as earnest and touching exhortation. That it is a pleasant book to read I do not contend, nor that it is free from language that is rude and nasty. But whether the language deserves the name of ribaldry depends on the

---

* "Luther's most earnest remonstrances were directed not against bad but against good works, and the stress laid upon them by the advocates of the old religion. If that religion had been in its practice so generally corrupt as it is represented to have been by modern writers, such denuntiations were idle " (Dr. Brewer, Introduction to *Letters and Papers*, p. 228). Tindale used to call zeal for good works " popeholiness ".

† Atterbury's *Epistolary Correspondence*, etc., iii. 452.

question whether, when Shakespeare's Ajax boxes the ears of Thersites and calls him a "whoreson cur," he thereby places himself on a level with Thersites, pouring out his foul venom on Agamemnon, Achilles, and all the princes of the army. Sir Thomas More complains that he could not clean the mouth of Luther without befouling his own fingers.

But let us understand the facts. In 1520, Luther published his treatise called the *Babylonian Captivity* in which he finally broke with the Church, railed at the Pope, and called on the world to embrace an entirely new religion, under the name of genuine Christianity. In 1521, Henry printed his book called *Defence of the Seven Sacraments*. Luther replied in a treatise so scurrilous, that it has probably no parallel in literature. Certainly such language had never before been addressed to a king or prince. It cannot be said that Henry had drawn this upon his own head. He had not attacked Luther, but stepped in as the Church's champion, to ward off the blows Luther was aiming at her. On the whole his defence is dignified, and he uses language no stronger than had been used in all ages, by saints and doctors, against inventors of novelties and disturbers of unity. In this book of Henry's More had no other share than that, after it was written, he had arranged the index.* But, against his will, he was drawn into the controversy. It was not possible for the king to reply to an attack such as Luther's. When Luther, a few years later, wrote an insincere apology for his virulence, Henry answered as it became him ; but even had he wished it, his advisers could

---

* The words of Sir Thomas are that "after it was finished, by His Grace's appointment, and consent of the makers of the same, *he* was only a sorter out and placer of the principal matters therein contained " (*Life of Roper*, p. 25). Mr. Bruce in the *Archæol.* (xxiii. 67) has a dissertation on the authorship of the *Assertio Septem Sacramentorum*. He understands the words of Sir Thomas as I have taken them. I do not enter further into this matter, since I have published an essay on the subject, called " Defender of the Faith ". (Catholic Truth Society.)

not have allowed him in 1523 to carry on a war of words with a foul-mouthed German boor. Some of his subjects undertook to avenge the "Defender of the Faith". Fisher, Bishop of Rochester, weighed as a theologian the original contentions of Luther, the English king's replies, and Luther's scornful reiterations. The king, however, in all probability, himself suggested to More that his wit would be well employed in chastising the insolent friar. This I gather from More's own words. Apologising for certain expressions, he says: "I doubt not, good reader, that your fairness will pardon me that in this book you read so often what causes you shame. Nothing could have been more painful to me than to be forced to speak foul words to pure ears. But there was no help for it, unless I left Luther's scurrilous book utterly untouched, *which is a thing I most earnestly desired.*"

It does not follow that, because More engaged in the controversy against his inclination, his method of conducting it was contrary to his conscience or his better judgment. He saw that Luther deserved to be trounced; he merely regretted that the task had been committed to him. He pleaded for leave to wear a mask while performing the unpleasant duty, and took the name of William Ross, an Englishman, supposed to be on a visit to Italy. His book is not a treatise on Lutheranism, for Lutheranism as a system had not yet been enunciated, and was still incomplete in the brain of its author. He refutes indeed both the denials and the assertions of Luther as they occur, but it is with Luther himself and Luther's language to Henry that he is dealing. The Wittenburg doctor, in the midst of his paroxysms of fury and hurling of nicknames, still wished to be taken for a prophet, zealous for his master's honour; and More's object was to turn into utter ridicule this pretension, by showing that he was simply an enraged and fanatical buffoon.*

---

* If such a designation seems too strong, let me cull a few specimens of his language. The king is "rex infelix, stolidissimus, delirus, nugigerulus, sceleratissimus, sacrilegus ; latro, asinus, porcus, truncus, antichristus,

He did not consider that his own book was to have any permanent value.   He therefore thus concluded it : "I confess
that my book is not such a one as the world must needs read ;
but, on the other hand, I trust it is one that need not be despised
by anyone who has condescended to read Luther's follies. As for
those who have simply disdained his ranting (*nænias*) there is
no need for them, nor do I wish them, to waste their time over
my book."

Of "reasoning," though Dr. Atterbury could not find "a
grain," there was far more than was necessary to overthrow any
arguments advanced by Martin Luther.   After a specimen or
two of More's lighter style of controversy, I will give a few
passages which will explain the earnest and determined opposition to the new opinions, in which he spent the rest of his life.
His method is to give Luther's words in full, and after each
paragraph to make a commentary.

Words of Luther.—"Where are you, my Lord Henry?
Bring forth your fine book against Luther. What is it that
your Lordship is defending—the seven sacraments ?   By whose
teaching—that of God, or of men ?   Let then your Thomistical
Lordship hear the judgment, not of Luther, but of Him before
whom the poles of the earth tremble, ' In vain do they worship
Me, teaching doctrines and commandments of men '."   (*Matt.*
xv. 9)."

Words of More.—" Reader, did you ever see a blind man
in a rage, and eager to revenge himself with his fists?   To
know where to hit out, he gets his adversary to speak, and
strikes where he thinks the sound comes from, but hits nothing,
since the speaker steps back.   Such is Luther, but far more

stultitiæ monstrum, rex mendacii ; damnabilis putredo, fæces latrinæ ;
vecors et indoctissima papistici corporis belua ; scurra levissimus ; insul-
sissimus Thomista, stropha Thomistica ; porcus Thomista," etc., etc.
Sir Thomas More's contention is : "Quis non rideat nebulonem miserrimum
tam furiosas efflantem glorias, quasi sederet in Christi pectore, cum
clausus jaceat in culo diaboli ?   Inde crepat ac buccinat " (Lib. i. cap. 7).

ridiculous ; for when the king answers him on his right hand, he strikes out towards the left. See him with his blind eyes standing ready to give his blow. 'Where are you, Lord Henry?' he cries. 'Here I am, close by you.' 'Come nearer, bring out your pretty book against Luther.' 'Here it is.' 'Nearer still, what is it your lordship defends—the seven sacraments?' 'Certainly.' 'A little nearer. By what teaching—that of God or of man?' 'Of God.' Now he is going to strike; mark with what precision. 'Listen,' he says, 'your highness: In vain do they worship Me with the doctrines of men'! and then he bursts out laughing and cannot contain himself for joy, at the crushing blow he has inflicted on his opponent." *

Luther had boldly declared that his only foundation was the written word of God, that he might get rid of all ecclesiastical tradition and all exercise of ecclesiastical authority. But the written word of God would not have served his purpose unless it were free to him to interpret it in a new sense by his own private judgment. We may listen to a specimen of his reasoning and of More's reply :—

Words of Luther.—"It is written, 'All things are yours, whether Apollo or Cephas or Paul, and you are Christ's' (1 *Cor.* iii. 22). If we are Christ's only, who is this stupid king, who strives with his lies to make us the Pope's? We are not the Pope's, but the Pope is ours. It is ours, not to be judged by the Pope, but to judge him. 'For the spiritual man is judged by none, but he judges all men' (*omnes*) (1 *Cor.* ii. 15). If it is true that all things are yours, even the Pope, how much more that dirt and disgrace of men, the Thomists and Henricians?"

Words of More.—"May I die if phrenzy itself is so phrenetical, or madness itself so mad, as this waggish head of Luther's. The Pope is ours, he says ; therefore it is ours to judge him, not to be judged by him. By the same reasoning : The physician is ours, therefore it is ours to cure him, not to be cured by him ;

and the schoolmaster belongs to the scholars, therefore it belongs to them to teach him, and not to learn from him !

"It is ours, he says, not to be judged by the Pope, but to judge him. What does he mean by 'ours'? Does he mean 'of the whole' collectively, or 'of each one' in particular? If he means 'of the whole,' he advances nothing for himself, since the whole of the Church is for the Pope, and against Luther. And in the matter of the sacraments still less, since people and Pope, both present and past, are in favour of the sacraments, and against Luther. But if it belongs to each one to judge the Pope and the sacraments, and the true sense of Scripture— since, among so many judges, the judgment of Luther alone is on one side—by what prerogative must his vote outweigh the votes of all the rest? Because, he says, the spiritual man judges all, and he is judged by none; and because 'all things are yours, even the Pope'. Reader, do you not seem to be listening to raving? Luther alone is spiritual; the Pope alone is unspiritual; so Luther must judge all and be judged by none, and the Pope must judge none, and be judged by all! And this raver does not see that, while he is raving against the Pope, he is raving also against Peter and Paul. For when the Apostle said 'all things are yours,' he did not add 'the Pope,' but Apollo, Cephas, and Paul. Hence Luther must reason consistently : We are not Peter's or Paul's, but Peter and Paul are ours ; therefore it is ours to judge Peter and Paul, and not to be judged by them. Nay, not so much ours as 'mine,' for it is the prerogative of the spiritual man to judge and not be judged. Hence the spiritual man, Luther, shall judge, not Thomists and Henricians only, but Peter and Paul and the rest of the Apostles. Come now, reader, deny if you can that one Minerva was born from the head of Jupiter, when you see the one head of Luther give birth to so many phrensies." *

Words of Luther.—"Everyone at his own risk believes truly

* Lib. i. cap. 14.

or falsely ; therefore everyone must take care for himself that he believes aright, so that common sense and the necessity of salvation prove that the judgment regarding doctrine is necessarily in the hearer. Otherwise to no purpose is it said : 'Prove all things, hold fast that which is good'."

Words of More.—"So then, because every one must take care to believe aright, he must have no care for Pope or councils, or church or holy fathers, or the people, or Peter or Paul, but he must himself judge boldly about everything ; and because he believes at his own risk, therefore without any risk he may believe in himself against the whole world, according to that advice of the Wise Man, 'Son, rely not on thy own prudence, and be not wise in thine own eyes'." *

In many places of this book Sir Thomas foretold the consequences to which this method of private illumination would lead, not only in the interpretation of Scripture, but in the acceptance or rejection of Scripture itself. His previsions have been justified, though slowly, in the rationalism and universal uncertainty in religious matters that prevails at the present day. But quite independently of what would come by a sure process of dissolution, contrary to the will or expectation of the original innovators, Sir Thomas saw quite enough in the immediate results of Luther's revolt to fill his soul with horror, whether as a Christian or a statesman. The following passage is from the peroration of his answer to Luther :—

"Reader, you will easily know the tree from its fruit. Recall to your memory what you have read, and you will see that, whatever the leaders of the Church, from the very cradle of Christianity, worshipped as most holy, is held by these Lutherans in the utmost contempt. What was celebrated with such veneration as the most holy sacrifice of the Mass ? and what has been more befouled and trampled on by these swine ? As regards prayer, not only have they abolished the liturgy of the fixed

* Lib. ii. cap. 22.

hours, but all the prayers which, from the very beginning, the Church has been accustomed to chant for the dead. Who will not abominate such cruelty? Even if it were altogether doubtful (as they falsely contend) whether the prayers of the living can profit the dead, yet what harm would there be to exercise our affections of piety, and to risk our prayers, since, even if we were doubtful of their efficacy, we are certain they cannot be injurious? What was reverenced more religiously than fasting, or observed so exactly as Lent? Yet now these wretches, 'made perfect in the Spirit,' in order not to distinguish day from day, give up every day to bacchanalian festivities. In how great esteem was continence held, how strictly was conjugal chastity prescribed, how approved was the chastity of widows, how assiduously and emphatically was virginity extolled, and all this from the teaching of Christ Himself. But now this antichrist has destroyed almost everything that bears the name of chastity. Priests, monks, virgins once dedicated to God, now at the instigation of the devil, in this 'church of the malignant,' under the name of lawful marriage, with a great pomp of attendant demons, celebrate their hateful nuptials; and, while none but evil men violate a pact made with a fellow-man, these fear not to violate a pact made with God, safe in the indulgence granted by Luther, who is already beginning to establish polygamy." He goes on to quote some sayings of Luther about marriage, and to relate his rage against the cultus of the saints and their images, Our Blessed Lady, and the Crucifix, at the very time that he was proud that his own portrait was being everywhere carried about with ludicrous veneration. "These, then," he exclaims, "are the spiritual fruits of this sect, this is the point which Luther's 'piety' has already reached. And all the crimes which flow from this heresy are supported and justified by one great impiety, since they contend that they are compelled to be what they are by the certain and predestined will of God.

"O illustrious Germany, can you doubt, can you doubt, when

they sow such spiritual things, what kind of corporal things they will reap? Indeed the thistles, as I hear, are already showing an ugly crop, and God is beginning to make known how He regards that sect, when He does not permit the priests who marry to take other wives than public prostitutes. In former days He forbade His priests to be joined in lawful matrimony to any but the purest virgins;* and now He does not suffer these incestuous and villainous nuptials to be contracted except with the foulest outcasts. And these bride-grooms, first sunk deep in infamy, and then ruined with disease and want, and giving themselves up to robbery, His justice is at last punishing with public executions. Would that His anger might stop short in the punishment of these dregs of men; but unless it is propitiated it will go farther. For many of the princes see, not without pleasure, the apostasy of the clergy, gaping as they do after the possessions of the apostates, which they hope to seize as derelict. And they rejoice to see obedience withdrawn from the Sovereign Pontiff, conceiving then the hope that they may dispose of everything, and may divide and dissipate it among themselves at home. On the other hand, they need not doubt, but that the people in their turn will throw off the yoke of the princes, and deprive them of their possessions. And when they shall come to do this, drunk with the blood of the princes, and exulting in the slaughter of the nobles, they will not submit even to plebeian governors; but following the dogma of Luther [about Christian liberty], and trampling the law under foot, then, at last without government and without law, without rein and without understanding, they will turn their hands against each other, and, like the earth-born brothers of old, will perish in mutual conflict. I beg of Christ that I may be a false prophet."

. This prevision of evil was both written and printed two years before the dreadful war of the peasants proved that More was

---

* *Levit.* xxi. 13.

no false prophet. What he thought of that calamity, and especially what he thought of Luther's conduct and writings, both before and during it, can be seen from the following extract from a Latin letter written about 1526 : *   " God does indeed sometimes, by means of such followers of the devil, either try the patience of the good members of His Church, or chastise the sins of Christians ; yet He is faithful, and with the temptation will provide an issue, and at last will wipe every tear from the eyes of those whom He has purified. But you, who are the impious and bloodthirsty slaughterers of the faithful, will by His anger be reduced to cinders, and driven away like dust from the face of the earth. Of this vengeance He has just given a fearful example, when those most wretched and villainous peasants, seduced by your teaching, after having destroyed so many monasteries, and for a time wandered hither and thither, giving themselves up to murder and plunder with impunity, just when they thought they had attained unrestrained and unrestrainable licence for every crime—behold the God of Majesty spoke in thunder, and sudden destruction came upon them. More than seventy thousand perished by the sword, and those who remained were reduced to cruel bondage.

"And are you not in this matter ashamed of your great master, Luther, first the most wicked leader, and then the most villainous deserter ; who after arousing, arming, and exciting the peasants to every kind of crime, when he saw that fortune threatened them with ruin, by his truculent

---

* *Epistola contra Pomeranum* (Lovanii, 1568). This letter is not contained in More's collected works. It was published by John Fowler, an English exile, from More's autograph, which he had probably obtained from John Harris, More's secretary. In the Preface More says that some one placed in his hand a letter from John Pomeranus (Bugenhagen), a German Lutheran, to "the faithful in England". He wrote his reply evidently with the view of publication, but may have laid it aside, preferring his English controversy with Tindall, Frith and Fish.

writings, betrayed and denounced them, and gave them up to be torn to pieces by the nobles; and by his shameful flatteries tried to smother the odium that was felt against himself in the blood of the poor wretches, of whose rebellion and slaughter he was the sole cause? Who that has a drop of human blood in his breast would not prefer to die ten times over, than to prolong a life hateful to God and man by such foul and cruel flattery?"

One other passage must be quoted from the first answer to Luther of 1523, described by Atterbury as "downright ribaldry, without a grain of reason". In it we have Sir Thomas More's declaration of allegiance to the Sovereign Pontiff:—

"As regards the primacy of the Roman Pontiff, the Bishop of Rochester has made the matter so clear from the Gospels, the Acts of the Apostles, and from the whole of the Old Testament, and from the consent of all the holy fathers, not of the Latins only, but of the Greeks also (of whose opposition Luther is wont to boast), and from the definition of a General Council, in which the Armenians and Greeks, who at that time had been most obstinately resisting, were overcome, and acknowledged themselves overcome, that it would be utterly superfluous for me to write again on the subject.

"I am moved to obedience to that See not only by what learned and holy men have written, but by this fact especially, that we shall find, that on the one hand every enemy of the Christian faith makes war on that See, and that, on the other hand, no one has ever declared himself an enemy of that See who has not also shortly after shown most evidently that he was the enemy of the Christian religion.

"Another thing that moves me is this, that if, after Luther's manner, the vices of men are to be imputed to the offices they hold, not only the papacy will fall, but royalty, and dictatorship, and consulate, and every other kind of magistracy, and the people will be without rulers, without law, and without order. Should such a thing ever come to pass, as it seems

indeed imminent in some parts of Germany, they will then feel
to their own great loss how much better it is for men to have
bad rulers than no rulers at all.   Most assuredly as regards the
Pope, God, who set him over His Church, knows how great an
evil it would be to be without one, and I do not think it desirable that Christendom should learn it by experience.   It is far
more to be wished that God may raise up such Popes as befit
the Christian cause and the dignity of the Apostolic office :
men who, despising riches and honour, will care only for
heaven, will promote piety in the people, will bring about peace,
and exercise the authority they have received from God against
the ' satraps and mighty hunters of the world,' excommunicating
and giving over to Satan both those who invade the territories
of others and those who oppress their own.   With one or two
such Popes the Christian world would soon perceive how much
preferable it is that the papacy should be reformed than abrogated.   And I doubt not that long ago Christ would have
looked down on the pastor of His flock if the Christian people
had chosen rather to pray for the welfare of their Father than
to persecute him, and to hide the shame of their Father than
to laugh at it.

" But be sure, Luther, of this : God will not forsake His own
vicar.   He will one day cast His eyes of mercy on him ; nay,
He is perhaps now doing it, in allowing a most wicked son to
scourge so painfully his father.   You are nothing else, Luther,
but the scourge of God, to the great gain of that See, and to
your own great loss.   God will act as a kind mother does, who,
when she has chastised her child, wipes away his tears, and, to
appease him, throws the rod into the fire."

What Sir Thomas More here writes of the coercitive power
of the Sovereign Pontiff, and the desirability of its vigorous
exercise, will probably surprise some readers, as the words of
an English statesman writing under the eye and in defence of
an English king, and that king Henry VIII.   But it was in strict
conformity with the international law of Europe.

The following clause was introduced, in 1515, into the commission appointing English ambassadors to treat of peace, etc. : "To take any oath upon our soul, and to do this personally on the Holy Gospels. Also, to obtain an Apostolic bull or rescript in due form, in which all the contents of such treaty will be confirmed by the authority of the Holy See, with pains and censures against ourselves and our heirs, and the sentence of interdict against our kingdom and dominions, if and in so far as we do and consent to the doing of anything contrary to the aforesaid treaty or any part of it, renouncing at the same time all exceptions of fact or law, even such as require special mention, for us and in our name, for the strengthening of such treaty." *

This clause recognised the Pope as the guardian of Christendom, and in 1523 Henry had no wish to quarrel with its letter or its spirit. If in 1534 his views had changed, we must remember that, according to the same Horace Walpole, who wrote so brilliantly about More :—

> From Catharine's wrongs a nation's bliss was spread,
> And Luther's light from Henry's lawless bed.

Henry in his reply to the apology of Luther, in which the heresiarch affected to believe that the book on the sacraments was not the king's, but the work of some of his ecclesiastics, such as Wolsey or Lee, had plainly declared the book to be his own, yet at a later period, when it rose up to condemn him, he had the meanness to insinuate, what he dared not assert, that Luther's contention was true ; and he had Luther's letter translated into English and spread abroad.†

His meanness and effrontery went even further than this. He charged some members of his Council to reproach Sir Thomas More that "he, by subtle sinister slights most unnaturally procuring and provoking him to set forth a book of the assertion of the seven sacraments, and maintenance of the

* Rymer, xiii. 496, 500. An. 1515.
† Letter of Chapuys (4th Feb., 1534). *Letters and Papers*, vii. 152.

Pope's authority, had caused him, to his dishonour throughout all Christendom, to put a sword in the Pope's hand to fight against himself". Sir Thomas's answer, which will be given in full in its proper place, was an utter denial that he had in any way whatever suggested the king's book. * No allusion seems to have been made to his defence of it against Luther. In his answer to Luther's apology in 1525 the king had referred to it as follows: "I see that, both in England and other places, some have replied to what you wrote against me. Some have treated you according to your deserts, and handled you after your own fashion, except that they have given reasons as well as insults, while you give only the latter." Ingratitude is the most conspicuous feature of the later life of Henry VIII. Scarce one of all those who laboured for him, whether nobly or ignobly, met any other return than insults and cruelty. †

* Roper's *Life of More*, n. 25.

† In this chapter I have taken for granted that the book of Gulielmus Rosseus is by More. The Latin style, the wit, and parallel passages in More's English works make this quite certain, nor have I found it anywhere questioned. Stapleton, however, tells us that during More's lifetime no one suspected him to be the author (cap. 6). More kept his secret by sometimes referring to Ross. Thus in his English work against Tindale, written in 1532, he says: "I doubt not but that Tindale hath read both Rosseus and Luther in those places, and seeth his master made a fool therein already" (p. 490). And again: " This reason was by one Rosseus proved so foolish and so unreasonable, that Tindale and Barns be both ashamed thereof" (p. 817). So also p. 513: "Luther was in that point by Rosseus shamefully soused in the mire". Stapleton does not tell us when the truth was discovered, nor how. There is no allusion to the book against Luther in Roper's notes, but its authorship was known to Harpsfield. Stapleton (cap. 4) says that William Ross was an Englishman, who had died in Italy just before More published his book. The author of the *Life of More* printed by Wordsworth says he was a well-known wild companion. Had either of these writers authority for these statements? I may add that if More did not acknowledge the work of Ross to be his own, Fisher in his book against Œcolampadius in 1526 refers to More's having written against Luther, and his words can only refer to this work (Pref. ad Lib. ii.).

CHAPTER XII.

CHANCELLOR.

I T is recorded in every English history how Cardinal Wolsey by his failure to secure the royal divorce lost the favour of the king whom he had served better than his God; and how on 19th October, 1529, the great seal of his chancellorship was taken from him. The Bishop of Bayonne, the French ambassador in England, wrote on 22nd October: "The Duke of Norfolk is made head of the Council; in his absence the Duke of Suffolk; over all is Mademoiselle Anne. It is not yet known who will have the seal. I think no priest will touch it, and that in this parliament the clergy will have terrible alarms." Wolsey is said to have declared that no man was so fit for the office of Lord High Chancellor as Sir Thomas More;* but there is no likelihood that he was consulted on the appointment, and the remark was probably made when the name of his successor was announced to him. The imperial envoy, Eustace Chapuys, who had only recently arrived in England, wrote to Charles V. on 25th October: "The chancellor's seal has remained in the hands of the Duke of Norfolk till this morning, when it was transferred to Sir Thomas More. Everyone is delighted at his promotion, because he is an upright and learned man, and a good servant of the Queen."† From the official act we learn that on Monday, the 25th October, at East Greenwich, the seal was delivered

---

* Erasmus. *Ep.* 426, in App. Harpsfield and Stapleton.
† *Letters and Papers*, iv. 6026.

by the king to Sir Thomas More, in the presence of Sir Christopher Hales, attorney general, in the king's privy chamber, and on the next day, 26th October, More took his oath as chancellor in the great hall at Westminster, in the presence of the Dukes of Norfolk and Suffolk, and a large number of the nobility and prelates.* Roper remembered five-and-twenty years later the great eulogy passed on Sir Thomas by the Duke of Norfolk, speaking in the king's name, and especially the way in which he had acquitted himself in his late embassy at Cambrai; and how Sir Thomas in reply had alluded to his predecessor: " Considering how wise and honourable a prelate had lately before taken so great a fall,† he had no cause to rejoice in his new dignity. And as the Dukes had charged him, on the king's behalf, uprightly to administer justice without corruption or partiality, so did he likewise charge them if they saw him at any time in anything to digress from his duty, even as they would discharge their own duty and fidelity to God and the king, so should they not fail to disclose it to His Grace, who otherwise might have just occasion to lay his fault wholly to their charge."‡ Of course More's old friend Erasmus was delighted to hear of his elevation, though he wrote to Mountjoy, to Tunstall and to Pace, almost in the same words : " I do not at all congratulate More, nor

* *Ib.*, 6025.

† Lewis, in his edition of Roper, has " fault," but Harpsfield's MS. has " fall ". Wolsey had been prosecuted by the order of Henry in the King's Bench, and had pleaded guilty. The charge was that he had kept his legatine court, contrary to the statute of Premunire.

‡ Stapleton has amplified Roper's account by composing two long and eloquent speeches, one for the duke and one for Sir Thomas. These have been well translated by Cresacre More. I omit them, as they are mere exercises in rhetoric. Stapleton makes More say of Wolsey : *acerbo casu dejectus occubuit inglorius.* The word *occubuit* may perhaps mean "fell"; Cresacre translates it "died"; but Wolsey survived another year after More's speech. Sir James Mackintosh has given the speeches in full without suspecting their authenticity.

literature ; but I do indeed congratulate England, for a better or holier judge could not have been appointed ".*

Cardinal Pole writes that the object of the king was to win over, or in plain words, to bribe More by this dignity, to side with him in what was called his "great matter," his divorce from Queen Catharine, and marriage with Anne Boleyn.† Roper confirms this, adding that the king was led into this hope by Dr. Stokesly, whom he had made Bishop of London. We shall see that the king and his bishop both underrated More's integrity. It has surprised many, that More, who knew this design, and the difficult and intricate path on which he was entering, should have accepted the chancellorship. The truth would seem to be, that a subject had no choice as to accepting or rejecting an office pressed upon him by Henry VIII. The danger to life and fortune might be as great in obstinately refusing to accept the office, as in resisting the king's will in its execution ; while he might hope that the king would soon be wearied of him and allow him to resign. As to the danger to his own conscience, More had taken care to clear his way before him regarding the only matter which then presented a difficulty, that of the divorce.

With respect to this unhappy question, the source of so many woes, there will be no need to enter into any details in this memoir. Its general history will be sufficiently familiar to the reader. Sir Thomas More, in a letter written to Cromwell on 5th March, 1534, drew up a full and minute account of his own course of action with regard to the king's divorce, both before, during, and after his chancellorship. The substance is as follows : Before going beyond sea with Wolsey, in July, 1527, he had heard of the difficulties that had been started concerning the impediment of affinity, but he then thought that the

---

* *Epist. Erasm.* 1034, 28th March, 1530 (not 1529).

† Certe ipse rerum exitus satis declarat illum hac de causa cancellarium esse factum, quo hac quasi mercede corruptus se eo trahi pateretur.

"hopes" and "comfort" of the king and his advisers were founded on supposed flaws in the bull of dispensation. On his return in September he was, therefore, surprised when, on his visiting the king at Hampton Court, while they were walking in the gallery, His Highness suddenly told him that he had found that his marriage was in such way contrary to Divine law, "that it could in no wise by the Church be dispensable". The king laid the Bible open before him, read him the words of *Leviticus* and *Deuteronomy*, and asked his opinion. Not thinking that his opinion on such a subject could have much weight for or against, he gave it, in obedience to the command. His Highness accepted benignly his sudden unadvised answer (which was apparently contrary to his own view), and commanded him to confer with his almoner, Dr. Fox, and to read with him a book that was then in preparation. This book was laid before a number of learned men at Hampton Court, and, after some modifications, it was again read at York Place in the cardinal's chamber, and the bishops and doctors present agreed that the king had reasons sufficient to conceive scruples about his marriage, and "to procure to have his doubt decided by judgment of the Church". While the cause was before the legates, Sir Thomas held himself entirely aloof, "for the matter was in hand by an ordinary process of the spiritual law, whereof he could little skill". Besides, while the legates were still sitting, he was sent on an embassy to Cambrai. On his return, having been appointed chancellor, the king again moved him to consider the matter. Should he be able to take the king's point of view, His Majesty would gladly use him among other of his counsellors in that matter. He would, however, in no way force his conscience; "he must first look to God, and after God to the king". He, therefore, studied the matter more attentively, taking for his instructors or advisers those whom the king selected: the Archbishops of Canterbury and York (Warham and Lee), the almoner, Dr. Fox, and Dr. Nicholas De Burgo, an Italian friar. Though he greatly desired to do the king all the service in his power, yet, as he could not bring his mind to the king's view, he was left "free and used in other business," retaining the royal favour. Thenceforward he meddled no more in the matter, refused to read any books on the side he had himself embraced, and finding one by chance in his study, that had been written against the divorce by Dr. Clark, Bishop of Bath, he offered to send it back, but was told to burn it, and did so. Since the king's second marriage, he had in no way discussed it with any, but had prayed and would continue to pray for the king, for the noble lady who had been anointed queen (Anne Boleyn), and their noble issue "long to live and well, in such way as may be to the pleasure of God, honour and surety to themselves, wealth, peace, and profit to the realm".

This account of the king's designs upon More, and how he contrived to baffle them, has led us beyond the period of his chancellorship. We must now return to the time of his appointment. This is not the place, nor is the present writer a fit person, to explain the nature and growth of the office of Lord High Chancellor of England. A word or two, however, may be allowed, in order to prevent confusion, especially in the minds of foreign readers of this memoir.* The word "chancellor," or "cancellarius," is ambiguous. It has been used to indicate a doorkeeper in a court of law, a law clerk, a diocesan official, a dignitary in a cathedral church, the president of a university, as well as in later times a great judge in a court of equity and minister of state. The chancellor of the kings of England was formerly a chaplain and secretary to the king. As spiritual adviser he was called the keeper of the royal conscience. As chief secretary he prepared royal mandates, grants and charters, and affixed the royal seal. Hence he became (and still remains) keeper of the great

* The following account is derived from Lord Campbell's *Introduction*, Bohn's *Cyclopædia of Political Knowledge*, and similar sources.

seal. The king, as the fountain of justice, appointed judges of the various courts, but when plaintiffs appealed to the king for justice, his secretary directed the royal *writs* to the judges to try the case.

So far, the functions of the chancellor were only ministerial. His jurisdiction as judge originated in the discretionary powers of the king, whose special interference was frequently sought, either against the decisions of his courts of law, or in matters which were not cognisable by the ordinary courts, or lastly, in cases where powerful misdoers set ordinary jurisdiction at defiance. Hence arose the practice of Equity as distinguished from the Common as well as the Statute Law; and as the chancellor, from his skill and experience, was naturally a chief adviser of the king and his Council, in course of time he came to hold (by royal appointment) a special court, in which the validity of royal grants was decided, and matters that regarded the possessions and transmission of land, as well as such other extraordinary cases as had formerly been referred to his opinion. His office, therefore, was twofold. His *hanniper* or hamper contained the royal writs, his *petty bag* the records of his decisions; and at a later period, the two sides or functions of the court of chancery were thus designated.

In the reigns of the early Anglo-Norman kings, the chancellor was but the sixth of the officials in the *Aula Regia*. The chief justiciar, constable, mareschal, steward, and chamberlain preceded him. But already St. Thomas Beckett was reckoned *secundus a rege*, and had fifty clerks under him. In the time of the Tudors the chancellor's was the highest dignity after that of the monarch, and even when not a peer he was by his office prolocutor of the House of Lords. Erasmus, who, from his long residence in England, and familiarity with the two chancellors, Warham and Wolsey, was well acquainted with the subject, wrote to a German bishop that "in England the cancellarius is not, as under the empire, a mere secretary of State, but the supreme judge,

and the right eye and right hand, so to say, of the king and
Council. When he appears solemnly, a gold sceptre is carried
at his right, at the top of which is an imperial crown, and at
his left a book. By these emblems, the supreme power,
under the king, and the knowledge of the laws, is symbolised."*
The great seal, however, was the principal emblem as well as
instrument of the chancellor's office. It had originally been
carried in a bag of white leather; in the time of Wolsey this
was enclosed in another of crimson velvet, embroidered with
the royal arms.†

There was in the functions of the chancellor nothing of an
ecclesiastical character, yet the office had been hitherto held,
with very few exceptions, by ecclesiastics, and not unfrequently
by great prelates, since they alone were fitted, by their superior
education and knowledge of the Roman civil law as well as
canon law, to form equitable judgments, and to fulfil the
other requirements of the office. ‡ The appointment of Sir
Thomas More marked a great change in English public life.
Thenceforward the chancellors, with very few exceptions, were
laymen.§

The chancellor was also at that period president of the
Court of Star Chamber. The name of this tribunal suggests
memories of tyranny, but its action in the time of Henry VIII.
was by no means oppressive. It rather provided security for
the humbler members of the community against oppression by
their richer or more powerful neighbours, according to the
original purpose of its institution. Its authority was derived

* *Epist. Erasm.*, 426, in App.

† During More's office this was renewed at a cost of £5 5s. 8d.
(*Letters and Papers*, v. 445).

‡ Sir James Mackintosh, in his *Life of More*, p. 120.

§ The last Catholic chancellor was Archbishop Heath, under Queen
Mary. To this day Catholics are excluded from the office created by
Catholic churchmen, and which has made English law what it now is.
[Should this book ever reach another edition I trust that this note will
have to be cancelled.]

from the Statutes 3 Henry VII., cap. 1, and 21 Henry VIII., cap. 20. The first of these recites that the orderly government of the realm was impeded by unlawful maintenances (on the part of noblemen), untrue demeaning of sheriffs in the returns and panels of juries, riots and unlawful assemblies, and it enacts that the chancellor, the treasurer, and certain other dignitaries should have power to summon persons so offending, and others, and to punish the misdoers just as if they had been convicted in the due course of law. The second statute enlarged the tribunal. There exist records of cases that came before this court, but not of the pleadings or judgments; nothing, therefore, that throws any light on Sir Thomas as judge.*

His new dignities seem to have made little change in the simplicity of More's domestic life; yet, as they brought with them the obligation of greater state in public, they were supported by a greater salary. This however was insufficient for the expenses entailed, at least to a man of More's integrity, for the office seems to have given to some other chancellors abundant opportunities of enriching themselves. We find a warrant to the treasurer to allow Sir Thomas More, as chancellor, the yearly sum of £142 15s., and for his attendance in the Star Chamber £200 a year; also to the chief butler to allow him £64 a year for the price of 12 tuns of wine, and to the keeper of the great wardrobe £16 for wax.† If we add together these sums, and multiply them by 12 for modern value, we find that his income was about £5000 a year; and according to Roper, his professional income before he entered on the royal service was nearly as much. He had, however, acquired certain estates and other emoluments which he still retained.‡

* See Appendix to 49th Report concerning Public Records, pp. 376-594.
† *Letters and Papers*, iv. 6079.
‡ Lady More mentions that his lands forfeited at his attainder were worth £60 a year. I find mention also of a corrody in the monastery of Glastonbury (*Letters and Papers*, vii. 1601-32), and a pension from the Order of St. John of Jerusalem (*Ib.*, 1675).

Though only in his fifty-second year, Sir Thomas More was what was then called an old man, such as he had depicted "the old sage father sitting in his chair" in the pageants which he had illustrated in his youth :—

> Old age am I, with locks thin and hoar,
> Of our short life the last and best part ;
> Wise and discreet ; the public weal, therefore,
> I help to rule to my labour and smart.

What has been recorded of his chancellorship, which lasted only about two years and a half, may be grouped under two heads. We will consider him first as a minister and next as a judge.

The famous parliament which lasted seven years, and which before its close pronounced an attainder upon Sir Thomas More, was solemnly opened by him as chancellor only a few days after he had received the seal. It met at Blackfriars* on Wednesday, 3rd November, 1529, and in his speech Sir Thomas declared "the cause of its assembly to be to reform such things as had been used or permitted by inadvertence, or by changes of time had become inexpedient". The Parliamentary Rolls add that "of these errors and abuses he discoursed in a long and eloquent speech ".†

The chroniclers put a very different speech into More's mouth. After showing that the king was the shepherd of his people, he added : "As you see that amongst a great flock of sheep some be rotten and faulty, which the good shepherd sendeth from the good sheep, so the great wether which is of late fallen (as you all know), so craftily, so scabbedly, yea and so untruly juggled with the king, that all men must needs guess and think that he thought in himself that he had no wit to perceive his crafty doing, or else he presumed that the king would not see nor know his fraudulent juggling and attempts.

---

* An adjournment took place to Westminster on account of the plague.
† *Rolls of Parliament*, i. 151.

But he was deceived, for His Grace's sight was so quick and penetrable that he saw him, yea and saw through him, both within and without, so that all thing to him was open, and according to his desert he hath had a gentle correction, which small punishment the king will not to be an example to other offenders." *

I confess to a profound distrust of all such records of speeches in our sixteenth century annalists, unless when they are borne out by official documents, or are the reports of witnesses. In this case Hall's version of the chancellor's speech has no such confirmation, nor is it in harmony with the course of events. Wolsey had pleaded guilty, as regards the Statute of Premunire, for exercising the office of legate, and had surrendered his property to the king. Sir Thomas could, therefore, allude to his "fall" at the time of his own installation without injustice. But the references in this supposed speech at the opening of parliament can only be to the forty-four articles or charges of maladministration. Now these were not brought before parliament until 1st December, and though Sir Thomas More's name, with the names of other members of the Council, was then placed upon the bill, he was not the man to prejudge Wolsey, and to call him by opprobrious names a month before a charge was formulated against him. There is also an evident anachronism in speaking of his "gentle correction" for his "fraudulent juggling". The only correction hitherto was for the public exercise of his legatine powers.†

---

* Hall, followed verbatim by Grafton and Holinshed.

† The bill of attainder was either withdrawn or rejected in parliament; but the cardinal was convicted before the King's Bench (*Letters and Papers*, iv. 6075). It must have been under the influence of these fabricated speeches that a Catholic writer in the *Dublin Review* (June, 1858, p. 258) allowed himself to speak of More as moved by "feelings of the meanest and most malignant nature," and of repaying the friendship of Wolsey "by supplanting, and then co-operating in his ruin". Supplanting! Why Erasmus tells us that it was Wolsey himself who proposed More as his only fit successor. (*See* Appendix D.)

The same chroniclers tell us that, on the 30th March, 1531, the chancellor thus addressed the House of Commons: " You of this worshipful House, I am sure, be not ignorant, but you know well, that the king, our sovereign lord, hath married his brother's wife ; for she was both wedded and bedded with his brother, Prince Arthur. If this marriage be good or no, many clerks do doubt ; " then, after the opinions of some foreign universities had been read out to them, More concluded (according to Hall) as follows: " Now you of the Common House may repeat in your countries what you have seen and heard, and then all men shall openly perceive that the king hath not attempted this matter of will or pleasure, as some strangers report, but only for the discharge of his conscience and surety of the succession of his realm." Burnet has founded on these words an argument that More was a partisan of the divorce. " He was a man," says Burnet, " of greater integrity than to have said this if he had thought the marriage good, so that he has either afterwards changed his mind, or did at that time dissemble too artificially with the king."* More was neither a dissembler nor did he change his mind. Hall and his followers have twisted a message he spoke in the king's name into a declaration of his own opinions. This is not a conjecture, but is proved by the words of Roper, as well as of one who knew More intimately, and wrote at the very time. Roper says he carried the king's message, " not showing of what mind himself was therein ". The Imperial ambassador, Chapuys, in a letter to Charles V. on the 2nd April, 1531, says that " on the 30th March the chancellor declared to the lords in parliament, by command of the king, that there were some who had said that the king was pursuing the divorce out of love for some lady, and not out of scruples of conscience, and that this was not true ". (Such was the king's message ; the responsibility for it, if it were false, rested, of course, with the king.) Chapuys adds : " Hereupon some

* *History of the Reformation.* In his Appendix against Sander, iv 552 (ed. Pocock).

asked the chancellor for his opinion; on which he said that
he had many times already declared it to the king, and said no
more. The chancellor then went down to the Commons, and
made the same declaration on the part of the king." *

The life of Sir Thomas More may be told intelligibly without
entering into the details of the momentous crisis through which
the Church in England was then passing. It will be sufficient
to allude to the then ambiguous and mysterious title of Supreme
Head of the Anglican Church, the recognition of which the king
was requiring from the clergy, before accepting their subsidy
and withdrawing the prosecution for violating the Statute
of Premunire by accepting Wolsey as papal legate. I have
shown elsewhere † that, though this title was not then put
forward in opposition to the supremacy of the Holy See, it had
something novel and perilous about it, that boded evil to the
liberties and rights of the Church in England. The title was
given, with the saving clause "so far as the law of Christ
allows," on 11th February, 1531. On the 20th Chapuys wrote:
"There is no one that does not blame this usurpation, except
those who have promoted it. The chancellor is so mortified
at it that he is anxious above all things to resign his office." ‡
It is clear from this that his voice had ceased to have any weight in
the royal councils ; § yet either his name gave prestige to the
government, or the king was still in hopes of gaining him to
his side, or there was no pretext for his deposition. A year
later, 13th May, 1532, Chapuys again wrote : " Parliament is

---

* *Letters and Papers*, v. 171. Chapuys' despatches were not known
to Burnet, but More's own declaration to Cromwell was known to him.
He read it so carelessly, or with such prejudice, that what More says
about the king's *hope* and *comfort* regarding the invalidity of the bull of
dispensation Burnet has supposed to be More's hope. The words of
More show that he did not even make a pretence that the king was eager
to calm his scrupulous conscience.

† In my *Life of Blessed John Fisher*, ch. ix.

‡ *Letters and Papers*, v. 112.

§ The council books of this period are lost.

discussing the revocation of all synodal and other constitutions made by the English clergy, and the prohibition of holding synods without express licence of the king. This is a strange thing. Churchmen will be of less account than shoemakers, who have the power of assembling and making their own statutes. The king also wishes bishops not to have the power to arrest persons accused of heresy. The chancellor and the bishops oppose him. *He is very angry, especially with the chanceller* and the Bishop of Winchester, and is determined to carry the matter." * This was written only three days before More resigned the office he could no longer hold with a good conscience. †

It is clear that, throughout these critical years, the chancellor had taken as little part as might be in political life, and had confined himself to his duties as a judge. To these we must now turn.

* *Letters and Papers*, v. 1013.

† It may be of interest to many to know what Sir Thomas thought of synods and convocations. I take the following passage from his *Apology*, written in 1533 : "I suppose he calleth those assemblings at their convocations by the name of confederacies, and he giveth a good thing and a wholesome, an odious, heinous name. For if they did assemble oftener, and there did the things for which such assemblies of the clergy in every province through all Christendom from the beginning were institute and devised, much more good might have grown thereof than the long disuse can suffer us now to perceive. But as for my days, as far as I have heard, nor as I suppose a good part of my father's neither, they came never together to convocation, but at the request of the king, and at their such assemblies concerning spiritual things have very little done. Wherefore, that they have been in that great necessary point of their duty so negligent, whether God suffer to grow to a secret, un-perceived cause of division and grudge against them, God, whom their such negligence hath, I fear me, sore offended, knoweth. But surely if this 'Pacifier' call those assemblies confederacies, I would not greatly wish to be confederate with them, for I could never wit them yet assemble for any great winning, but come up to their travail, labour, cost and pain, and tarry and talk, *et cetera*, and so get them home again " (*English Works*, p. 914).

Sir James Mackintosh, by the aid of researches into legal records, has shown how greatly the business in chancery increased after the time of More. "At the utmost, he did not hear more than two hundred cases and arguments yearly, including those of every description. No authentic account of any case tried before him, if any such be extant, has been yet brought to light. No law book alludes to any part of his judgments or reasonings. Nothing of this higher part of his judicial life is preserved which can warrant us in believing more than that it must have displayed his never-failing integrity, reason, learning and eloquence."* In the absence, then, of official documents we are grateful for the reminiscences of his son-in-law, Roper, and the notes of Stapleton.

Though Wolsey had been a diligent as well as an impartial judge, the business of the court of chancery, owing to the multitude of his political cares, had fallen into arrears, and very shortly before his removal from office, a commission had been issued to assist him.† Stapleton writes: "The chancellor's court is so loaded with business that it scarcely ever happens that there are not innumerable causes pending there. Certainly when More took the office there were causes that had remained undecided for twenty years. He presided so dexterously and successfully that once, after taking his seat and deciding a case, when the next case was called it was found that there was no second case for trial. Such a thing is said never to have happened before or since." ‡

"Courts of law," writes Mackintosh, "were jealous then, as since, of the power assumed by chancellors to issue injunctions to parties to desist from doing certain acts which they were by law entitled to do, until the court of chancery should determine whether the exercise of the legal right would not work injustice." Roper relates that though Sir Thomas granted but few injunc-

---

* *Life of More*, p. 125.   † 11th June, 1529.
‡ *Vita Mori*, cap. 3.

tions, yet the judges complained, and their complaints coming to Roper's ears he informed his father-in-law. Thereupon he caused the chief clerk to make a docket of the injunctions already passed by him or still depending in any of the courts. Which done he invited all the judges to dine with him in the council chamber at Westminster; where, after dinner, when he had broken with them what complaints he had heard of injunctions, and moreover showed them both the number and causes of every one of them, upon full debating they were forced to confess that they, in like case, could have done no otherwise themselves. He then offered that if they would at their own discretion, as they were, he thought, in conscience bound, mitigate and reform the rigour of the law themselves, he would issue no more injunctions. This they refused. After that he said secretly to me : 'I perceive, son, why they like not so to do ; for they see that they may, by the verdict of the jury, cast off all quarrels upon them, which they do account their chief defence '."

"He used commonly," says Roper, "every afternoon to sit in his open hall,* to the intent that if any person had any suit unto him, they might the more boldly come to his presence and then open their complaints before him. Whose manner was also to read every bill himself, before he would award any *subpœna*, and then would either set his hand to it or cancel it." †

"One of his sons-in-law on a time said merrily to him that when Cardinal Wolsey was lord chancellor, not only they of his privy chamber, but also his door-keeper, got great gain under him, and seeing he had married one of his daughters, he thought he might reasonably look for some ; but as the chancellor now kept no doors shut, and all had access to his presence, this state of things might be very commendable to the judge, but was not very profitable to his son-in-law, since

* This seems to mean his hall at Chelsea. The chancellors frequently heard cases in their own houses.

† Roper, p. 13.

he could not accept a fee for getting for those who asked his assistance what they could get equally well without him. Sir Thomas praised his scrupulous conscience. 'But there are many other ways, son,' said he, 'that I may do you good and pleasure your friend also—I might help your client by word or letter, or give his case precedence, or if I saw his case not the best I might move the parties to arbitration. Howbeit this one thing, son, I assure thee on my faith, that if the parties will at my hands call for justice, then were it my father stood on one side and the devil on the other, the devil should have his right, if his cause were good.' " *

It is right to say that Sir James Mackintosh thinks the favours indicated by Sir Thomas would have been " altogether dishonest," and that he would have recoiled from these in practice.†

Another son-in-law, Giles Heron, presuming in Sir Thomas's favour, would in no way make a compromise with his opponent, and the result was that when the pleadings were at an end, the chancellor made a decree against him.

Cresacre More tells a tale which, if it is not to be classed with the judgment of Solomon, shows at least that humour could be allied with justice. A beggar woman had lost her dog, and the finder had presented it to Lady More, who kept it a fortnight and grew fond of it. The owner, having traced the dog, complained to Sir Thomas. He sent at once for the lady and the dog. He was sitting in his hall, and, asking his wife to go to the upper end and the beggar to the lower end, while he himself held the dog, he bade them both call it. The dog at once ran to the poor beggar woman, and the judge decided in her favour; but Lady More purchased it from her

---

* *Ib.*, p. 12.

† Sir James, however, is mistaken in saying that the story is due to Cresacre More, who was not a lawyer, and only wrote what had reached him by tradition. Roper is the authority, and he was a lawyer, and reported what More said to himself.

with a piece of gold that would have bought three dogs, so that all parties were agreed as well as amused.

Stapleton has preserved a story that perhaps belongs to the time when More was under-sheriff rather than to his chancellorship. While More was presiding in court, assisted by other magistrates, a gang of cut-purses was brought up for trial. One of the magistrates, an old man, thereupon broke out into a vehement tirade against the citizens, who, by looking so carelessly after their purses, encourage these thefts. More found means to postpone the case till the next day, and meanwhile arranged with one of the thieves what should be done, promising him favour if he succeeded. The next day, when the case came on for trial, the thief declared that he could clear himself, but could only do so by making a secret and important communication to one of the judges. More told him to choose whom he would, and he at once chose the old magistrate who had spoken so sharply. While pretending to whisper something into his ear he managed (as had been arranged by More) to abstract the old man's purse, and returned to his place, giving to More a sign that he had been successful. Soon after More proposed a collection in court for some special object of pity, but when the old magistrate looked for his purse to make his contribution, to his dismay it was gone. He declared that he had it when he took his seat. More thereupon, amid much laughter, called on the thief to restore the purse, and gently admonished the magistrate not to be so severe in censuring other men's carelessness.*

These and similar stories may seem both insignificant and misplaced in the record of the supreme judge of a nation, but it often happens that a jest is immortal, while a legal judgment filled with ancient saws and modern instances finds no chronicler. There remains another aspect of More's chancellorship that will demand special treatment. Stories are told

* *Vita*, cap. 13.

not merely of severity, but of cruelty to heretics. I will
reserve the examination of these for a separate chapter, in
which both his acts and writings against the Lollards and
Lutherans must be dealt with in some detail.

What is rightly called the submission of the clergy, or their
surrender of the right of independent legislation, coincided
with the resignation of the great seal by Sir Thomas More.
The official memorandum informs us that he delivered it into
the king's hands in the garden of York Place, near Westminster,
at 3 p.m., on 16th May, 1532, in presence of the Duke of
Norfolk.* Chapuys wrote on 22nd : "The chancellor has
resigned, seeing that affairs were going on badly and likely to
be worse, and that if he retained his office he would be obliged
to act against his conscience, or incur the king's displeasure, as
he had already begun to do, for refusing to take his part against
the clergy. His excuse was that his salary was too small, and
that he was not equal to the work. Everyone is concerned, for
there never was a better man in the office." †

A characteristic story has been preserved by Roper, which
must be given in his own words : "Whereas upon the holy days
during his high chancellorship one of his gentlemen, when service at the church was done, ordinarily used to come to my lady
his wife's pew door, and say unto her, 'Madam, my lord is gone';
the next holy day after the surrender of his office, and departure
of his gentlemen from him, he came unto my lady his wife's
pew himself, and making a low courtesy said unto her :
'Madam, my lord is gone'. But she, thinking this at first to
be one of his jests, was little moved, till he told her sadly
[seriously] that he had given up the great seal. Whereupon,
she speaking some passionate words, he called his daughters
then present to see if they could not spy some fault about their
mother's dressing ; but they after search saying they could not
find none, he replied : 'Do you not perceive that your

---

* Rymer, xiv. 433.   † *Letters and Papers*, v. 1046.

mother's nose standeth somewhat awry ? ' Of which jeer the provoked lady was so sensible that she went away from him in a rage." * Roper seems here somewhat to have spoilt his story by omitting the words of the lady, which may have given some occasion and point to this otherwise rather rude bantering.

Sir John More had lived to witness his son's elevation, but died before his resignation.† It has been already mentioned that the chancellor, passing the court of King's Bench on his way to the chancery, if his father was already seated, would go in and ask his blessing on his knees. " When Sir John lay on his deathbed," says Roper, " Sir Thomas, according to his duty, oftentimes with comfortable words most kindly came to visit him, and at his departure out of this world with tears, taking him about the neck, most lovingly kissed and embraced him, commending him into the hands of Almighty God." If the son who thus honoured his father did not enjoy a long life, it was because God had better things in store for him in the land of the living.

* Roper's *Notes*, n. 18.   † His will was proved 5th Dec., 1530.

CHAPTER XIII.

AFTER THE RESIGNATION.

ROPER writes as follows : " After he had given over the chancellorship, and placed all his gentlemen and yeomen with noblemen and bishops, and his eight watermen with my Lord Audely, that in the same office succeeded him, to whom also he gave his great barge—then, he called us all that were his children to him, and asked our advice how we might now live. By the surrender of his office he could not, as he had been wont, bear the whole charges of the family himself, yet he was unwilling they should separate. When he saw us silent, he said : ' Then I will show my poor mind to you. I have been brought up at Oxford, at an Inn of the Chancery, at Lincoln's Inn, and also in the king's court, and so from the least degree to the highest. And yet have I in yearly revenues at this present left me a little over a hundred pounds a year.* So that now must we hereafter, if we like to live together, be contented to become contributors together. But by my counsel it shall not be best for us to fall to the lowest fare first. We will not, therefore, descend to Oxford fare, nor to the fare of New Inn ; but we will begin with Lincoln's Inn diet, where many right worshipful and of good years do live full well together. Which, if we find not ourselves able to maintain the first year, then will we the next year go one step down to New Inn fare, wherewith many an honest man is well contented. If that exceed our ability too, then we will the next year after descend to Oxford fare, where many grave, learned and ancient

* Say £1200 in modern value.

fathers be continually conversant. Which if our power stretch
not to maintain, then may we yet with bags and wallets go a-
begging together, and hoping that for pity some good folks will
give us their charity, at every man's door to sing *Salve Regina*,
and so still keep company and be merry together." It would
seem, however, that his sons-in law were too generous to accept
this offer. Stapleton informs us that the family was broken up,
only Roper and his wife remaining in Chelsea, though not in
their father's house.*

Thus, as Roper remarks, he had given up a most lucrative
position to enter the king's service, in which he had spent the
most vigorous and best part of his life; he had never been extravagant, yet when his official salary ceased he had not saved
enough for household expenses. "The lands that he had purchased were not," says his son-in-law, "I am assured, above the
value of 20 marks a year (£13 6s. 8d.), and after his debts
paid he had not, I know (his chain excepted), in gold and silver
left him the worth of £100." He had sold his plate, says
Stapleton, for about £400. Roper speaks only of lands *purchased*. Sir Thomas, in a work written in 1533, called *The
Apology*, says: "As for all the lands and fees that I have in
all England, besides such lands and fees as I have of the king's
most noble grace, is not at this day, nor shall be while my
mother-in-law liveth (whose life and good health I pray God
long keep and continue) worth yearly to my living the sum of
full £50. And thereof have I some by my wife, and some by
my father (whose soul Our Lord assoil), and some have I also
purchased myself.†

* *Vita*, cap. 15.

† *English Works*, p. 867. Harpsfield mentions a circumstance which
shows how far economy had to be practised: " He was compelled for the
lack of other fuel, every night before he went to bed, to cause a great
burden of fern to be brought into his own chamber, and with the blaze
thereof to warm himself, his wife and his children, and so without any
other fires to go to their beds " (MS. *Life*). This was of course before
the dispersion of the family.

When Archbishop Warham resigned the chancellorship, in 1515, More had written to him a letter of congratulation that may be applied to himself in 1532: "I ever judged your paternity happy in the way you exercised your office of chancellor, but I esteem you much happier now that you have laid it down and entered on that most desirable leisure, in which you can live for yourself and for God. Such leisure, in my opinion, is not only more pleasant than the labour you have forsaken, but more honourable than all your honours. To be a judge is the lot of many, and sometimes of very bad men. But you possessed that supreme office which, when relinquished, is as much exposed to calumny as it formerly conferred authority and independence; and to give up this willingly is what none but a moderate-minded man would care, and none but an innocent man dare, to do."*

Sir Thomas now was in this position. The king had, indeed, both promised him his continued favour, and commanded the Duke of Norfolk to pronounce his eulogy when inducting his successor. It was, however, well known that the king was dissatisfied and disappointed, and that the late chancellor had enemies at court, especially in the party of Anne Boleyn, so that it was not without hope of success that some serious charges were brought against him. He was accused by a man named Parnell that a Mrs. Vaughan, the wife of his adversary, had carried to the chancellor a large silver-gilt cup as a bribe, and that a decree had been given in favour of Vaughan. Sir Thomas was called before the Council. He acknowledged that such a cup had indeed been offered to him as a New-Year's gift, though long after the decree, and that he had accepted it out of courtesy. The Earl of Wiltshire (the father of Anne Boleyn) at once exclaimed: "Ah! did I not tell you, my lords, that you would find the matter true?" Sir Thomas begged leave to complete the tale. When he had, not without much ado, received the

---

* The letter, which is in Latin, is in full in Stapleton, cap. 6.

cup, he called his butler to fill it with wine, drank to the lady, and made her pledge him again. He had then obliged her to receive back the cup once more, and to take it as his New-Year's gift to her husband. The lady was summoned, and deposed to the truth of this.

He had made a decree in favour of a Mrs. Croker, a widow, against Lord Arundell. At the New-Year she presented him with a pair of gloves and £40 in angels within them. He said to her : " Mistress, it were against good manners to forsake a gentlewoman's New-Year's gift. I am, therefore, content to take your gloves; but as for your money, I must utterly refuse it."

A Mr. Gresham, who had a cause pending, had sent him at the New-Year a silver-gilt cup, of which he much admired the shape. He had accepted it, but by the messenger had sent him one in return of greater value.

Roper says he could have related many similar instances of his integrity.[*]

More did not forget to inform his old friend Erasmus of his retirement from office :—

" From the time I was a boy I have longed, dear Desiderius, that what I rejoice in you having always enjoyed I myself might some day enjoy also—namely, that being free from public business, I might have some time to devote to God and myself ; that, by the grace of a great and good God, and by the favour of an indulgent prince, I have at last obtained. I have not, however, obtained it as I wished. For I wished to reach that last stage of my life in a state, which, though suitable to my age, might yet enable me to enjoy my remaining years healthy and unbroken, free from disease and pain. But it remains in the hand of God whether this wish, perhaps unreasonable, shall be accomplished. Meanwhile a disorder of I know not what nature has attacked my chest, by which I suffer less in present

* *Notes*, n. 24, 25.

pain than in fear of the consequence. For when it had plagued me without abatement some months, the physicians whom I consulted gave their opinion that the long continuance of it was dangerous, and the speedy cure impossible ; but that it must be cured by the gradual alterative effects of time, proper diet, and medicine. Neither could they fix the period of my recovery nor ensure me a complete cure at last. Considering this, I saw that I must either lay down my office or discharge my duty in it incompletely. . . .

"From my house at Chelsea, 14th June, 1532." *

This letter was detained some months in Saxony before it reached its destination at Basle, as Erasmus informs his friend, John Faber, Bishop of Vienna. In the meantime the report spread rapidly over Europe that More had been deposed, and that his successor had at once liberated all those whom More had cast into prison for their religious teachings or professions. The bishop had written to Erasmus to learn the truth. Erasmus replied that he had been quite sure the report was false before he received More's letter, a copy of which he enclosed to the bishop. He explained the nature of the chancellorship in England, and made the highest eulogy of the manner in which More had held that charge.

"As to what is said about the opening of the prisons," continues Erasmus, "I do not know what the truth may be. One thing is certain : that More is a man by nature most gentle, and that he never molested anyone, who, after being admonished, was willing to relinquish the sectarian contagion. Do these newsmongers mean that the supreme judge in such a country as England should have no prison ? Certainly More hates the seditious doctrines which are disturbing the whole world. He does not conceal this nor wish it to be secret, being a man so devout that if he inclines to any extreme it is rather towards superstition than impiety. But it is a great

* *Epist. Erasm.*, 1223.

proof of his clemency that, while he was chancellor, not one underwent capital punishment for condemned doctrines, while so many have suffered in Germany and France. Certainly that man has a clement hatred of the impious who, when he has the power of putting them to death, strives only to cure the vices and save the vicious. Do they wish that he who fills the place of the king should favour seditious novelty against the judgment of the king and the bishops? Let us suppose— what, however, is far from the truth—that he had no great aversion from these new doctrines, either he would be bound to conceal his partiality or to resign his office.

"But let us pass over here all contention about doctrines; who does not know how many light and seditious men are ready, under the pretence of doctrine, to commit freely every crime, unless the severity of the magistrates put a rein on their growing audacity? Yet these newsmongers are indignant when the supreme judge in the kingdom of England does what, in the cities which have embraced the new opinions, the senate is sometimes forced to do. And had it not been done long ago, these false evangelicals would have burst into the inner-most chambers and store-rooms of the rich, and everyone would have been called a papist who had anything to lose. Already so great is the audacity and so unbridled the malice of many, that even those who are the inventors and propa-gators of the new dogmas, have written sharply against them. And yet they want the supreme judge in England to connive at the innovations, until the whole *swarm* of sects shall have spread with impunity over the kingdom—a kingdom flourishing beyond others in riches, in learning, and in religion. It may be indeed that, in honour of the new chancellor, some have been set free from prison, such as were harmless or confined for lighter crimes; for such is also the custom at the accession of a new king, in order to gain the goodwill of the people; and I fancy that was done when More entered on his office. But what is it that these scatterers of false tales propose? Is it to convince the sects, and favourers of sects, that a safe retreat is at hand for them in England? Why, from letters that have reached me from most trustworthy men, it appears that the king is even less tolerant of the new doctrines than the bishops and priests. There is no man of any piety who would not wish to see a reform of morals in the Church, but no one of any prudence considers it right to tolerate universal confusion."

Erasmus then goes on to express his satisfaction at More's timely escape from the absorbing cares of State; he describes his house on the banks of the Thames, and his delightful household, which he compares to a Platonic academy, but of a Christian Plato. "In the church of his village he has constructed a family tomb, to which he has translated the bones of his first wife, so little does he approve of any divorce.* On the wall he has placed a tablet, with the record of his life and his intentions, which my secretary has written out for you, word for word. I see I have been too talkative, but it is pleasant to converse with a friend about a friend." †

In the summer of 1533,‡ More refers to this epitaph in a letter to Erasmus: "The heretic Tyndale, my fellow-countryman, who is in exile nowhere and everywhere, has written to England lately that Melanchthon is now with the king of France; that he himself has spoken with one who saw him received at Paris with a retinue of 150 horse. Tyndale added that he was afraid that should France receive the word of God from Melanchthon, it would be confirmed in his belief con-

---

* *Usque adeo illi non placet ullum divortium.* Besides their obvious meaning, the words would appear to hint at More's aversion to the royal divorce.

† *Ep.* 426, in App. There is no date, but the letter must have been written at the end of 1532 or early in 1533.

‡ The letter (inter. Epist. Erasm., 461, in App.), has no date, but refers to Cranmer, the new archbishop, and his liberality to Erasmus. Cranmer was consecrated March 30, 1533.

cerning the Eucharist in opposition to Wycliffe's sect. See how carefully these fellows treat this matter, as if God had committed to them the instruction and nurture of the world in the rudiments of faith.

"As to what you wrote, that you had hesitated about publishing my letter, though there were reasons that made you wish to publish it, you need not hesitate at all. Some gossips here have been spreading it about that I had to resign against my will, though I pretend it was not so. So when I set up my tomb, I determined to state the matter as it is in my epitaph, that any one might refute it who could. As soon as they had taken note of it, as they could not show it to be false, they found fault with it as boastful. I preferred this to allowing the other rumour to gain ground, not indeed for my own sake, for I do not care very much what men say of me, provided that God approves of me; but since I had written in our own tongue some little books against some of our defenders of contentious doctrines, I considered that I ought to defend the integrity of my name; and that you may know how boastfully I have written you shall receive my epitaph, by which you will see that in my security of conscience I by no means flatter them, to prevent them from saying about me whatever they please. I have waited now till the meeting of parliament, since I exercised and resigned my office, but as yet no one has come forward to attack me· Either I have been so innocent or else so cautious, that my opponents must let me boast of one or other of these qualities.

"But as regards this business, the king has spoken many times privately, and twice in public. For in words which I am ashamed to repeat, when my successor (a most illustrious man) was installed, the king, by the mouth of the Duke of Norfolk, the Lord High Treasurer of England, ordered an honourable testimony to be given that with difficulty he had yielded to my request to retire. And not contented with this, the king, out of his singular goodness to me, had the same thing repeated by my successor in his own presence, at the solemn assembly of the peers and commons, in the speech which is made at the opening of parliament.

"If then you think it expedient you need not hesitate to publish my letter. As to what I profess in my letter that I gave trouble to heretics, I took pride in writing this.* For I so entirely detest that race of men, that there is none to which I would be more hostile, unless they amend. For every day more and more, I find them to be of such a sort, that I greatly fear for what they are bringing on the world." †

I give this famous epitaph in the old translation of Rastell: "Thomas More, a Londoner born, of no noble family, but of an honest stock, somewhat brought up in learning; after that in his young days he had been a pleader in the laws of this hall ‡ certain years, being one of the under-sheriffs of London, was of noble King Henry the Eight (which alone of all kings worthily deserved both with sword and pen to be called the Defender of the Faith, a glory afore not heard of) called into the court, and chose one of the Council and made knight; then made first under-treasurer of England, after that chancellor of the Duchy of Lancaster, and last of all, with great favour of his prince, lord chancellor of England. But in the mean season, he was chosen speaker of the parliament, and besides was divers times in divers places the king's ambassador, and last of all at Cambray, joined fellow and companion with Cuthbert Tunstal, chief of that embassy, then Bishop of London, and within a while after Bishop of Durham, who so excelleth in learning, wit and virtue, that the whole world scant hath at this day any more learned, wiser or better; where he both joyfully saw and was present ambassador when the leagues

---

* Hoc ambitiose feci.

† Inter Epist. Erasm , 466, in App.

‡ Perhaps a misprint for "realm".

between the chief princes of Christendom were renewed again, and peace so long looked for restored to Christendom, which peace Our Lord stablish and make perpetual.

"When he had thus gone through this course of offices or honours, that neither that gracious prince could disallow his doings, nor he was odious to the nobility nor unpleasant to the people, but yet to thieves, murderers and heretics grievous, at last John More, his father, knight, and chosen of the prince to be one of the justices of the King's Bench, a civil man, pleasant, harmless, gentle, pitiful, just and uncorrupted, in years old, but in body more than for his years lusty, after that he perceived his life so long lengthened, that he saw his son lord chancellor of England. thinking himself now to have lived long enough, gladly departed to God. His son then, his father being dead, to whom as long as he lived being compared was wont both to be called young and himself so thought too, missing now his father departed, and seeing four children of his own, and of their offspring eleven, began in his own conceit to wax old; and this affection of his was increased by a certain sickly disposition of his breast, even by and by following, as a sign or token of age creeping upon him. He, therefore, irked and weary of worldly business, giving up his promotions, obtained at last by the incomparable benefit of his most gentle prince, if it please God to favour his enterprise, the thing which from a child in a manner always he wished and desired: that he might have some years of his life free, in which he little and little withdrawing himself from the business of this life, might continually remember the immortality of the life to come. And he hath caused this tomb to be made for himself, his first wife's bones hither too, that might every day put him in memory of death that never ceases to creep on him. And that this tomb made for him in his life-time be not in vain, nor that he fear death coming upon him, but that he may willingly, for the desire of Christ, die and find death not utterly death to him, but the gate of a wealthier life, help him, I beseech you, good

reader, now with your prayers while he liveth, and when he is
dead also."

The epitaph concludes with some Latin verses, which I give
in the very literal translation of Archdeacon Wrangham :—

> Within this tomb Jane, wife of More, reclines;
> This More for Alice and himself designs.
> The first, dear object of my youthful vow,
> Gave me three daughters and a son to know;
> The next—ah! virtue in a stepdame rare!—
> Nursed my sweet infants with a mother's care.
> With both my years so happily have past,
> Which most my love, I know not—first or last.
> Oh! had religion destiny allowed,
> How smoothly mixed had our three fortunes flowed!
> But, be we in the tomb, in heaven allied,
> So kinder death shall grant what life denied. *

* From Cayley's *Life of More*, i. 134.

CHAPTER XIV.

TREATMENT OF HERETICS.

IN his epitaph More designedly and emphatically stated that he had been "troublesome to thieves, murderers, and heretics" (*furibus, homicidis, hæreticisque molestus*). We have seen Erasmus's commentary on these words. It is necessary, however, to study their force, not as apologists, but as historians. Whom does More designate as heretics? In what way did he trouble or "molest" them? In molesting them, did he contradict the principles he had laid down in his *Utopia* about toleration? Did he remain within, or did he go beyond the law as it existed in his time?

There is a long-standing tradition that he was not merely severe, which may seem to be justified by his own words, but even arbitrary and unjust. And as his amiable and upright character is admitted on all hands, the blame of this warp in his character and blot on his fame is cast on the religion which he professed. We have seen Horace Walpole writing of "that cruel judge whom one knows not how to hate, who persecuted others in defence of superstitions he had himself exposed". It is probable that Walpole derived this view of Sir Thomas More from Burnet's *History of the Reformation*.

Burnet writes : " More was not governed by interest, nor did he aspire so to preferment as to stick at nothing that might contribute to raise him ; nor was he subject to the vanities of popularity. The integrity of his whole life and the severity of his morals cover him from all these suspicions. If he had been formerly corrupted by a superstitious education, it had been no extraordinary thing to see so good a man grow to be misled by the force of prejudice. But how a man who had emancipated himself, and had got into a scheme of free thoughts, could be so entirely changed cannot be easily apprehended, nor how he came to muffle up his understanding and deliver himself up as a property to the blind and enraged fury of the priests. It cannot, indeed, be accounted for but by charging it on the intoxicating charms of that religion, that can darken the clearest understandings and corrupt the best natures ; and since they wrought this effect on Sir Thomas More, I cannot but conclude that 'if these things were done in the green tree, what shall be done in the dry ? ' " *

In our own day the same accusation of cruelty, and the same explanation, have been renewed by a popular historian. Mr. Froude writes · "Wolsey had chastised them [the innovators] with whips ; Sir Thomas More would chastise them with scorpions, and the philosopher of the *Utopia*, the friend of Erasmus, whose life was of blameless beauty, whose genius was cultivated to the highest attainable perfection, was to prove to the world that the spirit of persecution is no peculiar attribute of the pedant, the bigot, or the fanatic, but may co-exist with the fairest graces of the human character. The lives of re- markable men usually illustrate some emphatic truth. Sir Thomas More may be said to have lived to illustrate the necessary tendencies of Romanism, in an honest mind convinced of the truth ; to show that the test of sincerity in a man who professes to regard orthodoxy as an essential of salvation is not the readiness to endure persecution, but the courage that will venture to inflict it."†

* *History of Reformation*, iii. 98 (Pocock). When Burnet thus wrote the penal laws against the Catholics were making their lives a burden.

† *History of England*, ii. 73. It is instructive to mark that what Burnet calls vaguely "intoxicating charms" Froude calls dogmatic faith, and a belief that faith is required by God for salvation.

Such is the accusation. Let us now hear Sir Thomas's own statement of the case, made in the spring of 1533 : "As touching heretics, I hate that vice of theirs and not their persons, and very fain would I that the one were destroyed and the other saved. And that I have toward no man any other mind than this—how loudly soever these blessed new brethren and professors and preachers of heresy belie me—if all the favour and pity that I have used among them to their amendment were known, it would, I warrant you, well and plain appear ; whereof, if it were requisite, I could bring forth witnesses more than men would ween.

"Howbeit, because it were neither right nor honesty that any man should look for more thank than he deserveth, I will that all the world wit it on the other side, that who so be so deeply grounded in malice, to the harm of his own soul and other men's too, and so set upon the sowing of seditious heresies, that no good means that men may use unto him can pull that malicious folly out of his poisoned, proud, obstinate heart, I would rather be content that he were gone in time, than overlong to tarry to the destruction of other." *

If, then, Sir Thomas More requires a defence, no such apology can be set up for him as may be valid for the judges, who administered our cruel penal code with regard to theft, in the early years of the present century—viz., that not being legislators they were not responsible for the barbarity of the laws, and that being judges they were bound to pass sentence according to the laws as they found them. Such a defence is not applicable to the case of Sir Thomas More. It would exonerate him from any charge of *injustice*, if it can be shown (as it certainly can) that he did not go beyond the law. But as regards the imputation of a cruel disposition, Sir Thomas would reject a defence based on the supposition that he was the reluctant administrator of laws, the existence of which he

* *Apology*, ch. xlix. ; *English Works*, p. 925.

regretted. In his *Apology*, written after he had ceased to act as judge, he fully and heartily approves of the laws, both ecclesiastical and civil, that then existed in England against heresy, and he maintains that these laws had been administered with the utmost leniency and indeed with a dangerous laxity.*

The first question then that occurs is with regard to More's consistency. Did his later theories and practice contradict the more generous philosophy of his youth? That the reader may judge for himself, I will give without abridgment a passage from *Utopia* in Burnet's translation.

After stating that in Utopia there were several sorts of religion— some idolatrous, some monotheistical—and that the higher views were gradually setting aside the others, Raphael (the supposed traveller) says that Christianity also had been lately introduced by himself and his companions. He then continues as follows:—

"Those among them that have not received our religion do not fright any from it, and use none ill that goes over to it, so that all the while I was there one man only was punished on this occasion. He being newly baptised did, notwithstanding all that we could say to the contrary, dispute publicly concerning the Christian religion, with more zeal than discretion, and with so much heat, that he not only preferred our worship to theirs, but condemned all their rites as profane, and cried out against all that adhered to them as impious and sacrilegious persons, that were to be damned to everlasting burnings. Upon his having frequently preached in this manner he was seized, and after trial he was condemned to banishment, not for having disparaged their religion, but for his inflaming the people to sedition; for this is one of their most ancient laws, that no man ought to be punished for his religion.

"At the first constitution of their government, Utopus understood that, before his coming among them, the old inhabitants had been engaged in great quarrels concerning religion, by

---

* So also in his defence of his *Apology* (Salem and Bizance, ch. xiv., p. 958), etc.

which they were so divided among themselves, that he found it an easy thing to conquer them, since, instead of uniting their forces against him, every different party in religion fought by themselves. After he had subdued them he made a law that every man might be of what religion he pleased, and might endeavour to draw others to it by the force of argument and by amicable and modest ways, but without bitterness against those of other opinions ; but that he ought to use no other force but that of persuasion, and was neither to mix with it reproaches nor violence ; and such as did otherwise were to be condemned to banishment or slavery.

"This law was made by Utopus, not only for preserving the public peace, which he saw suffered much by daily contentions and irreconcilable heats, but because he thought the interest of religion itself required it. He judged it not fit to determine anything rashly ; and seemed to doubt whether those different forms of religion might not all come from God, who might inspire man in a different manner, and be pleased with this variety ; he therefore thought it indecent and foolish for any man to threaten and terrify another to make him believe what did not appear to him to be true.* And supposing that only one religion was really true, and the rest false, he imagined that the native force of truth would at last break forth and shine bright, if supported only by the strength of argument, and attended to with a gentle and unprejudiced mind ; while, on the other hand, if such debates were carried on with violence and tumults, as the most wicked are always the most obstinate, so the best and most holy religion might be choked with superstition, as corn is with briars and thorns ; he therefore left men

---

* Burnet's translation is here rather free. The Latin is " Certe vi ac minis exigere ut, quod tu verum credis idem omnibus videatur, hoc vero et insolens et ineptum censuit," *i.e.*, " To require by violence and threats that what you believe to be true should be accepted as true by all, he thought both indecent and foolish ".

wholly to their liberty, that they might be free to believe as they should see cause.

"Only he made a solemn and severe law against such as should so far degenerate from the dignity of human nature, as to think that our souls died with our bodies, or that the world was governed by chance, without a wise overruling Providence: for they all formerly believed that there was a state of rewards and punishments to the good and bad after this life; and they now look on those that think otherwise as scarce fit to be counted men, since they degrade so noble a being as the soul, and reckon it no better than a beast's: thus they are far from looking on such men as fit for human society, or to be citizens of a well-ordered commonwealth; since a man of such principles must needs, as oft as he dares do it, despise all their laws and customs: for there is no doubt to be made, that a man who is afraid of nothing but the law, and apprehends nothing after death, will not scruple to break through all the laws of his country, either by fraud or force, when by this means he may satisfy his appetites. They never raise any that hold these maxims either to honours or offices, nor employ them in any public trust, but despise them, as men of base and sordid minds. Yet they do not punish them, because they lay this down as a maxim, that a man cannot make himself believe whatever he likes."

This passage of the *Utopia* was no doubt in Burnet's mind when he referred to More's having once "got into a scheme of free thoughts". Sir James Mackintosh, a real lover of liberty, very different from Burnet, has written on this subject as follows: "It is evident that the two philosophers (More and Erasmus), who found all their fair visions dispelled by noise and violence, deeply felt the injustice of citing against them, as a proof of inconsistency, that they departed from the pleasantries, the gay dreams, at most the fond speculations, of their early days, when they saw these harmless visions turned into weapons of destruction in the blood-stained hands of the boors of

Saxony, and of the ferocious fanatics of Munster. The virtuous love of peace might be more prevalent in More: the Epicurean desire of personal ease predominated more in Erasmus. But both were, doubtless from commendable or excusable causes, incensed against those odious disciples, who now, with no friendly voice, invoked their authority against themselves." *

Though I have cited with pleasure this passage from an eminent writer, because it has a bearing on several things written by More in his *Utopia*, I can scarcely adopt it as regards the special matter of toleration we are now consider-ing; for I do not find that More's early theories on this subject were ever brought as a reproach against him during his own lifetime, much less that the innovators whom he resisted and prosecuted ever appealed, in favour of their own liberty, to general principles of toleration. More himself has put the following wish into the mouth of his interlocutor in his *Dialogue* : "I would," says his friend, "all the world were agreed to take all violence and compulsion away, upon all sides, Christian and heathen, and that no man were con-strained to believe but as he could be, by grace, wisdom and good works, induced ; and then he that would go to God, go on in God's name, and he that will go to the devil, the devil go with him".† This is perhaps the modern theory put in a homely way ; but before giving More's answer, let me say that this was not the theory of the Lutherans with whom More had to do. They pleaded for liberty as having exclusively the truth, but they never thought of giving liberty to Catholics. The Mass was to be forcibly abolished as a horrible idolatry, the monks to be dragged from their cloisters, and if necessary whipped at a cart's tail till they would marry and work,‡ and the gospel of Luther forced by the civil power upon the world.

---

* *Life of More*, p. 98.

† *Dialogue*, iv. 13, *English Works*, p. 275.

‡ See Fish's *Supplication of Beggars*. " Tie these holy idle thieves to the carts, to be whipped naked about every market town."

The state of things that More supposes in his *Utopia* had
nothing parallel in that age either among Catholics or Protestants. Some may think that he approximately describes the
present state of England; in which case, could he rise again,
himself unchanged, in our changed state of society, he would
doubtless plead for quiet and mutual forbearance, as did his
Portuguese friend, Raphael, in the conversation at Antwerp.

For my own part, I can find no evidence of change of views,
or of inconsistency in the author of the *Utopia*. In that work
More is discoursing of people who had no revelation from
God, and he condemns their acrimonious disputes and intoler-
ance in matters of pure reason or natural tradition. Before he
can be accused of inconsistency, it should be shown that the
social and religious problems, discussed by him in his later
English writings, were analogous to those contemplated by
King Utopus, and if so, that he solved them differently. Did
he, in later years, teach that men left by God to the pure
exercise of their reason, should not also be left free by their
rulers, "to seek God, if happily they may feel after Him and
find Him"?* Did he ever teach that the unbaptised heathen
should be compelled by force to accept the true faith? Did
he ever teach that men brought up from childhood in heresy,
and in atheism and materialism, and dazed and bewildered by
the multitude of opinions around them, should be punished
because they could not see their way to certainty or unity?
On the contrary, it was because he foresaw this very state of
things as the result of Luther's revolt, and grieved over it
because he foresaw that if once unity were broken up, and
the Catholic faith called in question, the people would be
"tossed about with every wind of doctrine, by the wickedness
of men, by cunning craftiness, by which they lie in wait to
deceive,"† he therefore met these innovations with an energy
inspired no less by his love of freedom of thought, than by his

* *Acts* xvii. 27.   † *Eph.* iv. 14.

love of his country. He thought, and he wrote over and over again, that there was no slavery like the slavery of sectarianism, and no freedom like that enjoyed where all have one unchangeable faith. Did More understand the word heretic as it is generally understood in England at the present day? I am not proposing a theological, but a historical question. I am not asking whether More was right or wrong in his judgment regarding heresy, but what did he mean by it? To most Protestants, orthodoxy can only mean for each man his private opinion or conviction in matters of religion, while heresy can only be a nickname for his neighbour's views. It does not require a mind of More's acuteness, or a character of his fairness, to see at a glance that, in such circumstances, mutual forbearance is the strictest of duties, and that no one should be violently repressed but he who violently disturbs his neighbour.

To More the word heresy conveyed a very different meaning. It was the private choice, by an individual, of a doctrine contradictory to that held to be clearly revealed by the divinely guided society to which that individual had belonged. More himself points out * (and it is his views we are discussing), that according to St. Paul, not only is heresy or faction in religion classed with grievous sins like murder, theft, and adultery,† but it is supposed by him to be as easily recognised and proved; so that the ruler of the spiritual society can admonish and reprove and ultimately reject the criminal, and cast him forth from the society, either delivering him over to Satan, like Hymeneus and Alexander, that he may learn not to blaspheme, or at least warning and commanding the society to avoid him as a pestilence. ‡

To More a heretic was neither a simp'e man erring by ignor-

* *English Works*, p. 823.
† *Gal.* v. 20.
‡ *Tit.* iii. 10; 1 *Tim.* i. 20; 2 *Tim.* ii. 17—passages frequently quoted by More.

ance, nor a learned man using his freedom in doubtful points: he was a man whose heart was "proud, poisoned, and obstinate," because he denied the Divine guidance of the Church into which he had been baptised, while he claimed special Divine inspiration for himself.

But this is not an adequate explanation of More's aversion to Lutheranism and of his conduct towards it. What has been said would apply to all heresy, though it were limited to the most abstruse points of revelation, and though its holder took no pains to propagate it. The zeal, the indignation and the horror of Sir Thomas More were aroused, because to him the Lutheran doctrines, as they first came before the world, appeared as the denial of everything that the Christian people had hitherto held in veneration, and as uprooting the foundation of all morals. We have seen what he wrote about it in his Latin work, under the name of Ross. As time went on he painted it in still darker colours, as fuller accounts came of the excesses in Germany and Switzerland. "Is it not a wonderful thing," he asks, in his *Dialogue*, written in 1528—"Is it not a wonderful thing, that we should now see a lewd friar so bold and shameless to marry a nun and bide thereby, and be taken still for a Christian man, and over that, for a man meet to be the beginner of a sect, whom any honest man would vouchsafe to follow? If our Lord God, whose wisdom is infinite, should have set and studied to devise a way whereby He might cast in our face the confusion of our folly, how might He have founden a more effectual than to suffer us that call ourselves Christian folk, to see such a rabble springing up among us, as let not to set at nought all the doctors of Christ's Church, and lean to the only authority of Friar Tuck and Maid Marion?" *

We have not, however, yet reached the full motive of More's conduct. It was because the buffooneries and infamies of Friar

* *Dialogue*, iv. ch. 9. *English Works*, p. 260. It is perhaps needless to say that Friar Tuck and Maid Marion were the low buffoons in the pageants of Robin Hood.

Tuck were united with the outrages and violence of Robin Hood that More justified their suppression by force. This is the answer he gives to his friend who wished that everyone might be left free to go to the devil if he chose. Yes, replies More, but he shall not drag society with him. It is here I find a perfect consistency with the opinions he had expressed in *Utopia*. King Utopus, he says, having no means of attaining unity, enforced moderation and mutual toleration, where he had found nothing but confusion and bitterness, because that contention had weakened the country and laid it open to foreign conquest. More, on the contrary, was the highest magistrate in a country hitherto in perfect peace and unity in religious matters. The Catholic Church had held exclusive possession of England for nearly a thousand years, and its doctrines, discipline, and institutions had leavened every part of English life. The policy of Utopus would certainly have allowed no heated dissensions to be introduced to break up this unity. He who would not allow the materialists to propagate their opinions, would have given no licence to false spiritualists "to bring in sects blaspheming".

This is the contention of Sir Thomas More throughout his many voluminous works of controversy. He says that "it was the violent cruelty first used by the heretics themselves against good Catholic folk that drove good princes thereto, for preservation not of the faith only, but also of peace among the people".[*] He enters fully into the history of the treatment of heretics. The Church, he maintains, had in no age punished them by death. The State had done it in self-defence, and had called on the Church to define heresy, to judge the fact and deliver the relapsed heretic into the hands of the civil power. The State (he maintains) only did this when it had attained peace and unity by means of the Church, and when it was found by experience that heretics ever stirred up sedition and rebellion,

[*] *English Works*, p. 275. See also p. 570, where he enters into much detail.

and if allowed to spread, brought about division and ruin. He points to the history of Lollardy in England in the time of Henry IV. and Henry V.; and to the fearful results of Lutheranism in Germany, in the violent destruction of the Catholic Church in some lands, the wars of the peasants in others; to the division of the empire making it unable to resist the threatened invasion of the Turks; and to that general break-up of what was called Christendom, which would be the inevitable consequence of the spread of these principles. *

Let us now turn from the theories of More to his personal practice. Was he ever cruel or unjust? It is surely a bold thing to accuse him of this after his own challenge. In 1532 an anonymous writer under the character of a peace-maker had thrown great blame on the proceedings of the clergy, but always in general terms, as, "Some say," "Many say," etc. Sir Thomas writes: "Let this pacifier come forth and appear before the king's Grace and his Council, or in what place he list, and there prove, calling me thereto, that any one of all these had wrong—but if it were for that they were burned no sooner. And because he shall not say that I bid him trot about for naught, this shall I proffer him, that I will bind myself for surety, and find him other twain besides of better substance than myself, that for every one of these whom he proveth wronged, his ordinary or his other officer by whom the wrong was done, shall give this pacifier all his costs about the proo₁ and a reasonable reward besides. And yet now, though no man would give him nothing, it were his part, perdie! to prove it for his own honesty, since he hath said so far." †

This public challenge met with no response in More's life-

* Sir James Mackintosh thinks him unfair in attributing the awful outrages of the Sack of Rome in 1527 mainly to the Lutherans. Dr. Brewer, however, seems to distribute the guilt between the Lutherans and the semi-christianised Saracens in the army of the Constable of Bourbon. What More tells on this subject (Dialogue iv. ch. 7) is too hideous to transcribe.

† Apology, ch. xxv.

time. Thirty years after his death the Protestant martyrologist Foxe brought forward some stories of More's cruelty, which are the sole foundation on which Burnet and other writers have grounded their accusations of his having "delivered himself up as a property to the blind and enraged fury of the priests".

In his account of John Tewkesbury, a pouchmaker or leather-seller of London, Foxe writes as follows : "He was sent from the Lollard's Tower * to my Lord Chancellor's, called Sir Thomas More, to Chelsea, with all his articles [*i.e.*, the articles of accusation], to see whether he could turn him, and that he might accuse others ; and there he lay in the porter's lodge, hand, foot and head in the stocks, six days without release. Then was he carried to *Jesu's Tree* in his privy garden, where he was whipped and also twisted in his brows with a small rope, that the blood started out of his eyes, and yet would not accuse no man. Then was he let loose in the house for a day, and his friends thought to have him at liberty the next day. After this he was sent to be racked in the Tower, till he was almost lame and there promised to recant." †

Again, of James Bainham, a lawyer, Foxe writes that he also was whipped in Sir Thomas's garden at the *Tree of Truth*, and then sent to the Tower to be racked, "and so he was, Sir Thomas More being present himself, till in a manner he had lamed him ".‡

Burnet says that Sir Thomas "looked on, and saw him put to the rack". §

Foxe wrote in the time of Elizabeth, and he has been proved to have picked up every bit of traditional gossip, and to have added so many inventions and embellishments of his own, that unless where he gives documents his testimony is of no value.

As regards Tewkesbury, his first examination, after which he

* Part of old St. Paul's, not of Lambeth.
† *Book of Martyrs,* iv. 689 (ed. Townsend).
‡ *Ib.,* iv. 698.
§ *History of Reformation,* i. 270 (ed. Pocock).

retracted, was on 8th May, 1529, and this was several months
before Sir Thomas was chancellor.   The story, therefore, of
his torture in More's garden is clearly mythical.   Foxe has
strangely mixed up the stories of Tewkesbury and Bainham ;
both are whipped at a tree in Sir Thomas More's garden, though
whether the Tree of Jesus was the same as the Tree of Truth
we are not told ; both are sent to the Tower and racked ; both
retract ; both are afterwards overcome by remorse, and publicly
bewail their retractation to their friends in a conventicle in Bowe
Lane, and then afterwards make a public protest in a church,
and so both are condemned to be burnt.   These are strange
coincidences ; but it is still more strange that a part of what
Foxe had written of Tewkesbury in one edition, in another
edition he omitted, and tacked on to his account of Bainham.*
The accuracy of Foxe may be judged from the fact that he im-
putes the death of Frith to More, yet Frith died in 1533, and
More had resigned his office a year before.†

Foxe does not seem to have been the inventor of the story
of the whippings and racking, for in the 36th chapter of his
Apology Sir Thomas refers to some such lies as then in
circulation.   The passage is very important, and shall be given
with little abridgment : " They that are of this brotherhood be
so bold and so shameless in lying, that whoso shall hear them
speak, and knoweth not what sect they be of, shall be very sore
abused [misled] by them.   Myself have good experience, for
the lies are neither few nor small that many of the blessed
brethren have made, and daily yet make by me.

" Divers of them have said that of such as were in my house
while I was chancellor I used to examine them with torments,
causing them to be bound to a tree in my garden, and there
piteously beaten.   And this tale had some of those good

---

* See vol. iv. p. 702, and Appendix, p. 769 (ed. Townsend).

† In his *Apology* (p. 887), written in the spring of 1533, More refers to
Frith as then in the Tower, not by his means, but by "the king's grace
and his Council".

brethren so caused to be blown about, that a right worshipful friend of mine did of late, within less than this fortnight, tell unto another near friend of mine that he had of late heard much speaking thereof.

"What cannot these brethren say that can be so shameless to say thus? For of very truth, albeit that for a great robbery or a heinous murder, or sacrilege in a church, with carrying away the pix with the Blessed Sacrament, or villainously casting it out, I caused sometimes such things to be done by some officers of the Marshalsea, or of some other prisons, with which ordering of them, and without any great hurt that afterwards should stick by them, I found out and repressed many such desperate wretches as else had not failed to have gone farther; yet, saving the sure keeping of heretics, I never did cause any such thing to be done to any of them in all my life, except only twain. Of which the one was a child and a servant of mine in mine own house, whom his father had, ere ever he came with me, nursled up in such matters, and had set him to attend upon George Jay or Gee, otherwise called Clerk, which is a priest, and is now for all that wedded in Antwerp, into whose house there the two nuns were brought which John Birt, otherwise called Adrian, stole out of their cloister to make them harlots. This George Jay did teach this child his ungracious heresy against the Blessed Sacrament of the altar, which heresy this child afterwards, being in service with me, began to teach another child in my house, which uttered his counsel. And upon that point perceived, I caused a servant of mine to stripe him like a child before mine household, for amendment of himself and ensample of such other.

"Another was one, which after that he had fallen into that frantic heresy, fell soon after into plain open frenzy besides." More then tells how he was confined in bedlam, and when set free disturbed public service in churches, and committed acts of great indecency: "Whereupon I, being advertised of these

pageants, and being sent unto and required by very devout
religious folk to take some other order with him, caused him,
as he came wandering by my door, to be taken by the constables
and bound to a tree in the street before the whole town, and
there they striped him with rods till he waxed weary, and somewhat longer. And it appeared well that his remembrance was
good enough, save that it went about grazing till it was beaten
home. For he could then very well rehearse his faults himself,
and speak and treat very well, and promise to do afterwards as
well. And verily God be thanked, I hear none harm of him
now.

"And of all that ever came in my hand for heresy, as help
me God, saving (as I said) the sure keeping of them, had never
any of them any stripe or stroke given them, so much as a fillip
on the forehead.

"But now tell the brethren many marvellous lies, of much
cruel tormenting that heretics had in my house, so far forth
that one Segar, a bookseller of Cambridge, which was in mine
house about four or five days, and never had either bodily harm
done him, or foul word spoken him, hath reported since, as I
hear say, to divers, that he was bound to a tree in my garden,
and thereto too piteously beaten, and yet besides that bound
about the head with a cord and wrung till he fell down dead in
a swoon. And this tale of his beating did Tyndale tell to an
old acquaintance of his own, and to a good lover of mine, with
one piece farther yet, that while the man was in beating, I spied
a little purse of his hanging at his doublet, wherein the poor
man had, as he said, five marks, and that caught I quickly to
me, and pulled it from his doublet and put it in my bosom, and
that Segar never saw it after, and therein I trow he said true,
for no more did I neither, nor before neither, nor I trow no
more did Segar himself."*

From this it would seem that Tindale's report of Segar's false
tale of the whipping and the twisted cord had, by the time of

* *English Works*, p. 901.

Foxe, got into the legend of Tewkesbury. On this declaration of Sir Thomas More, Sir James Mackintosh writes as follows : "This statement, so minute, so easily contradicted, if in any part false, was made public after his fall from power, when he was surrounded by enemies and could have no friends but the generous. He relates circumstances of public notoriety, or at least, so known to all his household, which it would have been rather a proof of insanity than of imprudence to have alleged in his defence, if they had not been indisputably and confessedly true. Wherever he touches this subject, there is a quietness and a circumstantiality, which are among the least equivocal marks of a man who adheres to the temper most favourable to the truth, because he is conscious that the truth is favourable to him. . . . Defenceless and obnoxious as More then was, no man was hardy enough to dispute his truth. Foxe was the first who, thirty years afterwards, ventured to oppose it in a vague statement, which we know to be in some respects inaccurate ; and on this slender authority alone has rested such an imputation on the veracity of the most sincere of men."*

Since the days of Sir James Mackintosh another charge has been made against More. Mr. Anthony Froude writes: "I do not intend in this place to relate the stories of his cruelties in his house at Chelsea, which he himself partially (!) denied, and which at least we may hope were exaggerated"; but Mr. Froude goes on to relate what he asserts to have been acts of illegal imprisonment committed by More. The first is that of Thomas Philips ; the second, that of John Field. The evidence against

* *Life of More*, pp. 101, 105. Such tales die hard. In 1889 appeared a book called *Old Chelsea*, by Mr. B. G. Martin. It gives a most interesting account both of Sir Thomas More and his house. Mr. Martin writes affectionately of More's " sweet and wholesome nature," yet he repeats Foxe's story of the floggings (p. 39), and that " he was imprisoned in the very cell, it is said, wherein he had sat as grand inquisitor aforetime racking heretics " (p. 42). Thus visitors to Chelsea and the Tower, instead of a mental vision of the real Blessed Thomas More, will shudder at the spectres of scourge and rack.

Sir Thomas is merely that Mr. Froude found petitions to the king drawn up by the men themselves. Of the result of Field's petition Mr. Froude can tell nothing; of that of Philips he has to tell that his complaint was against the Bishop of London rather than against More, and that it was cast aside by the House of Lords as frivolous.*

Mr. Froude does not seem to be aware that More himself has spoken of these very petitions. In the 38th chapter of his *Apology* he relates how Thomas Philips, a leatherseller, was brought before him when he was chancellor; he was examined with great leniency ("in as hearty loving manner as I could") and at last "I by indenture delivered him to his ordinary," but afterwards, for reasons enumerated, "I advised, and by my means helped that he was received prisoner into the Tower. And yet after that he complained thereupon, not against me but against the ordinary. Whereupon the king's highness commanded certain of the greatest lords of his Council to know how the matter stood; which known and reported, his highness gave unto Philips such answer as, if he had been half so good as I would he were, or half so wise as himself weeneth he were, he would forthwith have followed, and not stand still in his obstinacy so long, as he hath now put himself thereby in another deeper peril."

Sir Thomas continues: "Others have besides this complained that they have been unjustly handled, and they have nothing gotten but rebuke and shame. And some hath been heard upon importunate clamour, and the cause and handling examined by the greatest lords temporal of the king's most honourable council, and that since I left the office, and the complainour found in his complaining so very shameless false, that he hath been answered that he was too easily dealt with, and had wrong that he was no worse served."† Sir Thomas

<hr>

* *History of England*, ii. 74. Field's petition is also in *Letters and Papers*, vi. 1059.

† *English Works*, p. 906.

does not mention the names in these latter cases, nor does he say that the petitions of redress were made against himself; yet it seems likely that Field's complaint is the one last enumerated. In any case history contains no record that when Cromwell and the Earl of Wiltshire, and More's other enemies, were seeking charges against him, Field's complaints were considered worthy of attention. Yet Mr. Froude takes the fact that complaints were made as equivalent to a proof that they were well founded. Surely the great chancellor's integrity can survive a ruder shock than this. In the *Debellacion* of Salem and Bizance, Sir Thomas More again referred to the accusations of harshness as follows: " The untruth of such false fame hath been before the king's honourable council of late well and plainly proved, upon sundry such false complaints by the king's gracious commandment examined. And albeit that this is a thing notoriously known, and that I have myself in mine *Apology* spoken thereof, and that, since that book gone abroad, it hath been in likewise before the lords well and plainly proved in more matters afresh, and albeit that this water washeth away all his matter, yet goeth ever this water over this goose's back, and for anything that any man can do, no man can make it sink unto the skin, that she may once feel it, but ever she shaketh such plain proofs off with her feathers of 'Some say,' and ' They say' the contrary." *
The goose is still shaking her feathers in Mr. Froude's pages.

From all that has been gathered together in this chapter, I venture to conclude that there is no evidence of change in More's views as regards religious liberty, nor did his genial character become deteriorated or soured. He held strongly that the dogmatising heretics of those days, in the then circumstances of England and Christendom, should be forcibly repressed, and if necessary punished even by death, according to the existing laws. Yet in the administration of those laws he was not only rigidly upright, but as tender and merciful as

* *English Works*, p. 962.

is compatible with the character and office of a judge. "What other controversialist can be named," asks Sir James Mackintosh, "who, having the power to crush antagonists whom he viewed as the disturbers of the quiet of his own declining years, *the destroyers of all the hopes which he had cherished for mankind*, contented himself with severity of language?" *

* *Life of More*, p. 111. [See, on the subject of this chapter, a correspondence in the *Academy*, 2nd, 9th, 16th, 23rd May, 1891, between Mr. W. Lloyd and Mr. G. Gairdner ; also Mr. Gairdner's review of this book in *Academy* of 25th April. Note to 2nd Edition.]

CHAPTER XV.

ENGLISH CONTROVERSY.

SECTION I. ZEAL FOR THE FAITH.

THE task before me in this chapter is beset with no ordinary difficulties. The English controversial works of Sir Thomas More fill more than a thousand of the large, double column, closely printed pages of the great collection of his works, equal to perhaps six volumes like the present. To pass these by with a general allusion would be as incongruous in a biographer of More as for the writer of Lord Macaulay's life to say nothing of, or to refer vaguely to, his Essays. But the biographer of Macaulay supposes his readers familiar with the Essays, or that they will turn with eager interest to those with which they are yet unacquainted when told of their character or of the circumstances in which they were written, whereas probably not more than one or two of my readers has ever read a page of More's polemics, or will ever cast an eye on the volume that contains them. Perhaps they may have read in Burnet that More was "no divine," that "he knew nothing of antiquity," that "his writings were designed rather for the rabble than for learned men".* Were I to retort that there is more solid Divinity, scriptural and patristic learning, force of reasoning, to say nothing of wit, in the most hastily written treatise of More's than in Burnet's *Exposition of the Thirty-Nine Articles*, I

* *History of Reformation*, i. 557 (ed. Pocock).

should be far below the truth, yet I could not ask a reader to accept my bare assertion. At most I could beg him to suspend his judgment as concerning a thing unknown to him. On the other hand, I cannot reproduce by long quotations the somewhat antiquated and very bitter controversy of the first twenty years of Lutheranism; nor would it be to much purpose to analyse minutely works that are quite unlikely to be read. The only course left to me is to give some account here—as much as possible in More's own words—of the reasons and the method of his controversy, and to print in a separate volume extracts of permanent interest and characteristic of his style.

We have already seen in the last chapter that Sir Thomas More was moved to his opposition to the new doctrines by his keen prevision of their consequences, as well religious as social. It is no exaggeration to say that he clearly anticipated and foretold such results of the Lutheran revolt as history reveals to us in the sudden overthrow by the Scotch fanatics of the whole fabric of the Catholic religion and of every venerated monument of antiquity, the national madness of the English Puritans, the impieties and atrocities of the various French revolutions, or the brutal agnosticism of modern secularists in England and America. When he was chancellor More wrote as follows : " In good faith, I never thought other yet, soon after the beginning, but that when those folk fell once to their horrible heresies, which Tindale in his books has taught us, they should not fail to fall soon after unto these others too" (*i.e.*, the tenets of the Munster Anabaptists, denying all obligation of law spiritual or temporal, rejecting all government, introducing communism in property, and abolishing all marriage), " and then that Our Blessed Saviour Christ was but only Man, and not God at all. And, as help me God, I verily fear that they shall fall unto that at last, that there is no God. And then, reckoning neither upon God nor devil, nor immortality of their own souls, but jesting and scoffing that ' God is a good fellow,' and ' as good a soul hath an owl as a cuckoo,' and ' when thou seest my soul hang in the hedge then hurl stones at it hardily and spare not'; and, as Tindale saith, 'When thou speakest with St. Peter then pray him to pray for thee'; thus reckoning upon nothing but only upon this world,* and therefore reckoning for nothing but only for the body, they shall at the last fall in a new rage, and gather themselves together (but if their malice be the better suppressed) to make other manner masters than ever they made yet, whereof the mischief shall fall in their own necks. But yet if this may be suffered once to rise, all the mischief will not fall in their own necks alone, but much harm shall hap upon many good men's heads, ere these rebellious wretches be well repressed again."†

More did not find many Englishmen to share his anxieties; he thus expresses and laments the general apathy of good Catholics: " If because we know our cause so good we bear ourselves thereupon so bold, that we make light and slight of our adversaries, it may happen to fare between the Catholics and heretics at length, as it fareth sometimes in a suit at the law by some good man, against whom a subtle, wily shrew ‡ beginneth a false action, and asketh from him all the land he hath. This good man sometimes, that knoweth his matter so true, persuadeth to himself that it were not possible for him to lose it by the law. And when his counsel talketh with him, and asketh him how he can prove this point or that for himself, answereth again : 'Fear ye not for that, sir, I warrant you all the country knoweth it. The matter is so true and my part so plain, that I care not what judges, what arbiters, what twelve men go thereon. I will challenge no man for any labour that mine adversary can make therein.' And with such good hope the good man goeth him home, and there sitteth still and putteth no doubt in the matter. But in the mean-

* The very profession from which so many of our own artisans call themselves *Secularists*.

† *English Works*, pp. 656, 657.

‡ A shrew, in More's works, is not a scold, but a rogue.

while his adversary, which for lack of truth of his cause must
needs put all his trust in craft, goeth about his matter busily,
and by all the false means he may, maketh him friends, some
with good fellowship, some with rewards, findeth a fellow to
forge him false evidence, maketh means to the sheriff, getteth
a partial panel, laboureth the jury, and when they come to the
bar hath all his trinkets ready; whereas good Tom Truth
cometh forth upon the other side, and because he weeneth all
the world knoweth how true his matter is, bringeth never a
witness with him, and all his evidence unsorted.   And one
wist I once that brought unto the bar, when the jury was
sworn, and openly delivered his counsel, his tinder box, with
his flint and his matches, instead of his box of evidence, for that
had he left at home.   So negligent are good folk sometimes,
when the known truth of their matter maketh them over bold.

" And surely much after this fashion in many places play
these heretics and we.   For like as a few birds, always chirk-
ing and flying from bush to bush, seem a great many, so these
heretics be so busily walking, that in every ale-house, in every
tavern, in every barge, and almost every boat, as few as they be,
a man shall always find some.   And there be they so busy
with their talking (and in better places also where they may
be heard), so fervent and importune in putting forth of anything which may serve for the furtherance of their purpose, that
between their importunate preaching and the diligence or
rather the negligence of good Catholic men, appeareth oft times
as great a difference as between frost and fire.

" And surely between the true Catholic folk and the false
heretics, it fareth also much like as it fared between false Judas
and Christ's faithful Apostles.   For while they, for all Christ's
calling upon them to wake and pray, fell fast in a slumber, and
after in dead sleep, the traitor neither slept nor slumbered, but
went about full busily to betray his Master, and bring himself
to mischief." *

* *English Works*, p. 921.

Roper tells us : " It fortuned, before the matter of the king's matrimony brought in question, when I, in talk with Sir Thomas More, of a certain joy commended unto him the happy estate of this realm, that had so Catholic a prince that no heretic durst show his face, so virtuous and learned a clergy, so grave and sound a nobility, and so loving, obedient subjects, all in one faith agreeing together. 'Truth it is indeed, son Roper,' quoth he, and in all degrees and estates of the same went far beyond me in commendation thereof; 'and yet, son Roper, I pray God,' said he, 'that some of us, as high as we seem to sit upon the mountains, treading heretics under our feet like ants, live not the day that we would gladly be at league and composition with them, to let them have their churches quietly to themselves, so that they would be contented to let us have ours quietly to ourselves.' After that I had told him many considerations why he had no cause to say so : 'Well,' said he, ' I pray God, son Roper, some of us live not till that day,' showing me no reason why he should put any doubt therein. To whom I said, 'By my troth, sir, it is very desperately spoken ' (that vile term, I cry God mercy, did I give him). Who, by these words, perceiving me in a fume, said merrily unto me, 'It shall not be so, it shall not be so'."*

In the year 1526, before he had begun any of his own English works against the heretics, More showed his great zeal and anxiety in the matter in the following letter to Erasmus. After some expressions of sympathy for his physical sufferings, he says that the Christian world can ill spare him and is expecting some more of his excellent works. "But especially what is still wanting of your *Hyperaspistes*.† You can conceive nothing more fruitful to all, more pleasing to your friends, more honourable to yourself or more necessary. You cannot believe how eagerly all good men expect it ; on the contrary, the bad,

---

* *Notes*, no. xiii.

† The title of the answer of Erasmus to Luther's book *De Servo Arbitrio*. *Hyperaspistes* means " champion " or " protector ".

who favour Luther or envy you, seem to grow more bold and numerous from your delay in replying. If you have merely postponed this work to finish some other things, such as the *Institution of Christian Matrimony*, which her Majesty the Queen esteems so much (as you will soon, I trust, feel), I can bear the delay. If you are taking your time to treat the matter more accurately, I am delighted, for I desire that part to be treated with the utmost diligence. But if the reason of your delay is, as some report, that fear has caused you to give it up, I cannot repress my sorrow or sufficiently express my surprise. O my dearest Erasmus, God forbid that, after all your Herculean labours and your dangers, after all the toils and vigils to benefit the world, in which you have spent the best years of your life, you should begin now so miserably to love these sick souls, that rather than lose their suffrage you should desert the cause of God.

"As regards myself I can neither promise nor hope what all expect from you, from the well-known examples you have given of a soul strong and trustful in God. I can never doubt that to your life's end, whatever catastrophe may befall, you will manifest the same fortitude, since you cannot but trust that God, who has allowed this tragedy, will come in due time to our aid.

"Besides there is, as I conceive, just now no great reason to fear, much less to be overwhelmed by it. If the Lutherans intended to do anything, they would have been more likely to do it before you answered at all, for so they would have prevented your answering. Or if they wished to be revenged for what you have written, they would have poured out their fury on you when your first book appeared, in which you so painted the wild beast, and so pointed out the evil spirit that drives him on, that you have made that smoky and infernal demon as visible to men's eyes as if you had dragged Cerberus out of hell. What danger, therefore, now remains I do not see, which would not equally threaten if you write no more. You have

answered his calumnies against yourself, and transfixed him
with your pen; there now remains only to treat the passages
of Holy Scripture; and since in the thousand copies of your
first part you have promised the whole world, as by so many
bonds, that you would diligently execute that second part, you
cannot refuse to pursue the cause of God after having successfully achieved your own, or to perform what you have publicly
promised, especially since you can do it so easily. Nor is
Luther such a fool as to hope you will refrain, nor so unjust as
to dare to ask it. That he desires you to keep silence I have
no doubt, however much he may pretend a magnificent contempt of you in his letter, of which it is hard to say whether it
is more boastful or more foolish. He is conscious enough how
the miserable glosses by which he has tried to obscure the
most clear passages of Holy Scripture, cold as they were already, become under your criticism the merest ice." More
then begs his friend to write a confidential letter, if there is
really some danger that in England is not known. Then after
a short digression about the visit of Holbein, he concludes:
" You have done well to confute in a pamphlet the opinion
that had been wickedly spread about that you favoured the
heresy of Carldstadt.* But, although I would gladly see some
day, if God grants you leisure, a treatise on this subject [the
Holy Eucharist] to confirm our faith, proceeding from that
heart of yours which is made to defend the truth, yet I am so
solicitous regarding the *Hyperaspistes*, that I trust you will take
nothing to heart so as to call off your care and thought from
the finishing of that work. Farewell, dearest of all mortals,
Erasmus. From Greenwich, the 18th December, 1526. Yours,
with more than my whole heart, THOMAS MORE." † Whether

* This refers to a book published by Erasmus in 1526 called *Detectio
Prætigiarum*, etc.

† *Letter* 334, in App. inter Epist. Erasmi. The date 1525 given by Le
Clerc is wrong, for the first part of *Hyperaspistes* was not published till
1526, nor the *Detectio* above referred to.

or not the admonition of More was needed to stir up the zeal of Erasmus, it was not thrown away. The second book of the *Hyperaspistes* appeared in 1527. Luther and Erasmus were for ever separated, and Luther never ceased to denounce his opponent as a free-thinker, an empty pedant, a man to be avoided like the plague.

The accusation did not on that account cease to be made by many Catholics that Luther had merely carried out the principles of Erasmus, and boldly denied where Erasmus only hinted doubts, that Luther hatched the egg laid by Erasmus;* yet Erasmus could now repudiate the charge with some force: "They lie most impudently who say that this Lutheran conflagration has been kindled by my writings, for no one has been able to point out one condemned proposition which I have in common with Luther. Collusion between me and Luther! Yes, as Hector colluded with Achilles. Read my *Diatribe* (on Free Will) and Luther's answer, than which nothing can be more hostile, and read also the two books of my *Hyperaspistes* in reply to him. . . . There are some whose only study it is to gather out of my many treatises, some of which I wrote when I was young and when all was peaceable, and some not seriously, whatever they can twist towards a suspicion of Lutheran doctrines. Even this they do most impudently and calumniously. But if they really side with the Sovereign Pontiff, how much better would it be to select those things which show that I differ from the paradoxes of Luther." †

But to return to England.

The anxiety felt by More at the spread of heresy and its probable results was shared by the Bishop of London, Cuthbert Tunstall. There existed between him and More the closest friendship and mutual admiration. They had acted together in several embassies, as we have seen. On the subject of the

---

* The words are quoted by Erasmus himself.

† *Ep.* 345, in App. The whole letter, to John Gacchus, a Franciscan, is one of Erasmus' best. It was written from Basle in 1527.

supremacy of the Holy See, Tunstall's views were erroneous,* and led him to acquiesce in Henry's schism, though experience made him wiser, and he was not only reconciled with the Church, but died in resistance to the renewal of the schism in the first year of Elizabeth. But as regards Lutheranism and the denial of the sacraments and visible Church as taught by Tindale, Barns, and the other English heretics, he was always orthodox, and no one was more anxious to stop the spread of heretical books. English books were being printed on the continent and energetically scattered in England. The very novelty and startling nature of their denial of hitherto received belief, and of their attack on ancient and universal practice, excited men's curiosity, and won for them an attention quite disproportioned to their intrinsic importance. As modern evolutionist theories, by giving a new explanation of the universe, and overthrowing the old foundations of morality, have excited the imagination far beyond the influence of their scientific appeals to reason; so did the sweeping negations of Luther, Zwingle, and their followers fascinate the minds of the young, and their satire on the clergy was greedily read by the irreligious and discontented. It appeared to Tunstall and More that the mischief being wrought by these books could not be effectually met either by measures of suppressions or by the learned refutations published in Latin by professed theologians. Engglish books written in a popular style, to defend Catholic doctrines and expose the sophisms of the heretics, were urgently needed; and there was no man in England so fitted for the task as More. Whether the thought of More's devoting his life to this work originated with him or with Tunstall, we cannot know. In Tunstall's Register is the following document, dated March, 1527, and addressed to Sir Thomas More: "Because you, most dear brother, are able to emulate Demosthenes in our vernacular tongue no less than in Latin,

* I judge from his own MS. treatise, which will be quoted in a later chapter.

and are wont to be an ardent defender of Catholic truth whenever you hear it attacked, you cannot spend the occasional hours that you can steal from your official duties better than in composing in our own language such books as may show to simple and unlearned men the cunning malice of the heretics, and fortify them against these impious subverters of the Church ". (The Bishop, therefore, by the powers received from the Holy See, gives to Sir Thomas faculty to read the books of heretics for their refutation.) " For it is of great help towards victory to know thoroughly the plans of the enemy, what they hold and whither they tend ; for if you go about to refute what they protest that they do not hold, you lose your pains. Engage therefore courageously in this holy work, by which you will benefit the Church of God, make for yourself an immortal fame, and win eternal glory in heaven." *

Section II. Fruits of Zeal.

I. " The Dialogue."

More's first work is in the form of a dialogue, and in his other books he refers to it by this title. In *Utopia*, and in the Latin book against Luther, there was an ingenious fiction as to their composition ; so also is this. A friend of More's is supposed to have sent a messenger, a young man studying at one of the universities, and somewhat bitten with the new opinions, to consult More, who encourages him to speak out quite freely his own difficulties, and to state as strongly as he can what he has heard said by others. This gives More an opportunity of stating the Lutheran doctrines and objections as forcibly as their maintainers could have themselves desired, and with far more wit than the best of them possessed. More and the messenger begin by discussing the lawfulness and reasonableness of troubling people for their religious belief or teaching They soon get into the question of the use of images and

* Burnet, iv. p. 13 ; Wilkins, iii. 711.

pilgrimages, and of praying to saints, then very prevalent topics. Thus they are brought to discuss the truth of miracles, and at last the possibility of miracles, and (I may say in passing) Hume's famous argument is thoroughly anticipated and solved. Thence they come to the criterion of miracles, and whether they are worked by the devil to lead the Church into error. This brings them to the possibility of the Church being deceived, and the means provided by God to learn the truth, to Scripture and its interpretation; the test of inspiration, and the presence of the Holy Ghost in the visible Church. In the third book much is said of Tindale's recent translation of the New Testament into English, of its heretical bias. The fourth book gives the history of Luther's own fall, of his self contradiction, and the results of his teaching.

More is supposed to write a full account of all this discussion to the friend who sent him the messenger. Hence he uses perpetually the phrases, Quoth he, Quoth I, and Quoth your friend; so that the book was popularly known as *Quod he and Quod I. The Dialogue*, though redundant in words, as was the style of the age, is never dull, and theological disputes are enlivened by amusing illustrations and merry tales. When Sir Thomas was told that the lightness of his style was brought as an objection against him, he replied that the matter required no defence : " For, as Horace saith, a man may sometimes say full sooth in game; and one that is but a layman as I am, it may better haply become him merrily to tell his mind than seriously and solemnly to preach. And over this, I can scant believe that ' the brethren ' find any mirth in my books, for I have not much heard that they very merrily read them." *

II. "SUPPLICATION OF SOULS."

The book called *The Dialogue* appeared in 1528, and Sir Thomas soon found occupation for his pen in composing a second controversial work, called *The Supplication of Souls.*

* *English Works*, p. 927.

This was an answer to *The Supplication of Beggars*, an incendiary tract that appeared late in the same year, or early in 1529.

Simon Fish, its author, was a member of the University of Oxford, and a law student in London. Having publicly ridiculed Wolsey, he fled into the low countries, and became intimate with some of the English exiles, and imbibed their heresy. It was there he composed, in 1528, his *Supplication of the Beggars*. Foxe gives two contradictory accounts of the way in which this book was brought to the knowledge of the king, and of the way in which the king secretly connived at its propagation. Mr. Creighton thinks it probable that Henry saw in it a convenient means of preparing men's minds for the ecclesiastical revolutions he was already meditating in 1529.[*] In any case it was widely spread through London before the meeting of the parliament, which was to begin its work by drawing up grievances against the Church, and to end in formal schism and heresy.

Fish's book is vigorously written, and in a form likely to take the popular fancy. Its statistics of the number of parishes in England, and the wealth of the Church, are acknowledged to have been greatly exaggerated; but such a defect would be little cared for by the men likely to read it. Its great literary merit was that it was very short—it fills only fourteen pages of the reprint of the Early English Text Society. An answer can seldom be as short as an objection; yet it seems a pity that More never saw the advantage of connecting brevity with wit. Fish had drawn up his booklet in the form of a petition, addressed by the beggars of England to the king, complaining that the mendicant friars consumed what belonged by right to the diseased, the aged, and the impotent. In the course of the petition they allude to the alms given to the friars to say Masses for the dead, and deny the existence of purgatory.

[*] *Dictionary of National Biography*, Art. *Fish*.

More's religious faith was outraged no less than his social instincts. His answer is divided into two books, in the former of which he examines the accuracy of the charges made against the friars and the clergy in general, and shows how the principles on which the author demands the confiscation of ecclesiastical goods would involve the general plunder of the rich by the poor. In the second book he defends the doctrine of purgatory, and of suffrages for the dead.

The book must have been very quickly written, and perhaps when More adopted his opponent's literary form and made his answer a *Supplication of Souls* he scarcely foresaw the incongruities into which he would be led as his book gradually developed into a political and theological treatise. The souls give a learned dissertation on the laws of mortmain, on the value of the currency, and (for the refutation of the beggars' calumnies) enter into all the details of the treatment and death of a certain Richard Hun. Perhaps they could do all this better than the "foul unhappy sort of lepers and other sore people" could have discussed economical problems and illustrated them from the history of King Arthur and King John, as they do in Fish's address to the king. But we are rather startled when, in More's pages, the souls begin to relate merry tales and to make jokes. In fact, in one place they go so far that they have to apologise to their readers : "Surely," they say, "we cannot but here confess the truth, these nice and wanton words do not very well with us ; but we must pray God and you to pardon us, for, in good faith, his matter of monks' marriages is so merry and so mad, that it were able to make one laugh that lieth in the fire".* We are more easily reconciled to political discourse, for are we not listening to ancient legislators and statesmen? As the parliament was about to meet, and the news had reached purgatory that plots were being contrived against the clergy, it was natural for these holy souls to give the

* *English Works*, p. 306.

benefit of their experience: "Ye would peradventure ween,"
they say, "that the man (Simon Fish) would now devise some
good, wholesome laws for help of all these matters.　Nay, he
will none thereof, for he saith that the clergy is stronger in the
parliament than the king himself.　For in the higher house he
reckoneth that the spirituality is more in number and stronger
than the temporality ; and in the common house he saith that
all the learned men of the realm, except the king's learned
Council, be feed with the Church to speak against the king's
crown and dignity, and therefore he thinketh the king unable
to make any law against the faults of the clergy.　This beggars'
proctor would fain show himself a man of great experience, and
one that had great knowledge of the manner and order used in
the king's parliaments.　But then he speaketh so savourly
hereof, that it well appeareth of his wise words he neither
canneth any skill thereof, nor never came in the house.　For,
as for the higher house, first the king's own royal person alone
more than counterpoiseth all the lords spiritual present with
him and the temporal too.　And over this the spiritual lords
can never in number exceed the lords temporal, but must needs
be far underneath them if it please the king.　For His Highness
may call thither by his writ many more temporal lords at his
own pleasure.　And, being as they be, there was never yet
seen that the spiritual lords banded themselves there as a
party against the temporal lords ; but it hath been seen that
the thing which the spiritual lords have moved and thought
reasonable, the temporal lords have denied and refused, as
appeareth upon the motion made for the legitimation of the
children born before the marriage of their parents, wherein
albeit that the reformation which the lords spiritual moved was
a thing that nothing pertained to their own commodity, and
albeit they laid also for their part the constitution and
ordinance of the Church, and the laws of other Christian
countries, yet could they not obtain against the lords temporal,
that nothing alledged to the contrary but their own wills."　The

souls then go on to refute what had been said of the lower house : "And surely if he had been in the common house as some of us have been, he should have seen the spirituality not gladly spoken for," etc.*

There is a great deal worth studying from a historical and political point of view in this treatise. On its religious aspect I will not here dwell ; but I may promise the reader that he will find no dry theological treatise on sin and its punishment. More makes everything picturesque. The souls thus bewail the care they gave before death for pompous funerals, and how little they took heed of their real wants : " Much have we left in our executors' hands, which would God we had bestowed upon poor folk for our own souls and our friends' with our own hands. Much have many of us bestowed upon rich men in gold rings and black gowns, much in many tapers and torches, much in worldly pomp and high solemn ceremonies about our funerals, whereof the brittle glory standeth us here, God wot, in very little stead, but hath on the other side done us great displeasure. For albeit that the kind solicitude and loving diligence of the quick, used about the burying of the dead, is well allowed and approved afore the face of God ; yet much superfluous charge used for boast and ostentation, namely, devised by the dead before his death, is of God greatly misliked. And most especially the kind and fashion thereof, wherein some of us have fallen, and many besides us that now lie damned in hell. For some hath there of us, while we were in health, not so much studied how we might die penitent and in good Christian plight, as how we might be solemnly borne out to burying, have gay and goodly funerals, with heralds at our hearses, and offering up our helmets, setting up our escutcheon and coat armours on the wall, though there never came harness on our backs, nor never ancestor of ours ever bare arms before. Then devised we some doctor to make a sermon at our Mass in

* *English Works*, p. 301.

our month's mind, and there preach to our praise with some fond fantasy devised of our name; * and after Mass, much feasting, riotous and costly; and finally, like madmen made we men merry at our death and take our burying for a bride-ale. For special punishment whereof, some of us have been by our evil angels brought forth full heavily, in full great despite, to behold our own burying, and to stand in great pain invisible among the press, and made to look on our carrion corpse carried out with great pomp, whereof Our Lord knoweth we have taken heavy pleasure."†

Much more of this treatise should I like to quote, but I must be content with one short passage. The evil angels appointed to punish the souls "convey us (say the souls) into our own houses, and there double is our pain, with spite sometimes of the self-same thing, which while we lived was half our heaven to behold. There show they us our substance and our bags stuffed with gold, which, when we now see, we set much less by them than would an old man that found a bag of cherry stones which he laid up when he was a child."

Even in the pathetic description given by the souls of their forgetful relatives More's humour breaks out: "Yet we hear sometimes our wives pray for us warmly; for in chiding with her second husband, to spite him withal, 'God have mercy,' saith she, 'on my first husband's soul, for he was a wise and honest man, far unlike you'. And then marvel we much when we hear them say so well by us, for they were ever wont to tell us far otherwise. "‡

More had adopted this style to get his book read. He knew the temper of the times, and probably had forecast in his mind the avarice of the monarch, which glutted itself only a few

---

* Not only were More's contemporaries fond of rebuses, but the Christian or surname was taken as a text of a funeral oration, and tortured into silly moralities.

† *English Works*, p. 335.

‡ *Ib.*, p. 336.

years later in the plunder of the monasteries. The following passage contains his warning on this head: "He (Simon Fish) reckoneth all the clergy idle because they labour not with their hands till their faces sweat. But Our Saviour Christ reckoned far otherwise in Blessed Mary Magdalen, whose idle sitting at her ease and hearkening he accounted and declared for better business than the busy stirring and walking about of His good hostess Martha, which was yet of all worldly business occupied about the best; for she was busy about alms and hospitality, and the guesting of the best Poor Man and most gracious Guest that ever was guested in this world. Now, if this cannot yet content this good man, because of God's commandment given unto Adam, that he should eat his bread in the sweat of his face, then would we fain wit whether himself never go to meat till he have wrought so sore with his hands that his face sweateth. Howbeit he thinketh it peradventure enough for him that he sitteth and studieth till he sweat in seeking out old heresies and devising new. And verily, if he look that such business should serve him for a discharge of hand-labour, much better may we think discharged thereof many good men whom he would have beaten thereto, living their lives in fasting, prayer, and preaching, and studying about the truth.

"But it is good to look betime what this beggars' proctor meaneth by this commandment of hand-labour. For if he confess that it bindeth not every man, then is it laid to no purpose against the clergy, for there was small clergy when that word was said to our first father, Adam. But now, if ye call it a precept as he doth, and then will that it extend unto all the whole kind of man, then, though he say little now, he meaneth to go further hereafter. For if he might first have the clergy put out of their living, and all that they had clean taken from them . . . this pageant once played . . . he would after make another bill to the people against merchants, gentlemen, kings, lords, and princes, and complain that they have all, and sav that they do nothing for it but live idle, and that they be com manded in *Genesis* to live by the labour of their hands in the sweat of their faces, as he sayeth by the clergy now. . . . Whoso will advise princes or lay people to take from the clergy their possessions, alledging matters at large, as laying to their charge that they live not as they should, nor use not well their possessions, and that therefore it were well done to take them from them by force and dispose of them better. . . . We would give you counsel to look well what will follow. For he shall not fail . . . to find reasons enough that should please the people's ears, wherewith he would labour to have lords' lands and all honest men's goods to be pulled from them by force, and distributed among beggars. . . . We be content that ye believe us not, but if it have so proved already by those uplandish Lutherans that rose up in Almaine."*

Simon Fish died of the plague about a year after the publication of his book, and More tells us that, before his illness "God gave him such grace, that he repented and came into the Church again, and forsook and forswore all the whole bill of those heresies".†

III. CONFUTATION OF TINDALE'S ANSWER.

Fish had written that all the abuses came because "the king's chief judge (the chancellor) was always a spiritual man".‡ He lived long enough to witness Wolsey's fall and a layman's elevation to the dignity. The cares of that great office, far from blunting More's zeal, sharpened it by bringing clearly and frequently before him the mischief that was being worked by the spread of heresy. It was during his chancellorship that he made time to write the most voluminous of all his works, his confutation of Tindale's answer to his *Dialogue*. This work of More's, including his answer to Friar Barns, is divided into nine books, and would make three good octavo volumes.§

* *English Works*, p. 304. † *Ib.*,.p. 881.

‡ Reprint by Early English Text Society, p. 13.

§ It was brought out in two separate parts. The printer was More's brother-in-law, John Rastell.

William Tindale's name is so prominent among the first English Protestants, and his history so well known, that it is needless to speak of it here. More's controversy with him is pretty well summed up in the following passage, which is of special interest because Tindale threatened More with a bad end for resisting the truth. More died at the block; Tindale outlived him, but died at the stake.

"It liketh Tindale to liken me to Balaam, Pharaoh, and to Judas too. Since the pith of all his process standeth in this one point, that his heresies be the true faith, and that the Catholic faith is false; that the holy days nor the fasting days no man need to keep; that the Divine services in the church is all but superstition; that the church and the alehouse is all one, saving for such holy preaching; that men have no free will of their own to do good nor ill; that to reverence Christ's Cross or any saint's image is idolatry; that to do any good work, fast give alms, or other, with intent the rather to get heaven or to be the better rewarded there, is deadly sin afore God and worse than idolatry; to think that the Mass may do men any good more than the priest himself were a false belief; a false faith also to pray for any soul; great sin to shrive us or to do penance for sin; friars may well wed nuns and must needs have wives; and the sacraments of Christ must serve for Tindale's jesting stock. These be the truths that Tindale preacheth. And because I call these truths heresies, therefore, Tindale calleth me Balaam, Judas, and Pharaoh, and threateneth me sore with the vengeance of God and with an evil death.

"What death each man shall die, that hangeth in God's hands, and martyrs have died for God and heretics have died for the devil. But since I know it very well, and so doth Tindale too, that the holy saints dead before these days, since Christ's time till our own, believed as I do, and Tindale's truths be stark devilish heresies; if God give me the grace to suffer for saying the same, I shall never in my right wit wish to die better. And, therefore, since all the matter standeth in this point alone, that if his heresies be the true faith, then I stand in peril, and if they be a false faith I may be safe enough; let him leave his sermon hardily for the while, and first go prove his lies true, and then come again and preach, and Friar Luther also, and his leman with him too, and then may the geese provide the fox a pulpit." *

IV. LETTER AGAINST FRITH.

Another of More's antagonists was a young man named John Frith, who, after being educated at Henry VI.'s foundations at Eton and Cambridge, had been made by Cardinal Wolsey a junior canon of Cardinal College (afterwards Christ's Church), Oxford. Having imbibed the new heresies and got into trouble, he went abroad in 1528 and married. When More's book against Frith appeared, Frith wrote a book against the doctrine of purgatory, in which he attempts to reply not only to More, but to what the Bishop of Rochester (Fisher) and John Rastell, More's brother-in-law, had written on the same subject. He returned to England in 1532, was arrested upon a warrant of the chancellor (More), and committed to the Tower. He was allowed much liberty, and wrote a short treatise against the Catholic doctrine of the Holy Eucharist, of which several copies were made by his friends, three of which came into the hands of Sir Thomas, to which he made an answer. This answer is in the form of a letter to a friend, who had sent him the first copy. It is about a dozen folio pages, and is remarkable amongst all his polemical writings for its reserve and the almost compassionate tone in which he treats the misguided youth who has dared to attack the most august of mysteries. Frith had said that it was the philosophical impossibility of accepting the literal sense of Our Lord's words regarding the Eucharist that obliged him to interpret them in a figurative sense. More meets very candidly whatever argu-

* End of second book against Tindale. *English Works*, p. 443.

ments he had advanced, but at the same time he says that if the faith of the whole Catholic Church is to be set aside in this way, "I were able myself to find out [*i.e.*, to invent] fifteen new sects in one forenoon, that should have as much probable hold of Scripture as this heresy has". *

Frith had compared the Holy Eucharist to a ring given by a husband to his wife for a remembrance, when going to a far country. More allows the comparison, but adds that Frith himself is like "a man to whom a bridegroom had delivered a goodly gold ring with a rich ruby therein, to deliver over to his bride for a token, and then he would like a false shrew, keep away that gold ring and give the bride in the stead thereof a proper ring of a rush,† and tell her that the bridegroom would send her no better ; or else like one that when the bridegroom had given such a gold ring to his bride for a token, would tell her plain and make her believe that the ring were but copper or brass to minish the bridegroom's thanks".‡

V. "THE APOLOGY".

After More had resigned the chancellorship he wrote a book called *The Apology.* Certain things had been objected against his writings. One was their extreme length. He replies that "every way seemeth long to him that is weary ere he begin, but I find some men again, to whom the reading is so far from tedious, that they have read the whole book over thrice, and some that make tables thereof for their own remembrance. But the objectors will, if they be reasonable men, consider in themselves that it is a shorter thing and sooner done to write heresies than to answer them. For the most foolish heretic in

* *English Works*, p. 836.

† Pretended or mock marriages were sometimes made with rush-rings (Brand).

‡ *Ib.*, p. 835. More did not immediately publish this letter, but he had it printed for distribution, to those who had read Frith's tract (*English Works*, p. 904). A year later he gave it to the public.

a town may write more false heresies in one leaf than the
wisest man in the whole world can well and conveniently by
reason and authority confute in forty. * But greatly can I
not marvel, though these evangelical brethren think my works
too long. For everything think they too long that aught is.
Our Lady's psalter [the rosary] think they too long by all the
Ave Maries and some good piece of the Creed too. Then the
Mass think they too long by the secrets, and the canon, and all
the collects wherein mention is made either of saints or souls
Instead of a long porteous [breviary], a short primer shall
serve them ; and yet the primer think they too long by all
Our Lady's matins. And the seven psalms think they long
enough without the litany ; and as for dirge or commemoration
for their friends' souls, all that service think they too long by
altogether." †

Another complaint had been made that More used opprobrious words, and the example was quoted against him of an
anonymous Catholic writer called the Pacifier, who treated his
opponents gently. More replies : "I cannot say nay, but that
is very truth. Howbeit every man hath not the like wit, nor
like inventions in writing. For he findeth many proper ways
of uttering evil matter in good words, which I never thought
upon, but am a simple plain body, much like the Macedonians,
for whom Plutarch writeth that King Philip, their master, made
a reasonable excuse. For when they were in the war, some of
their enemies fled from their own king and came into King
Philip's service against their own country. With whom when
the Macedonians fell sometimes at words, as it often happeneth
among soldiers, the Macedonians in spite would call them
traitors. Whereupon they complained to King Philip, and
made the matter sore and grievous, that whereas they had not
only left their own native country but did also fight against it
and help to destroy it for the love and service they had towards

him, his own people letted not, in anger and despite, to call them false traitors. Whereupon King Philip answered them : 'Good fellows, I pray you be not angry with my people, but have patience. I am sorry that their manner is no better. But I wis ye know them well enough; their nature is so plain, and their utterance so rude, that they cannot call a horse but a horse.' And in good faith, like those good folk am I. For though Tindale and Frith in their writings call me a poet, it is but of their own courtesy, undeserved on my part. For I can neither so much poetry, nor so much rhetoric neither, as to find good names for evil things, but even as the Macedonians could not call a traitor but a traitor, so can I not call a fool but a fool, nor a heretic but a heretic." *

But he then compares seriously his own freedom of speech with the abuse these man poured out on the whole Catholic Church. "For they say that this eight hundred years all the corps of Christendom hath been led out of the right way from God, and have lived all in idolatry and died in the service of the devil, because they have done honour to Christ's Cross, and prayed unto saints, and reverenced their relics, and honoured their images, and been baptised in Latin, and taken matrimony for a sacrament, and used confession and done penance for sins, and prayed for all Christian souls, and been anealed in their deathbed, and have taken their housel after the rite and usage of the Church, and have set more by the Mass than they should do, and believed that it was a sacrifice, a host, and an oblation, and that it should do them good; and have believed that there was neither bread nor wine in the Blessed Sacrament of the altar, but instead of bread and wine the very Body and Blood of Christ.

"And these things, say Tindale and Barns both, be very false belief and great damnable sin in the doing, and so damn they to the devil the whole Catholic Church, both temporal and

---

* *English Works*, p. 864. (*Apology*, ch. ix.)

spiritual, and (except heretics) leave not one man for God's part this eight hundred years past, by their own limitation; and of truth, if these false heresies were true, not in the other seven hundred before that neither.

"Now, when that against all the whole Catholic Church, both that now is and that ever before hath been from the Apostle's days hitherto, both temporal and spiritual, laymen and religious, and against all that good is, saints, ceremonies, service of God, the very sacraments and all, and most against the best, that is to wit, the precious Body and Blood of Our Saviour Himself in the holy sacrament of the altar, these blasphemous heretics in their ungracious books, so villainously jest and rail; were not a man, ween you, very far overseen, and worthy to be counted discourteous, that would, in writing against their heresies, presume without great reverence to rehearse their worshipful names?

"If any of them use their words at their pleasure, as evil and as villainous as they list, against myself, I am content to forbear any requiting thereof, and give them no worse words again, than if they speak me fair. For all shall be one to me, or rather the worse the better. For the pleasant oil of heretics cast upon mine head can do my mind no pleasure, but contrariwise, the worse that such folk write of me, for hatred that they bear to the Catholic Church and faith, the greater pleasure, as for my own part, they do me. But surely their railing against all other I purpose not to bear so patiently, as to forbear to let them hear some part of like language as they speak. Howbeit utterly to match them therein, I neither can though I would, nor will neither though I could; but am content, as I needs must, to give them therein the mastery, wherein to match them were more rebuke than honesty."*

More had also been accused that he treated Tindale, Barns, and Frith, as if they were wanting in talent and learning. To this, he replies that he had never called in question their

* English Works, p. 865.

ability, but asserted that it appeared to small advantage in their works, which was probably owing to the badness of their cause. If they were really as learned and clever as their followers boasted, it must be admitted that God had shown His indignation in causing them to write so foolishly; and in this, he adds, they have been treated with more severity than the fallen angels, who in their fall retain their natural gifts. This gives occasion to a bit of delicate banter about devils, ladies, and heretics, which is so characteristic of More's genius, that I must transcribe it :—

"Father Alphonse,* the Spanish friar, told me that the devils be no such deformed, evil-favoured creatures as men imagine them, but they be in mind proud, envious, and cruel. And he bade me, that if I would see a very right image of a fiend, I should no more but even look upon a very fair woman that hath a very shrewd,† fell, cursed mind. And when I showed him that I never saw none such, nor wist not where I might any such find, he said he could find four or five; but I cannot believe him. Nor verily no more can I believe that the fiends be like fair shrewd women, if there were any such. Nor, as the world is, it were not good that young men should ween so, for they be so full of courage, that were the fiends never so cursed, if they thought them like fair women, they would never fear to adventure upon them once. Nor, to say the truth, no more can I believe neither that the damned spirits have all their natural gifts as whole and as perfect as they had before their fall. But surely if they have, then God hath on Tindale, Barns, and Frith, and those other heretics, more showed His vengeance in some part than He did upon the devil. For in good faith God hath, as it seemeth, from these folk taken away the best part of their wits."‡

* Perhaps Alphonso de Castro, the emperor's confessor and a learned writer—but more probably another Father Alphonsus, also a minorite, who was confessor to Queen Katharine.

† Shrewd—*i.e.*, shrewish, malicious.

‡ *English Works*, p. 863.

The Apology was written by More, not so much to defend
his own polemical style as to answer accusations that had been
made against the clergy as regards their treatment of heretics.
This had been done especially by the writer, who is called by
More the Pacifier, because his professed object was to allay the
quarrel that was springing up between the clergy and the laity.
But his mode of pacifying was, according to Sir Thomas, like
that of a man who should step in between two combatants,
and putting one of them gently back with his hand, should
commence to buffet the other about the face; "some men
would say (I suppose), that he had as lieve his enemy were
let alone with him, and thereof abide the adventure, as
have such a friend step in to part them".* Though the
Pacifier writes as a good Catholic, yet it is the clergy who
receive all the buffets at his hand, and that too without
distinct charges, but with repetition of every kind of malicious
gossip, brought in with a "Some say" or "They say". Of
the principal of these accusations I have given some account
in the preceding chapter. (*See* Appendix E.)

VI. "Debellation of Salem and Bizance".

More's *Apology* came out in the spring of 1533. He heard
that several opponents were busily engaged in elaborating
answers, to which he thus laughingly refers: "Like as a
husband, whose wife were in her travail, hearkeneth and would
fain hear good tidings, so, since I so much heard of so sore
travail of so many, I longed of their long labour to see some
good speed, and some of those fair babes born. And when
these great hills had thus travailed long, from the week after
Easter till as much afore Michaelmas, the good hour came on
as God would that one was brought a-bed with sore labour at
last delivered of a dead mouse. The mother is yet but green,
good soul, and hath need of good keeping; women wot what
caudle serveth against her after-throes."† It must be pardoned

* *Apology*, ch. xiii., *English Works*, p. 872.   † *Ib.*, p. 930.

More's adversaries if they made a sorry pun upon his name, and called him "Master Mock,"* for certainly all men cannot relish jests at their own expense as More is said to have done. The "dead mouse" to which he here alludes was written by the Pacifier, or Sir John Somesay, as More calls him, and whom he had handled rather sharply in his *Apology*. His book was in the form of a dialogue, and called *Salem and Bizance*. In less than a month More's answer was printed, called *The Debellacion of Salem and Bizance*. I need here say no more than that it should be consulted by those who would wish to see the treatise of a clever man, and learned lawyer, on the ancient ecclesiastical and civil processes against heresy.

VII. ANSWER TO "SUPPER OF THE LORD".

Nor will I delay upon the last of the series of More's controversial works, his answer to a book called *The Supper of the Lord*. After the death of Frith, a book of his on the Eucharist, written in answer to More's letter on the same subject, was being printed on the Continent, and was daily expected in England in August, 1533,† when another book appeared, without author's name, but written, as More thought, either by William Tindale or George Jay.‡ More intended his answer to consist of two parts, but the troubles that fell on him early in 1534 prevented his composing the second part. The first is in five books, and is mainly a scriptural exposition of the sixth chapter of St. John's Gospel. On no subject could he write more gladly and feelingly than on that mystery which had been so dear to him from his boyhood.

SECTION III. SOME REMARKS.

1. Among the various points of Christian faith controverted in

* *English Works*, p. 1037.
† *Ib.*, p. 1046.
‡ The author is called by More "The Masker". He is now known to have been Tindale.

the sixteenth century, there is one of which there is little mention in Sir Thomas More's English works, one which he may be said to have studiously avoided—that of the supremacy of the Roman Pontiff; and yet for this, and not for any of those articles on which he had written so copiously, was he destined to die. We have seen how clearly he stated his belief in his book against Luther in 1523. His belief had not varied in the six or seven years devoted to the defence of the Church in the English tongue; but there were good reasons for avoiding this topic.

It must be remembered that, during the whole of this period, Henry VIII. was the main obstacle to the spread of the Lutheran heresy in England. With the exception (perhaps) of conniving at Fish's pamphlet—the *Supplication of Beggars*—Henry was more zealous even than the bishops in suppressing heretical books. It was therefore of great importance to More in no way to irritate or alienate him. Now, although the king had not committed any overt act of formal schism while More was writing, he was engaged on his divorce, which brought him into collision with the Sovereign Pontiff. It was simple prudence in More to keep aloof the question of the nature and extent of the Pope's authority, until the passions of the king were again calmed, and would allow him to take up his old position as the foremost champion of the Pope in Europe.

It has been said by some that Sir Thomas More did not consider the supremacy of the Pope as being essential to the Catholic Church. The only ground for this assertion is his own remark that he made no mention of the Pope in his definition of the Church. Tindale, professing to answer More's *Dialogue*, placed the following words as the title of one of his chapters : " Whether the Pope and his sect be Christ's Church or no ". In his reply to Tindale, More writes as follows : " I have, in places enough, well and plainly declared, that I call the Church of Christ 'the Catholic known Church of all Christian nations, neither gone out nor cut off'. And albeit

all these nations now do and long have recognised and acknowledged the Pope, not as the Bishop of Rome but as the successor of St. Peter, to be their chief spiritual governor under
God, and Christ's vicar on earth ; yet did I never put the Pope
for part of the definition of the Church, defining the Church to
be 'the common known congregation of all Christian nations
under one head, the Pope'. Thus did I never define the
Church, but purposely declined therefrom, because I would not
intricate and entangle the matter with two questions at once
. . . since if he be the necessary head he is included in the
name of the whole body, and whether he be or not, if it be
brought in question, were a matter to be treated and disputed
beside."*

It is a strange thing that, because a writer refuses to assume
a point in carrying on a controversy, or to complicate a controversy by introducing a matter that will entail dispute, and is
therefore content with a serviceable definition abstracting from
the point in question, he should be represented as admitting
that the point is unessential.

The words Papist and Popish had been very early imported
into the Lutheran controversy, and were used where there was
not the most distant reference to the Pope. More calls this a
mere spiteful nickname, since the matters denied by the heretics
were held unanimously by the ancient doctors whom they had
not yet learnt to call Papists. If, however, they are willing to
include those holy doctors under the name of Papist, which
they count odious, no wise man will be ashamed of it.† When
the Masker taunted More with his zeal "to stablish the Pope's
kingdom," More replied : "What great cause should move me
to bear that great affection to the Pope as to feign all these
things for stablishment of his kingdom ? He thinketh that
every man knoweth already that the Pope is my godfather, and
goeth about to make me a cardinal."‡ Such answers were

* *English Works*, p. 615   † *Ib.*, p. 1101.   ‡ *Ib.*, p. 1120.

sufficient for such writers and for the occasion. What sentiments More entertained on the Divine government of the
Church will be seen in a future chapter.

2. It would be a curious and interesting study to gather from
the various writings of Sir Thomas More, Latin and English, what
he considered to be the principal causes of the rapid spread of
heresy in his day, in England and elsewhere. Such a study,
however, would belong rather to the history of his times than
to that of his life. Two passages I am about to quote bear
on this subject, but I choose them rather to illustrate his amusing style and his insight into character :—

"A certain priest, as it was said, after that he fell from the
study of the law, wherein he was a proctor and partly well
learned, unto the study of Scripture, he was very fearful and
scrupulous, and began at the first to fall into such a scrupulous
holiness, that he reckoned himself bound so straitly to keep
and observe the words of Christ after the very letter, that because our Lord biddeth us when we will pray enter into
our chamber and shut the door to us, he thought it therefore sin to say his service abroad, and always would be sure
to have his chamber door shut unto him when he said his
matins. Howbeit, I tell you not this thing for any great hurt
in the man, for it was more peevish and painful than evil and
sinful. But surely men say that, in conclusion, with the weariness of that superstitious fear and servile dread, he fell as far to
the contrary ; and under pretext of love and liberty waxed so
drunk of the 'new must' of lewd lightness of mind and
vain gladness of heart, which he took for spiritual consolation,
that whatsoever himself listed to take for good, that thought he
forthwith approved by God. And so framed himself a faith,
framed himself a conscience, framed himself a devotion, wherein
him list, and wherein him liked he set himself at liberty.*

* Of scrupulosity leading to license More had a domestic example in
Roper. Luther's revolt and whole system of theology may be traced to
the same cause. Latimer's history is another illustration.

" ' And if it so were,' quoth your friend, 'then ye see, lo! what cometh of this saying of service.'

" 'Of saying service!' quoth I; 'that is much like as at Beverley late, when much of the people being at a bear-baiting, the church fell suddenly down at evensong time, and over-whelmed some that then were in it; a good fellow, that after heard the tale told, "Lo!" quoth he, "now may you see what it is to be at evensong, when ye should be at the bear-baiting". Howbeit, the hurt was not there in being at evensong, but in that the church was falsely wrought. So was in him or any man else none harm but good in saying of Divine service, but the occasion of harm is in the superstitious fashion that their own folly joineth thereunto, as some think they say it not, but if they say every psalm twice.'

" 'In faith,' quoth your friend, 'then if I were as he, I would mumble it up apace, or else say none at all.'

" 'That were as evil,' quoth I, 'on the other side. There is a mean may serve between both.'

" 'Yea,' quoth he, 'but wot ye what the wife said that com-plained to her gossip of her husband's frowardness. She said her husband was so wayward that he would never be pleased. For if his bread, quoth she, be dough-baked, then is he angry. Marry, no marvel, quoth her gossip. Marry, and wot ye what, gossip? quoth she, and if I bake it all to hard coals, yet is he not content neither, by Saint James. No, quoth her gossip, ye should bake it in a mean. In a mean! quoth she, marry, I cannot happen on it. And so in a pair of matins,* it is much work to happen on the mean. And then to say them too short is lack of devotion, and to say them too

---

* A popular use of the word pair. They said a pair of beads, of stairs, of cards, where we say a string, a flight, a pack. A pair of matins, either because matins comprises many psalms and prayers, or because in addi-tion to matins of the day, matins of Our Lady or of the dead were often recited.

seriously is somewhat superstitious; and therefore the best way were, to my mind, to say none at all.'

"'Yea,' quoth I, 'but then is God as wayward a husband, as ye spake of, that will neither be content with His bread burned to coals, nor dough-baken neither?'

"'By Our Lady,' quoth he, 'but be He contented or not, I ween He hath much dough-baken bread among. For the matins, I tell you, be in some places sungen faster than I can say them.'

"'Peradventure,' quoth I; 'so were it need, for if they should sing matins no faster than ye say them, they should I ween sing very few matins in a year.'

"'In faith,' quoth he, 'and some that say them make me to doubt much, whether the bees in their hives use to say matins among them; for even such a buzzing they make.'

"'Surely,' quoth I, 'that is as true as it is evil done.'" *

From the above it will be seen that Sir Thomas was not inclined to hide the abuses or deficiencies on the Catholic side. Let us hear now what he thought of the Protestant preaching of his day. He had been saying that the new teachers in Saxony denounced all bodily affliction as mere superstition. Even "heaviness of heart and weeping for our sins, this they reckon shame almost and womanish peevishness. Howbeit (thanked be God) their women wax there now so mannish, that they be not so peevish, nor so poor in spirit, but that they can sin on as men do, and be neither afraid, nor ashamed, nor weep for their sins at all. And surely I have marvelled much the less ever since that I heard the manner of their preachers there. For as you remember, when I was in Saxony,† these matters were in a manner but in a mammering, nor Luther was not then wed yet, nor religious men out of their habit, but

* *English Works*, p. 208.

† More never was in Saxony. He is putting these words in the mouth of a supposed Hungarian. The sermon described by More must have been heard by himself in England.

suffered were those that would be of the sect freely to preach what they would unto the people.

"And forsooth I heard a religious man myself, one that had been reputed and taken for very good, and which, as far as the folk perceived, was of his own living somewhat austere and sharp. But his preaching was wonderful—methink I hear him yet—his voice was so loud and shrill, his learning less than mean. But whereas his matter was much part against fasting, and all affliction for any penance, which he called men's inventions, he cried ever out upon them to keep well the laws of Christ, let go their peevish penance, and purpose then to mend, and seek nothing to salvation but the death of Christ. 'For He is our justice, and He is our Saviour, and our whole satisfaction for all our deadly sins. He did full penance for us all upon His painful Cross, He washed us there all clean with the water of His sweet side, and brought us out of the devil's danger with His dear precious blood. Leave, therefore, leave, I beseech you, these inventions of men, your foolish Lenten fasts, and your peevish penance, minish never Christ's thank, nor look to save yourself. It is Christ's death, I tell you, that must save us all; Christ's death I tell you yet again, and not your own deeds. Leave your own fasting, and lean to Christ alone, good Christian people, for Christ's dear bitter Passion.'

"Now, so loud and so shrill he cried Christ in their ears, and so thick he came forth with Christ's bitter Passion, and that so bitterly spoken, with the sweat dropping down his cheeks, that I marvelled not though I saw the poor women weep, for he made my own hair stand upon my head. And with such preaching were the people so brought in, that some fell to break their fasts on the fasting days, not of frailty or of malice first, but almost of devotion, lest they should take from Christ the thank of His bitter Passion. But when they were awhile nuzzelled in that point first, they could abide and endure after many things more, with which had he then begun they would have pulled him down. God amend that man, whatsoever he be, and God keep all good folk from such manner of preachers ! Such one preacher much more abuseth the name of Christ and of His bitter Passion, than five hundred hazarders that in their idle business swear and forswear themselves by His holy bitter Passion at dice. They carry the minds of the people from the perceiving of their craft, by the continual naming of the name of Christ; and crying His Passion so shrill into their ears, they forget that the Church hath ever taught them that all our penance without Christ's Passion were not worth a pease." *

3. After the varied examples given in this chapter and elsewhere, no minute criticism can be necessary as to Sir Thomas More's literary style. But as I could only illustrate his work by detached fragments, I will conclude with one or two general remarks. Not one of his treatises is cast in a scientific form. They were intended, not as Burnet says, for " the rabble," but for the gentry of England. They are never merely didactic. The dialogue was More's favourite form, a preference he had probably derived from his study of Plato. In his first English controversial work, the *Quoth He and Quoth I*, as well as in his last devotional treatise, his *Comfort against Tribulation*, the speakers are fictitious and the style is very lively. In the other works the authors whom he is controverting are his partners in the dialogue; for he does not merely refer to their arguments or give their substance, he quotes them in full. It is greatly owing to this that his treatises run to so great a length. But no one could complain that he was misrepresented, or even that his book was suppressed, since it appeared again in More's pages, though accompanied by its antidote.

4. Another matter that could scarcely be gathered from the fragments I have quoted is More's deep learning in Holy Scripture. We have seen in his letter to Dorpius, written, be it remembered, some years before Luther's first appearance as

* *English Works*, p. 1175.

a reformer, how eagerly More upheld the study of Holy Scripture as the most fruitful occupation of a theologian. It had been his favourite study from his boyhood, and he was engaged on a commentary on the Gospel when his writing materials were taken from him in the Tower. On the other hand, nothing pained him more than to see souls deluded by fair but false pretences ; to see their reverence for Our Lord and His sacred Passion, and their belief in the inspiration of Holy Scripture—a reverence and a belief derived solely from the Holy Church—used as weapons against herself, by her own revolted and ungrateful priests. This consideration is very important in judging of Sir Thomas More's character and action, since he has been often represented as an enemy of the Bible or of its diffusion, because he concurred in the suppression of Tindale's erroneous translation. His genuine sentiments may be seen from the following passages :—

"Holy Scripture is the highest and best learning that any man can have, if one take the right way in the learning. It is, as a good holy saint saith, so marvellously tempered, that a mouse may wade therein, and an elephant be drowned therein. For there is no man so low, but if he will seek his way with the staff of his faith in his hand, and hold that fast and search the way therewith, and have the old holy fathers also for his guides, going on with a good purpose and a lowly heart, using reason and refusing no good learning, with calling of God for wisdom, grace, and help, that he may well keep his way and follow his good guides, then shall he never fall in peril, but well and surely wade through, and come to such end of his journey as himself would well wish. But surely if he be as long as Longinus, and have a high heart, and trust upon his own wit, look he never so lowly that setteth all the old holy fathers at nought, that fellow shall not fail to sink over the ears and drown. And of all wretches worst shall he walk, that forcing little * of the faith of Christ's Church, cometh to the Scripture

* Making but slight account of.

of God to look and try therein whether the Church believe right or not.   For either doubteth he whether Christ teach His Church true or else whether Christ teacheth it at all or not. And then he doubteth whether Christ in His words did say true, when He said He would be with His Church to the end of the world." *

Elsewhere he writes of the misuse of Scripture by the preachers of his day :—

"I have known right good wits that have set all other learning aside, save the study of Scripture, partly for sloth, partly for pride, which affections their inward secret favour to themselves cloaked under the pretext of simplicity and good Christian devotion.   But in a little while after, the damnable spirit of pride, that unaware to themselves lurked in their hearts, hath begun to put out his horns and show himself. For then have they longed, under the praise of Holy Scripture, to set out to show their own study.   Which, because they would have seem the more to be set by, they have first fallen to the dispraise and derision of all other disciplines.   And because, in speaking or preaching of such common things as all Christian men knew, they could not seem excellent, therefore, marvellously they set out paradoxes and strange opinions against the common faith of Christ's whole Church.   And thus once proudly persuaded a wrong way, they take the bridle in the teeth and run forth like a headstrong horse, that all the world cannot pluck them back.   But, with sowing sedition and setting forth of errors and heresies, and spicing their preaching with rebuking of priesthood and prelacy, for the people's pleasure, they turn many a man to ruin, and themselves also. And then the devil deceiveth them in their blind affections. They take for good zeal to the people their malicious envy, and for a great virtue their ardent appetite to preach, wherein they have so great pride for the people's praise, that preach I ween

* *English Works*, p. 162.

they would, though God would with His own mouth command them the contrary.

"And some have I seen, which, when they have for their perilous preaching been by their prelates prohibited to preach, have proceeded on still. And for maintenance of their disobedience have amended the matter with a heresy, boldly and stubbornly defending that, since they had cunning to preach, they were by God bound to preach, and that no man, nor no law that was made or could be made, had any authority to forbid them; and this they thought sufficiently proved by the words of the Apostles: 'We must obey God rather than men'. As though these men were Apostles, now specially sent by God to preach heresies and sow seditions among Christian men.

"One of this new kind of preachers, being demanded why that he used to say in his sermons that now-a-days men preached not well the gospel, answered that he thought so because he saw not the preachers persecuted, nor no strife nor business arise upon their preaching, which things he said and wrote was the fruit of the gospel, because Christ said: 'I am not come to send peace into the world but the sword'. Was not this a worshipful understanding, that because Christ would make a division among infidels, from the remnant of them to win some, therefore these apostles would sow some cockle of dissension among the Christian people, whereby Christ might lose some of them?"*

It had been the contention of Luther when asked whence he got his Bible, except from the Church, that the visible Church had indeed been divinely and infallibly guided to distinguish between inspired and uninspired writings, to collect and to preserve the written word of God. Sir Thomas had replied that by the same divine guidance she distinguishes between divine and human traditions, divine sacraments and human ceremonies, and especially that if she can know which

* *Ib.,* p. 150.

is the true Scripture she must know which is the true sense of
Scripture, since Our Lord wishes to preserve His Church, not
from erring in one particular way, but from erring at all. *
This argument he pursues at great length in his English works ;
but he puts it all in a short and epigrammatic form in the following words : " Since ye reckon Christ none otherwise present
with His Church than in [*i.e.*, by means of] Holy Scripture,
doth He give His Church the right understanding of Holy
Scripture or not ? ' What if he do not ? ' quoth he. ' Marry,'
quoth I, ' then yourself seeth well, that they were as well without.   And so should the Scripture stand them in as good
stead, as a pair of spectacles should stand a blind friar.' " †

I will conclude this notice of More's controversial writings by
the well-weighed judgment of one of the greatest of controversial
theologians, Thomas Stapleton :—

" In the English works of More, which I read through for
the most part thirty years ago, I found him most thoroughly
versed in the Holy Scriptures, and not unfamiliar with the
Fathers and even with scholastic theology.   He quotes, not
frequently indeed, but appositely when necessary, Augustine,
Jerome, Chrysostom, Cyril, Hilary, Bernard, Gerson.   He
himself, when placed on his defence, affirmed that for seven‡
years he had carefully read the Fathers to know their teaching
as to the primacy of the Roman Pontiff.   And though he was
then intent only on one subject, who can doubt how many
things a man of such talent and marvellous memory would note
in passing regarding our present heresies ?   Running my eye
lately over many parts of his works, I have noticed that he had
well studied dogmatic theology, so that when he touches on
grace, free-will, merit, the nature and acts of faith, charity or
other virtues, on original sin, even on predestination, he so
manages his pen, and writes according to the rules of true

* *Responsio ad Lutherum*, Lib. i. cap. 9.
† *English Works*, p. 147.
‡ The printed letter has seven, the original MS. ten.

theology, that a professed theologian could hardly do it more accurately and fitly.

"A proof that he studiously read St. Thomas is in a fact related by John Harris, his secretary. A book by some heretic, which had just been printed, was brought to More, and he read it as he was being rowed from his house to London. After a little he pointed with his finger to some places and said to Harris : ' See, the arguments of this rascal are precisely the objections placed by St. Thomas in such an article of the second question of his second part of the *Summa*. But the villain says nothing about the solutions made by the holy doctor to the objections.' I myself have seen a certain disputation between More and Father Alphonsus, a minorite, the confessor of Queen Catharine, in which the former maintains the opinion of Scotus about attrition and contrition, as more safe and more probable, against the opinion of Occam ; so that one cannot but marvel to see how a man, who throughout his life was immersed in civil and political matters, and was so excellently versed in profane literature, had not merely dipped into theological and even scholastic questions, but made himself master of them." *

More's controversy with his pen in defence of the Catholic faith came to an end at Christmas, 1533. Henceforth we have to follow him in a controversy of a very different nature, not with heretics and communists, but with the " Defender of the Faith," and the despotic master of England. One matter connected with these writings must be mentioned in conclusion. Sir Thomas More's labours were in all respects disinterested. It is not easy to discover what were the relations in the first century after the invention of printing between authors and their publishers. It would seem, however, that the latter, who were also printers, binders, and booksellers, took all the cost and all the profit. They left the author a certain number of copies, which he might present to his friends and especially to

* *Vita*, cap. 4.

his patrons.   In return for a dedication or the presentation of a book, the author would sometimes receive a gift in money, an office, or a benefice.   There are no dedications prefixed to More's English works.   It was, however, put about that More had become a wealthy man by means of his writings.   In his *Apology* he enters on this matter fully, showing how small was his income from land or other source ; and that, except from the royal grants or salaries belonging to his offices, "not one groat" of his yearly revenue had come to him since he wrote his first book.   He continues : "But then say the brethren that I have taken great rewards in ready money of divers of the clergy".   He allows that a liberal offer had been made, "but (he says) I dare take God and the clergy to record, that they could never fee me with one penny thereof ; but as I plainly told them I would rather have cast their money into the Thames than take it.   For albeit they were good men and honourable, yet look I for my thanks of God that is their better, and for whose sake I take the labour and not for theirs. . . . Although they (the heretics) should call me Pharisee for the boast, and Pelagian for my labour, I am not fully so virtueless, but that of mine own natural disposition, without any special peculiar help of grace thereto, I am both over proud and over slothful also, to be hired for money to take half the labour and business in writing, that I have taken in this gear since I began." *

His son-in-law gives us further details.   The clergy agreed to make up a sum of four or five thousand pounds at the least. The Bishops of Durham (Tunstall), Bath (Clark), and Exeter (Voysey), were charged to convey this present, and pressed it on him ; on his refusal, they urged him to bestow it on his wife and children.   It was all to no purpose, and the money was restored to the subscribers.†

* *Apology*, ch. x. ; *English Works*, p. 867.

† Roper's *Notes*, xiv.   Sir J. Mackintosh remarks that " £5000 was a hundred times the amount of his income ; and according to the rate of interest at that time would have yielded him £500 a year".

This honourable testimonial had been offered probably soon after the resignation of the chancellorship in the summer of 1532. Still more honourable to himself was his own conduct when chancellor, as related by Roper. The water-bailiff of London, who had formerly been in his service, heard certain merchants—probably those trafficking with Germany, and who were infested with Lutheranism—railing against More. He made it known to the chancellor, and begged him to punish their malice. Sir Thomas replied : "Why, Mr. Bailiff, would you have me punish them by whom I receive more benefit than by you that be my friends ? Let them, in God's name, shoot never so many arrows at me ; as long as they do not hit me, what am I the worse ?"*

A man who would neither receive recompense from his friends, nor resent injury from his enemies, was a worthy champion of the Catholic faith.

* Roper, n. viii.

CHAPTER XVI.

FIRST TROUBLES.

THE subject of the last two chapters has somewhat interrupted the chronological course of this narrative, since
it was necessary to group together matters extending
over several years, both before, during and after More's chancellorship. The record of his literary labours has brought us to
the period of his troubles, which begins with the year 1534.
Even before his elevation he was full of anxiety, not on his
own account, but for the evils he saw impending over the
Church and over England. "Walking with me," writes Roper,
"along the Thames' side at Chelsea, in talking of other things,
he said to me: 'Now would to Our Lord, son Roper, upon
condition that three things were well established in Christendom, I were put in a sack and here presently cast into the
Thames'. 'What great things be those, sir,' quoth I, 'that
you should so wish?' 'In faith, son, they be these,' quoth
he; 'the first is, that whereas the most part of Christian
princes be at mortal wars, they were all at universal peace.
The second, that whereas the Church of Christ is at this present
sore afflicted with many errors and heresies, it were settled in
perfect uniformity of religion; the third, that whereas the
matter of the king's marriage is now come in question, it were
to the glory of God and quietness of all parties brought to a
good conclusion.'" Roper does not give the date of this
conversation; from the mention of war, it would seem to

have been in 1528, before More's last embassy to Cambrai. He did his best to bring about peace from national strife, and to prevent the spread of heresy; with regard to the divorce, as he could do no good, he prudently kept aloof.

When he laid down the chancellorship, he had received the assurance from the king of his continued favour, but he had good reasons to distrust one so capricious and despotic, now carried forward by passion and surrounded by bad advisers. Roper tells us of the advice he gave to Thomas Cromwell. "Mr. Cromwell," said More, "you are now entered into the service of a most noble, wise, and liberal prince; if you will follow my poor advice, you shall, in your counsel-giving to his Grace, ever tell him what he ought to do, but never what he is able to do; for if the lion knew his own strength, hard were it for any man to rule him." Unfortunately, Cromwell did the very opposite, and became the evil genius of the king, finding prey for the lion, until at last he was himself devoured. During the later months of 1532 and the whole of 1533 Sir Thomas avoided Henry's court as much as possible, and gave himself to the composition of his books. He was, however, a careful observer, and while meditating his own course, was preparing for the worst. When the divorce was pronounced by Cranmer, Sir Thomas said to his son-in-law: "God grant, son, that these matters within a while be not confirmed with oaths". At Pentecost, 1533, Anne Boleyn, who had been secretly married to the king before the pretended divorce, and afterwards publicly acknowledged as queen, made her magnificent entry into London for her coronation. More's holy friend, Fisher, had been arrested, and kept out of the way, for it was known he would take no part in such an act. It was, no doubt, supposed that Sir Thomas would not dare to absent himself. Yet this he did. The matter is thus related by Roper: "He received a letter from the Bishops of Durham, Bath, and Winchester (Tunstall, Clerk, and Gardiner), requesting him both to keep their company from the Tower to the coronation, and also to take £20 (that by the bearer thereof they had sent him), to buy him a gown; which he thankfully receiving, still tarried at home. At their next meeting he said merrily: 'My lords, you required two things of me, the one I was so well content to grant, that I thought I might be the bolder to deny the other'. He then explained that he took the money because the bishops were rich and he was poor; but his reason for refusing the invitation he illustrated by one of his merry tales, the moral of which was that the bishops were in danger of losing their honour first, and being afterwards destroyed, but as for himself, destroyed he might be, but dishonoured he was resolved he would not be.

It was noticed in his family that he would now often speak of "the joys of heaven and the pains of hell, of the lives of the holy martyrs, of their marvellous patience, and what a happy and blessed thing it was for the love of God to suffer the loss of goods, of liberty, and even life. He would add that for himself, if he could perceive himself encouraged by his wife and children to die in a good cause, for joy thereof he would merrily run to death." * Notwithstanding this interior readiness to suffer, no one could be more cautious to give no unnecessary offence. Sir James Mackintosh remarks that "he most warily retired from every opposition but that which conscience absolutely required. He displayed that very peculiar excellence of his character, which, as it showed his submission to be the fruit of sense of duty, gave dignity to that which in others is apt to seem and to be slavish." †

He had himself written as follows: "Our Lord advised His disciples that if they were pursued in one city, they should not come forth and foolhardily put themselves in peril of denying Christ by impatience of some intolerable torments, but rather flee thence into some other place, where they might serve Him in quiet, till He should suffer them to fall in such point that there were no way to escape. And then would He have them

* Roper.   † *Life of More*, p. 150.

abide by their tackling like mighty champions, wherein they shall not in such case fail of His help." *

It seems probable that Anne Boleyn, indignant at the slight offered her by More's absence from her coronation, and his known disapproval of the divorce, plotted either his humiliation or his ruin.

About Christmas, 1533, a book or proclamation of nine articles was devised by the king's Council in justification of his marriage. The principal points were the following:—

1. That Cranmer's judgment was founded on the decisions of the most famous universities and of the whole English clergy.

2. That causes should not be removed from the country where they are initiated; and that parliament did not desire the inheritance of this realm to depend on the Bishop of Rome, by some men called Pope.

4, 5, 6. That the General Council is superior to all bishops; that any man, especially a prince, may appeal from the Bishop of Rome to the Council, and after his appeal may despise the Pope's censures.

8. That bishops are bound to admonish before excommunicating; which course has been followed by "our good Archbishop of Canterbury admonishing the king that he lived in unlawful matrimony".

9. That the Pope is by birth illegitimate, guilty of simony (at his election), and of heresy in refusing the king's appeal. †

It seems that some pamphlet appeared in answer to the above proclamation, and More was suspected of being its author. His nephew, William Rastell, son of John Rastell and Elizabeth More, afterwards a lawyer and a judge, was at that time following his father's business of a publisher. He was called before the Council, and denied any knowledge of the book. This caused More to write the following letter to

* *English Works*, p. 278.   † *Letters and Papers*, vii. 1.

Cromwell, at that time Master of the Jewel House and secretary to the king:—

"RIGHT WORSHIPFUL,—

"In my most hearty wise I recommend me unto you.

Sir,—My cousin,* William Rastell, hath informed me, that your mastership of your goodness showed him that it hath been reported that I have, against the book of certain articles, which was late put forth in print by the king's honourable Council, made an answer, and delivered it unto my said cousin to print. And albeit that he for his part truly denied it, yet because he somewhat remained in doubt whether your mastership gave him therein credence or not, he desired me for his farther discharge to declare you the very truth. Sir, as help me God, neither my said cousin nor any man else never had any book of mine to print, one or other, since the said book of the king's Council came forth. For of truth the last book that he printed of mine was that book that I made against an unknown heretic, which hath sent over a work that walketh in over many men's hands, named the *Supper of the Lord*, against the Blessed Sacrament of the Altar. My answer whereunto, albeit that the printer, unware to me, dated it *anno* 1534, by which it seemeth to be printed since the Feast of the Circumcision, yet was it of very truth both made and printed, and many of them gone, before Christmas. And myself never espied the printer's oversight in the date, in more than three weeks after. And this was in good faith the last book that my cousin had of mine. Which being true, as of truth it shall be found, sufficeth for his declaration in this behalf.

"As touching my own self, I shall say thus much farther, that

---

* W. Rastell was Sir Thomas's nephew. Cousin (*consanguineus*) is a general term for kin. Nephew (*nepos*) meant grandson or descendent in remote degree. More thus writes (p. 638): "Whether the old doctors, whom these men call grandfathers, or else these young new naughty nephews, be better to be believed"

on my faith I never made any such book nor never thought to do. I read the said book [the proclamation] once over, and never more. But I am for once reading very far off from many things, whereof I would have meetly sure knowledge ere ever I would make an answe:, though the matter and the book both concerned the poorest man in a town, and were of the simplest man's making too. For of many things which in that book be touched, in some I know not the law, and in some I know not the fact. And, therefore, would I never be so childish, nor so play the proud, arrogant fool, by whomsoever the book had been made, and to whomsoever the matter had belonged, as to presume to make an answer to the book, concerning the matter whereof I never was sufficiently learned in the laws, nor fully instructed in the facts. And then, while the matter pertained unto the king's Highness, and the book professeth openly that it was made by his honourable Council, and by them put in print with His Grace's license obtained thereto, I verily trust in good faith that, of your good mind towards me, though I never wrote you word thereof, yourself will both think and say so much for me, that it were a thing far unlikely that an answer should be made thereunto by me.

"I will by the grace of Almighty God, as long as it shall please Him to lend me life in this world, in all such places as I am of my duty to God and the king's Grace bound, truly say my mind and discharge my conscience as becometh a poor, honest, true man, wheresoever I shall be by His Grace commanded. Yet surely if it should happen any book to come abroad in the name of His Grace or his honourable Council, if that book to me seemed such as myself would not have given mine own advice to the making, yet I know my bounden duty to bear more honour to my prince, and more reverence to his honourable Council, than that it could become me for many causes to make an answer to such a book, or to counsel and advise any man else to do it. And, therefore, as it is a thing I never did nor intended, so I heartily beseech you, if you shall happen to perceive any man, either of evil will or of lightness any such thing report by me, be so good master to me as help to bring us both together. And then never take me for honest after, but if you find his honesty somewhat impaired in the matter. Thus am I bold upon your goodness to encumber you with my long, rude letter, in the contents whereof I eftsoon heartily beseech you to be, in manner aforesaid, good master and friend unto me ; whereby you shall bind me to be your bedes-man while I live, as knoweth Our Lord, whose especial grace both bodily and ghostly long preserve and keep you.

"At Chelsea in the vigil of the Purification of Our Blessed Lady [1534],

"By the hand of,

"Assuredly all your own,

"THOMAS MORE, Knight." *

* *English Works*, p. 1422. Chelsea is written Chelchithe; in other letters it is Chelsey.

CHAPTER XVII.

THE HOLY MAID OF KENT:

NO further mention occurs in any paper now extant of the charge related in the last chapter; but in the meantime another had been in preparation : a charge of misprision of treason, that is, of knowledge and concealment of treason in the matter of the Holy Maid of Kent.

Very few words will be sufficient as an introduction to the letters that follow. Elizabeth Barton, a Kentish servant-maid, subject in her youth to falling sickness, was said to have been cured in a chapel of Our Lady, and had become a nun at Canterbury. She was supposed to receive revelations from God, and acquired so great a reputation that she was commonly spoken of as the Holy Maid of Kent. From the time the king's divorce from Queen Katharine was first mooted, her revelations took a political character; she declared herself commissioned by God to admonish and to threaten the king if he persisted, and she visited, for the making known of these celestial warnings, not only her diocesan, Archbishop Warham, but Cardinal Wolsey and Henry himself. At last, in the autumn of 1533, she was supposed to be the tool of a party opposed to the divorce, and was arrested and examined, together with some Benedictine monks, some Observant Franciscan friars, some secular priests and laymen. Of the truth of the accusations made against her and them we need not inquire. It is well-known that several, amongst whom was the Blessed John Fisher, Bishop of Rochester, were attainted of misprision of treason, and several others, including the nun, of treason, and that these were executed at Tyburn on 21st April, 1534. I shall here confine myself to what regards Sir Thomas More.*

From documents lately published it appears that it was Cromwell who, without a vestige of evidence and in the face of evidence to the contrary, sought to include More in a matter from which he had with the utmost circumspection kept himself free. Father Hugh Rich, one of the accused Franciscans, stated in reply to interrogations : " He confesseth that he hath shewed other revelations to Sir T. More, but none concerning the king, for he would not hear them ". This passage was struck through, and the name of More inserted by Cromwel himself among those to whom the revelations about the king were made known.† The Notes or Remembrances kept by Cromwell were seized at his attainder and are still in existence, betraying his action day by day. In January, 1534, we find : " To cause indictments to be drawn up for the offenders in treason and misprision concerning the nun of Canterbury " ; ‡ and " Eftsoons to remember Master More to the king ". § Another document, which is too mutilated to give us any positive information, shows how evidence was being sought against More, as regards his domestic conversation. ||

The following letter gives a minute statement of all the action of Sir Thomas in the matter. It bears no date, but it alludes to the confession of the nun at St Paul's Cross, which was on 23rd November, 1533, and was written before the bill of attainder was brought into parliament in the middle of the following February. The letter is addressed to Cromwell :—

* I have entered into more detail and discussed Blessed John Fisher's share in this matter in my *Life of Fisher*.

† *Letters and Papers*, vi. 1468.

‡ *Ib.*, vii. 48.

§ *Ib.*, 50, 108.

|| *Ib.*, 290.

" RIGHT WORSHIPFUL,—

"After my most hearty recommendation, with like thanks for your goodness, in accepting of my rude, long letter. I perceive, that of your further goodness and favour towards me, it liked your mastership to break with my son Roper, of that, that I had had communication not only with divers that were of acquaintance with the lewd * nun of Canterbury, but also with herself; and had, over that, by my writing, declaring favour towards her, given her advice and counsel; of which my demeanour, that it liketh you to be content to take the labour and the pain to hear, by mine own writing, the truth, I very heartily thank you, and reckon myself therein right deeply beholden to you.

"It is, I suppose, about eight or nine years ago since I heard of that housewife † first; at which time the Bishop of Canter-bury that then was (God assoil his soul) sent unto the king's Grace a roll of paper, in which were written certain words of hers, that she had, as report was then made, at sundry times spoken in her trances ; whereupon it pleased the king's Grace to deliver me the roll, commanding me to look thereon, and afterwards show him what I thought therein. Whereunto, at another time, when His Highness asked me, I told him, that in good faith I found nothing in these words that I could any thing regard or esteem; for seeing that some part fell in rhythm, and that, God wot, full rude also, for any reason, God wot, that I saw therein, a right simple woman might, in my mind, speak it of her own wit well enough. Howbeit, I said, that because it was constantly reported for a truth, that God wrought in her, and that a miracle was shewed upon her, I durst not, nor would not, be bold in judging the matter.

---

* The word "lewd" in the sixteenth century had not the definite mean-ing now attached to it. It was a contemptuous epithet for one who was ignorant, cunning, or malicious.

† A contemptuous term ; a hussy.

And the king's Grace, as me thought, esteemed the matter as light as it after proved lewd.

"From that time till about Christmas was twelvemonth, albeit that continually there was much talking of her, and of her holiness, yet never heard I any talk rehearsed, either of revelation of hers, or miracle, saving that I heard say divers times, in my lord cardinal's days, that she had been both with his lordship and with the king's Grace, but what she said, either to the one or to the other, upon my faith I had never heard any one word. Now, as I was about to tell you, about Christmas was twelvemonth, Father Risby, Friar Observant, then of Canterbury, lodged one night at mine house ; where, after supper, a little before he went to his chamber, he fell in communication with me of the nun, giving her high commendation of holiness, and that it was wonderful to see and understand the works that God wrought in her ; which thing, I answered, that I was very glad to hear it, and thanked God thereof. Then he told me that she had been with my lord legate in his life, and with the king's Grace too ; and that she had told my lord legate a revelation of hers, of three swords that God had put in my lord legate's hand, which if he ordered not well God would lay it sore to his charge. The first, he said, was the ordering the spirituality under the Pope, as legate. The second, the rule that he bore in order of the temporalty under the king, as his chancellor. And the third, she said, was the meddling he was put in trust with by the king, concerning the great matter of his marriage. And therewithal I said unto him, that any revelation of the king's matters I would not hear of ; I doubt not that the goodness of God should direct His Highness with His grace and wisdom, that the thing should take such end as God should be pleased with, to the king's honour and surety of the realm. When he heard me say these words, or the like, he said unto me, that God had specially commanded her to pray for the king ; and forthwith he brake again into her revelations concerning the cardinal, that his soul was saved by her mediation; and without any other communication went into his chamber. And he and I never talked any more of any such manner of matter, nor since his departing on the morrow I never saw him afterwards, to my remembrance, till I saw him at St. Paul's Cross.

"After this, about Shrovetide, there came unto me, a little before supper, Father Rich, Friar Observant of Richmond; and as we fell in talking, I asked him of Father Risby, how he did; and upon that occasion, he asked me, whether Father Risby had any thing showed me of the holy nun of Kent; and I said, yea, and that I was very glad to hear of her virtue. 'I would not,' quoth he, 'tell you again that you have heard of him already; but I have heard, and known, many great graces that God hath wrought in her, and in other folks, by her, which I would gladly tell you, if I thought you had not heard them already.' And therewith he asked me, whether Father Risby had told me anything of her being with my lord cardinal; and I said, 'Yea'. 'Then he told you,' quoth he, 'of the three swords?' 'Yea, verily,' quoth I. 'Did he tell you,' quoth he, 'of the revelations that she had concerning the king's Grace?' 'Nay forsooth,' quoth I, 'nor if he would have done, I would not have given him a hearing; nor verily no more I would indeed, for since she hath been with the king's Grace herself, and told him, methought it a thing needless to tell me, or to any man else.' And when Father Rich perceived that I would not hear her revelations concerning the king's Grace, he talked on a little of her virtue, and let her revelations alone; and therewith my supper was set upon the board, where I required him to sit with me; but he would in no wise tarry, but departed to London. After that night I talked with him twice, once in mine own house, another time in his own garden at the Friars, at every time a great space, but not of any revelations touching the king's Grace, but only of other mean folk, I knew not whom, of which things some were very strange, and some were very childish. But albeit that he said he had seen her lie in her trance in great pains, and that he had at other times taken great spiritual comfort in her communication ; yet did he never tell me that she had told him those tales herself ; for if he had, I would, for the tale of Mary Magdalen which he told me, and for the tale of the hostie, with which, as I have heard, she said she was housled at the king's Mass at Calais—if I had heard it of him as told unto himself by her mouth for a revelation, I would have both liked him and her the worse. But whether ever I heard the same tale of Rich or of Risby, or of neither of them both, but of some other man since she was in hold, in good faith I cannot tell : but I wot well when or wheresoever I heard it, methought it a tale too marvellous to be true, and very likely that she had told some man her dream, which told it out for a revelation. And in effect I little doubted but that some of these tales that were told of her were untrue ; but yet, since I never heard them reported as spoken by her own mouth, I thought nevertheless that many of them might be true, and she a very virtuous woman too ; as some lies be peradventure written of some that be saints in heaven, and yet many miracles indeed done by them for all that.

"After this, I being upon a day at Sion, and talking with the fathers together at the grate, they showed me that she had been with them, and showed me divers things that some of them misliked in her; and in this talking they wished that I had spoken with her, and said they would fain see how I should like her. Whereupon, afterwards, when I heard that she was there again, I came thither to see her, and to speak with her myself. At which communication had, in a little chapel, there were none present but we two ; in the beginning whereof I showed that my coming to her was not of any curious mind, any thing to know of such things as folks talked that it pleased God to reveal and show unto her, but for the great virtue that I had heard so many years, every day more and more spoken and reported of her; I, therefore, had a great mind to see her and be acquainted with her, that she might have somewhat the

more occasion to remember me to God in her devotion and
prayers; whereunto she gave me a very good, virtuous answer,
that as God did of His goodness far better by her than she, a
poor wretch, was worthy, so she feared that many folk, yet
beside that, spoke of their own favourable minds many things
for her, far above the truth, and that of me she had many such
things heard, that already she prayed for me, and ever would;
whereof I heartily thanked her.　I said unto her: 'Madam, one
Helen, a maiden dwelling about Tottenham, of whose trances
and revelations there hath been much talking, she hath been
with me of late, and showed me that she was with you, and
that after the rehearsal of such visions as she had seen, you
showed her that they were no revelations, but plain illusions of
the devil, and advised her to cast them out of her mind; and
verily she gave therein good credence unto you, and thereupon
hath left to lean any longer unto such visions of her own;
whereupon she saith she findeth your words true, for ever since
she hath been the less visited with such things as she was wont
to be before'.　To this she answered me, 'Forsooth, sir, there
is in this point no praise unto me, but the goodness of God, as
it appeareth, hath wrought much meekness in her soul, which
hath taken my rude warning so well, and not grudged to hear
her spirit and her visions reproved'.　I liked her, in good faith,
better for this answer, than for many of these things that I
heard reported by* her.　Afterwards she told me, upon that
occasion, how great need folk have, that are visited with such
visions, to take heed, and prove well of what spirit they come
of; and in that communication she told me, that of late the
devil, in likeness of a bird, was flying and fluttering about
her in a chamber, and suffered himself to be taken; and being
in hands, suddenly changed, in their sight that were present,
into such a strange, ugly-fashioned bird, that they were all
afraid, and threw him out at a window.

"For conclusion, we talked no word of the king's Grace, or

* *i.e.*, of her; concerning her.

any great personage else, nor in effect, of any man or woman, but of herself and myself; but after no long communication had, for or [ere] ever we met my time came to go home, I gave her a double ducat, and prayed her to pray for me and mine, and so departed from her, and never spake with her after. Howbeit, of a truth, I had a great good opinion of her, and had her in great estimation, as you shall perceive by the letter that I wrote unto her. For afterwards, because I had often heard that many right worshipful folks, as well men as women, used to have much communication with her; and many folk are of nature inquisitive and curious, whereby they fall sometimes into such talking, and better were to forbear, of which thing I nothing thought while I talked with her of charity; therefore, I wrote her a letter thereof, which, since it may be, peradventure, that she brake* or lost, I shall insert the very copy thereof in this present letter.

" These were the very words :—

" ' Good Madam and my right dearly beloved Sister in our Lord God,

" ' After most hearty commendation, I shall beseech you to take my good mind in good worth, and pardon me, that I am so homely as of myself unrequired, and also without necessity, to give counsel to you, of whom for the good inspirations, and great revelations that it liketh Almighty God of His goodness to give and show, as many wise, well-learned, and very virtuous folk testify, I myself have need, for the comfort of my soul, to require and ask advice. For surely, good madam, since it pleased God sometime to suffer, such as are far under and of little estimation, to give yet fruitful advertisement to such other as are in the light of the Spirit so far above them, that there were between them no comparison—as He suffered His high prophet Moses to be in some things advised and counselled

* *i.e.*, tore up.

by Jethro—I cannot, for the love that in Our Lord I bear you, refrain to put you in remembrance of one thing, which in my poor mind I think highly necessary to be by your wisdom considered, referring the end and the order thereof to God and His Holy Spirit to direct you. Good madam, I doubt not but that you remember that in the beginning of my communication with you I shewed you that I neither was, nor would be, curious of any knowledge of other men's matters, and least of all of any matter of princes, or of the realm, in case it so were that God had, as to many good folks before-time He hath, any time revealed unto you such things; I said unto your ladyship, that I was not only not desirous to hear of, but also would not hear of. Now, madam, I consider well that many folk desire to speak with you which are not all peradventure of my mind in this point; but some hap to be curious and inquisitive of things that little pertain unto their parts; and some might peradventure hap to talk of such things as might after turn to much harm; as I think you have heard how the late Duke of Buckingham, moved with the fame of one that was reported for an holy monk, and had such talking with him, as after was a great part of his destruction, and disheriting of his blood, and great slander and infamy of religion.* It sufficeth me, good madam, to put you in remembrance of such things as I nothing doubt your wisdom and the Spirit of God shall keep you from talking with any person, specially with high persons, of any such manner things as pertain to princes' affairs, or the state of the realm, but only to commune and talk with any person, high and low, of any such manner things as may to the soul be profitable for you to show, and for them to know. And thus, my good lady and dearly beloved sister in Our Lord, I make an end of this my needless advertisement unto you, whom the Blessed Trinity preserve and increase in grace, and put in your mind to recommend me and mine unto Him in your devout prayers.

* Executed in May, 1521, on a charge of treason.

" 'At Chelsey, this Tuesday, by the hand of your hearty loving brother and beadsman,

" ' THOMAS MORE, Kt.'

" At the receipt of this letter, she answered my servant that she heartily thanked me : soon after this there came to mine house the prior of the Charterhouse at Shene, and one Brother Williams with him, who nothing talked to me but of her, and of the great joy that they took in her virtue, but of any of her revelations they had no communication.   But at another time Brother Williams came to me, and told me a long tale of her, being at the house of a knight in Kent, that was sore troubled with temptations to destroy himself, and none other thing we talked of, nor should have done of likelyhood, though we had tarried together much longer, he took so great pleasure, good man, to tell the tale, with all the circumstances at length. When I came again another day to Sion, on a day in which there was a profession, some of the fathers asked me how I liked the nun.   And I answered that, in good faith, I liked her very well in her talking ; ' howbeit,' quoth I, ' she is never the nearer tried by that ; for I assure you, she were likely to be very bad, if she seemed good, ere I should think her other, till she happened to be proved naught ' ; and in good faith, that is my manner indeed, except I were set to search and examine the truth upon likelyhood of some cloaked evil ; for in that case, although I nothing suspected the person myself, yet no less than if I suspected him sore, I would, as far as my wit would serve me, search to find out the truth, as yourself hath done very prudently in this matter ; wherein you have done, in my mind, to your great laud and praise, a very meritorious deed, in bringing forth to light such detestable hypocrisy ; whereby every other wretch may take warning, and be feared to set forth their own devilish, dissembled falsehood, under the manner and colour of the wonderful work of God ; for verily, this woman so handled herself, with help of that evil spirit hath inspired her, that after her own confession declared at Paul's Cross,* when I sent word by my servant unto the Prior of the Charterhouse, that she was undoubtedly proved a false, deceiving hypocrite, the good man had had so good opinion of her so long, that he could at the first scantly believe me therein. Howbeit it was not he alone that thought her so very good, but many another right good man besides, as little marvel was upon so good report, till she was proved naught.

"I remember me further, that in communication between Father Rich and me, I counselled him, that in such strange things as concerned such folk as had come unto her, to whom, as she said, she had told the causes of their coming ere themselves spake thereof, and such good fruit as they said that many men had received by her prayer, he and such other so reported it, and thought that the knowledge thereof should much pertain to the glory of God, should first cause the things to be well and sure examined by the ordinaries, and such as had authority thereunto ; so that it might be surely known whether the things were true or not, and that there were no letters intermingled among them, or else the letters might after hap to aweigh the credence of these things that were true. And when he told me the tale of Mary Magdalen, I said unto him : 'Father Rich, that she is a good, virtuous woman, in good faith, I hear so many good folk so report, that I verily think it true; and think it well-likely that God worketh some good and great things by her ; but yet are, you wot well, these strange tales no part of our creed ; and, therefore, before you see them surely proved, you shall have my poor counsel, not to wed yourself so far forth to the credence of them as to report them very surely for true, lest that if it should hap that they were afterwards proved false it might minish your estimation in your preaching, whereof might grow great loss'. To this he thanked me for my counsel, but how he used it after that I cannot tell.

* On 23rd November, 1533.

"Thus have I, good Mr. Cromwell, fully declared to you, as far as myself can call to remembrance, all that ever I have done or said in this matter, wherein I am sure that never one of them all shall tell you any further thing of effect; for if any of them, or any man else, report of me, as I trust verily no man will, and I wot well truly no man can, any word or deed by me spoken or done, touching any breach of my legal * truth and duty towards my most redoubted sovereign, and natural liege lord, I will come to mine answer, and make it good in such wise as becometh a poor true man to do ; that whosoever any such thing shall say, shall therein say untrue ; for I neither have in this matter done evil, nor said evil, nor so much as any evil thing thought, but only have been glad, and rejoiced of them that were reported for good ; which condition I shall nevertheless keep towards all other good folk, for the false, cloaked hyprocisy of any of these, no more than I shall esteem Judas the true apostle, for Judas the false traitor.†

"But so purpose I to bear myself in every man's company while I live, that neither good man nor bad, neither monk, friar, nor nun, nor other man or woman in this world shall make me digress from my truth and faith, either towards God or towards my natural prince, by the grace of Almighty God ; and as you therein find me true, so I heartily therein pray you to continue towards me your favour and good-will, as you shall be sure of my poor daily prayer ; for other pleasure can I not do you. And thus the Blessed Trinity, both bodily and ghostly, long preserve and prosper you.

"I pray you pardon me, that I write not unto you of mine own hand, for verily I am compelled to forbear writing for a while, by reason of this disease of mine, whereof the chief occasion is grown, as it is thought, by the stooping and leaning

---

* Is not this a copyist's error for loyal or leal ?

† *i.e.*, He will not count the apostle St. Jude (Thaddeus) a traitor, because Judas (Iscariot) was a traitor.

on my breast, that I have used in writing. And thus, eft-soons, I beseech Our Lord long to preserve you." *

That the letter written by Sir Thomas to the nun was not considered a sufficient exculpation can only be accounted for by the supposition that it was not taken as authentic, that he was suspected not to have really kept a copy of his letter, but to have now invented this in self-defence. This is not a supposition merely, for it appears, from a paper in the British Museum, that inquiries were made as regards More's letter, and the answer was signally corroborative of More's veracity. There is neither name nor date to this paper. I give what relates to More verbatim, but not in its uncouth spelling : " The phrase of Master More's letter I have utterly (as God knoweth) forgotten, for I read it only superficially. In the which I perceived at that time no hurt. Whereupon I counselled and desired Master Golde, also the woman, to keep it safe, for the discharge of the said Master More, whom I conjectured to have heard, after his departing from Sion, something considering her being with the king's Grace, and revelations touching this

* This letter is not in Rastell's collection. It was published by Burnet in the *Records* (n. xxi.) of his second book. He took it from the Norfolk MSS. of Gresham College. " This collection," says Mr. Pocock, " has been destroyed." Of the 562 MSS. which it contained this letter formed part of n. 150, and is catalogued as 3049 in the *Catalogi*. It was probably not an original. Burnet has charged Rastell with suppressing this letter, because of its condemnation of the Holy Maid. Mr. Bruce has vindicated the honesty of Rastell in an article in the *Archæologia* (vol. xxx. p. 149). From comparison with MSS. now existing, Mr. Bruce is of opinion that Rastell printed, not from the letters which were sent—to which he had no access—but from rough drafts that had remained among Sir Thomas's papers. Of the above letter he had no copy. As to the nun, she is not placed among the Church's heroines. Catholics entertained different views of her before Rastell published More's collected works, as they do now. Blessed More's language is strong in reprobation of her, so was Blessed Edmund Campion's. Blessed John Fisher abstained from pronouncing any judgment.

laudable marriage (but the truth I know not), whereby I suspected that he was moved to write that letter. In which he
gave her thanks for her familiar communication, desiring her
to be a testimonial that he never moved nothing appertaining
to our sovereign prince at his being with her. Then also he
desired her no otherwise to disdain his counsel than did Moses,
who had all the revelations, the counsel of Jethro, whose counsel was, as I remember, to show her revelations not to every
man, but to the spiritual and godly persons, not to wordly
men, who receive (as the other honey and wax) poison of
everything.* After he touched the Duke of Buckingham, that
had much displeasure by consorting to a religious person and
monk of Hinton,† but for what his displeasure ensued I remember not there to be expressed, nor yet for what extent he moved
that matter, nor yet how it was ordered in his style, but that he
annexed in the conclusion of his letter this petition to be numbered as one most desirous of her prayers, and such pleasure
as he might do it should always be ready." The paper concludes with an acknowledgment of guilt and folly, and a piteous
appeal for mercy, among other things in consideration of the
writer's youth. ‡

Cromwell, of course, kept this document to himself, and
neither communicated it to Sir Thomas More, nor to the tribunal before which he was to be accused. The parliament
that More had opened in 1529 had not yet been dissolved, and
was summoned for a new session on 15th January. On the
21st of February, a bill of attainder was introduced in the
upper house against all whom it was sought to implicate with
the nun. Sir Thomas heard (perhaps without surprise) that

* It was a common saying that the bee sucks honey from the flower,
and the spider poison.

† "Mount Grace" was first written and cancelled.

‡ Cotton MSS. Cleopatra E., vi. f. 154. This paper seems to be
written by one of the friars, Rich or Risby. From the words, "your
goodness, your mastership," it is clearly addressed to Cromwell.

his name was included, and he wrote the following letter to Cromwell :—

"RIGHT WORSHIPFUL,—

"After right hearty recommendations, so it is that I am informed that there is a .bill put in against me into the higher house before the lords, concerning my communication with the nun of Canterbury, and my writing unto her. Whereof I not a little marvel, the truth of the matter being such as God and I know it is, and as I have plainly declared unto you by my former letters, wherein I found you then so good, that I am now bold eftsoon upon your goodness to desire you to show me the favour, that I might the rather by your good means have a copy of the bill.

"Which seen, if I find any untrue surmise therein, as of likelihood there is, I may make my humble suit unto the king's good Grace, and declare the truth, either to His Grace, or by His Grace's commandment, wheresover the matter shall require. I am so sure of my truth towards His Grace, that I cannot mistrust His Grace's favour towards me upon the truth known, nor the judgment of any honest man. Nor never shall their loss in this matter grieve me, being myself so innocent as God and I know me, whatever should happen therein by the grace of Almighty God, who, both bodily and ghostly, preserve you.

"At Chelsea, this present Saturday,
"By the hand of,
"Heartily all your own,
"THO MORE, Knight." *

This letter was soon followed by another to the king, but as it is unusually verbose and contains no new facts, it will be enough to give the substance. More reminds Henry of his gracious promise of protection in case of any suit that might concern More's honour. For honour or profit he cares nothing, but a charge is being made that touches him more deeply,

* *English Works*, p. 1423.

for his allegiance is called in question. He is perfectly clear in his conscience, but cannot endure the suspicion of ingratitude and baseness. If he should lose his Majesty's good opinion he cares not about goods, liberty or life. These things "could never do me pennyworth of pleasure; but only should my comfort be, that after my short life, and your long (which with continual prosperity to God's pleasure Our Lord of His mercy send you), I should once meet Your Grace again in heaven, and there be merry with you; where, among mine other pleasures, this should yet be one, that Your Grace should surely see there then, that, howsoever you take me, I am your true bedesman now, and ever have been, and will be till I die, howsoever your pleasure be to do by me".*

Rastell gives this as written "in February or March," the draft from which he printed bearing no date or signature. The Cotton MS. concludes: "At my poor house of Chelsith, the fifth day of March, by the known rude hand of your most humble and heavy faithful subject and bedeman, Thomas More, Knight".

The bill had been read a second time on 26th February, and a third time on 6th March. The entry in the Lords' Journal of that date is as follows (in Latin): "A bill, written on paper, concerning the due punishment of Elizabeth Barton, nun and hypocrite, formerly called the Holy Maid of Kent, with her adherents, was thrice read. Their lordships thereupon thought it fit to find whether it was according to the king's will that Sir Thomas More, and the others named with him in the said bill (with the exception of the Bishop of Rochester, who is laid up with illness, and whose answer is already known by his letters), should be required to appear before their lordships in the Star Chamber, that it may be heard what they can say for themselves."

The Imperial Ambassador, Chapuys, wrote to the Emperor

* *English Works*, p. 1423, and in Ellis. *Orig. Let.* (1st ser.) ii. 47, from Cleop E., vi. 132.

on 7th March : " More, the late chancellor, has been examined by the chancellor [Audley] and Cromwell, for a letter which he wrote to the nun, which could not have been more prudent, as he exhorted her to attend to devotion and not meddle in the affairs of princes. As the king did not find, as it seems he hoped, an occasion for doing him more harm, he has taken away his salary." *

His name was indeed struck out of the bill of attainder ; but I must relate in a separate chapter how this came about, because the narrative will bring us into a matter of a very different nature—More's views regarding the supremacy of the Holy See.†

* *Letters and Papers*, vii. 296.

† In More's *English Works* will be found some very interesting and amusing discussions on miracles, apparitions, and revelations. He relates with much wit some examples of imposture (see his *Dialogue English Works*, p. 134), but with great earnestness an instance of what he considered a true diabolical possession and miraculous deliverance (*Ib.*, 137). False miracles and imposture he considers no disproof of the existence of true miracles and real revelations, but a proof of the need of careful tests : " I am sure though ye see some white sapphire or berill so well counterfeit, and so set in a ring, that a right good jeweller will take it for a diamond, yet will ye not doubt, for all that, but that there be in many other rings already set right diamonds indeed. Nor ye will not mistrust St. Peter for Judas."

CHAPTER XVIII

BEFORE THE COUNCIL.

ROPER relates a strange, pathetic history. Sir Thomas More, the virtuous and accomplished gentleman, the perfect statesman, the most loyal of subjects, the man who had spent the best years of his life in the single-hearted service of his king and country—this man was hated by his king for his very goodness, for his uprightness and honour, and the king was bent on his ruin unless he could bring him to dishonour. Without a shred of evidence against him, with the clearest proofs of his loyalty in his hands, both in More's own declaration, in the letter he had written to the nun, and in the testimony of Father Hugh Rich, Henry had caused his former friend, whose neck he had clasped so lovingly as they walked in the Chelsea garden, to be attainted before those noblemen and prelates, over whose assembly he had so lately presided as chancellor, on a charge of misprision of treason, a crime involving confiscation of all property and imprisonment at the king's pleasure; and all this, says Roper, " presupposing of likelihood that this bill would be to Sir Thomas More so troublous that it would force him to relent and condescend to his request " (to approve his divorce). "wherein," adds his son-in-law proudly, " His Grace was much deceived".

Sir Thomas had petitioned to be heard by the lords; the lords also, who knew his innocence, had petitioned for leave to hear him. A strange thing—that such a petition should have been necessary when men's honour, property and liberty were at stake! "The king," continues Roper, "not liking this proposal, assigned that he should appear before four members of his Council: Cranmer, Archbishop of Canterbury; Audley, the Lord Chancellor; the Duke of Norfolk, and Thomas Cromwell. At which time I, thinking I had a good and fit opportunity, earnestly advised him to labour to those lords for his discharge out of the bill; who answered me that he would." The instructions, however, of these royal tools were not to inquire into truth and justice, but to seek by promises and threats to make Sir Thomas More one like themselves.

"At his coming before them they entertained him very friendly, willing him to sit down with them, which in no wise he would. Then began the lord chancellor to declare unto him how many ways the king had showed his love and favour towards him, how fain he would have had him continue in his office, how glad he would have been to have heaped more benefits upon him, and finally how he could ask no worldly honour nor profit at His Highness's hands that were likely to be denied him; hoping by this declaration to provoke him to recompense His Grace with the like again, and unto those things which the parliament, the bishops, and the universities had already passed to add his consent. To this Sir Thomas mildly made answer: 'No man living is there, my lords, that would with better will do the thing that should be acceptable to the king's Highness. Howbeit, I verily hoped I should never have heard of this matter more, considering that I have from time to time always from the beginning so plainly and truly declared my mind unto His Grace; which His Highness ever seemed to me, like a most gracious prince, very well to accept, never minding, as he said, to molest me more therewith.'

"Many things more were there of the like sort uttered on both sides. But in the end, when they saw they could by no manner of persuasions remove him from his former determination, then began they more terribly to touch him, telling him

that the king's Highness had given commandment, if they could
by no gentleness win him, in his name with his great ingratitude to charge him—that never was there servant so to his
sovereign so villainous, nor subject to his prince so traitorous
as he.   For he, by subtle, sinister slights most unnaturally provoking the king to set forth his book on the seven sacraments
and maintaining of the Pope's authority, had caused him, to
his dishonour throughout all Christendom, to put a sword in
the Pope's hand to fight against himself.

"When thus had they laid forth all the terrors they could
imagine against him, 'My lords,' quoth he, 'these terrors be
arguments for children, and not for me.   But to answer to
that wherewith you do chiefly burden me, I believe the king's
Highness of his honour will never lay that to my charge, for
none is there that can in this point say in my excuse more than
His Highness himself.   He right well knoweth that I was never
procurer nor counsellor of His Majesty thereto ; but after it
was finished, by His Grace's appointment and consent of the
makers of the same, I was only a sorter out and placer of the
principal matters therein contained.   Wherein, when I found
the Pope's authority highly advanced, and with strong arguments mightily defended, I said unto His Grace : I must put
Your Highness in remembrance of one thing, and that is this—
the Pope, as Your Grace knoweth, is a prince as you are, and in
league with all other Christian princes.   It may so hereafter
fall out that Your Grace and he may vary upon some point of
leagues, whereupon may grow breach of amity and war between
you both.   I think it best, therefore, that that place be amended
and his authority more slenderly touched.'   'Nay,' quoth His
Grace, 'that shall it not.   We are so much bounden to the See
of Rome that we cannot do too much honour to it.'   Then did
I farther put him in remembrance of the statute of Premunire,
whereby a good part of the Pope's pastoral cure here was pared
away. To that answered His Highness : 'Whatsoever impediment
be to the contrary, we will set forth that authority to the utter-

most, for we receive from that See our crown imperial; which I never heard of before till His Grace told it me with his own mouth'.

"Thus displeasantly departed they. Then took Sir Thomas his boat towards his house at Chelsea, wherein by the way he was very merry; and for that I was nothing sorry, hoping that he had gotten himself discharged out of the parliament bill. When he was landed and come home, then walked we twain alone in his garden together, where I, desirous to know how he had sped, said: 'I trust, sir, that all is well because you are so merry?' 'It is so indeed, son Roper, I thank God,' quoth he. 'Are you, then, put out of the bill?' quoth I. 'By my troth, son Roper,' quoth he, 'I never remembered it.' 'Never remembered it!' said I; 'a cause that toucheth yourself too near, and us all for your sake. I am sorry to hear it, for I verily trusted, when I saw you so merry, that all had been well.' Then said he: 'Wilt thou know, son Roper, why I was so merry? In good faith I rejoiced that I had given the devil a foul fall, and that with those lords I had gone so far as, without great shame, I could never go back again.' At which words waxed I very sad, for though himself liked it well, yet liked it me but a little.

"Now, upon the report made to the king of all their discourse, the king was so highly offended, that he plainly told them he was fully determined that the bill should proceed against him. To whom the lord chancellor and the rest of the lords said that they perceived the lords of the upper house so bent to hear him in his own defence, that if he were not put out of the bill, it would, without fail, be utterly an overthrow of all. But for all this needs would the king have his own will, or else (he said) that at the passing thereof he would be personally present himself.

"Then the Lord Audley and the rest, seeing him so vehemently set thereupon, on their knees most humbly besought His Grace to forbear, considering that if he should in his own presence receive an overthrow, it would not only encourage his subjects ever after to contemn him, but also through all Christendom redound to his dishonour for ever; adding that they mistrusted not in time against him to find some meet matter to serve his time better; for in this cause of the nun, he was accounted (they said) so innocent and clear, that for his dealing therein men reckoned him far worthier of praise than of reproof. Whereupon at length, through their earnest persuasion, he was content to condescend to their petition. And on the morrow after, Mr. Cromwell meeting me in the parliament house,* willed me to tell my father that he was put out of the parliament bill. But because I had appointed to dine that day in London, I sent the message by my servant to my wife to Chelsea. Whereof when she informed her father, ' Meg,' quoth he, ' *quod differtur non aufertur* '. After this, as the Duke of Norfolk and Sir Thomas More chanced to fall in familiar talk together, the Duke said unto him : ' By the Mass, Mr. More, it is perilous striving with princes ; therefore, I would wish you somewhat to incline to the king's pleasure ; for by God's Body, Mr. More, *indignatio principis mors est* '. ' Is that all, my lord ? ' quoth he ; ' then, in good faith, between Your Grace and me is but this, that I shall die to-day and you to-morrow.' "

Immediately on returning home from his interview with the Council,† Sir Thomas More thought it best to make a statement in writing, to the same effect as he had spoken, on the three points which had been brought forward—the matter of the nun, that of the divorce, and the supremacy of the Holy See. This he did in a letter to Cromwell, asking him to be his spokesman and advocate with the king.

He repeats in a few words what he had said in a previous letter with regard to the faultlessness of his conduct in the matter of the nun's revelations. I have given already from

* Roper was M.P. for Canterbury.
† The letter is dated 6th March in the MS. copy.

this letter his account of the way he had studied the question of the divorce, and the entirely neutral position he had kept. We must now hear his own declaration as to the history of his mind on the doctrine of the Pope's supremacy. To secure his exact words I have transcribed the following from the corrected copy which he signed and sent to Cromwell,* not from the printed version that was made from the rough draft.† The variations, however, are very insignificant, except in two instances that will be mentioned in the notes :—

"As touching the third point, the primacy of the Pope, I nothing meddle in the matter. Truth it is, that as I told you when you desired me to show you what I thought therein,‡ I was myself sometime not of the mind that the primacy of that See § should be begun by the institution of God, until that I read in that matter those things that the king's Highness had written in his most famous book against the heresies of Martin Luther. At the first reading whereof I moved the king's Highness either to leave out that point or else to touch it more slenderly, for doubt of such things as after might hap to fall in question between His Highness and some Pope, as between princes and Popes divers times have done. Whereunto His Highness answered me that he would in nowise anything minish of that matter, of which thing His Highness showed me a secret cause, whereof I never had anything heard before.

"But surely after that I had read His Grace's book therein, and so many other things as I have seen in that point by this continuance of this ten‖ years since and more, I have found in effect the substance of all the holy doctors, from St. Ignatius, disciple to St. John the Evangelist, unto our own days, both

---

* Cleopatra E., vi. f. 150-152.

† *English Works*, p. 1426.

‡ That is, in the appearance before the Council the same day.

§ The words "See apostolique" were first written, but "apostolique" is cancelled. It occurs, however, below.

‖ Rastell's version has seven. It is clearly x. in the MS.

Latins and Greeks, so consonant and agreeing in that point, and the thing by such General Councils so confirmed also, that in good faith I never neither read nor heard anything of such effect on the other side that ever could lead me to think that my conscience were well discharged, but rather in right great peril, if I should follow the other side, and deny the primacy to be provided by God.

"Which if we did, yet can I nothing (as I showed you) perceive any commodity that ever could come by that denial. For that primacy is at the leastwise instituted by the corps of Christendom, and for a great urgent cause in avoiding of schisms, and corroborate by continual succession more than the space of a thousand years at the least (for there are passed almost a thousand years since the time of the holy St. Gregory). And, therefore, since all Christendom is one corps, I cannot perceive how any member thereof may, without the common consent of the body, depart from the common head. And then if we may not lawfully leave it by ourself, I cannot perceive, but if* the thing were a treating in a General Council, what the question could avail, whether the primacy were instituted immediately by God, or ordained by the Church.

"As for the General Councils assembled lawfully, I never could perceive, but that in the declaration of the truths, to be believed and to be standen to, the authority thereof ought to be taken for undoubtable.† Or else were there in nothing no certainty, but through Christendom upon every man's affectionate reason all things might be brought from day to day to continual ruffle and confusion. From which by the General Councils, the Spirit of God, assisting every such Council well assembled, keepeth, and ever shall keep, the corps of His Catholic Church.

* "But if," *i.e.*, except in the case that.

† Rastell has: "In the declaration of the truth, it is to be believed and to be standen to, the authority whereof ought to be taken for undoubtable".

"And verily, since the king's Highness hath (as by the book of his honourable Council appeareth), appealed to the General Council from the Pope, in which Council I beseech Our Lord send His Grace comfortable speed, methinketh in my poor mind it could be no furtherance there unto His Grace's cause if His Highness should in his own realm before, either by laws making, or books putting forth, seem to derogate and deny, not only the primacy of the See Apostolic, but also the authority of the General Councils too. Which I verily trust His Highness intendeth not.

"For in the next General Council it may well happen, that this Pope may be deposed and another substituted in his room, with whom the king's Highness may be very well content. For albeit that I have for my own part such opinion of the Pope's primacy * as I have showed you, yet never thought I the Pope above the General Council, nor never have I in any book of mine, put forth among the king's subjects in our vulgar tongue, advanced greatly the Pope's authority.† For albeit that a man may peradventure so find therein that, after the common manner of all Christian realms, I speak of him as primate, yet never do I stick thereon with reasoning and proving of that point. And in my book against the Masker I wrote not, I wot well, five lines,‡ and yet of no more but only St. Peter himself, from whose person many take not § the primacy, even of those that grant it none of his successors. And yet was that book made, printed, and put forth of very truth before that any of the books of the Council ‖ was either printed or spoken of. But whereas I had written thereof at length in my confutation before, and for the proof thereof had compiled together all that I could find therefor, at such time as I little looked that there should fall between the king's Highness and the Pope

* Rastell has "supremacy".
† He had done this in his Latin work, as we have seen.
‡ Rastell has "times". § i.e., take not away.
‖ i.e., the King's Council.

such a breach as is fallen since; when I after that saw the thing likely to draw towards such displeasure between them I suppressed it utterly, and never put word thereof in my book, but put out the remnant without it." *

There are two points in this profession of faith that seem to require elucidation. How could a highly educated Catholic man hold, as More confesses that he did for a time, that the supremacy of the Roman Pontiff was only of ecclesiastical institution? I should reply that his error, being at that time purely theoretical, can be easily conceived to have existed quite innocently in such a man. He had made no special study of theology in his youth, and there was nothing before the rise of Luther's heresy to call his special attention to the subject of the nature and origin of the Pope's primacy. He was not living in schism, and seeking to justify his position, but in loyal obedience to the Holy See, certain of the duty of obedience, and for that reason not careful to examine the origin of the authority whose claim he in no way contested. Of course it should be known to every Catholic man that the Pope is the divinely appointed successor of St. Peter. But the great schism and the action of the Councils of Constance and Basle, and the theories to which that action had given rise, had much disturbed and confused men's minds. A new but necessarily imperfect knowledge of early Church history, and of the writings of the Fathers, had made students acquainted with difficulties for which they found no solutions. Erasmus had put out historical doubts on this as on many other subjects ; and his writings or conversations had probably much influence with More.†

* Cleopatra E., f. 150; also *English Works*, p. 1426.

† De monarchia Pontificis nunquam dubitavi, sed an hæc monarchia fuerit agnita tempore Hieronymi aut exserta, dubito alicubi. Sed ut alicubi noto quod videtur facere ad hanc opinionem, ita rursus aliis locis annoto quæ faciunt ad diversam opinionem. Et tot aliis locis voco Petrum principem apostolici ordinis, pontificem Romanum vicarium Christi et Ecclesiæ principem (Erasmus, *Ep.* 667).

But I should conjecture that the main source of his error was his intimate familiarity with Tunstall. More held his friend's learning, as well as his virtue, in the highest esteem. Now Tunstall declares, in his answer to Pole's treatise on ecclesiastical unity, that his opinions on the Holy See were, and ever had been, not such as we call Gallican, but like those of modern Anglicans. It will not be a digression to give a specimen of Tunstall's language, since what he wrote to Pole in 1536 he must have often said to More, during their long intimacy. He declares that the king, in making himself head of the Anglican Church, was desirous " to reduce his Church of England out of all captivity of foreign powers, heretofore usurped therein, into the pristine estate that all Churches of all realms were in at the beginning, and to abolish and clearly put away such usurpation as theretofore in this realm the Bishops of Rome have, to their great advantage and impoverishing of the realm and the king's subjects, of the same. . . . Would to God you had been exercised in reading the ancient councils, that you might have known from the beginning, from age to age, the continuance and progress of the Catholic Church, by which you should have perceived that the Church of Rome had never of old such a monarchy as of late it hath usurped." * In a dignified answer Pole reminds Tunstall that men, learned and holy as Fisher and More, held the contrary, and were so thoroughly convinced of the Divine institution of the primacy of the Holy See, that they had shed their blood for it.

When, in 1520, More's attention was called to this matter, he must at first have been perplexed between Fisher and Tunstall ; but when he gave himself to earnest study he soon came to share the conviction and faith of Fisher, and he tells Cromwell that more than ten years' continual study had in no

* MS. in British Museum, Cleopatra E., vi. f. 389. I am not aware whether this letter is anywhere printed. Pole's answer to it is in *Strype Mem.*, i. pt. ii. n. 83, p. 306.

wise altered his mind, so that it was not a matter of opinion but of conscience.

What More adds about the possibility of a General Council deposing the Pope is somewhat *male sonans*, but it must be remembered that More is taking the king at his own word; he had not only appealed to a future General Council against the Pope, but he accused the Pope himself of being a usurper of the Apostolic See by simony, and (in any case) of having forfeited it by heresy. More, therefore, knowing full well that Henry wished for nothing less than the meeting of a General Council, wished His Majesty good speed. It would be rash to quote More as holding that a Council may depose a Pope for evil and scandalous life, as some have held. More refers only to the two things mentioned by Henry, viz., simony and heresy. Now, it is admitted by all that simony invalidates a Pope's election. Could it be proved against him, he would not, strictly speaking, be deposed, but he would be declared never to have been Pope.* Again, if manifest and obstinate heresy were proved against a Pope, a Council might declare his See vacant, since he would be deposed by the invisible Head of the Church, the everlasting Truth.†

In these cases only is a Council above the Pope, according to the highest " ultramontane " doctrine, nor would it be just to cite our great chancellor for more than this. His words were all weighed in a learned balance. It was not many days after this declaration that More had to prove, by loss of bodily liberty, the freedom of his soul and his steadfast allegiance to conscience.

---

* His acts, however, would have been valid *ex titulo colorato* (see *Franselin, De Ecclesia. Bouix, De Papa,* vol. iii).

† The case has never occurred, and many hold that it cannot occur.

CHAPTER XIX.

REFUSAL OF THE OATH.

A LL attempts to entangle More in the meshes of the law for his own actions had entirely failed. He had proved his innocence in every point. His ruin was to be accomplished by the course of public events in which he had had no share. The day that he had foretold, and for which he was preparing himself, soon came, when Henry's divorce and marriage with Anne Boleyn, as well as the succession to the crown in her offspring, were to be confirmed by oaths. A bill limiting the succession, making it high treason to oppose it, and misprision of treason to speak against it, was passed in parliament and received the royal assent on 30th March, 1534. It enacted "that all the nobles of the realm, spiritual and temporal, and all other subjects arrived at full age, should be obliged to take corporal oath, in the presence of the king or his commissioners, to observe and maintain the whole effect and contents of the Act". The penalties of refusal were those of misprision of treason. Parliament, however, omitted to prescribe a formula. That which was drawn up by the commissioners was wider than the scope of the Act, and included an affirmation of the truth of its preamble, declaring the invalidity of Henry's first marriage and the validity of the second. As the Sovereign Pontiff had, on 23rd March, 1534, given his final decision in favour of the marriage with Katharine of Aragon, such an oath implied the rejection of his authority. At the same time the formula recalled and repudiated any oath taken "to any foreign authority, prince, or potentate". This, for the clergy, was a violation and renunciation of their oath of fidelity and obedience to the Pope.   By an evident abuse of this Act of parliament an oath was administered to all the clergy throughout the realm, expressing total rejection of any authority of the Bishop of Rome in England.   For the laity the form chosen dwelt rather on the succession to the crown.

The members of the two houses took the oath in presence of the king before the prorogation of parliament on the 30th March.   What formula was used on that occasion we do not know.   That which appears in the Lords' Journal, and to which reference has just been made as having been drawn up by the commissioners, did not receive parliamentary sanction until the next session, towards the close of the year, though that sanction declared it valid in the past.

Sir Thomas now took a singular way of preparing his family for the catastrophe, if we may believe Cresacre.   This was to give them some false alarms.   He hired an official to come suddenly to his house, as if with a summons, so as to startle all the inmates, and thus give him an opportunity to speak on the subject of detachment and martyrdom.   On 28th March John Graaynfyld, an official of the Court of Chancery, wrote to Lord Lisle : " My old master, Sir Thomas More, is clearly discharged of his trouble ".*   Sir Thomas knew that he was only at the beginning of his troubles.

On Low Sunday, which, in 1534, fell on 12th April, More went into London with his son-in-law, Roper, to hear the sermon at St. Paul's, and afterwards went to the house of John Clements.   His presence had been remarked, and the official, following him to Clements' house, served him with a citation to appear next morning before the royal commissioners at Lambeth, to take the new oath.†   What follows must be told

* *Letters and Papers*, vii. 384.

† This circumstance is not noted by Roper, but by Stapleton (cap. 15), who no doubt learnt it from Mrs. Clements.   There is a misprint of *Dom. in palmis* for *in albis*.

in the very words of Roper, the eye-witness: "Then Sir Thomas More, as his accustomed manner always was ere he entered into any matter of importance (as when he was first chosen of the Privy Council, when he was sent ambassador, appointed speaker of the parliament-house, made lord chancellor, or when he took any other like weighty matter upon him), to go to Church to be confessed,* to hear Mass, and to be houseled; so did he likewise in the morning early the self-same day that he was summoned to appear before the lords at Lambeth". This was Monday, 13th April. The commissioners were: Cranmer, Archbishop of Canterbury; Audley, lord chancellor; Cromwell, secretary of state; to whom was added the Abbot of Westminster.

Roper continues: "And whereas he evermore used before, at his departure from his wife and children, whom he tenderly loved, to have them bring him to his boat, and there to kiss them, and bid them all farewell, *then* would he suffer none of them forth the gate to follow him, but pulled the wicket after him and shut them all from him; and with a heavy heart, as by his countenance it appeared, with me and our four servants took boat towards Lambeth. Wherein sitting still sadly a while, at the last he suddenly rounded me in the ear and said: 'Son Roper, I thank Our Lord the field is won'. What he meant thereby I then wist not, yet, loth to seem ignorant, I answered: 'Sir, I am therefor very glad'. But, as I conjectured afterward, it was for that the love he had to God wrought in him so effectually that he conquered all his carnal affection utterly."

I may here supplement Roper's narrative from the beautiful treatise composed by Sir Thomas in the Tower on Our Lord's Agony in the Garden. In it will be found the true explanation of his own conduct throughout his trials and martyrdom, because he had ever this model before his eyes. Thus, of the interior

---

* The old English phrase "to be confessed" (where we say "to confess") indicates the sacramental character of the act, and its passive nature as regards absolution.

conflict he endured in parting with his family and his liberty, after mentioning that some of the martyrs of their own accord gladly went to meet persecution, he writes : " But yet God of His infinite mercy doth not require us to take upon us this most high degree of stout courage, which is so full of hardness and difficulty.   And therefore I would not advise every man at adventure rashly to run forth so far forward that he shall not be able fair and softly to come back again, but unless he can attain to climb up to the hill-top, be haply in hazard to tumble down even to the bottom headlong.   Let them yet whom God especially calleth thereunto set forth in God's name and proceed, and they shall reign.   But yet before a man falleth in trouble, fear is not greatly to be discommended, and so that reason be always ready to resist and master fear, the conflict is then no sin nor offence at all, but rather a great matter of merit. . . . Unto one that were likely to be in such a case, Christ saith : ' Pluck up thy courage, faint heart ; what though thou be fearful, sorry and weary, and standest in great dread of most painful torments, be of good comfort ; for I Myself have vanquished the whole world, and yet felt I far more fear, sorrow, weariness, and much more inward anguish too, when I considered My most bitter, painful Passion to press so fast upon Me.   He that is strong-hearted may find a thousand glorious valiant martyrs whose ensample he may right joyously follow.   But thou now, O timorous and weak, silly sheep, think it sufficient for thee only to walk after Me, which am thy Shepherd and Governor, and to mistrust thyself and put thy trust in Me.   Take hold of the hem of My garment, therefore ; from thence shall thou perceive strength and relief to proceed.' " *

Sir Thomas will now himself tell us what happened to him at Lambeth.   It was a great crisis in English history, the first overt and total renunciation of the authority of the Sovereign Pontiff and separation from the rest of Christendom ; for such in reality and in effect it was, though few realised at the time

* *English Works*, p. 1357.

the full significance of their act.   A letter to his daughter Margaret, written a few days later, has been preserved: "When I was before the lords at Lambeth I was the first that was called in, albeit that Master Dr. the Vicar of Croydon was come before me and divers others.   After the cause of my sending for declared unto me (whereof I somewhat marvelled in my mind, considering that they sent for no temporal men but me), I desired the sight of the oath, which they showed me under the great seal.   Then desired I the sight of the Act of Succession, which was delivered me in a printed roll.   After which read secretly by myself, and the oath considered with the Act, I answered unto them that my purpose was not to put any fault either in the Act or any man that made it, or in the oath or any man that sware it, nor to condemn the conscience of any other man : but as for myself, in good faith my conscience so moved me in the matter, that though I would not deny to swear to the succession, yet unto that oath that there was offered me I could not swear without the jeoparding of my soul to perpetual damnation.   And that if they doubted whether I did refuse the oath only for the grudge of my conscience or for any fantasy, I was ready therein to satisfy them by my oath which if they trusted not, what should they be the better to give me any oath ?   And if they trusted that I would therein swear true, then trusted I that of their goodness they would not move me to swear the oath that they offered me, perceiving that for to swear it was against my conscience.

"Unto this my lord chancellor said, that they all were very sorry to hear me say this, and see me thus refuse the oath. And they said all, that on their faith I was the very first that ever refused it, which would cause the king's Highness to conceive great suspicion of me and great indignation towards me. And therewith they showed me the roll and let me see the names of the lords and the commons which had sworn and subscribed their names already.   Which notwithstanding, when they saw that I refused to swear the same myself, not blaming

23

any other man that had sworn, I was in conclusion commanded to go down into the garden. And thereupon I tarried in the old burned chamber that looketh into the garden, and would not go down because of the heat.

"In that time I saw Master Dr. Latimer come into the garden, and there walked he with divers other doctors and chaplains of my lord of Canterbury. And very merry I saw him, for he laughed and took one or twain about the neck so handsomely, that if they had been women I would have weened he had been waxen wanton. After that came Master Dr. Wilson * forth from the lords, and was with two gentlemen brought by me, and gentlemanly sent straight unto the Tower. What time my Lord of Rochester + was called in before them, that can I not tell. But at night I heard that he had been before them, but where he remained that night, and so forth till he was sent hither, I never heard.‡ I heard also that Master Vicar of Croydon and all the remnant of the priests of London that were sent for, were sworn; and that they had such favour at the Council's hand, that they were not lingered or made to dance any long attendance to their travail and cost, as suitors were sometimes wont to be, but were sped apace to their great comfort; so far forth that Master Vicar of Croydon, either for gladness or for dryness, or else that it might be seen, *Quod ille notus erat pontifici*, went to my lord's buttery bar and called for drink, and drank *valde familiariter*.

"When they had played their pageant and were gone out of the place, then was I called in again. And then was it declared unto me, what a number had sworn ever since I went aside, gladly without any sticking. Wherein I laid no blame in no man, but for mine own self answered as before. Now, as well before as then, they somewhat laid unto me for obstinacy, that whereas before, since I refused to swear, I would not declare any

* Dr. Wilson had been royal chaplain.
+ Blessed John Fisher.
‡ He was kept at Lambeth in the custody of Archbishop Cranmer.

special part of that oath that grudged my conscience, and open
the cause wherefore.   For thereunto I had said unto them, that
I feared lest the king's Highness would, as they said, take displeasure enough towards me for the only refusal of the oath.
And that if I should open and disclose the causes why, I should
therewith but further exasperate His Highness, which I would in
nowise do, but rather would I abide all the danger and harm
that might come towards me, than give His Highness any occasion of further displeasure, than the offering of the oath unto
me of pure necessity constrained me.

"Howbeit, when they divers times imputed this to me for
stubbornness and obstinacy, that I would neither swear the
oath, nor yet declare the causes why, I declined thus far towards
them, that rather than I would be accounted for obstinate, I
would upon the king's license, or rather his such commandment
had, as might be my sufficient warrant, that my declaration
should not offend His Highness nor put me in the danger of any
of his statutes, I would be content to declare the causes in writing, and (over that) to give an oath in the beginning, that if I
might find those causes by any man in suchwise answered, as I
might think mine own conscience satisfied, I would after that
with all my heart swear the principal oath too.   To this I was
answered, that though the king would give me license under
his letters patent, yet would it not serve me against the statute.
Whereto I said, that yet if I had them, I would stand unto the
trust of his honour at my peril for the remnant.   But yet
thinketh me,* lo! that if I may not declare the causes without
peril, then to leave them undeclared is no obstinacy.

"My lord of Canterbury taking hold upon that that I said,
that I condemned not the consciences of them that swear, said
unto me, that it appeared well, that I did not take it for a very
sure thing and a certain, that I might not lawfully swear it, but
rather as a thing uncertain and doubtful.   'But then,' said my
lord, 'you know for a certainty, and a thing without doubt, that you

* It seems to me.

be bound to obey your sovereign lord your king. And therefore are you bound to leave off the doubt of your unsure conscience in refusing the oath, and take the sure way in obeying of your prince, and swear it.' Now all was it so, that in mine own mind methought myself not concluded,* yet this argument seemed me suddenly so subtle, and namely with such authority coming out of so noble a prelate's mouth, that I could again answer nothing thereto, but only that I thought myself I might not well do so, because that in my conscience this was one of the cases in which I was bounden that I should not obey my prince, since that (whatsoever other folk thought in the matter, whose conscience or learning I would not condemn nor take upon me to judge), yet to my conscience the truth seemed on the other side. Wherein I had not informed my conscience neither suddenly nor slightly, but by long leisure and diligent search for the matter. And of truth, if that reason may conclude, then have we a ready way to avoid all perplexities ; for in whatsoever matter the doctors stand in great doubt, the king's commandment, given upon whether side he list, solveth all the doubts.

"Then said my lord of Westminster to me, that howsoever the matter seemed unto mine own mind, I had cause to fear that mine own mind was erroneous, when I see the great Council of the realm determine of my mind the contrary, and that therefore I ought to change my conscience. To that I answered that if there were no more but myself upon my side, and the whole parliament upon the other, I would be sore afraid to lean to mine own mind only against so many. But, on the other side, if it so be that in some things for which I refuse the oath, I have (as I think I have) upon my part as great a council and a greater too, I am not then bounden to change my conscience and conform it to the Council of one realm against the general council of Christendom.

"Upon this Master Secretary,† as he that tenderly favoureth

---

* Although it seemed to me that this reasoning was not conclusive.
† Thomas Cromwell.

me, said and sware a great oath, that he had lever that his own only son (which is of truth a goodly young gentleman, and shall, I trust, come to much worship) had lost his head, than that I should thus have refused the oath. For surely the king's Highness would now conceive a great suspicion against me, and think that the matter of the nun of Canterbury was all contrived by my drift. To which I said that the contrary was true and well known; and whatsoever should mishap me, it lay not in my power to help it without the peril of my soul.

"Then did my lord chancellor repeat before me my refusal unto Master Secretary, as to him that was going unto the king's Grace; and in the rehearsing his lordship repeated again that I denied not but was content to swear unto the succession. Whereunto I said, that as for that point I would be content, so that I might see my oath in that point so framed, in such a manner as might stand with my conscience. Then said my lord: 'Marry, Master Secretary, mark that too, that he will not swear that neither but under some certain manner'. 'Verily no, my lord,' quoth I, 'but that I will see it made in such wise first as I shall myself see that I shall neither be forsworn nor swear against my conscience.' Surely as to swear to the succession I see no peril; but I thought and think it reason that to mine own oath I look well myself, and be of counsel also in the fashion; and never intended to swear for a piece and set my hand to the whole oath. Howbeit, as help me God, as touching the whole oath I never withdrew any man from it, nor never advised any to refuse it, nor never put nor will put any scruple in any man's head, but leave every man to his own conscience. And methinketh in good faith that so were it good reason that every man should leave me to mine." *

Although this letter was written by More to his daughter, yet there are, if I mistake not, several passages intended rather for the eyes of others than for hers. There was every likelihood that sooner or later the letter might come before the Council or

* *English Works*, p. 1428.

the king, and he wished to have an accurate record of what had passed, and of his reasons for refusing the oath.

Sir Thomas mentions that the Bishop of Rochester has been sent "hither". He means to the Tower, for it is known from Roper that, after refusing the oath, Sir Thomas was kept in the custody of the Abbot of Westminster for four days while the king consulted with his Council as to his future treatment. On Friday, 17th April, he was sent to the Tower, whence he wrote to his anxious daughter the letter that has just been given.

His committal to the Tower was the result of the following correspondence between Cranmer and Cromwell:—

"RIGHT WORSHIPFUL MASTER CROMWELL,—

"After most hearty commendations, etc. I doubt not but you do right well remember that my Lord of Rochester and Master More were contented to be sworn to the Act of the king's succession, but not to the preamble of the same. What was the cause of their refusal I am uncertain, and they would by no means express the same. Nevertheless, it must needs be either the diminution of the authority of the Bishop of Rome, or else the reprobation of the king's first pretensed matrimony. But if they do obstinately persist in their opinions of the preamble, yet meseemeth it should not be refused, if they will be sworn to the very Act of Succession, so that they will be sworn to maintain the same against all powers and potentates.

"For hereby shall be a great occasion to satisfy the princess-dowager and the Lady Mary, which do think that they should damn their souls if they should abandon and relinquish their estates. And not only it should stop the mouths of them, but also of the emperor and other their friends, if they give as much credence to my Lord of Rochester and Master More speaking or doing against them, as they hitherto have done, and thought that all should have done, when they spake and did with them.

"And, peradventure, it should be a good quietation to many

other within this realm, if such men should say that the succession comprised within the said Act is good and according to God's laws. For then, I think, there is not one within this realm that would once reclaim against it. And whereas divers persons, either of a wilfulness will not, or of an indurate and invertible conscience cannot, alter from their opinions of the king's first pretensed marriage (wherein they have once said their minds, and percase have a persuasion in their heads that if they should now vary therefrom their fame and estimation were distained for ever), or else of the authority of the Bishop of Rome ; yet, if all the realm with one accord would apprehend the said succession, in my judgment it is a thing to be amplected and embraced. Which thing, though I trust surely in God that it shall be brought to pass, yet hereunto might not a little avail the consent and oaths of these two persons, the Bishop of Rochester and Master More, with their adherents, or, rather, confederates.

" And if the king's pleasure so were, their said oaths might be suppressed, but [*i.e.*, except] when and where His Highness might take some commodity by the publishing of the same. Thus Our Lord have you ever in His conservation.

" From my manor at Croydon, the 17th day of April.
" Your own assured ever,
" THOMAS CANTUAR." *

The last clause about *suppressing* the exact nature of the oath to be taken by More and Fisher is worthy of Cranmer. It was to be given out (such was the scheme) that they had yielded, so as to induce others to yield ; but occasionally it might " suit the king's commodity," as when dealing with persons of similar scruples, to reveal and use the modified form.

Cromwell laid the archbishop's letter before the king. His Majesty did not deny that another form of oath would satisfy the Act, but it would by no means satisfy his intentions and policy, for his whole object was to humble Sir Thomas, and

* Burnet, i. 255. Also (in abridgment) in *Letters and Papers*, vii. 499.

bend him to his will in the matter of the divorce. Without any regard, therefore, to justice, he bade his minister return the following answer :—

"My lord, after mine humble commendation, it may please Your Grace to be advertised that I have received your letter and showed the same to the king's Highness, who, perceiving that your mind and opinion is that it were good that the Bishop of Rochester and Master More should be sworn to the king's succession, and not to the preamble of the same, thinketh that if their oaths should be taken it were an occasion to all men to refuse the whole, or at least the like. For, in case they be sworn to the succession, and not to the preamble, it is to be thought that it might be taken not only as a confirmation of the Bishop of Rome's authority, but also as a reprobation of the king's second marriage. Wherefore, to the intent that no such things should be brought into the heads of the people by the example of the said Bishop of Rochester and Master More, the king's Highness in no wise willeth but that they shall be sworn as well to the preamble as to the Act. Wherefore, His Grace specially trusteth that ye will in no wise attempt or move him to the contrary ; for, as His Grace supposeth, that manner of swearing, if it shall be suffered, may be an utter destruction of his whole cause, and also to the effect of the law made for the same."

Roper had never seen these letters, but they entirely bear out his assertion, that "albeit in the beginning they (the commissioners) were resolved with an oath not to be acknown [*i.e.*, acknowledged] whether he had to the supremacy been sworn, or what he thought thereof, he should be discharged ; yet did Queen Anne, by her importunate clamour, so sore exasperate the king against him, that, contrary to his former resolution, he caused the said oath of supremacy to be ministered unto him ; who, albeit he made a discreet, qualified answer, nevertheless was forthwith committed to the Tower ".

The words used by Roper should be noted. Burnet and

others find fault with Catholic writers for speaking of an oath of supremacy instead of an oath of succession. Roper, however, who was a lawyer as well as a contemporary, knew perfectly well what he wrote. Had the oath been merely to the succession of the crown, as was the intention of parliament, More would have taken it, while regretting the motives or premisses that had led to the change. But because the oath was converted into one of supremacy, he refused it.

To clear up the matter, I may remark that, although the denial of the Pope's supremacy in the Church in no way logically involves the affirmation of the king's supremacy in the Church of England (as the whole of non-conformist England has perfectly well understood), yet at the period in question the two were inseparable in men's minds. The headship of the king was insisted on simply to get rid of the Pope's authority. The Pope's authority was denied simply to make place for the king's prerogative. Thus John Leek confesses that he had advised Blessed John Hall "not to go to Hounslow before the commissioners to take oath to renounce the papacy and acknowledge the king's supremacy"; and he is speaking of no other oath than that exacted in virtue of this Act of Succession in the spring of 1534.* Though the form of oath subscribed by the clergy was much more explicit on these points than any that was proposed to Sir Thomas More, yet there were in it clauses or words implying the same doctrines, as Cranmer's letter testifies.

Hence Sir Thomas, on his committal to the Tower, while accepting and even rejoicing in the Providence of God, did not conceal the injustice of his imprisonment on the part of men. "I may tell thee, Meg, they that have committed me hither for refusing of this oath, not agreeable with their statute, are not by their own law able to justify mine imprisonment. And surely, daughter, it is a great pity that any Christian prince should, by a flexible council, ready to follow his

* *Letters and Papers*, viii. 56.

affections, and by a weak clergy, lacking grace constantly to stand to their learning, with flattery be so shamefully abused." * Lest it be suspected that Margaret may not have exactly reported her father's words, or that Sir Thomas may have spoken hastily, I will add that the best legal authorities of modern times entirely accept More's view, as related by Roper; and that the government virtually acknowledged its error, by causing parliament to ratify their past arbitrary proceedings. A new session began on the 3rd of November, 1534. Roper says: "At length, the Lord Chancellor and Mr. Secretary, espying their own oversight, were fain to find the means that another statute should be made for the confirmation of the oath so amplified with their additions".

Sir James Mackintosh writes : "An Act was passed † which ratifies and professes to recite the form of oath promulgated on the day of prorogation; and enacts that the oath above recited shall be *reputed* to be the very oath intended by the former Act of Succession, though there were, in fact, some substantial and important interpolations in the latter Act". ‡ And Lord Chancellor Campbell, writing of the attainder of More in this same session, "for refusal to take the oath of supremacy," says it was "an offence created by no law"; since (as he explains elsewhere) the commissioners had no right to foist the question of the Pope's supremacy, or the king's supremacy, into an oath which should have been limited to the succession. An oath to the succession had never been refused by either More or Fisher, yet in the winter session they were both attainted of misprision of treason. In the Act which relates to More,§ the king's grants of land to him in 1523 and 1525 are resumed; it is alleged that he refused the oath since 1st May of 1534, with an intent to sow sedition, and he is reproached for having demeaned himself in other respects ungratefully and unkindly to the king, his benefactor.

---

* From a conversation reported by Roper.   † 26 Hen. viii. cap. 2.
‡ *Life of More*, p. 176.   § 26 Hen. viii. cap. 23.

CHAPTER XX.

THE TOWER.

"WHEN Sir Thomas was going to the Tower," says Roper, "wearing as he commonly did a chain of gold about his neck, Sir Richard Southwell, that had the charge of his conveyance thither, advised him to send home his chain to his wife or to some of his children. 'Nay, sir,' quoth he, 'that I will not; for if I were taken in the field (of battle) by my enemies, I would they should somewhat fare the better for me.' At whose landing Mr. Lieutenant* was ready at the Tower gate to receive him, where the porter demanded of him his upper garment. 'Mr. Porter,' quoth he, 'here it is,' and took off his cap and delivered to him, saying: 'I am very sorry it is no better for thee'. 'No, sir,' quoth the porter, 'I must have your gown.' And so was he by Mr. Lieutenant conveyed to his lodging, where he called unto him John à Wood, his own servant, there appointed to attend him, who could neither write nor read, and sware him before the lieutenant, that if he should hear or see him at any time speak or write any matter against the king, Council, or the state of the realm, he should open it to the lieutenant, that the lieutenant might incontinent reveal it to the Council."

Most of the buildings of the great fortified enclosure, then and now called the Tower of London, still stand as in the days of Henry VIII. Of these, none is more generally known than

* Sir Edmund Walsingham.

the Beauchamp Tower in the western ward, which is tradition-
ally said to have been the place of confinement of Sir Thomas
More.   According to the fixed scale of charges of the lieutenant, Sir Thomas as a knight paid fees of ten shillings a week
for himself and five shillings for his servant.   A bill of charges
drawn up a few years after his death contains the following

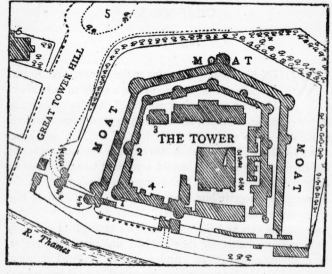

PLAN OF THE TOWER.

1. The Bell Tower.   4. The Lieutenant's Lodgings.
2. The Beauchamp Tower.   5. The Scaffold.
3. St. Peter's ad Vincula.   6. All Hallows, Barking.

entry: "Sir Thomas More for 3 m. [months] unpaid, after 40s.
and his servant after 5s. [a week] . . . £9".*   This heavy
charge of about £6 a week in modern value ought to have
purchased a generous diet, yet from details to be mentioned
presently it would seem that even the smallest comforts had to
be supplied by friends from outside.   Yet, in August, 1534,

* Cotton MSS. (B.M.) ; *Titus*, Bk. i.

Margaret Roper told her sister-in-law that "besides his old disease of his breast, he was now grieved in the reins by reason of gravel and stone, and with the cramp that divers nights griped his legs". *

This did not satisfy his spirit of mortification and penance. It had long been a practice with him on certain days to wear a rough hair shirt, and he continued this in the prison cell till his death. Roper relates that one summer evening when he sat at supper with his family and had laid aside his gown, his young daughter-in-law, Anne Cresacre, chanced to espy the hair shirt, and began to laugh at it. His daughter Margaret, perceiving this, acquainted her father, who was sorry that his austerities were detected. This beloved child entered into the secrets of her father's heart. She had been accustomed to wash the hair shirt for him, and to her the day before his death he had it secretly conveyed.† A part of this precious relic lies before me as I write. If the holy prisoner sought by penitential exercises to communicate more closely with the Passion of Our Lord, he kept up his sympathy with the Church during his isolation, by celebrating all her feasts, at least in spirit, within the walls of his dungeon. Stapleton learnt from one of those who cherished every detail of his martyrdom, that he was accustomed to dress more carefully, as far as his slender wardrobe allowed, when the great feasts came round.‡

The rigour of confinement varied much in English prisons of that date, according to the quality of the offender, the nature of his offence, or his means of purchasing the indulgence or connivance of his jailor. The lieutenant of the Tower, Sir Edmund Walsingham, had been a friend of Sir Thomas.

* *English Works*, p. 1434.

† It was from her that Roper learnt these details, and also that he was wont on certain days to punish his body with whips and knotted cords.

‡ That he had at least two "gowns" is clear from his own words in a letter, that, when summoned before the Council, "he changed his gown," and from the fact that, when about to go to the scaffold, he wished to put on his best apparel.

Roper tells us that soon after his illustrious prisoner's committal to his charge, he visited him, and declared that from old affection and from gratitude for favours he had himself received, he would gladly "make him good cheer," but that this he could not do without incurring the anger of the king. Sir Thomas replied : " Mr. Lieutenant, I verily believe as you say, and heartily thank you ; and assure yourself, I do not mislike my cheer; but whensoever I so do, then thrust me out of your doors ". Doubtless Sir Edward Walsingham in later days would often relate this merry saying of the martyr.

In a book written in the Tower, that will be described presently, Sir Thomas gives us a glimpse of his prison cell, if (as it seems certain) he is writing of himself and his wife. " I wist a woman once that came into a prison to visit of her charity a poor prisoner there, whom she found in a chamber (to say the truth) meetly fair, and at the leastwise it was strong enough. But with mats of straw the prisoner had made it so warm, both under the feet and round about the walls, that in these things, for the keeping of his health, she was on his behalf glad and very well comforted. But among many other displeasures that for his sake she was sorry for, one she lamented much in her mind, that he should have the chamber door shut upon him by night, and made fast by the jailor that should shut him in. ' For, by my troth,' quoth she, ' if the door should be shut upon me, I would ween it would stop up my breath.' At that word of hers the prisoner laughed in his mind ; but he durst not laugh aloud, nor say nothing to her, for somewhat indeed he stood in awe of her, and had his finding there much part of her charity for alms ; but he could not but laugh inwardly, while he wist well enough that she used on the inside to shut every night full surely her own chamber to her, both doors and windows too, and used not to open them of all the long night. And what difference, then, as to the stopping of the breath, whether they were shut up within or without ? " *

* *Dialogue of Comfort*, Bk. iii. ch. 2c.

From this and other details it would seem that Sir Thomas was treated at first with some leniency. Indeed, he appears to have been allowed the range of the Tower, or at least occasional exercise in the garden as well as access to the church ; for when this liberty had been restricted, his daughter wrote that she " cannot hear what moved them to shut him up again. She supposes that, considering he was of so temperate mind that he was content to abide there all his life with such liberty, they thought it not possible to incline him to their will, except by restraining him from the church, and the company of his wife and children. She remembers that he told her in the garden that these things were like enough to chance shortly after." *

So thoroughly had Sir Thomas More trained himself to make the best of everything, that he found in the solitude of the prison the realisation of his early aspirations to a monastic and contemplative life. " When he had remained in the Tower little more than a month," writes Roper, " my wife, longing to see her father, by her earnest suit at length got leave to go unto him. At whose coming, after the seven psalms and litany said (which whensoever she came unto him, ere he fell in talk of any worldly matter, he used accustomably to say with her), among other communication he said unto her : 'I believe, Meg, that they that have put me here ween they have done me a high displeasure : but I assure thee on my faith, mine own good daughter, if it had not been for my wife and ye that be my children, I would not have failed long ere this to have closed myself in as strait a room, and straiter too.† But since I am come hither without mine own desert, I trust that God of His goodness will discharge me of my care, and with His gracious help supply my lack among you. I find no cause, I thank God, Meg, to reckon myself in worse case here than at home; for methinketh God maketh me a wanton (*i.e.*, a spoiled child), and setteth me on His lap and dandleth me.' "

Prisoners have little or no history. From May, 1534, when

* Letter of Margaret Roper, *English Works, p.* 1446.
† See *supra*, p. 25.

he finally refused the oath, to May, 1535, when new troubles began, is almost a blank in the records of Sir Thomas More. It is hard to realise the monotony of his life. When he had been secluded from the church, Sunday and feast-day must have passed without bringing even that variety they give to modern prison discipline. There were, indeed, two churches within the precincts of the Tower, which may still be seen— the ancient Norman Church of St. John in the White Tower, and the Church of St. Peter ad Vincula, which had recently been burnt down and rebuilt; but into neither of these were prisoners conducted to hear Mass on days of precept; nor can I find in any records of those days the slightest trace of sermons preached or sacraments administered, with the one exception of confession before execution.

Lady More was allowed once or twice to visit her husband. He has told us of his amusement at her horror of suffocation under locks and bolts. Another interview is related by Roper, the details of which may have been witnessed by Margaret Roper or related by Sir Thomas to Margaret, or, perhaps, told by Lady More herself. "When Sir Thomas," writes Roper, "had continued a good while in the Tower, my lady, his wife, obtained licence to see him. Who, at her first coming, like a simple, ignorant woman and somewhat worldly too, with this manner of salutation homely saluted him : 'What a good year ! * Mr. More,' quoth she, 'I marvel that you, that hitherto have been taken for a wise man, will now so play the fool, to lie here in this close, filthy prison, and be content thus to be shut up among mice and rats, when you might be abroad at your liberty, and with the favour and goodwill both of the king and his Council, if you would but do as all the bishops and best learned of this realm have done. And seeing you have at Chelsea a right fair house, your library, your gallery, garden, orchard, and all other necessaries so handsome about you, where you might in the company of me, your wife, your children, and

* A well known exclamation in those days.

household, be merry, I muse what (a God's name!) you mean here still thus fondly to tarry.' After he had awhile quietly heard her, with a cheerful countenance, he said unto her : 'Is not this house as nigh heaven as mine own?' To whom she, after her accustomed homely fashion, not liking such talk, answered : 'Twittle, twattle, twittle, twattle!' 'How say you, Mrs. Alice, is it not so?' 'Bone Deus, bone Deus, man, will this gear never be left?' quoth she. 'Well then, Mistress Alice, if it be so, it is very well; for I see no great cause why I should much joy in my gay house, or in anything thereunto belonging, when, if I should but seven years lie buried under the ground, and then arise and come thither again, I should not fail to find some therein that would bid me get out of doors, and tell me it were none of mine. What cause have I, then, to like such a house as would so soon forget its master?'"

Lady More was evidently one of those good souls to whom respectability is the law of laws, and to whom a scruple to do what decent people do is simply unintelligible. She probably thought that too much learning or too much religion had driven Sir Thomas mad. Yet she meant well, and was kind and devoted, and was depriving herself of the very things she most cherished, in order to pay his weekly pension. Her husband, therefore, loved and esteemed her, though he could smile at her weaknesses, and did not expect from her a heroism of which she could not even frame a conception.

Very different was his correspondence and conversation with his daughter Margaret. According to a marginal note in Rastell's edition of More's works, she had taken the oath with the clause " as far as it would stand with the law of God," a manner of swearing that the government would occasionally connive at. She seems to have more than once by word or letter tried to persuade her father to conform his conscience to that of the men of learning and reputation who had yielded. The following letters will tell their own tale. Only one of them, however, is dated : this is a letter from Lady Alington,

More's step-daughter, to Margaret Roper. It was written on
the Monday after St. Lawrence (10th August), 1534. She
relates an interview she had had with Audley, the lord chancellor, whose help she had asked in favour of Sir Thomas.
Audley had easily promised this, though he declared that the
remedy was in More's own hands, if he would put aside his
foolish scruples; and he had joked on the matter, relating
some fables, of which Lady Alington says: " In good faith,
they pleased me nothing, nor I wist not what to say, for I was
abashed of this answer; and I see no better suit than to
Almighty God, for He is the comforter of all sorrows ".*
Margaret, however, took with her this letter on her next visit to
the Tower, the details of which are related in a very long letter
to Lady Alington, of which I must give merely an abridgment.
After the usual prayers and some conversation about his wife
and children, Margaret told her father that she had a letter
which proved how his persistence was alienating his friends.
More replied with a smile : " What, Mistress Eve ! hath my
daughter Alington played the serpent with you, and with a
letter set you at work to come and tempt your father again, and
for the favour that you bear him, labour to make him swear
against his conscience and so send him to the devil ? "   And
after that he said seriously and earnestly : " Daughter Margaret,
we two have talked of this thing more than twice or thrice, and
I have told you that if it were possible for me to do the thing
that might content the king's Grace, and God not offended, no
man had taken this oath more gladly than I would do ".   He
explained that he had long and well weighed the matter, and
had well considered all the possible consequences.   God's
providence had now placed him in that strait that he must
either deadly displease God or abide any worldly harm that
might fall for his other sins.   He read Lady Alington's letter
very carefully twice, spoke highly of her affection for him and
of his own love for her ; he laughed at Audley's fables as being

* *English Works*, p. 1433.

nothing to the point. Audley had said that "he marvelled that More was so obstinate in his own conceit in a matter that no one scrupled save the blind bishop and he". The blind, that is, the obstinate bishop, was, of course, Blessed John Fisher of Rochester. On this More remarked that no doubt many, both temporal and spiritual, looked on the taking of the oath as a mere trifle, though probably many did not really think this that said it; "But though they did, daughter, it would not make much to me, not though I should see my Lord of Rochester say the same. For albeit of very truth I have him in that reverent estimation, that I reckon in this realm no one man in wisdom, learning, and long approved virtue meet to be compared with him, yet that in this matter I was not led by him very plainly appeareth, in that I refused the oath before it was offered to him, and in that his lordship was content to have sworn of that oath (as I perceived since by you) either somewhat more or in some other manner than ever I minded to do. Verily, daughter, I never intend to pin my soul at another man's back, not even the best man that I know this day living. For I know not whither he may hap to carry it. There is no man living of whom, while he liveth, I may make myself sure. Some may do for favour, and some may do for fear, and so might they carry my soul a wrong way. And some might hap to frame himself a conscience, and think that if he did it for fear God would forgive it. And some may peradventure think that they will repent and be shriven thereof, and that so shall God remit it to them. And some may be, peradventure, of the mind that, if they say one thing and think the while the contrary, God more regardeth the heart than the tongue; and that, therefore, their oath goeth upon what they think and not upon what they say. But in good faith, Margaret, I can use no such ways in so great a matter."

Margaret told him he was not asked to swear against his conscience, in order to keep other men company, but to instruct and reform his conscience by the consideration that such and so many men considered the oath lawful, and even a duty since parliament required it. He replied that parliament might err, and explained at considerable length when a man is bound to give up his own private opinion or judgment. This should be done at the infallible decree of a general council, but not at the enactment of a parliament.

" But, Margaret," he concluded, " for what cause I refuse the oath I will never show you, neither you nor no body else, except the king's Highness should like to command me. I have refused and do refuse the oath for more causes than one. And this I am sure, that of them that have sworn it, some of the best learned, before the oath was required, plainly affirmed the contrary of such things as they have now sworn, and that not in haste, but often and after great diligence to seek out the truth." Margaret caught at this, and said that probably they now saw more than they saw before. More would not deny this or condemn them, but he at least had seen no reason to change. He told Margaret, also, that he was not in the minority, as some affirmed. Throughout Christendom the greater part thought with him. " But go we now to them that are dead before, and that are, I trust, in heaven; I am sure that it is not the fewer part of them that, all the time while they lived, thought in some of the things that way that I think now."

When he saw his daughter, after this discussion, sitting very sadly, not from any fear she had about his soul, but at the temporal consequences she foresaw, he smiled again and exclaimed : " How now, daughter Margaret? What now, Mother Eve? Where is your mind now? Sit not musing with some serpent in your breast, upon some new persuasion to offer Father Adam the apple yet once again."

" In good faith, father," replied Margaret, " I can no further go. For since the example of so many wise men cannot move you, I see not what to say more, unless I should look to persuade you with the reason that Master Harry Pattenson made."

(It will be remembered that Pattenson was More's fool, now in the service of the Lord Mayor.) "For," continued Margaret, "he met one day one of our men, and when he had asked where you were, and heard that you were in the Tower still, he waxed angry with you, and said : ' Why ? what aileth him that he will not swear ? Wherefore should he stick to swear ? I have sworn the oath myself.' And so," says Margaret, " have I sworn." At this More laughed, and said : " That word was like Eve, too, for she offered Adam no worse fruit than she had eaten herself ".

Margaret then told him that Cromwell had hinted that parliament was not yet dissolved, and might decree worse things against him. More replied that he had thought of this. However, no man could do him hurt without doing him wrong, and he trusted God would not suffer so good and wise a prince as Henry thus to requite the long service of his true, faithful servant. " Yet, since nothing is impossible, I forgot not in this matter the counsel of Christ in the Gospel, that ere I should begin to build this castle for the safeguard of mine own soul, I should sit and reckon what the charge would be. I counted, Margaret, full surely many a restless, weary night, while my wife slept, and thought I slept, too, what peril were possible to fall to me ; and in devising I had a full, heavy heart. But yet I thank Our Lord for all that I never thought to change, though the very uttermost should happen to me that my fear ran upon."

Margaret urged that things might appear still more terrible when they should actually take place, and thus perhaps it would be too late. This word roused her father. " Too late, daughter Margaret ! I beseech Our Lord that if ever I make such a change, it may be too late, indeed ; for well I wot the change can not be good for my soul." He went on to speak most tenderly of his trust in God to prevent his falling, or even to raise him up should he chance to fall like Peter, adding these solemn and heroic words :—

"And finally, Margaret, this wot I very well, that, without my fault, He will not let me be lost. I shall, therefore, with good hope, commit myself wholly to Him ; and if He suffer me for my faults to perish, yet shall I thus serve for a praise of His justice. But in good faith, Meg, I trust that His tender pity shall keep my poor soul safe, and make me commend His mercy. And, therefore, mine own good daughter, never trouble thy mind for anything that shall happen to me in this world. Nothing can come but what God wills!" He concluded by exhorting all his family to be resigned, to remain united, and to pray for him. "And if anything happen me that you would be loth, pray to God for me, but trouble not yourselves ; as I shall full heartily pray for us all that we may meet together once in heaven, where we shall make merry forever, and never have trouble after." *

I doubt whether, in the Acts of the Martyrs, there is a nobler scene than this. Did ever temptation come in a more subtle form ? The affectionate daughter had no thought of leading her father to do what was unworthy of him. When we see one so pure and wise as Margaret Roper thus deceived, we can estimate the enormity of the scandal given to the laity by the prelates and clergy of England, and we can also estimate the magnificence of More's loyalty to conscience, that he should be in no ways swayed by that example, thus pressed upon him by the mouth of his accomplished and beloved daughter.

The following letter, dealing with the same subject, has no date, and may perhaps have preceded the conversation related by Margaret to Lady Alington : "Our Lord bless you. If I had not been, my dearly beloved daughter, at a firm and fast point, I trust in God's great mercy this good great while before, your lamentable letter had not a little abashed me, surely far above all other things, of which I hear divers times not a few terrible towards me. But surely they all touched me never so near,

---

* *English Works*, pp. 1434-1443. Rastell doubts whether More himself may not have written this letter.

nor were so grievous unto me, as to see you, my well beloved
child, in such vehement piteous manner, labour to persuade
unto me that thing wherein I have, of pure necessity for respect unto mine own soul, so often given you so precise answer
before. Wherein as touching the points of your letter, I can
make none answer. For I doubt not but you well remember
that the matters which move my conscience (without declaration whereof I can nothing touch the points) I have sundry
times showed you that I will disclose them to no man.

"And therefore, daughter Margaret, I can in this thing no
further, but like as you labour me again to follow your mind,
to desire and pray you both again to leave off such labour,
and with my former answers to hold yourself content. A
deadly grief unto me, and much more deadly than to hear of
mine own death (for the fear thereof, I thank Our Lord, the fear
of hell, the hope of heaven, and the Passion of Christ daily
more and more assuage), is, that I perceive my good son, your
husband, and you, my good daughter, and my good wife, and
mine other good children and innocent friends, in great displeasure and danger of great harm thereby. The let whereof
while it lieth not in my hand, I can no further but commit all
to God. *Nam in manu Dei*, sayeth the Scripture, *cor regis est*
and *sicut divisiones aquarum quocunque voluerit impellit illud.*
Whose high Goodness I most humbly beseech to incline the
noble heart of the king's Highness to the tender favour of you
all, and to favour me no better than God and myself know
that my faithful heart towards him and my daily prayer for
him do deserve.

"For surely if His Highness might inwardly see my true mind
such as God knoweth it is, it would (I trust) soon assuage his
high displeasure : which, while I can in this world never in such
wise show but that His Grace may be persuaded to believe the
contrary of me, I can no further go, but put all in the hands of
Him for fear of whose displeasure for the safeguard of my soul,
stirred by mine own conscience (without insectation or reproach

laying to any other man's), I suffer and endure this trouble.
Out of which I beseech Him to bring me, when His will shall
be, into His endless bliss of heaven, and, in the meanwhile,
give me grace and you both in all our agonies and troubles,
devoutly to resort prostrate unto the remembrance of that
bitter agony, which Our Saviour suffered before His Passion at
the Mount.   And if we diligently so do, I verily trust we shall
find therein great comfort and consolation.

"And thus, my dear daughter, the blessed Spirit of Christ for
His tender mercy govern and guide you all, to His pleasure
and your weal and comforts both body and soul.

"Your tender, loving father,

"THOMAS MORE, Knight." *

To this letter Margaret returned the following answer :—

"MINE OWN GOOD FATHER,—

"It is to me no little comforth, since I cannot talk
with you by such means as I would, at the least way to delight
myself among in this bitter time of your absence by such means
as I may, by as often writing to you as shall be expedient, and
by reading again and again your most fruitful and delectable
letter, the faithful messenger of your very virtuous and ghostly
mind, rid from all corrupt love of worldly things, and fast knit
only in the love of God and desire of heaven, as becometh a
very true worshipper and a faithful servant of God, which I
doubt not, good father, holdeth His holy hand over you and
shall (as He hath) preserve you both body and soul (*ut sit mens
sana in corpore sano*), and namely, now when you have abjected
all earthly consolations and resigned yourself willingly, gladly
and fully for His love to His holy protection.

"Father, what think you hath been our comfort since your
departing from us?   Surely the experience we have had of your
life past, and godly conversation, and wholesome counsel, and
virtuous example, and a surety not only of the continuance of

* *English Works*, p. 1431.

that same, but also a great increase by the goodness of Our Lord, to the great rest and gladness of your heart, devoid of all earthly dregs, and garnished with the noble vesture of heavenly virtues, a pleasant palace for the Holy Spirit of God to rest in, who defend you (as I doubt not, good father, but of His goodness He will) from all trouble of mind and of body, and give me, your most loving, obedient daughter and hand-maid, and all us, your children and friends, to follow that that we praise in you; and to our only comfort remember and com-mune [*i.e.*, converse] together of you, that we may in conclusion meet with you, mine own dear father, in the bliss of heaven, to which Our most merciful Lord hath bought us with His precious Blood.

"Your own

"most loving obedient daughter and bedeswoman,

"MARGARET ROPER,

which desireth above all worldly things to be in John à Woode's stead to do you some service. But we live in hope that we shall shortly receive you again; I pray God heartily we may, if it be His holy will."*

From another very affectionate letter of the same daughter I have already given an extract regarding her father's seclusion from the church.† He replied that his "close keeping again did of likelihood grow of his negligent and very plain true word, which she would remember". He warned her to expect a new search in all their houses, since people would not believe he was really so poor as appeared by the first search. "Which thing," he says, "if ever it should happen, can make but game to us that know the truth of my poverty, unless they find out my wife's gay girdle and her golden beads. Howbeit, I verily believe that the king's Grace of his benign pity will take no-thing from her." He repeats what he had said before of his innocence and good conscience in refusing the oath, and the

* *English Works*, p. 1432.   † *Supra*, p. 367.

possibility of some new, but unjust, law being made against him. He assures her that he has never prayed to be released from prison or delivered from death, nor wavered one moment at the prospect of any pain, "albeit I found myself (I cry God mercy) very sensual and my flesh much more shrinking from pain and from death than methought it the part of a faithful Christian man ".* This letter was written with a coal or burnt wood, "and other pens have I none here ". In another letter he says : "That your fear of your own frailty, Margaret, nothing misliketh me. God give us both twain grace to despair of ourselves, and wholly to hang upon the strength of God. . . . Surely, Meg, a fainter heart than thy frail father hath canst thou not have. And yet I verily trust in the great mercy of God that He shall, of His goodness, so stay me with His holy hand that he shall not finally suffer me to fall wretchedly from His favour. . . . And verily, my dear daughter, in this is my great comfort, that albeit I am of nature so shrinking from pain that I am almost afraid of a fillip, yet in all the agonies that I have had, I thank the mighty mercy of God, I never in my mind intended to consent to do anything against my conscience." †

Opportunities of writing were rarer as time went on. The following short letter seems to belong to the later months of his imprisonment :—

" MINE OWN GOOD DAUGHTER,—

" Our Lord be thanked, I am in good health of body, and in good quiet of mind ; and of worldly things I no more desire than I have. I beseech Him make you all merry in the hope of heaven. And such things as I somewhat longed to talk with you all concerning the world to come, Our Lord put them into your minds, as I trust He doth and better too by His Holy Spirit, who bless you and preserve you all.

" Written with a coal by your tender loving father, who in his

---

* *English Works*, p. 1446.   † *Ib.*, p. 1446.

poor prayers forgetteth none of you all, nor your babes, nor your nurses, nor your good husbands, nor your good husbands' shrewd wives, nor your father's shrewd wife neither, nor our other friends.

"And thus fare ye heartily well for lack of paper,

"THOMAS MORE, Knight.

"Our Lord keep me continually true, faithful and plain, to the contrary whereof I beseech Him heartily never to suffer me live. For as for long life (as I have often told thee, Meg) I neither look for nor long for, but am well content to go, if God call me hence to-morrow. And, I thank Our Lord, I know no person living that I would had one fillip for my sake; of which mind I am more glad than of all the world beside.

"Recommend me to your shrewd Will* and mine other sons, and to John Harris, my friend, and yourself knoweth to whom else, and to my shrewd wife above all, and God preserve you all, and make and keep you His servants all." †

With the exception of the few visits from his wife and daughter in the earlier months of More's imprisonment, no relation or friend was allowed to communicate with him. This he expressly declares in a circular letter to all his friends, asking them to give credit to Margaret in case she should make known to them any necessity.‡ One or two letters were, however, given to him, perhaps by permission of the governor, and his answers have been preserved. A priest named Leader had heard that More had relented and taken the oath. He seems to have written to congratulate with him on the fact and on his approaching deliverance from prison. More replied :—

"The tale that is reported, albeit I cannot but thank you though ye would it were true, yet I thank God it is a very vanity. And I trust in the great goodness of God that He shall never suffer it to be true. If my mind had been obstinate

---

* William Roper.   † *English Works*, p. 1430.   ‡ *Ib.*, p. 1432.

in deed, I would not let for any rebuke or worldly shame plainly to confess the truth; for I propose not to depend upon the fame of the world. But I thank Our Lord that the thing that I do is not for obstinacy, but for the salvation of my soul, because I cannot induce mine own mind otherwise to think than I do concerning the oath. As for other men's conscience I will be no judge of, nor I never advised any man neither to swear nor to refuse. But as for mine own self, if ever I should mishap to receive the oath (which I trust Our Lord shall never suffer me), ye may reckon sure that it were expressed and extorted by duress and hard handling. For as for all the goods of this world, I thank Our Lord I set not much more by than I do by dust. And I trust both that they will use no violent forcible ways, and also that if they would, God would of His grace (and the rather a great deal through good folks' prayers) give me strength to stand. '*Fidelis Deus*,' saith St. Paul, '*qui non patitur vos tentari supra id quod potestis ferre, sed et dat cum tentatione proventum ut possitis sustinere.*' For this I am very sure that if ever I should swear it, I should swear deadly sore against mine own conscience. For I am very sure in my mind, that I shall never be able to change myne own conscience to the contrary. As for other men's I will not meddle of.

"It hath been showed me that I am reckoned wilful and obstinate, because that since my coming hither, I have not written unto the king's Highness, and by mine own writing made some suit unto His Grace. But, in good faith, I do not forbear it of any obstinacy, but rather of a lowly mind and a reverent, because that I see nothing that I could write, but that I fear me sore that His Grace were likely rather to take displeasure with me for it than otherwise, while His Grace believeth me not that my conscience is the cause, but rather obstinate wilfulness. But surely that my let is but my conscience that knoweth God, to whose order I commit the whole matter, '*In cujus manu corda regum sunt*'. I beseech Our Lord that all may prove as true faithful subjects to the king that have sworn, as I am in my mind very sure that they be which have refused to swear.

"In haste this Saturday, the 16 day of January [1535] By the hand of your bedesman,

"THOMAS MORE, Knight,
"Prisoner." *

Two other letters are addressed to Dr. Nicolas Wilson, one of the king's chaplains, who had refused the oath on the same day as More and Fisher, and had been committed to the Tower. It would seem that his strength of soul was exhausted by a long solitary confinement. He found means to write to his old friend, Sir Thomas, suggesting doubts that now occurred to him regarding the force of the conclusions that had made him refuse the oath. More replies that he is sorry to see him thus agitated, but that he cannot give him any relief. When the king had bidden them both study the subject, they had done so together as thoroughly as possible, and had arrived at the same conclusions. "Now," he says, "I neither murmur, nor grudge, nor make assertions, nor keep disputation on the matter; and, as touching the oath and the causes for which I refused it, no man knoweth what they be. For they be secret to my own conscience, some other, peradventure, than those that other men would ween, and such as I never disclosed to any man yet, nor never intend to do while I live." He meddles with no other man's conscience. "In mine own conscience (I cry God mercy) I find of mine own life matters enough to think upon. I have lived, methinketh, a long life, and now neither I look nor long to live much longer. *I have, since I came to the Tower, looked once or twice to have given up my ghost ere this,* and, in good faith, my heart waxed the lighter with hope thereof. Yet forget I not that I have a long reckoning and a great to give account of. But I put my trust in God, and in the merits of His bitter Passion, and I beseech Him to give me and

* *English Works*, p. 1450.

keep me the mind to look to be out of this world and to be
with Him. For I can never but trust, that who so long to be
with Him shall be welcome to Him; and, on the other side,
my mind giveth me verily that any that ever shall come to Him
shall full heartily wish to be with Him ere ever he shall come at
Him." With some affectionate words and commendation to
his prayers, he concludes, asking him to send the letter back,
"for though its contents are harmless, the bearer might get into
trouble by it".*

It seems, however, that Dr. Wilson kept it, and wrote him a
second letter, to which Sir Thomas answered shortly: "I perceive that you have promised to swear the oath. I beseech
Our Lord give you thereof good luck. And whereas I perceive
that you would gladly know what I intend to do, you wot well
that I told you when we were both abroad, that I would therein
neither know your mind nor no man's else; nor you nor no
man else should therein know mine. With God's grace I will
follow my own conscience. What my own shall be to-morrow,
myself cannot be sure; and whether I shall have finally the
grace to do according to mine own conscience or not hangeth
in God's goodness, not in mine, to whom I beseech you
heartily to remember me in your devout prayers, and I shall
and do daily remember you in mine, such as they be."†

Whether Dr. Wilson was moved to recall his promise to take
the oath I do not find recorded. From the bill of the governor's
expenses it appears that he remained prisoner for two years and
two months;‡ yet at a subsequent period he got promotions
that he could not have enjoyed without acquiescing in the
schism.

By comparing the various expressions of Sir Thomas together,
it seems that he was himself deterred from taking the oath of
succession, in the form in which it was proposed to him, by
several reasons, some of which were doctrinal, and held by the

* *English Works*, p. 1443.   † *Ib.*
‡ Cotton MS.; *Titus*, Bk. i.; also *Archæologia*, xviii. 294.

doctors of the Church ; but others were of a secret nature known to himself, and which he had never communicated to another, and would not reveal even to his daughter. Whether these had reference to Anne Boleyn's affinity with Henry, or her pre-contract of marriage with Percy, or some other impediment still more secret, we cannot now discover, any more than we can know the grounds on which Cranmer pronounced that Anne's marriage with Henry had been null from the beginning; it may be as well to anticipate somewhat, in order to conclude here what is told of the wreck of his property and home.*

Towards the end of the year 1534, the wife and children of Sir Thomas petitioned for his pardon and release. They alleged that he had remained more than eight months in the Tower "in great continual sickness of body and heaviness of heart". " The king during that time has allowed his wife to retain his moveable goods and the revenues of his lands, al-though forfeited for his refusal of the oath ; but lately an Act has been made in the last parliament, not only confirming the former forfeiture, but causing the inheritance of all the lands which the said Sir Thomas had from the king, amounting to the annual value of £60, to be forfeited. All that his wife brought him is expended in the king's service, and she is likely to come to want, as also her son, who stands charged with the payment of certain great sums due by Sir Thomas to the king. But above all this, Sir Thomas is likely to die, after his long and true service to the king. They beseech the king to grant this their petition, con-sidering that his offence is not of malice or obstinacy, but of such a long continued and deep-rooted scruple as passeth his power to avoid and put away."†

* Dr. Bailey, in his *Life of Fisher*, mentions several incidents of More's life in the Tower to which I have here made no reference—*e.g.*, a plot laid to gain him over by the report that Fisher had taken the oath. In my *Life of Blessed Fisher* I have given my reasons for taking all this as apochryphal.

† Arundel MS., 152, f. 300 b. *Archæologia*, xxvii. 369.

In May, 1535, Lady More made another appeal to Cromwell. She had been compelled of very necessity to sell her
apparel to provide 15s. weekly for the board wages of her poor
husband and his servant.* Neither of these petitions found
the slightest response in the heart of the monarch wholly given
to feasting and pageantry, and surrounded by greedy sycophants.

In January, 1535, the king granted to Henry Norris, "Esquire of the Royal Body," the fee simple of the manors of
Doglington and Fringeford, in Oxfordshire, the advowson of
Doglington Church, and Barly Park, which had come into the
king's hand by the attainder of Sir Thomas More.†

In April, the manor of South, in Kent, with advowsons
thereto belonging, likewise forfeited, were given to the queen's
brother, George Boleyn, Viscount Rochford.‡ And the king's
brother-in-law, the Duke of Suffolk, wrote to the king a few
days after the death of the martyr, begging him not to grant
any part of Sir Thomas More's land lying about Chelsea, because he himself wished to have the house and lands adjoining,
which (he says) are not above the yearly value of £16.§

* *Letters and Papers*, viii. 800.

† *Ib.*, viii. 149, n. 16. He had received these by royal grant in
1525.

‡ *Ib.*, 632, n. 13. The manor of South had been granted to Sir
Thomas in 1522.

§ *Ib.*, 1101. Whether the duke obtained his request I do not perceive.
The following are mentioned as the successive owners of More's house :
Sir William Paulet—Gregory, Lord Dacre—Sir William Cecil, Lord
Burghley—Sir Robert Cecil, Earl of Salisbury—The Earl of Lincoln—
Sir Arthur Gorges—Lionel Cranfield, Earl of Middlesex—King Charles
I.—The Duke of Buckingham —William Plummer—The Earl of Bristol—
—Lady Ann Russell—The Duke of Beaufort—Sir Hans Sloane (who
pulled it down in 1740).

CHAPTER XXI.

ASCETIC WRITINGS.

IT would seem that during the far greater part of his imprisonment, Sir Thomas was allowed the use of books to read, as well as of pen and ink and plenty of paper. He composed works in Latin and English that would fill two good octavo volumes. All these writings were devotional or ascetic, that is, meditations on the mysteries of faith or treatises on the exercise of Christian virtues.

If I mistake not, Blessed Thomas More stands quite alone among the ascetic writers of the Church ; for while he is not inferior to the best ecclesiastics in his use of Holy Scripture, his knowledge of the human heart, his analysis of the workings of passion and the counterworkings of grace, he considered it his layman's privilege to use a livelier style and to illustrate his matter with abundance of merry stories.

As far back as 1522, when he had lately been made a knight and treasurer of the kingdom, and was in the midst of all the splendours of Henry's court, he had sought to keep his heart pure and humble by composing a treatise in English on the words of Ecclesiasticus : " In all thy works remember thy last end, and thou shalt never sin ". * *Novissima*, the last things, were understood to be these four—Death, Judgment, Heaven, and Hell. Sir Thomas began a treatise that was to comprise all four, but he laid it aside before he had concluded

* *Ecclus*. vii. 40.

the first part, on Death, and the fragment was not published until 1557.

"This short medicine," he says, *i.e.*, the remembrance of the Last Things, "is of a marvellous force, able to keep us all our life from sin. This medicine, though thou makest a sour face at it, is not so bitter as thou makest for. He biddeth thee not take neither death, nor doom, nor pain, but only to remember them, and yet the joy of heaven therewith to temper them withal. Now, if a man be so dainty-stomached, that going where contagion is, he would grudge to take a little treacle, yet were he very nicely wanton if he might not, at the leastwise, take a little vinegar and rose water on his handkercher."* And, indeed, in More's treatment of the matter, though he has barely touched on heaven, and written merely of death, there is far more rose water than vinegar. Not that his descriptions or exhortations lack strength, but that they have a literary interest which entices the reader to linger over the most appalling subjects. A few samples will show my meaning. Here is an allusion to the famous pictures of Death in Pardon-Church-Haugh at St. Paul's, London : "We were never so moved by the beholding of the Dance of Death pictured in Paul's as we shall feel ourselves stirred by the imagination in our hearts, of our own deaths. And no marvel ; for those pictures express only the loathly figure of our dead, bony bodies ; which, though it be ugly to behold, yet neither the sight thereof, nor the sight of all the dead heads in that charnel house, nor the apparition of a very ghost, is half so grisly as the deep conceived phantasy of death in its nature by the lively imagination graven in thine own heart. For there seest thou not one plain grievous sight of the bare bones hanging by the sinews, but thou seest thyself—if thou die no worse death—yet at leastwise lying in thy bed, thy head shooting, thy back aching, thy veins beating, thine heart panting, thy throat rattling, thy flesh trembling, thy mouth gaping, thy nose sharping, thy legs cool-

* *English Works*, p. 71.

ing, thy fingers fumbling, thy breath shorting, all thy strength fainting, thy life vanishing, and thy death drawing on." *

He thus describes the pompous funerals that were so fashionable in those days : " Instead of sorrow for our sins and care of heaven, the devil putteth us in mind of provision for some honourable burying, so many torches, so many tapers, so many black gowns, so many merry mourners laughing under black hoods, and a gay hearse, with delight of goodly and honourable funerals, in which the foolish sick man is sometimes occupied, as though he thought he should stand in a window and see how worshipfully he shall be brought to church ". †

The certainty and uncertainty of death he illustrates by what he calls " a homely example, not very pleasent, but nathless very true ". " If there were two, both condemned to death, both carried out at once towards execution, of which two the one were sure that the place of his execution were within one mile, the other twenty miles off, yea, a hundred, if ye will, he that were in the cart to be carried a hundred miles would not take much more pleasure than his fellow in the length of his way, notwithstanding that it were a hundred times as long as his fellow's, and that he had hereby a hundred times as long to live, being sure and out of all question to die at the end.

" Reckon me now yourself a young man in your best lust, twenty year of age if ye will. Let there be another ninety. Both must ye die ; both be ye in the cart carrying forward. His gallows and death standeth within ten mile at the farthest, and yours within eighty. I see not why ye should reckon much less of your death than he, though your way be longer, since ye be sure ye shall never cease riding till ye come at it.

" And this is true, although ye were sure that the place of your execution stood so far beyond his. But what if there were to the place of your execution two ways, of which the one were fourscore mile farther about than your fellow's, the other nearer by five mile than his, and when ye were put in the

* *English Works*, p. 77.　　　　† *Ib.*, p. 79.

cart had warning of both ; and though ye were showed that it were likely that ye should be carried the longer way, yet it might happen ye should go the shorter ; and whether ye were carried the one or the other ye should never know till ye come to the place, I trow ye could not in this case make much longer of your life than of your fellow's. Now in this case are we all. For Our Lord hath not endented with us of the time. He that appointed what we may not pass, but not how soon we shall go nor where nor in what wise. And, therefore, if thou wilt consider how little cause thou hast to reckon thy death so far off, by reason of thy youth, reckon how many as young as thou have been slain in the self-same ways in which thou ridest, how many have been drowned in the self-same waters in which thou rowest.

" And thus shalt thou well see that thou hast no cause to look upon thy death as a thing far off, but a thing undoubtedly nigh thee, and ever walking with thee. By which, not a false imagination but a very true contemplation, thou shalt behold him and advise him such as he is, and thereby take occasion to flee vain pleasures of the flesh that keep out the very pleasures of the soul." *

From his considerations on death Sir Thomas draws many forcible conclusions, of which the following was suggested by his life at court :—

" Now, the high mind of proud fortune, rule and authority, Lord God ! how slight a thing it would seem to him that would often and deeply remember that death shall shortly take away all this royalty and his glory shall (as scripture saith) never walk with him into his grave. But he that overlooketh every man, and no man may be so homely (as) to come too near him, but thinketh that he doth much for them whom he vouchsafeth to take by the hand or beck upon, whom so many men dread and fear, so many wait upon, he shall within a few years, and only God knoweth within how few days, when death

* *English Works*, p. 82.

arresteth him, have his dainty body turned into stinking carrion, be borne out of his princely palace, laid in the ground, and there left alone, where every lewd lad will be bold to tread on his head. Would not, ween ye, the deep consideration of this sudden change, so surely to come, withdraw the wind that puffeth us up in pride upon the solemn sight of worldly worship?

" If thou shouldst perceive that one were earnestly proud of the wearing of a gay golden gown while the losel playeth the lord in a stage play, wouldest thou not laugh at his folly, considering that thou art very sure that when the play is done, he shall go walk a knave in his old coat? Now, thou thinkest thyself wise enough while thou art proud in thy player's garment, and forgettest that when thy play is done, thou shalt go forth as poor as he. Nor thou rememberest not that thy pageant may happen to be done as soon as his." * Clearly the Field of the Cloth of Gold, and the imperial pomps of Charles V., and the pageants of Whitehall and Hampton Court had but little blinding or dazzling power on the mind of Blessed Thomas More.

This book was written the year after the execution of the Duke of Buckingham on a charge of high treason. Sir Thomas, showing how the thought of death is a remedy against the temptation of envy, thus illustrates the subject : " If it so were that thou knewest a great duke, keeping so great estate and princely port in his house that thou, being a right mean man, haddest in thine heart great envy thereat, and specially at some special day in which he keepeth for the marriage of his child a great honourable court above other times ; if thou, being thereat, and at the sight of the royalty and honour showed him of all the country about resorting to him, while they kneel and crouch to him, and at every word barehead be-grace him ; if thou shouldst suddenly be advertised that for secret treason lately detected to the king, he should undoubtedly be taken the morrow, his court all broken up, his goods seized, his wife

* *English Works*, p. 84.

put out, his children disherited, himself cast in prison, brought forth and arraigned, the matter out of question, and he should be condemned, his coat armour reversed, his gilt spurs hewn off his heels, himself hanged, drawn, and quartered, how thinkest thou by thy faith, amid thine envy shouldest thou not suddenly change into pity ? " *

One is reminded of Buckingham's cry at his arrest :—

> . . . My life is spann'd already;
> I am the shadow of poor Buckingham :
> Whose figure even this instant cloud puts out,
> By dark'ning my clear sun. †

There is one passage in this book that derives a very deep interest from the reflection that the author of it was to spend fifteen months in the Tower and be thence led out to execution. " Mark this well, for of this thing we be very sure, that old and young, man and woman, rich and poor, prince and page, all the while we live in this world we be but prisoners, and be within a sure prison, out of which there can no man escape.   And in worse case be we than those that be taken and imprisoned for theft. For they, albeit their heart heavily hearkeneth after the sessions, yet have they some hope, either to break prison the while, or to escape there by favour, or after condemnation some hope of pardon.   But we stand all in another plight, we be very sure that we be already condemned to death, some one, some other, none of us can tell what death we are doomed to, but surely can we all tell that die we shall. And clearly know we that of this death we get no manner pardon. For the King, by whose high sentence we be condemned to die, would not of this death pardon His own Son.

" The prison is large, and many prisoners in it, but the Jailer can lose none ; He is so present in every place, that we can creep into no corner out of His sight.   For as holy David saith to this Jailer : 'Whither shall I go from Thy Spirit, and

* *English Works*, p. 86.   † Shakspere, *Henry VIII.*, Act i., sc. 1.

whither shall I flee from Thy face ?' as who saith—no whither. There is no remedy, therefore, but as condemned folk and remediless, in this prison of the earth we drive forth a while: some bound to a post, some wandering abroad ; some in the dungeon, some in the upper ward ; some building them bowers and making palaces in the prison ; some weeping, some laughing ; some labouring, some playing ; some singing, some chiding, some fighting ; no man almost remembering in what case he standeth, till that suddenly, nothing less looking for, young, old, poor and rich, merry and sad, prince, page, pope, and poor-soul priest, now one, now another, some time a great rabble at once, without order, without respect of age or of estate, all stripped stark naked, and shifted out in a sheet, be put to death in divers wise in some corner of the same prison, and even there thrown in a hole, and either worms eat him under ground or crows above.

"Now come forth, ye proud prisoners, for I wis ye be no better, look ye never so high, when ye build in the prison a palace for your blood, is it not a great royalty if it be well considered? Ye build the tower of Babylon in a corner of the prison and be very proud thereof, and some time the jailer beateth it down again with shame. Ye leave your lodging for your own blood, and the jailer, when ye be dead, setteth a strange prisoner in your building, and thrusteth your blood into the other cabin. Ye be proud of the arms of your ancestors set up in the prison ; and all your pride is because ye forget that it is a prison. For if ye took the matter aright, the place a prison, yourself a prisoner condemned to death, from which ye cannot escape, ye would reckon this gear as worshipful as if a gentleman thief, when he should go to Tyburn, would leave for a memorial the arms of his ancestors painted on a post in Newgate.

"Surely, I suppose that if we took not true figure for a phantasy, but reckoned it (as it is indeed) the very express fashion and manner of all our estate, men would bear them-

selves not much higher in their hearts, for any rule or authority
that they have here in this world, which they may well perceive
to be indeed no better but one prisoner bearing a rule among
the remnant, as the tapster doth in the Marshalsea ; or at the
uttermost, one so put in trust with the jailer, that he is half
an under-jailer over his fellows, till the sheriff and the cart
come for him." *

When at last, twelve years later, Sir Thomas found himself
locked up in the upper ward of the Beauchamp Tower, very
naturally all these thoughts recurred to his mind, and, strange
as it may seem, he comforted himself by the consideration that
he was in reality no more a prisoner than when he was at liberty
or than the rest of the world.   He worked out the parallel with
great ingenuity and infinite wit in his *Dialogue of Comfort
against Tribulation.*   One of the interlocutors, Vincent, asserts
that the whole argument is ingenious yet unreal—in a word,
sophistical. Antony, the other speaker, replies : "In good faith,
cousin, such an old fool am I, that this thing, in the persuading
whereof unto you I had weened I had quit me well, and when
I have all done, appeareth to your mind but a trifle and a
sophistical phantasy, myself have so many years taken for so
substantial truth that as yet my mind cannot give me to think
it any other.   Wherefore, lest I play as the French priest played,
that had so long used to say *Dominus*, with the second syllable
long, that at the last he thought it must needs be so, and was

---

* *English Works*, p. 84.   More had already expressed similar thoughts
in a Latin epigram :—

> Damnati ac morituri in terræ claudimur omnes
>   Carcere, in hoc mortem carcere nemo fugit.
> Carceris in multas describitur area partes,
>   Inque aliis alii partibus ædificant.
> Non aliter quám de regno de carcere certant,
>   In cæco cupidus carcere condit opes.
> Carcere obambulat hic vagus, hic vincitur in antᵣo,
>   Hic servit, regit hic ; hic canit, ille gemit.
> Jam quoque dum carcer non tanquam carcer amatur.
>   Hinc aliis alii mortibus extrahimur.

ashamed to say it short; to the intent that you may the better perceive me, or I the better myself, we shall here between us a little more consider the thing. And hardily spit well on your hands, and take good hold, and give it not over against your mind." Vincent does his best, but Antony replies to his objections and difficulties with such skill that at last, as regards the matter of liberty, he has to admit that all men are God's prisoners. "But," says he, "that God, our chief Jailer, useth any such prisonly fashion of punishment, that point I must needs deny. For I neither see Him lay any man in the stocks, or strike fetters on his legs, or so much as shut him up in a chamber either." Antony replies: "Is he no minstrel, cousin, that playeth not on a harp? Maketh no man melody, but he that playeth on a lute? He may be a minstrel and make melody, you wot well, with some other instrument, some strange-fashioned, peradventure, that never was seen before. God, our chief Jailer, as Himself is invisible, so useth He in His punishment invisible instruments, and, therefore, not of like fashion as the other jailers do, but yet of like effect, and as painful in feeling as those. For He layeth one of the prisoners with a hot fever as evil at his ease in a warm bed as the other jailer layeth his upon the cold ground. He wringeth by the brows with a megrim, He collareth them by the neck with a quinsy, He bolteth them by the arms with a palsy, that they cannot lift their hands to their heads, He manacleth their hands with the gout in their fingers, He wringeth them by the legs with a cramp in their shins, He bindeth them to the bed board with the crick in the back, and layeth one there along, and as unable to rise as though he lay by the feet fast in the stocks. Some prisoner of another gaol singeth, danceth in his two fetters, and feareth not his feet for stumbling at a stone; while God's prisoner, that hath but his one foot fettered by the gout lieth groaning on a couch, and quaketh and crieth out if he fear there would fall on his foot no more than a cushion." *

* *English Works*, p. 1246.

The above must suffice as specimens of More's ascetic writings. The reader will not be disappointed who goes to the *Dialogue of Comfort* in search of holy precepts, acute reasoning, or brilliant wit. Indeed, in none of his writings does Sir Thomas so abound in humour as in these pages written while waiting for a traitor's death, in the dim light let in by the loopholes of dungeon walls eleven feet thick.

It does not appear to be recorded how he managed to have his MS. safely conveyed out of prison. The *Dialogue* was written primarily for the instruction and comfort of his own family; yet its form was adapted for publication at some future day. He entitled it: "*A Dialogue of Comfort against Tribulation*, made by a Hungarian in Latin, and translated out of Latin into French, and out of French into English; now newly set forth, with many places restored and corrected by conference of sundry copies".* He wished to speak clearly of the dangers to faith and liberty menacing England, and yet to do this under cover of a parable, as in his *Utopia*. The device was ingenious. The Hungarians were expecting an invasion of the Turks, and the choice between apostasy on the one hand, and death, imprisonment, or at least exclusion from public life and impoverishment, on the other. In this crisis a Hungarian noble, named Vincent, is supposed to visit his uncle Antony, who is near his death, and who is famed for wisdom and piety. He seeks advice and consolation in the tribulations that menace them. In the conversations which ensue the purposes and advantages of trials and sufferings are thoroughly considered, both in general and in their various species. The form of dialogue, as managed by More's skilful hand, lends itself to objections, explanations, digressions, amusing illustrations, which make this one of the most instructive and interesting

* It was printed by Serjeant Rastell in the complete works in 1557, and by John Fowler, in Antwerp, in 1573, and in modern spelling by Dolman in 1847. (*See Wisdom and Wit of Sir T. More*, by the present writer.)

books ever written "to justify the ways of God to man". Its earnest and pathetic arguments are relieved by mirth, yet its very mirth is full of pathos when we remember the writer, and the time and place of its composition. Vincent is asking whether a man in tribulation may seek some worldly recreation, and amongst other things he quotes St. Thomas, that "proper, pleasant talking, which is called εὐτραπελία, is a good virtue, serving to refresh the mind". Antony will not deny it, and confesses: "Of truth, cousin, as you know very well, myself am of nature even half a giglot and more. I would I could as easily mend my fault as I can well know it; but scant can I refrain it, as old a fool as I am. . . . Howbeit, let such recreations serve us but for sauce, and make them not our meat, and let us pray unto God that we may feel such a savour in the delight of heaven, that in respect of the talking of the joys thereof all worldly recreation be but a grief to think on." * The reader may remember how the mirthfulness of More's conversation, as well as the earnestness and sincerity with which, as a young man, he would talk of eternal life, were among the characteristics that had most impressed Erasmus. Neither business nor literature, nor the wiles of diplomacy, nor the pomps and pleasures of courts, had robbed him of his mirth or dimmed his vision of eternity. The secret strength of his heart was this, to use his own expression, that to him "the sayings of Our Saviour Christ were not a poet's fable, nor a harper's song, but the very holy word of Almighty God Himself". †

I have said that the trials of fines, confiscations, imprisonment and death which were now falling on the writer of this *Dialogue*, and which (he foretells) would soon fall on all the faithful followers of Christ, are supposed to come from the Turk. Had the book fallen into the hands of Henry, the Defender of the Faith could only have found treason lurking in its pages by identifying himself with the enemy of the

---

* Book ii. ch. i.   † *Ib.*, Bk. iii. ch. 15.

Christian name. It is probable, however, that Margaret Roper secretly conveyed the MS. from the Tower and kept it for a safer day.

His other devotional writings, as prayers, meditations, and the treatise on the Passion, may have been seized by those who were sent to take from him his books and writing material upon the discovery of his correspondence with Blessed John Fisher in June, 1535; but as they were seen to be harmless they were given to his family. Of the treatise on the Passion, which though imperfect is very lengthy, I must say a few words. It was written by Sir Thomas partly in Latin and partly in English. He begins with long meditations on the creation and fall of angels and of men, and the redemption. Then for the Passion, adopting the concordance of the Gospels by Gerson, he develops each word in very learned and devout reflections. These were evidently the result of his life-study of Our Lord's Passion. The long catena of quotations from Greek and Latin Fathers on the Blessed Sacrament proves that he had either many books at hand or (more probably) that his note-books were already well stored. The plotting of Judas, the washing of the disciples' feet by Our Lord, and the institution of the Holy Eucharist, complete the part written by Sir Thomas in English.* In Latin he had continued the history of the Agony in the Garden, and had just reached the words, "They laid hands on Jesus," when the hands of Henry's officials were laid on his books and he knew that the time of his own passion had come. The second part was translated by a daughter of Margaret Roper, Mistress Basset, who was attendant on Queen Mary, and who, with her mother's learning in the Latin tongue, has caught perfectly her grandfather's English style. †

I conclude this notice of More's ascetic writings by a trans-

---

* *English Works*, pp. 1270-1349. This part is not in the Latin works.

† She is called "niece" in the old folio; but the words "nephew" and "niece" in those days were equivalent to our "grandson" and "granddaughter" (*nepotes*).

lation of a few lines of a Latin tract found among the martyr's
papers, with the title: "Death for the faith is not to be
shunned":—

"If you save your life to-day by offending God, you will hate
it to-morrow, and lament that you did not undergo death yes-
terday. For you will call to mind that death has still to be endured, and you will not know what kind of death it will be,
nor how soon it will come. And you will have reason to fear
lest your death, thus postponed a little, shall be followed by the
torments of hell, in which men will desire to die, but death
will flee from them; whereas the eternal joys of heaven would
have followed that death from which you have fled. What
folly by trying to avoid temporal death to incur death eternal,
while you do not really avoid temporal death but merely postpone it! If you escape death now, can you live for ever, or die
without pain? When the fatal sickness comes and the pains
of death begin to press upon you, oh! how you will wish that
you had already endured for your soul's salvation a death however cruel." *

Clearly the holy prisoner, before the charge of treason was
made against him, had a presentiment of a violent death, and
that his death would be endured not only without crime against
his sovereign, but for the faith of his Divine Master: or, in
other words, that a martyr's crown would in all likelihood be
offered to him; and for this he prepared himself with fear and
trembling, as well as with peace and hope.

* *Quod mors pro fide non sit fugienda*—a short treatise of about two
pages. I do not recognise the phrase of Sir Thomas, though no doubt it
was printed from a paper in his handwriting.

CHAPTER XXII.

EXAMINATIONS IN PRISON.

THE parliament which More had opened in 1529 met for another session in November, 1534. It passed the following Acts, to which he owes his martyrdom :—

Chapter I. says : "Albeit the king's Majesty justly and rightfully is, and ought to be, supreme head of the Church of England, and so is recognised by the clergy of this realm in their convocations; yet, nevertheless, for corroboration and confirmation thereof, and for increase of virtue in Christ's religion within this realm of England, and to repress and extirpate all errors, heresies, and other enormities and abuses heretofore used in the same, be it enacted, by the authority of this present parliament, that the king, our sovereign lord, his heirs and successors, kings of this realm, shall be taken, accepted, and reputed, the only supreme head in earth of the Church of England, called *Anglicana Ecclesia*, and shall have and enjoy, annexed and united to the imperial crown of this realm, as well the title and style thereof as all honours, dignities, immunities, profits, and commodities to the said dignity of supreme head of the said Church belonging and appertaining.

" And that our said sovereign lord, his heirs and successors, kings of this realm, shall have full power and authority, from time to time, to visit, repress, redress, reform, order, correct, restrain, and amend all such errors, heresies, abuses, offences, contempts, and enormities, whatsoever they be, which by any manner of spiritual authority or jurisdiction, ought to be or may lawfully be reformed, repressed, ordered, redressed, corrected, restrained, or amended, most to the pleasure of Almighty God, the increase of virtue in Christ's religion, or for the conservation of the peace, unity, and tranquillity of this realm, any usage, custom, foreign laws, foreign authority, pre-scription, or any other thing or things to the contrary hereof notwithstanding."

By the thirteenth chapter of the same year it was made high treason for any person after the first day of February next coming (*i.e.*, February, 1535, *new style*) "maliciously to wish, will, or desire by words or writing, or by craft imagine, invent, practise, or attempt any bodily harm to be done or committed to the king's most royal person, the queen's, or their heirs ap-parent, or deprive them or any of them of their dignity, title or name of their royal estates, or slanderously and maliciously publish and pronounce, by express writing or words, that the king, our sovereign lord, should be heretic, schismatic, tyrant, infidel, etc."

There was a good deal of hesitation at making hasty words treason, and the word "maliciously" had been purposely intro-duced to exempt from the penalties of high treason words uttered incautiously, or words spoken soberly and as the result of conviction, but with no purpose of rebellion or sedition. This parliamentary precaution proved vain, for the judges (as we shall see) not only explained the word "maliciously" as belonging necessarily to all words spoken, but made even silence malicious and equivalent to denial.

Sir Thomas, whose imprisonment was in itself a perpetual profession of faith, had all along resolved to maintain a perfect silence, so as in no way to provoke persecution, but to wait quietly on the Providence of God. Silence, however, was too loud a protest to please the king, and the wretched monarch, angry that a year's imprisonment had wrung no compliance from his former councillor and friend, determined to try the force of the new instrument that parliament had placed in his hand.   It did not, indeed, authorise scrutiny into anyone's opinions, but his slavish Council made no such objection when he commissioned some of them to proceed to the Tower and interrogate More and Fisher.   More has himself told the result in the following letter :—

"MY DEARLY BELOVED DAUGHTER,—

"Our Lord bless you.   I doubt not but by the reason of the king's councillors resorting hither, in this time in which (Our Lord be their comfort) these fathers of the Charterhouse and Master Reynoldes of Sion, be now judged to death for treason (whose matters and causes I know not), may hap to put you in trouble and fear of mind concerning me being here a prisoner, specially for that it is not unlikely that you have heard that I was brought also before the Council here myself.   I have thought it necessary to advertise you of the very truth, to the end that you should neither conceive more hope than the matter giveth, lest upon another term it might agrieve your heaviness ; nor more grief and fear than the matter giveth on the other side.

"Wherefore, shortly ye shall understand, that on Friday, the ast day of April, in the afternoon, Master Lieutenant came in here unto me, and showed me that Master Secretary would speak with me.   Whereupon I shifted my gown, and went out with Master Lieutenant into the gallery to him, where I met many—some known and some unknown—in the way.   And in conclusion, coming into the chamber where his mastership sat, with Master Attorney, Master Solicitor, Master Bedyll, and Master Dr. Tregonwell, I was offered to sit down with them, which in no wise I would.

"Whereupon Master Secretary showed unto me that he doubted not but that I had, by such friends as hither had resorted to me, seen the new statutes made at the last sitting of the parliament. Whereunto I answered, yea, verily. How beit, for as much as being here I have no conversation with any people, I thought it little need for me to bestow much time upon them, and, therefore, I redelivered the book shortly, and the effect of the statutes I never marked nor studied to put in remembrance. Then he asked me, whether I had not read the first statute of them of the king being head of the Church. Whereunto I answered, yes. Then his mastership declared unto me, that since it was now by Act of Parliament ordered that His Highness and his heirs be, and ever of right have been, and perpetually should be, supreme head on earth of the Church of England under Christ, the king's pleasure was, that those of his Council there assembled should demand mine opinion and what my mind was therein. Whereunto I answered, that in good faith I had well trusted that the king's Highness would never have commanded any such question to be demanded of me, considering that I ever from the beginning well and truly from time to time declared my mind unto his Highness; and since that time (I said) unto your mastership, Master Secretary, also, both by mouth and by writing. And now I have in good faith discharged my mind of all such matters, and neither will dispute kings' titles nor Popes'; but the king's true, faithful subject I am and will be, and daily I pray for him, and all his, and for you all that are of his honourable Council, and for all the realm. And otherwise than this I never intend to meddle. Whereunto Master Secretary answered, that he thought this manner of answer should not satisfy nor content the king's Highness, but that His Grace would exact a more full answer. And his mastership added thereunto, that the king's Highness was a prince, not of rigour, but of mercy and pity. And though that he had found obstinacy at some time in any of his subjects, yet when he should find them at another time conformable and submit themselves, His Grace would show mercy; and that concerning myself, His Highness would be glad to see me take such conformable ways, as I

might be abroad in the world again among other men, as I have
been before.   Whereunto shortly (after the inward affection of
my mind) I answered for a very truth, that I would never meddle
in the world again, to have the world given me.   And to the
remnant of the matter I answered in effect as before, showing
that I had fully determined with myself neither to study nor
meddle with any matter of this world, but that my whole study
should be upon the Passion of Christ, and mine own passage
out of this world.

"Upon this I was commanded to go forth for a while, and
after called in again.   At which time Master Secretary said unto
me, that though I were a prisoner condemned to perpetual
prison, yet I was not thereby discharged of mine obedience and
allegiance unto the king's Highness.   And thereupon demanded
me, whether that I thought that the king's Grace might not
exact of me such things as are contained in the statutes, and
upon like pains as he might upon other men.   Whereto I
answered that I would not say the contrary.   Whereunto
he said, that likewise as the king's Highness would be gracious
to them that be found conformable, so His Grace would follow the course of his laws towards such as he shall find
obstinate.   And his mastership said farther, that my demeanour in that matter was a thing that of likelihood made
other so stiff therein as they be.   Whereto I answered, that I
gave no man occasion to hold any point one or other, nor
never gave any man advice or counsel therein one way or
other.   And for conclusion I could no farther go, whatsoever
pain should come thereof.   'I am (quoth I) the king's true,
faithful subject and daily bedesman, and pray for His Highness,
and all his, and all the realm.   I do nobody no harm, I say
none harm, I think none harm, but wish everybody good.
And if this be not enough to keep a man alive, in good faith
I long not to live.   And I am dying already, and have, since
I came here, been divers times in the case that I thought to
die within One hour.   And I thank Our Lord I was never sorry

for it, but rather sorry when I saw the pang past. And, therefore, my poor body is at the king's pleasure. Would God my death might do him good.' After this Master Secretary said : 'Well, ye find no fault in that statute ; find you any in any of the other statutes after?' Whereto I answered: 'Sir, whatsoever thing should seem to me other than good in any of the other statutes, or in that statute either, I would not declare what fault I found, nor speak thereof'. Whereunto finally his mastership said full gently, that of any thing that I had spoken there should none advantage be taken. And whether he said farther that there was none to be taken I am not well remembered. But he said that report should be made unto the king's Highness, and his gracious pleasure known.

"Whereupon, I was delivered again to Master Lieutenant, which was then called in. And so was I by Master Lieutenant brought again into my chamber. And here am I yet in such case as I was, neither better or worse. That that shall follow lieth in the hand of God, whom I beseech to put in the king's Grace's mind that thing that may be to His high pleasure, and in mine to mind only the weal of my soul, with little regard of my body, and you with all yours, and my wife, and all my children, and all our other friends, both bodily and ghostly heartily well to fare.

"And I pray you and them all pray for me and take no thought whatsoever shall happen me ; for I verily trust in the goodness of God, seem it never so evil to this world, it shall indeed in another world be for the best.

"Your loving father,
"THOMAS MORE, Knight."

On receiving this letter Margaret again made earnest suit to visit her father, and it was probably in the hope that her presence would bend him that her suit was granted. Something very different took place. Her visit was on 4th May, the day of the martyrdom of the Carthusians and others. Roper's words have made this interview famous: "As Sir Thomas

More was looking out of his window, he chanced to behold one Master Reynolds, a religious, learned, and virtuous father of Sion, and three monks of the Charterhouse, for the matter of the supremacy and matrimony going out of the Tower to execution; he, as one longing in that journey to have accompanied them, said unto my wife, then standing there beside him : ' Lo, dost thou not see, Meg, that these blessed fathers be now as cheerfully going to their deaths as bridegrooms to their marriage ? Wherefore, thereby mayest thou see, mine own good daughter, what a great difference there is between such as have in effect spent all their days in a strait and penitential and painful life religiously, and such as have in the world, like worldly wretches (as thy poor father hath done), consumed all their time in pleasure and ease licentiously. For God, considering their long-continued life in most sore and grievous penance, will no longer suffer them to remain here in this vale of misery, but speedily hence taketh them to the fruition of His everlasting Deity. Whereas thy silly father, Meg, that like a wicked caitiff hath passed forth the whole course of his miserable life most sinfully, God, thinking him not worthy so soon to come to that eternal felicity, leaveth him here still in this world further to be plagued and turmoiled with misery.' " *
On 7th May, some members of the Council again visited the Tower and interrogated both Fisher and More. The following letter has no date, but from the names of the councillors being different from those who are known to have visited the Bishop of Rochester on that day, it seems to refer to a subsequent interrogation on 3rd June. It is addressed to Margaret Roper :—

* The martyrs of the 4th May were : Blessed John Houghton, Blessed Augustine Webster, Blessed Robert Lawrence, all Carthusian priors ; Blessed Richard Reynolds, a Bridgetine monk ; and Blessed John Hale, vicar of Isleworth. They were drawn on hurdles from the Tower to Tyburn, where they were hung, cut down alive, brutally mutilated and quartered.

" Our Lord bless you and all yours. Forasmuch (dearly beloved daughter) as it is likely that you either have heard or shortly shall hear that the Council were here this day, and that I was before them, I have thought it necessary to send you word how the matter standeth. And verily, to be short, I perceive little difference between this time and the last. For as far as I can see, the whole purpose is, either to drive me to say precisely the one way, or else precisely the other.

" Here sat my Lord of Canterbury, my Lord Chancellor, my Lord of Suffolk, my Lord of Wiltshire, and Master Secretary. And after my coming Master Secretary made rehearsal in what wise he had reported unto the king's Highness what had been said by His Grace's Council to me, and what had been answered by me to them, at mine other being before them here last, which thing his mastership rehearsed in good faith very well, as I knowledged and confessed, and heartily thanked him therefore. Whereupon he added thereunto that the king's Highness was nothing content nor satisfied with mine answer ; but thought that by my demeanour I had been occasion of much grudge and harm in the realm, and that I had an obstinate mind and an evil towards him, and that my duty was, being his subject (and so he had sent them now in his name upon mine allegiance to command me), to make a plain and a terminate answer, whether I thought the statute lawful or not. And that I should either knowledge and confess it lawful that His Highness should be supreme head of the Church of England, or else utter plainly my malignity. Whereto I answered that I had no malignity, and, therefore, I could none utter. And as to the matter, I could none other answer make than I had before made, which answer his mastership had there rehearsed. Very heavy I was that the king's Highness should have any such opinion of me. Howbeit, if there were one that had informed His Highness many evil things of me that were untrue, to which His Highness for the time gave credence, I would be very sorry that he should have that opinion of me the space of one day.   Howbeit, if I were sure that other should come on the morrow by whom His Grace should know the truth of mine innocency, I should in the mean while comfort myself with consideration of that. And in likewise now, though it be great heaviness to me that His Highness hath such opinion of me for the while, yet have I no remedy to help it, but only to comfort myself with this consideration, that I know very well that the time shall come when God shall declare my truth towards His Grace before him and all the world.   And whereas it might haply seem to be but small cause of comfort, because I might take harm here first in the mean while, I thanked God that my case was such here in this matter, through the clearness of mine own conscience, that though I might have pain I could not have harm.   For a man may in such a case lose his head and have none harm.   For I was very sure that I had no corrupt affection, but that I had always from the beginning truly used myself, looking first upon God, and next upon the king, according to the lesson that His Highness taught me at my first coming to his noble service, the most virtuous lesson that ever prince taught his servant, whose Highness to have of me now such opinion is my great heaviness. But I have no mean, as I said, to help it, but only comfort myself in the mean time with the hope of that joyful day, in which my truth toward him shall well be known.   And in this matter further I could not go, nor other answer thereto I could not make.

"To this it was said by my Lord Chancellor and Master Secretary both, that the king might by his laws compel me to make a plain answer thereto either the one way or the other. Whereto I answered that I would not dispute the king's authority what His Highness might do in such a case.   But I said that verily, under correction, it seemed to me somewhat hard.   For if it so were that my conscience gave me against the statute (wherein how my conscience giveth me I make no declaration), then I nothing doing nor nothing saying against the statute, it were a very hard thing to compel me to say, either precisely with it against my conscience to the loss of my soul, or precisely against it to the destruction of my body.

" To this Master Secretary said, that I had, ere this, when I was chancellor, examined heretics, and thieves, and other male-factors, and gave me great praise above my deserving in that behalf. And he said, that I then, as he thought, and at the least wise bishops, did use to examine heretics, whether they believed the Pope to be head of the Church, and used to compel them to make a precise answer thereto. And why should not then the king, since it is a law made here that His Grace is head of the Church here, compel men to answer precisely to the law here, as they did then concerning the Pope. I answered and said, that I protested that I intended not to defend my part or stand in contention. But I said there was a difference between those two cases, because that at that time, as well here as elsewhere through the corps of Christendom, the Pope's power was recognised for an undoubted thing; which seemeth not like a thing agreed in this realm, and the contrary taken for truth in other realms. Whereto Master Secretary answered, that they were as well burned for the denying of that as they be beheaded for the denying of this ; and, therefore, as good reason to compel them to make precise answer to the one as to the other. Whereto I answered, that since in this case a man is not by a law of one realm so bound in his conscience, where there is a law of the whole corps of Christendom to the contrary in a matter touching belief, as he is by a law of the whole corps, though there happen to be made in some place a law local to the contrary, the reasonableness or the unreasonableness in binding a man to precise answer standeth not in the respect or difference between beheading and burning, but because of the difference in change of conscience, the difference standeth between beheading and hell. Much was there answered unto this, both by Master Secretary and my Lord Chancellor, over long to rehearse.

" And, in conclusion, they offered me an oath by which I should be sworn to make true answer to such things as should be asked me on the king's behalf, concerning the king's own person. Whereto I answered, that verily I never purposed to swear any book oath more while I lived. Then they said, that I was very obstinate, if I would refuse that, for every man doth it in the Star Chamber and everywhere. I said that was true; but I had not so little foresight, but that I might well conjecture what should be part of mine interrogatories, and as good it was to refuse them at the first as afterwards. Whereto my Lord Chancellor answered, that he thought I guessed truth, for I should see them. And so they were showed me, and they were but twain : the first, whether I had seen the statute ; the other, whether I believed that it were a lawful made statute or not. Whereupon I refused the oath and said further by mouth, that the first I had before confessed, and to the second I would make none answer ; which was the end of our communication, and I was thereupon sent away.

" In the communication before, it was said it was marvelled that I stuck so much in my conscience, while at the uttermost I was not sure therein. Whereto I said, that I was very sure that mine own conscience, so informed as it is by such diligence as I have so long taken therein, may stand with mine own salvation. I meddle not with the conscience of them that think otherwise. Every man *suo damno stat aut cadit*.* I am no man's judge. It was also said unto me, that if I had as lief be out of the world as in it, as I had there said, why did I not then speak even plain out against the statute. It appeared well I was not content to die, though I said so. Whereto I answered, as the truth is, that I have not been a man of such holy living as I might be bold to offer myself to death, lest God, for my presumption, might suffer me to fall ; and, therefore, I put not myself forward, but draw back. Howbeit, if

* So in print. It should probably be *domino*.

God draw me to it Himself, then trust I in His great mercy that He shall not fail to give me grace and strength. In conclusion, Master Secretary said, that he liked me this day much worse than he did the last time. For then, he said, he pitied me much, and now he thought I meant not well. But God and I know both that I mean well, and so I pray God do by me.

"I pray you be, you and mine other good friends, of good cheer, whatsoever fall of me, and take no thought for me, but pray for me, as I do, and shall do, for you and all them.

    "Your tender, loving father,

      "THOMAS MORE, Knight."

About this time it was discovered that some letters had passed at different times between More and Fisher. It was hoped that something treasonable might be discovered, or something that could be interpreted as conspiracy. The Council thereupon proceeded to make inquisition into the matter. Questions were drawn up and ministered to the three servants, Wilson, Golde, and Wood, and to any others known to have visited the prisoners or acted as messengers.

Wilson, Fisher's servant, examined on 7th June, acknowledged that when he found how much importance the bishop attached to the word "maliciously" in the statute, he suspected that he had been counselled by More, but found that it was not so. It was Robert Fisher who had spoken of it to the bishop, and he thinks the bishop told George to call More's attention to it. He had heard from George that More told him the secretary had given him good words, but More would say nothing about his answer. Wilson had carried and had received little presents of food but no letters. "He had sent Mr. More's servant half a custard on Sunday last, and long since green-sauce. More, or his servant, sent him an image of St. John, and apples and oranges, after the snow that fell last winter. On New Year's Day More sent him a paper

with writing, 2000*l.* in gold,* and an image of the Epiphany."
He had often suspected George of carrying letters between Mr.
More and the bishop, indeed he gave George a letter to More
from my lord, since the first examination. The servants had
agreed to deny any letters being sent, but not to forswear
themselves. Had heard the bishop tell George he might say
he had never carried any letters on the king's business.

Interrogated again on 8th June, he admitted that the bishop
wrote a letter to More, which was not closed, and told Wilson,
if George was sober, to give it him to be delivered, which he
did. Does not know whether George brought any answer,
but heard him say that Mr. More was merry, and that my
lord was satisfied. The bishop had told him that the Council
had blamed the lieutenant very sore for his negligence in keeping himself and Mr. More, thinking they had had counsel of
each other, which was an error.

George Golde, the lieutenant's servant, examined on 8th
June, acknowledged that he had carried about a dozen letters
between More and Fisher, some written with ink and some
with coal, and that he had been told both by Fisher and
More to burn some of these. More had also written four letters
to his daughter, Mrs. Roper. Examined again on 9th June, he
said that Bonvisi sent to More, two or three times a week, meat
and a bottle of wine, till a quarter of a year ago, since when he
had sent none.

John à Wood, More's servant, was examined on the 10th; said
that about a fortnight after the first being of the Council in the
Tower, George, the lieutenant's servant, came to More, and
asked him from the bishop what answer he had made. More
replied that he would not dispute of the king's title, but give
himself to his beads and think on his passage hence; and this
he wrote in a letter to be given to Fisher. Soon after he sent
another letter by George, to the effect that he would counsel

---

* As More had not a piece of gold of his own, was this New Year's
present a drawing of bags of gold ?

Fisher not to make the same answer, lest the Council might think they had agreed, and that he could meddle with no man's conscience but his own. After the Council were at the Tower, the bishop sent to tell More what answer he had made ; does nor know if More replied. Next day he declared that on the morning after the Council came to the Tower his master told him that his daughter, Roper's wife, wished to know what had taken place, and he wrote her three letters.*

Nothing of any importance regarding Sir Thomas was elicited from any of the other messengers. On 12th June, the Bishop of Rochester was interrogated. Of his answer I give only what regards More. About four letters had passed between them concerning the matters mentioned in the question. More's first letter was to ask him what answer he had given to the Council in the matter for which he was first committed. He had sent a reply.† George Golde showed him a letter from More to his daughter, stating that when the Council had proposed to him the matter about which they came, he said he would not dispute about the king's title, and the secretary had given him good words. He had then sent a letter by George to know his answer more precisely, but does not recollect his reply. Wrote also to More about the word "maliciously" in the statute, but did not ask More's advice. More thought that their answers would be much alike, and that the Council would suppose that one had taken light of the other, and he wrote to Fisher to avoid this suspicion. After the Council was last at the Tower, and Mr. More's books were taken from him, George told the bishop that More was in a "peck of troubles," and wished to know Fisher's answer. He wrote that he had appealed to the statute, and had begged not to be forced to reply to the

* *Letters and Papers*, viii. 856. Mr. Gairdner, with great difficulty, has put together and read the twenty-one mutilated papers containing the above and other details.

† This was in July, 1534, as appears from More's answers.

interrogations. He had burnt the letters lest they should bring any blame on the lieutenant.*

On the 14th, interrogations were administered to Sir Thomas More. He denied that any communication had passed between himself and any one else concerning the Acts of Succession, of supreme head, or the Act making it treason to speak certain words of the king. He had written divers scrolls to Dr. Fisher, and received others from him, containing for the most part nothing but comforting words and thanks for meat and drink sent by one to the other. But about a quarter of a year after his coming to the Tower he wrote to Fisher, saying he had refused the oath, and never intended to tell the Council why; and Fisher answered that he had not refused to swear to the succession. No other letters passed touching the king's affairs till the Council came to examine upon the Act of Supreme Head, but after his examination he received a letter of Fisher desiring to know his answer. He had replied stating that he meant not to meddle, but fix his mind on the Passion of Christ, or words to that effect. He afterwards received another letter from Fisher stating that he was informed the word "maliciously" was used in the statute, and suggesting that, therefore, a man who spoke nothing of malice did not offend the statute. He replied that he agreed, but feared it would not be so interpreted. Did not report to Fisher his answer to the Council, with the advice to make his own answer different, lest the Council should suspect confederacy.† After his last examination, sent Fisher word by a letter, that Mr. Solicitor had informed him that it was all one not to answer, and to say against the statute what a

* *Letters and Papers*, n. 858.

† This seems contrary to the testimony of the bishop and of More's own servant. Perhaps the discrepancy may be explained by supposing that it was John à Wood who officiously gave the advice as if from More, and that Fisher's memory was inaccurate as to its being in a letter. More was so circumspect as regards writing or speaking, that it is very unlikely he should have written so compromising a document and have communicated its contents to a gossiping servant. John à Wood could not read.

man would, as all the learned men of England would justify. He therefore said he could only reckon on the uttermost, and desired Fisher to pray for him, as he would for Fisher.

And considering that it would come to the ears of his daughter, how the Council had been with him, and other things might be reported which would cause her to take sudden fright;* and fearing that, being, as he thought, with child, she might take harm, he sent to her, both after his first examination and after his last, letters telling her the answers he had given, and that he could not tell what the end might be, but, whatever it were, he prayed her to take it patiently and pray for him.

She had written him before divers letters, advising him to accommodate himself to the king's pleasure, especially urging this in her last.

Other letters he neither sent nor received from any person. George, the lieutenant's servant, carried the letters to and fro. There is none of these letters forthcoming. He would have had George keep them, and George always said there was no better keeper than the fire. When he saw this he desired George to let some trusty friend of his read them, and if he saw any matter of importance in them, he might report it to the Council and get thanks ; otherwise that he should deliver them. But George said he feared the lieutenant, who had ordered him not to meddle with such matters, and so burned them.

After this the Council proposed the three great questions :—

1. Whether he would obey the king as supreme head ? He can make no answer.

2. Whether he will acknowledge the king's marriage with Queen Anne to be lawful and that with Lady Katharine invalid ? Never spoke against it ; can thereunto make no answer.

* The original word is "flight," which is not to be understood in its modern sense. We still use the word "flighty," of one subject to sudden emotions.

3. Where it was objected to him that by the said statute he, as one of the king's subjects, is bound to answer the said question, and recognise the king as supreme head, like all other subjects. He can make no answer.*

On the discovery of the correspondence between More and Fisher, the Council sent Mr. Rich the Solicitor-General, Sir Richard Southwell, and a servant of Cromwell named Palmer, to take from Sir Thomas all his books and writing materials.† Of a conversation which took place on this occasion an account will be given in the next chapter. Stapleton adds that when his books were gone Sir Thomas closed the shutters of his narrow window and sat in the dark, not in gloomy despair, but to meditate more freely on the joys of heaven. The lieutenant, finding him thus one day, asked him the reason. Sir Thomas replied merrily that as the wares were all gone the shop windows might as well be shut. Cresacre More, his great-grandson, says : " Yet still, by stealth, he would get little pieces of paper, in which he would write divers letters with a coal ; of which my father left me one which was to his wife [*i.e.*, to More's wife] which I account as a precious jewel, afterwards drawn over by my grandfather's son with ink ".

* *Letters and Papers*, n. 867.   † Roper's *Notes*.
Life of More, ch. ix.

CHAPTER XXIII.

THE TRIAL.

"O CITY of London," exclaimed Cardinal Pole, " you saw led out from prison on a charge of treason the man at whose tribunal you had so lately beheld others standing for a similar crime ; the man whom you had known as a boy, a youth, and whom you had marked in later life, as, amid the applause and congratulations of all, he mounted through every grade of honour, until he reached the very highest office. And because he was your own citizen and child, not without a secret sense of joy you beheld his prosperous career tending always to your own praise and honour. You saw him at last led out as a criminal from prison, in sordid dress, and grown old, not by the lapse of years, but by the squalor and sufferings of his dungeon, and for the first time you beheld his head made white by long confinement ; you saw his weak and broken body leaning on a staff, and even so scarcely able to stand, and dragged along the way that led to the place of trial, or rather of certain condemnation. Could you see this spectacle with dry eyes ? Or could you without tears see him return by the same road condemned to the penalty of traitors, while you knew that his fidelity towards yourself could never be shaken by bribes or threats ? How, indeed, could the citizens of London be unmoved, when I see utter strangers, who never knew him and never received benefit from him, conceive such sorrow in reading the story of his trial as not to be able to restrain their tears. I myself, who have loved and venerated him, not because of private affection, but because of his virtue and integrity and benefits to my country, writing now about his death, in my exile far from England, feel the tears gush to my eyes against my will, so that—as God is my witness—they hinder my writing, and blot the words that I have written." *

I will try to give as accurately as I can what has been recorded of this trial, designated by Lord Campbell as a "judicial murder," and as "the blackest crime that ever has been perpetrated in England under the form of law". On the 26th June, 1535, a special commission of Oyer and Terminer for Middlesex had been issued, directed to Sir Thomas Audley, chancellor; Thomas, Duke of Norfolk; Charles, Duke of Suffolk; the Earl of Huntingdon, the Earl of Cumberland, the Earl of Wiltshire (father of Anne Boleyn), Lord Montague, Lord Rochford (brother of Anne Boleyn), Lord Windsor, Thomas Cromwell, secretary; Sir John Fitz-James, chief justice of the king's bench; Sir John Baldwin, chief justice of the common pleas; Sir Richard Lister, chief baron of the exchequer; Sir William Paulet, Sir John Porte, Sir John Spelman, Sir Walter Luke, Sir William Fitz-William, Sir Antony Fitz-Herbert, justices. †

The trial of the second band of Carthusian fathers, and of the Bishop of Rochester, had already taken place. The Carthusians won the crown of martyrdom on 19th June; Blessed John Fisher on the 22nd. Perhaps the king had hoped that these deaths would intimidate More, and he was kept for the last. His trial was fixed for the 1st July, and a jury-panel was formed of the following inhabitants of the liberties

---

* *Pro Ecclesiae Unitatis Defensione*, f. xciii. This book was written and sent to Henry VIII. a few months after More's death, though not published till some years later.

† *Baga de Secretis*, pouch 7, bundle 3. See also Third Report of the Deputy-keeper of Public Records (1842), pp. 16-240.

of the Tower, within which the crime was alleged to have been committed: Sir T. Palmer, Sir T. Bent, *knights*; George Lovell, Thomas Burbage, *esquires*; Geoffrey Chamber, Edward Stockmore, William Brown, Jaspar Leake, Thomas Bollington, John Parnell, Richard Bellamy, and George Stoakes, *gentlemen*.

The indictment is in Latin, and of enormous length.* It is founded, not on the Act of Succession, but on that of Supremacy 26, Hen. VIII. cap. 1 and cap. 13. It sets forth that on the 7th May, at the Tower, before Thomas Cromwell, Thomas Bedyll and John Tregonell and divers others the king's councillors, being examined on the king's supremacy, he replied: "I will not meddle with such matters". That afterwards, on the 12th May, the said Sir Thomas, "knowing that John Fisher, clerk, was then and had been detained in the Tower for divers great misprisions committed by him against the king, and that the said Fisher, being examined, had denied to accept the king as before mentioned, wrote a letter to him, by which he agreed with Fisher in his treason, and intimated the silence which he (More) had observed; he also used the expression: ' The Act of Parliament is like a two-edged sword, for if a man answer one way it will confound his soul, and if the other way it will confound his body'". Then afterwards More, fearing lest Fisher on his renewed examination should reveal what More had written, he (More) on the 26th May sent other letters, requesting Fisher not to give the same answer, but to speak his own mind, lest the king's councillors should suspect confederacy. Nevertheless, Fisher, on the 3rd June, when examined by Sir Thomas Audley, the Duke of Suffolk, the Earl of Wiltshire, and others, did refuse a direct answer, and said: "The statute is like a two-edged sword, etc., therefore, I will make no answer in that matter". That on the same

---

* It is in the *Baga de Secretis*; there is also a copy in the Arundel MS. 151. Sir James Mackintosh did not know of this, and erroneously thought that Sir Thomas More was indicted under the Act of Succession.

3rd June More gave the same answer. Lastly, that on 12th June there was a dialogue between Richard Rich, the solicitor-general, and More, which is there detailed.

The said Richard Rich charitably moved Sir T. More to be conformable to the before-mentioned laws, to which More replied: "Your conscience will save you and my conscience will save me". Rich then, protesting that he was speaking without authority, said: "Supposing that it were enacted by parliament that I, Richard Rich, should be king, and that it should be treason to deny the same, what would be the offence if you, Sir T. More, was to say that I, Rich, was king; for certain it is that in my conscience (said Rich) you would be obliged so to accept me for king, because you would be bound by the Act of Parliament". To which More then and there answered, "that he should offend if he were to say no, for he was obliged by the Act, because he could give his consent to the same". But he said that was a light case, wherefore the said Thomas More further said to Rich that he would put a higher case: "Suppose it should be enacted by parliament *quod Deus non esset Deus* [that God were not God], and that opposing the act should be treason; and if it were asked of you, Richard Rich, whether you would say that God were not God according to the statute, and if you were to say no, would you offend?" To which Rich answered More: "Certainly; because it is impossible that God were not God. But because your case is so high, I will put a medium one. You know that our lord the king is constituted chief head on earth of the Church of England; and why, Master More, can you not affirm to accept the same, just as you would in the preceding case that I should be made king, in which case you agree that you would be obliged to acknowledge and accept me as king?" To which More, persevering in his treasons, answered to Rich, that the cases were not similar; because "the king can be made by parliament and deprived by parliament, to which Act every subject being in parliament gives his consent; but in the first case the subject cannot be obliged, because his consent cannot be given for that in parliament, and although the king might be so accepted in England, yet many do not assent to the same in foreign parts ".*

Such was Rich's testimony as recited in the indictment. It bears on the face of it the evidence of forgery; for who can think for a moment that More would thus speak to a man like Rich on the power of parliament to depose kings, or on the recent statute of supremacy? But we shall hear More's own statement. Official documents do not give the pleadings at the trial; but a few days after More's death there appeared on the continent a French account of his speeches, which was immediately spread through Europe and translated into many languages. It bears intrinsic evidence of truth : in the first place, because it entirely corresponds with the indictment; and secondly, because More's answers are in exact conformity with what he had written in the various letters given in previous chapters—letters, of course, unknown to the writer.†

"On the 1st July, 1535, Master Thomas Morus, formerly chancellor of England, was brought before the judges, and the accusations against him read in his presence. The chancellor and the Duke of Norfolk turned to him and said : 'You, Master More, have gravely erred against the king; nevertheless we hope by his clemency that if you repent and correct your obstinate opinion, in which you have so rashly persevered,

* The account of the conversation in all previous biographies is that given by Roper. It is substantially the same, but contains a proposition about Rich being made Pope, which More rejects. Roper had probably no other authority than the indictment and More's answer as related to him. He mentions, however, that the supposed conversation took place in presence of Sir Richard Southwell and Mr. Palmer while More's books were being packed up.

† MS. Bibl. Nat., Paris. Castlenau's *Memoirs* i. 415 (ed. 1731, Brussels). The following is the translation given by Mr. Gairdner. I have compared it with the French, and added a few words that had been omitted (see *Letters and Papers*, viii. p. 394).

you will receive pardon'. He replied : 'My lords, I thank you very heartily for your good will. I pray God preserve me in my just opinion even to death. As to the accusations against me, I fear words, memory, and judgment would alike fail me to reply to such a length of articles, especially considering my present imprisonment and great infirmity.' A chair was then ordered to be placed for him, and he proceeded as follows :—

"'As to the first article, charging me with having always maliciously opposed the king's second marriage, I will only answer that what I have said has been according to my conscience. I never wished to conceal the truth, and if I had, I should have been a traitor. For this error, if error it should be called, I have been condemned to perpetual imprisonment, which I have already suffered for fifteen months, and my goods confiscated. For this reason I will only reply to the principal charge against me, that I have incurred the penalty of the statute made in the last parliament since I was in prison, by refusing to the king, maliciously, falsely, and traitorously, his title of Supreme Head of the Church of England, in proof of which you allege my reply to the secretary and Council, that as I was dead to the world, I did not care to think of such things, but only of the Passion of Christ. I reply that your statute cannot condemn me to death for such silence, for neither your statute nor any laws in the world punish people except for words and deeds—surely not for keeping silence.' To this the king's proctor replied that such silence was a certain proof of malice intended against the statute, especially as every faithful subject, on being questioned about the statute, was obliged to answer categorically that the statute was good and wholesome. 'Surely,' replied More, 'if what the common law * says is true, that he who is silent seems to consent, my silence should rather be taken as approval than contempt of your

* " Ce que l'on dit vulgairement." But the Spanish version says : " Lo que el direetio comun dire ". Erasmus translates it : " Si verum est quod habetur in legibus ".

statute. You say that all good subjects are obliged to reply; but I say that the faithful subject is more bound to his conscience and his soul than to anything else in the world, provided his conscience, like mine, does not raise scandal or sedition, and I assure you that I have never discovered what is in my conscience to any person living.

" 'As to the second article, that I have conspired against the statute by writing eight letters * to the Bishop of Rochester, advising him to disobey it, I could wish these letters had been read in public, but as you say the bishop has burnt them, I will tell you the substance of them. Some were about private matters connected with our old friendship. Another was a reply to one of his asking how I had answered in the Tower to the first examination about the statute. I said that I had informed my conscience, and so he also ought to do the same. I swear that this was the tenor of the letters, for which I cannot† be condemned by your statute.

" 'Touching the third article, that when I was examined by the Council, I answered that your statute was like a two-edged sword, for he who approved it would ruin his soul, and he who contradicted it his body; and that the Bishop of Rochester answered similarly, showing that we were confederates : I reply that I only answered thus conditionally, that supposing a statute to cut thus both ways like a two-edged sword, how could a man behave so as not to incur either danger? I do not know how the bishop replied, but if he answered like me, it must have been from the agreement between us in opinion, but not because we had ever arranged it between us. Be assured I never did or said anything maliciously against the statute, but it may be that this has been maliciously reported to the king.'

" Then they ordered an usher to summon twelve men, accord-

* "Huit paires de lettres." The Spanish says simply, "ocho letras". Erasmus, "octa paria". On the word "pair," see Note, p. 303.

† The negative is omitted in the French, but is given in the Spanish and in Erasmus.

ing to the custom of the country, and these articles were given
to them that they might judge whether More had maliciously
contravened the statute. After a quarter of an hour's absence,
they declared him guilty of death, and sentence was pronounced
by the chancellor, 'according to the tenour of the new law'.*

"More then spoke as follows : 'Since I am condemned
and God knows how, I wish to speak freely of your statute, for
the discharge of my conscience. For the seven years that I
have studied the matter, I have not read in any approved
doctor of the Church that a temporal lord could or ought to
be head of the spirituality.'† The chancellor, interrupting
him, said : 'What, More, you wish to be considered wiser and
of better conscience than all the bishops and nobles of the
realm ?' To this More replied : 'My lord, for one bishop
of your opinion I have a hundred saints of mine ; and for one
parliament of yours, and God knows of what kind, I have all
the General Councils for 1000 years ; and for one kingdom I
have France and all the kingdoms of Christendom'. Norfolk
told him that now his malice was clear. More replied : 'What
I say is necessary for discharge of my conscience and satisfaction of my soul, and to this I call God to witness, the sole
Searcher of human hearts. I say further, that your statute is
ill made, because you have sworn never to do anything against
the Church, which, through all Christendom, is one and undivided, and you have no authority, without the common consent
of all Christians, to make a law or Act of Parliament or Council
against the union of Christendom. I know well that the reason
why you have condemned me is because I have never been
willing to consent to the king's second marriage ; but I hope,
in the Divine goodness and mercy, that, as St. Paul and St.

* " Selon la lettre de la noble loi " (De Castelnau). Apparently a mis-
reading of " nouvelle ". The Spanish has, " segun la forma y tenor de
la nueva ley " ; Erasmus, " juxta tenorem novæ constitutionis ".

† Quod laicus, aut, ut vocant, secularis, possit aut debeat esse caput
status spiritualis aut ecclesiastici (Erasmus).

Stephen, whom he persecuted, are now friends in Paradise, so we, though differing in this world, shall be united in perfect charity in the other. I pray God to protect the king, and give him good counsel.'"

This account is accurate, but incomplete. The writer has omitted Sir Thomas More's answer to the evidence of Rich. The recital of the long dialogue, with its various suppositions, and More's rehearsal of the true conversation, were probably too complicated for the French writer to follow. More's answer is recorded by Roper, who says that, though he was not present at the trial, he gives the words of More as reported to him by Sir Anthony St. Leger, by Mr. Chaywood, and Mr. Webb, and others, as correctly as his memory would serve. "If I were a man, my lords, that did not regard an oath, I need not stand in this place, at this time, as an accused person. And if this oath of yours, Mr. Rich, be true, then I pray that I may never see the face of God, which I would not say were it otherwise to win the whole world." He then recited the conversation in the Tower as it had really taken place, adding: "In good faith, Mr. Rich, I am sorrier for your perjury than for my own peril; but neither I, nor any other man else, to my knowledge, ever took you to be a man of such credit, as that, in any matter of importance, I, or any other, would, at any time, vouchsafe to communicate with you. And I, as you know, of no small while, have been acquainted with you and your conversation, who have known you from your youth hitherto, for we long dwelled together in one parish. I am sorry you compel me so to say, that you were esteemed very light of your tongue, a great dicer, and of no commendable fame. And so in your house at the Temple, where hath been your chief bringing up, were you likewise accounted.

"Can it, therefore, seem likely to your honourable lordships that I would, in so weighty a cause, so unadvisedly overshoot myself as to trust Mr. Rich, a man of me always reputed of little troth, so far above my sovereign lord the king or any of his noble councillors, that I would utter unto him the secrets of my conscience touching the king's supremacy, the special point at my hands so long sought for—a thing that I never did, nor never would, after the statute thereof made, reveal unto the king's Highness himself? Can this, in your judgment, my lords, seem likely to be true?

"And yet, if I had so done indeed, seeing it was spoken but in secret, familiar talk, nothing affirming, and only in putting of cases, it cannot justly be taken to be spoken *maliciously*. I can never think, my lords, that so many worthy bishops, so many honourable personages as at the making of that law were assembled, ever meant to have any man punished by death in whom there could be found no malice, taking *malitia* for *malevolentia*, for if *malitia* be generally taken for sin, no man is there that can then excuse himself."

Thereupon Rich caused Sir Richard Southwell and Mr. Palmer to be sworn, but they both said that they were so engaged in packing the books that they paid little attention to the conversation—a paltry compromise between fear and conscience.

Roper also says that when Sir Thomas, after the verdict of the jury, was asked what he could allege against the sentence, he replied not only that supremacy in the Church could not belong to a layman, but that it "rightfully belonged to the See of Rome, as granted personally by Our Lord when on earth to St. Peter and his successors," and that, as the city of London could not make a law against the laws of the realm of England, so England could not make a law contrary to the general law of Christ's Catholic Church, and that the Magna Charta of England was that "the English Church should be free and enjoy all its right entire," and so the king had sworn at his coronation. He added that for England to refuse obedience to the See of Rome was the same as for a child to refuse obedience to a parent. As St. Paul said to the Corinthians: "I have begotten you in Christ," so might St. Gregory say to the English: "You are my children, because I have under Christ given to you everlasting salvation".

Lord Macaulay has called the state trials of those days "murder preceded by mummery". The trial was indeed an empty farce, since on 25th June, after the death of Blessed Fisher, the king had ordered the preachers to set forth to the people the treasons of the late Bishop of Rochester, and of Sir Thomas More; joining them together though the latter was still untried.*

But the martyr's earnest part was a spectacle to God, to angels, and to men.

In what follows not a word may be changed or omitted from Roper's narrative: " Now, after his arraignment departed he from the bar to the Tower again, led by Sir William Kingston, a tall, strong, and comely knight, constable of the Tower, and his very dear friend.† Who, when he had brought him from Westminster to the " Old Swan," towards the Tower, there, with a heavy heart, the tears running down his cheeks, bade him farewell. Sir Thomas More, seeing him so sorrowful, comforted him with as good words as he could, saying: "Good Mr. Kingston, trouble not yourself, but be of good cheer, for I will pray for you and my good lady your wife, that we may meet in heaven together, where we shall be merry for ever and ever". Soon after, Sir William Kingston, talking with me of Sir Thomas More, said: " In good faith, Mr. Roper, I was ashamed of myself that at my departing from your father I found my heart so feeble and his so strong, that he was fain to comfort me that should rather have comforted him ".

"When Sir Thomas," continues Roper, "came from West-minster to the Tower, his daughter, my wife, desirous to see

* *Letters and Papers*, viii. 921.

† According to the official record it was Sir Edmund Walsingham, he lieutenant, who conducted the prisoner to Westminster. Roper cannot have been mistaken in saying that it was the constable, Sir William Kingston, who conducted him back to the Tower.

her father, whom she thought she should never see in this world after, and also to have his final blessing, gave attendance about the Tower wharf, where she knew he should pass before he could enter into the Tower. There tarrying his coming, as soon as she saw him, after his blessing upon her knees reverently received, she hasting towards him, without consideration or care of herself, pressing in among the midst of the throng and company of the guard, that with halbards and bills went round about him, hastily ran to him, and there openly, in sight of them, embraced him, and took him about the neck and kissed him.* Who, well liking her most natural and dear daughterly affection towards him, gave her his fatherly blessing and many godly words of comfort besides. From whom after she was departed, she, not satisfied with the former sight of him, and like one that had forgotten herself, being all ravished with the entire love of her father, having respect neither to herself nor to the press of people that were about him, suddenly turned back again, ran to him as before, took him about the neck, and divers times kissed him lovingly, and at last, with a full and heavy heart, was fain to depart from him ; the beholding whereof was to many that were present so lamentable that it made them for very sorrow thereof to weep."†

Roper, in his modesty, says nothing here about himself, yet it seems evident that he was a spectator of all these things, and was supporting his wife in her great trial. Stapleton informs us that John More, Sir Thomas's son, also came to receive his father's blessing on his knees, probably as he left Westminster Hall; he adds also that Margaret Gigs and Dorothy Colly accompanied Margaret Roper, and ventured to follow her example in embracing the holy martyr.

* Cresacre More mentions her cry : " Oh ! my father ! Oh ! my father !"

† Erasmus, in the account he published under the name of Covrinus Nucerinus, gives the interview with Margaret with the same details, remarking that even the guards were melted to tears.

The sentence passed on More was that he should die at Tyburn with all the infamous brutalities then inflicted on traitors. The time, however, had not been fixed, and the decision of the king was awaited. Cresacre More, after Stapleton, tells us that he redoubled his penitential exercises, scourging himself, and meditating on death, with a sheet around him, as if he were a corpse prepared for burial. He was condemned on the 1st July, and executed on the 6th. "In the meantime," says Cresacre,* "came to him a light-headed courtier, talking of no serious matter, but only urging him this, that he would change his mind; and being wearied with his importunity, he answered him, that he had changed it, who presently went and told the king thereof. And being by him commanded to know wherein his mind was changed, Sir Thomas rebuked him for his lightness in that he would tell the king every word that he spoke in jest, meaning that whereas he had purposed to be shaven, that he might seem to others as before he was wont, now he was fully minded that his beard should take such part as his head did; which made the fellow blank and the king very angry."

On Monday, the 5th July, he wrote with a charred stick this his last letter to Margaret, at the same time sending to her his hair shirt:—

"Our Lord bless you, good daughter, and your good husband, and your little boy, and all yours, and all my children, and all my god-children and all our friends. Recommend me when ye may to my good daughter Cecily, whom I beseech Our Lord to comfort; and I send her my blessing and to all her children, and pray her to pray for me. I send her a handkercher, and God comfort my good son, her husband. My good daughter Daunce hath the picture in parchment that you delivered me from my Lady Coniers, her name on the back. Show her that I heartily

---

* Stapleton is his authority.

pray her that you may send it in my name to her again,
for a token from me to pray for me.

"I like special well Dorothy Colly. I pray you be good
unto her. I would wot whether this be she that you wrote me
of. If not, yet I pray you be good to the other as you may in
her affliction, and to my good daughter Jane Aleyn too.
Give her, I pray you, some kind answer, for she sued hither to
me this day to pray you be good to her.

"I cumber you, good Margaret, much, but I would be sorry
if it should be any longer than to-morrow, for it is St. Thomas's
even, and the utas of St. Peter; * and, therefore, to-morrow
long I to go to God. It were a day very meet and convenient
for me.

"I never liked your manner towards me better than when
you kissed me last; for I love when daughterly love and dear
charity hath no leisure to look to worldly courtesy. Farewell,
my dear child, and pray for me, and I shall for you and all
your friends, that we may merrily meet in heaven. I thank
you for your great cost. I send now my good daughter
Clement † her algorism stone, and I send her and my
godson and all hers God's blessing and mine. I pray you at
time convenient recommend me to my good son John More.
I liked well his natural fashion. Our Lord bless him and his
good wife, my loving daughter, to whom I pray him to be good,
as he hath great cause : and that, if the land of mine come to
his hands, he break not my will concerning his sister Daunce.
And the Lord bless Thomas and Austin, and all that they
shall have." ‡

In one of the last days of his life he wrote a Latin letter to
his friend of forty years' standing, Antonio Bonvisi, an erudite
and wealthy Italian merchant settled in London, who had sent

---

* Utas, *i.e.*, the octave day of the feast of St. Peter, 29th June ; the
7th July is the Translation of the Relics of St. Thomas of Canterbury.

† Margaret Gigs, who had married Dr. Clement.

‡ *English Works*, p. 1457.

both to him and to the Bishop of Rochester many little presents during their imprisonment. The letter is full of affection, and he bids him farewell till they meet again where there will be no need of letters, where no walls will keep them apart, and no jailer forbid their conversation, but where, with God the Father, and His only-begotten Son, Jesus Christ, and the Holy Ghost, who proceeds from both, they will enjoy eternal bliss.*

' *English Works*, p. 1455.

CHAPTER XXIV.

THE MARTYRDOM.

If love be strong, hot, mighty, and fervent,
　　There may no trouble, grief, or sorrow fall
But that the lover would be well content
　　All to endure, and think it eke too small,
　　Though it were death, so he might therewithal
The joyful presence of that person get
On whom he hath his heart and love yset.

Thus should of God the lover be content
　　Any distress or sorrow to endure,
Rather than be from God his love absent,
　　And glad to die, so that he may be sure,
　　By his departing hence, for to procure
After this valley dark the heavenly light,
And of his love the glorious blessed sight.

THUS More had written in his early manhood. They
were no empty, idle words. The thought of eternity,
the desire of the vision of God, run through the
texture of his whole life. Many a man, before and since, has
met death bravely. Not only in the excitement of a field of
battle, or the enthusiasm of a rescue from fire, but calmly in
the execution of duty, as when the captain stands erect upon
the sinking ship, while he sees the last boat depart with the
women and children. All admiration to such deaths! All
honour to such men! But it is not mere physical or moral

courage we honour in the death of Blessed Thomas More. It is that his death was willing, though not wilful. One word of compliance and he would have been carried from the Tower to the palace of the king triumphantly, and little shame would have been his where all had yielded. But his death was not only willing, it was desired. All the martyrs have accepted death to be faithful to their God, but not all have desired death; at least, they have not all, like More, desired it throughout their life. To him eternity had ever been the only reality, the only hope that makes life worth living. Pleasure, literary fame, wealth, the smiles of princes, had only proved to him how mean are all the goods this life can offer, and his soul thirsted for the strong God from the midst of weakness, for the living God from the midst of death: "As the hart panteth after the fountains of water, so my soul panteth after Thee, O God; my soul hath thirsted after the strong living God; when shall I come and appear before the face of God?" *

The details of More's glorious martyrdom have been made familiar to all by the narration of his son-in-law. Stapleton gathered a few additional circumstances from Margaret Clements and Dorothy Colly.† Shame caused the king to commute the sentence of drawing, hanging, mutilating and quartering at Tyburn into beheading on Tower Hill.‡ The day he chose was that which More had desired, the 6th July. Early in the morning of that day an old friend of More, Sir Thomas Pope, was sent by the king to announce to him that he must die that day before nine o'clock. Not one of the historians has a word about confession and communion; but as we know from a

* *Psalm* xli.

† Stapleton's history has been very literally followed by Cresacre More.

‡ Cresacre says that when this royal clemency was made known to More, he answered: "God forbid the king should use any more such mercy unto any of my friends, and God bless all my posterity from such pardons". The words seem authentic, but I do not find the authority for them.

letter of Chapuys' that a confessor was assigned to Fisher. and. as this was an ordinary concession before execution,* we may suppose that Sir Thomas had this consolation once more before he died, though probably not that of receiving the Viaticum of Our Lord's Body and Blood. More thanked Sir Thomas Pope for the news he brought, and expressed his gratitude to the king for placing him where he had had so much leisure to prepare for his last end. "And so, God help me, am I bounden to His Highness most of all, that it pleaseth him so shortly to rid me from the miseries of this wretched world; and therefore will I not fail earnestly to pray for His Grace both here and also in the world to come." "The king's pleasure is farther," said Pope, "that at your execution you shall not use many words." "Mr. Pope," replied More, "you do well to give me warning of His Grace's pleasure, for, otherwise, at that time had I purposed to have spoken, but of no matter wherewith His Grace or any should have had cause to be offended. I beseech you, good Mr. Pope, to be a mean to His Highness that my daughter Margaret may be at my burial." "The king is content already," replied Pope, "that your wife and children and other friends shall have liberty to be present thereat." "Oh, how much beholding, then, am I unto His Grace, that unto my poor burial vouchsafeth to have so gracious consideration." Sir Thomas Pope could not restrain his tears, but the martyr comforted him with his usual words about a happy meeting in heaven.†

His friend Bonvisi had sent to him a handsome dress of camelot (a kind of silk) to wear at his execution.‡ The lieutenant advised him to take it off, saying that he who should have it after his death—for it was the perquisite of the headsman—was but a rascal. "What! Mr. Lieutenant," replied

---

* "Whom the protector bade speed and shrive him apace, for, by St. Paul," quoth he, "I will not to dinner till I see thy head off" (More's *Richard III.*).

† The above is from Roper.

‡ Stapleton.

More, " shall I account him a rascal that shall do me this day
so singular a benefit? Were it cloth of gold I should think it
well bestowed on him, as St. Cyprian did who gave his executioner thirty pieces of gold." He yielded, however, to the
insistance of the lieutenant; but gave a gold angel to the
headsman on the scaffold, and he had before asked his son to
befriend him in any way he could.*

Stapleton says that Margaret Clements once showed him a
curiously wrought representation or statuette of Sir Thomas
More going towards the scaffold. This she had made, or
caused to be made, as the image of the martyr was present in
her memory. His face was very pale and emaciated, he wore
a poor dress of frieze, and carried a red cross in his hand. His
beard was long, and his eyes were raised to heaven.

Harpsfield says that as he left the Tower gate a woman asked
him to notify that he had certain evidences of hers, that were
delivered to him when he was chancellor, and that since he
had been imprisoned she had been unable to recover them.
"Good woman," he replied, "content thyself and take patience
a little while, for the king is so good and gracious to me, that
even within this half-hour he will disburden me of all worldly
business, and help thee himself." † Another woman followed
him crying that he had done her a great injury when he was
chancellor. He replied calmly that he remembered her case
well, and should still give the same decision.‡ The selfish
women were exceptions. One good woman came from her
house and offered him a cup of wine. He thanked her, but
refused it, saying that Christ at His Passion drank no wine, but
gall and vinegar. " Last of all," says Cresacre, " there came a
citizen of Winchester. This man had long laboured under a
temptation of despair and suicide. Sir Thomas, when chan-

* Stapleton, who says he gave the money himself. Roper says that
he sent it.

† Harpsfield's MS., from whom Stapleton relates this.

‡ Cresacre. This is not in Harpsfield.

cellor, had tried to console him, and had, by his prayers rather than his words, delivered him for three years. After Sir Thomas's committal to prison, the old temptation returned more violently. But now, hearing that his friend was to be executed, he came to London, and ran towards him as he was led out to execution, desiring, with great earnestness, that he would help him by his prayers; to whom Sir Thomas said : "Go and pray for me, and I will carefully pray for you". He went away with confidence, and was troubled no more.*

The scaffold, says Roper, was very unsteady, and putting his feet on the ladder, he said merrily to the lieutenant : " I pray thee see me safe up, and for my coming down let me shift for myself ". " Then desired he all the people to pray for him and to bear witness with him that he should there suffer death in and for the faith of the Catholic Church." This is Roper's account. The French report, copied by Erasmus, adds that he exhorted the people to pray for the king that God would send him good counsel, and protested that he died his faithful servant, but especially the servant of God.

He then knelt down and, according to Stapleton, recited the psalm *Miserere*, which had always been his favourite prayer.† The executioner as usual asked pardon, and he kissed him, saying cheerfully : " Pluck up thy spirits, man, and be not afraid to do thy office. My neck is very short ; take heed, therefore, thou strike not awry for saving of thine honesty." ‡ *Ridebit in die novissimo.*

The block used at that period was a mere low log, so that the victim had to lie at full length on the scaffold with his face

* Cresacre, from Stapleton. Ch. vi.

† " The martyrs in their agony made no long prayers aloud, but one inch of such a prayer so prayed in that pain was worth a whole ell and more, even of their own prayers prayed at some other time " (*English Works*, p. 1164).

‡ Roper.

downwards.* More had brought with him a handkerchief : he blindfolded himself, and placing his head upon the block, received the fatal but blessed blow that will surround his brow for ever with the martyr's aureole.† He had lived fifty-six years and five months.

The story of More's life and death is told. The reader will make his own reflections. As I have tried to say only what was strictly necessary on contemporary history, so I will forbear to speak of the consequences of More's life and death on England, and on the Church. With the record, then, of his earthly relics I will make an end. Of the disposal of his sacred head and body his own son-in-law says nothing, and Archdeacon Harpsfield, who could have learned every detail from Roper, and who wrote freely in the days of Mary, omitting all mention of the body, merely gives the well-known fact that the head was placed on London Bridge, and tells us nothing of its fate. The account given by Stapleton is as follows : " The head remained fixed on a stake on London Bridge for a month, when Margaret Roper bribed the man whose business it was to throw it into the river to give it to her ". Though it had been parboiled before being exposed (as Erasmus mentions, and as was the custom), yet it was easily recognised, not only by the absence o a tooth that he had lost before death, but because its appearance was almost as fair as during life. But the beard, which had been hoary before death, became of a reddish colour afterwards. Margaret had it preserved in spices, and kept it most reverently while she lived ; "and to this day," adds Stapleton, cautiously, "it is still preserved in her family ".‡ Even in the

* Thus Blessed John Fisher was executed (see my *Life of Fisher*, 2nd ed., App.).

† Cresacre adds that, having his head on the block, he bade the executioner stay until he had removed his beard, saying that it had committed no treason. This incident is not in Roper, Harpsfield, or Stapleton.

‡ Et hodie adhuc apud aliquem suorum custoditur.

next century Cresacre More thought it more prudent to say :
" She buried it where she thought fittest ".   Sir Richard Morison, on the contrary, writing in 1536 an answer to Cochlæus,
who in a little book had mentioned the removal of More's and
Fisher's heads from the bridge, boldly denies such removal.
" Come here," he says, " and you shall see both heads where
they were placed, and still warning men by the spectacle not
to conspire against the king or the laws of the kingdom." *
Morison, a protegé of Cromwell's, was seeking court favour,
and had been set up to defend Henry against the execrations
of Europe.   He could not deny that the most venerable heads
in England had been impaled on London Bridge.   He thought
it, therefore, best to pretend no shame and affirm relentless
justice.   His affirmations and denials are of little value.   I
prefer to believe the veracity of Stapleton, who says that Margaret was summoned before the Council for keeping her father's
head as a relic, as well as his books and writings.   She replied
that she had procured her father's head for burial that it might
not be the food of fishes ; and that she had, with the exception
of his printed books, few of his writings but familiar letters,
which she earnestly begged that she might keep for her solace.
Powerful men at court befriended her, and she was no more
molested.   " Carrying her love beyond the grave," writes Sir
James Mackintosh, " she desired that the head might be buried
with her when she died.   The remains of this precious relic
are said to have been since observed in the burial place, lying
on what had been her bosom."   Tennyson's words will occur
to the mind :—

> Morn broaden'd on the borders of the dark
>   Ere I saw her, who clasped in her last trance
>   Her murder'd father's head. †

This legend is so beautiful that it is almost cruel to question
it.   It is not, however, ancient, and it seems impossible to

* Apomaxis calumniarum, etc., f. 93, b.   (See Appendix I.)
† A Dream of Fair Women.

reconcile it with facts. The vault of the Ropers is in St. Dunstan's Church, Canterbury, and it is there that Margaret, with her father's head, is supposed to lie. Indeed, a leaden vessel, such as would contain a head, was seen in the Roper vault as late as 1835, though it was not lying in or on a coffin, but placed on a ledge behind an iron grating. That may, indeed, be the head of Blessed Thomas, and Margaret may, in obedience to the Council, have placed it where she hoped it would be safe. She died in 1544, nine years after her father, and thirty-four before her husband. But, though she has a monumental inscription at St. Dunstan's, she was buried at Chelsea; and William Roper, her husband, who died 4th January, 1578, directs in his will that his body be placed with that of his wife and children, at Chelsea, Co. Middlesex "in the vault with the body of my dearly beloved wife (whose soul Our Lord pardon), where my father-in-law, Sir Thomas More (whose soul Jesus bless), did mind to be buried". Margaret, it seems, had chosen to be buried with her mother, whom More had already placed in the family vault. For some reason Roper's injunction was not carried out, and he lies at St. Dunstan's, Canterbury.*

The headless body of More suffered no such outrages as were offered, by the express orders of the king, to that of Fisher. No doubt he wished to revenge on the cardinal what he called the wrongs done him by the Pope. He had no such reason for insulting More. By the governor's permission, then, the body was laid in the chapel of St. Peter ad Vincula in the Tower. This is expressly stated by Stapleton, who had all the details from Margaret Clements and Dorothy Harris. These two women assisted Margaret Roper in the burial. They used to relate that, when they came to take up the body they had all forgotten the winding sheet, and had brought no money with them, and, being far from their homes, had no credit in that

* See Roper Pedigree at Coll. Arms (MS. Norfolk, xii. p. 2). Information kindly communicated by E. Bellasis, Esq., *Lancaster Herald*.

quarter. Mrs. Harris, however, went to a draper's shop, and agreeing on the price, made as though she would look for money in her purse, and then try whether they would trust her; and to her great surprise she found the exact sum they had agreed on.*

In the British Museum there is a Latin *Life of Blessed John Fisher*, of which the greater part has been consumed by fire, and most of the remnant is illegible. But the following passage is easy to decipher.† After stating that Fisher's body remained for seven years in All Hallows' Churchyard, on Tower Hill, visited and venerated especially by foreigners, the writer continues : "The martyr's enemies were so angry at the concourse, that they had the body exhumed and carried to the Tower, and with the relics of Thomas More cast into an obscure place. But certain persons who have taken note of events have left in writing, that the bodies of these holy men did not even rest there ; but that, when the heat of persecution somewhat abated, they were devoutly carried to the village of Chelsea, where More had resided, and are there kept to this day entombed in a new monument which he had prepared for himself when he was in (royal) favour. But while I was endeavouring to discover from common report or from written records the real place where this precious treasure is hidden, I was hindered. May God grant that some day, when religion revives and peace is restored to the Church, it may be known to the faithful where are those longed-for relics." All this is very perplexing. The life is anonymous, but bears intrinsic evidence of having been written in the time of Queen Mary. How could there be any difficulty in discovering the truth of the removal when Roper was still alive and so many of More's grandchildren? It would seem that the writer was just

---

* This story is related by Stapleton and by Sander. Burnet reproaches Sander with inventing it. He merely, like Stapleton, told what he heard on the best authority.

† Arundel MS. 152, f. 233.

ST. PETER'S AD VINCULA.

To face p. 438.

making his inquiries when the death of Queen Mary drove him into exile and interrupted all communication with the family. Stapleton, who wrote in 1588, says nothing of this removal to Chelsea.*

Cresacre More, who had no doubt all the family traditions, writes that " the body was buried in the chapel of St. Peter, in the belfry, or as some say, as one entereth into the vestry, near unto the body of the holy martyr Bishop Fisher, who being put to death just a fortnight before, had small respect done unto him all this while ". This last phrase must point to the shameful outrages perpetrated on the body of Blessed Fisher, and imply that it was removed from All Hallows to the Tower, not seven years, but one fortnight after its burial. Cresacre's knowledge of Fisher's history may have been imperfect, or Margaret may really have got leave to take up the bishop's remains and lay them with her father's. Cresacre gives no hint of subsequent removal. He could scarcely have visited the chapel of St. Peter, for there was no *vestry* in the entrance to which the body could have been laid. The spot pointed out at present is near the entrance to the small bell-tower ; and if that was the resting-place of the holy ashes, they will not have been removed to the vaults, as was the case with those in the nave, when the church was repaired in 1876.†

Near the entrance door at the west end has been recently placed a memorial tablet with the following inscription :—

" List of remarkable persons buried in this chapel :

" 1.   Gerald Fitzgerald, Earl of Kildare,   ·   1534.
" 2.   John Fisher, Bishop of Rochester,   -   1535.
" 3.   Sir Thomas More, -   -   -   -   -   1535.

* Weever and others affirm the removal of More's body to Chelsea, but they give no authority. The Rev. J. Morris, S.J., argues in favour of the removal in the *Month* for Feb., 1891. Perhaps the vault at Chelsea may be some day opened, and the truth revealed. As yet the evidence to me seems in favour of the Tower.

† On this removal see *The Chapel in the Tower*, by Mr. C. Doyne Bell.

" 4.   George Boleyn, Viscount Rochford, -   1536.
" 5.   Queen Anne Boleyn,   -   -   -   1536.
" 6.   Thomas Cromwell, Earl of Essex,   -   1540.
" 7.   Margaret of Clarence, Countess of
                Salisbury,   -   -   -   -   1541,"
        etc. ; in all, 34, ending :
" 34.   Simon, Lord Fraser of Lovat,   -   -   1747."

These lines throw open many a dark and painful page of English history, and they remind us of More's words to Tindale : that violent death may come to saint or sinner, to martyr or heretic, to patriot or traitor.   They suggest bitter reflections on More's false friends and open enemies—on Cromwell, Anne Boleyn, and Henry VIII.   But I refrain.   I have said as little of these as I could, and I will not conclude a *Life of Blessed More* by reproaches of those for whom he prayed with his last breath.   A more fitting termination will be found in his own words, written in the Tower in the prospect of the block :—

" To this great glory of heaven can there no man come *headless*.   Our Head is Christ, and, therefore, to Him must we be joined, and as members of His must we follow Him, if we will come thither.   ' Know ye not that Christ must suffer passion and by that way enter into the kingdom ? '   Who can for very shame desire to enter into His kingdom of Christ with ease, when He Himself entered not into His own without pain ? " *

* *Dialogue of Comfort against Tribulation*, Bk. iii. ch. 26.

APPENDIX A.

I OWE the following notes to the courtesy of E. Bellasis, Esq., *Lancaster Herald*:—

I. SIR JOHN MORE.

The MS. in College of Arms, *Vincent*, cxi. p. 370, notes that Sir John More's grandfather More married Joanna, daughter of John Leicestre. It also states that Sir John had two brothers, Richard and Christopher, the latter of whom was married.

Sir John's first wife is called Alice, daughter of —— Hancombe of Hancombe, Co. Bedford.

This Latin pedigree ends with the three children of Christopher Cresacre More, who was born 3rd July, 1572.

This MS. also mentions Sir John's second wife as Alice, relict of Clarke, and notes that she had by her first husband a daughter, Agnes Clarke.

The date of this MS. is probably *circa* 1621-6, and it consists of imperfect copies of Glover's Visitation, 1584, and of St. George's Visitation in 1612, with many additions and pedigrees from Dodsworth's deeds, and other genealogies and arms not in the originals, and supposed to have been collected by Vincent.

The MS. (Coll. Arms, xlvii. D. xiv. p. 333) describes Sir John More's second wife as Alice, daughter of John and sister of Sir Christopher More of Losely, Surrey.

(441)

II. The Martyr's First Wife.

The MS. (Vincent, cxxiv. p. 291) has this entry in the Colt
pedigree: "Jana, nupta Thomæ Moore militi, Cancellario
Angliæ"; and she appears as the daughter of John Colt or
Cowlt of Essex by his wife Jane, daughter of Sir John Elring-
ton of Middlesex, knight. She had two brothers—Sir George
Colt of Candish, Suffolk, knight, and Thomas Colt—and four
sisters. All six married.

III. Arms.

A pedigree of four descents and arms of Colt appear in (Coll.
Arms) MS. D. xi. p. 32ᵇ. The descents begin with Jane
More's father, John Colt, and the arms are given thus "argent
a fess between 3 colts courant sable ".

In MS. (Coll. Arms) E.D.N. lvi. p. 148, being the grants
by Sir Christopher Barker (Norroy, 1536; Garter, 1536-50) and
other kings of arms in trick, occurs this entry: "Sir Tho. Moore
Lord Chancellor T. H. 8". The trick below this is: "4ly, 1st,
and 4th, *ar.* a chevron engrailed between 3 moorcocks sable;
2nd and 3rd argent on a chevron between 3 unicorns' heads
erased sable (not blazoned), 3 roundles (not blazoned)".

How the martyr quarters this unicorn coat is not shown in
the pedigrees. The coat is apparently intended for that of
Killingbeck, an old family of Chapel-Allerton in Yorkshire,
whom the heralds Flower, in 1584-5, and Dugdale, in 1665
duly visited; *i.e.*, "argent on a chevron sable between 3 unicorns' heads (couped, *Flower;* erased, *Dugdale*), azure, 3
annulets or ".

No crest given, but it is described officially in 1797 as "a
Moor's bust in profile proper, from the ear two annulets con-
joined, *or,* shirt also proper ".

APPENDIX B.

(*See page* 54.)

MORE'S LOVE OF FUN.

A practical joke perpetrated by Sir Thomas More is recorded by Erasmus, yet seems to have escaped the notice of any of his numerous biographers. I had marked it for quotation, yet it somehow eluded me when composing.

In the *Moriæ Encomium* of Erasmus, Folly says: " I know a *namesake of my own*, who made a present to his newly-married wife of some false jewels, persuading her easily (for he was a most eloquent jester) that they were not only genuine, but of inestimable value. Now, I ask, what difference did it make to the young lady, since she fed her eyes and mind on the glass with just as much delight as if it were diamond, and cherished her rubbish as if it were the rarest treasure? Her husband meanwhile saved his expenses, enjoyed his wife's mistake, and bound her to him by ties of gratitude, no less than if her gifts had cost him much."

Who can doubt that the eloquent jester, *facundus nugator,* was Thomas More? Whom else could Moria call a namesake of her own (*mei nominis*)? Erasmus had already said that he dedicated his book to More, because his family name was as like to Moria as he that bore it was unlike.

What is to be thought of such a trick? Was it honourable, was it lawful? Few, I think, would maintain this, had More carried out the deception to the end, and had it been detected and exposed by another. Though ignorance may sometimes be bliss, and though it may be lawful sometimes to leave people in blissful ignorance or self-deception, it would be strange and dangerous morality to maintain that we may cheat another on the ground that he suffers no real injury. Erasmus puts this plea in the mouth of Folly. But More did not carry out the deception. The book of Erasmus in which the story is told was written in More's house in 1508, during the lifetime of the lady who had been tricked. This was Jane Colt, his first wife. It would perhaps have been more difficult to hoodwink Mistress Alice Middleton. More, after enjoying his little joke for a few days, had doubtless soon undeceived the lady, and they both told the story to Erasmus. I note this, lest the Promotor Fidei should seek to make capital of the incident.

APPENDIX C.

ASTRONOMICAL SYSTEM.

BLESSED Thomas More was fond of astronomy. It is needless to say that he held the Ptolemaic or geocentric system, in which the earth is the centre of all things and various spheres revolve around it. The bookmark of his brother-in-law, John Rastell, which adorns the title pages of the first edition of More's works, illustrates this system. In the lower part are four concentric hemispheres. The smallest and central one—by hills, castles and trees upon it—is intended to represent the earth. Round this is another, by points or fine lines representing the atmosphere. Above this another, being the region of clouds, and higher still the region of fire. At the top of the plate is the bust of God the Father and under it the word *Fiat ;* and the space above the spheres is dotted over with sun, moon and stars. In the midst of these a merman and mermaid hold a tablet with the initials " J. R." Royal coats of arms fill up the top corners.

In one of Sir Thomas's controversial works an ignorant objection to the Divine presence in the Church is amusingly compared to a popular objection to the laws of gravitation. The illustration is correct, though More's astronomical system was incomplete. If the gentlewoman mentioned was Lady More, as seems pretty certain, the story illustrates More's domestic sphere as well as the heavenly spheres. Sir Thomas had been arguing that because the Church was before the sects,

(445)

and the sects came out from the Church; therefore, the Church is right and the sects wrong. Tindale mocked at this argument. It would prove, he said, that the synagogue was right, and Our Lord and His Apostles wrong. Sir Thomas answers that the cases are not similar unless the synagogue had the promise and gift of perpetuity on earth like the Church. Tindale's retort reminds him of a reply made by a gentlewoman to her husband. He was trying to teach her the treatise of the sphere, *i.e.*, the system of the universe. He began at the earth, and to make her perceive that the "earth hangeth in the midst of the world (the universe) by its own weight, 'you must,' he said, 'mark well this, that in the universe higher and lower mean simply outer and inner; so that of the whole world, earth, water, air, and all the spheres above, being each in a round compass over the other, the earth lieth in the very midst, and is the innermost place of the universe. Being, therefore, in the lowest place, its own weight keeps it there, because no heavy thing can of itself ascend upwards, and to fall out of its place on any side would be to fall from a lower place to a higher.

"'Imagine, therefore, that a hole were bored through the earth and a millstone thrown down here on this side from our feet; it would finally remain in the centre of the earth. It could not go farther, for then it would be falling outwards or upwards.'

"Now while he was telling her this tale, she nothing went about to consider his words, but as she was wont in all other things, studied all the while nothing else but what she might say to the contrary. And when he had, with much work and oft interrupting, brought at last his tale to an end: 'Well,' quoth she, as Tindale saith to me, 'I will argue like and make you a like sample. My maid hath yonder a spinning wheel, or else, because all your reason resteth in the roundness of the world: come hither, thou girl; take out thy spindle and bring me hither the whorl. Lo, sir, ye make imaginations, I cannot tell you what. But here is a whorl, and it is round as the world is, and we shall not need imagine a hole bored through, for it hath a hole bored through indeed.   But yet, because ye go by imaginations, I will imagine you.   Imagine me now that this whorl were ten mile thick on every side, and this hole through it still, and so great that a millstone might well go through it. Now, if the whorl stood at one end and a millstone were thrown in alone at the other end, would it go no farther than the midst, trow you?   By God, if one threw in a stone no bigger than an egg, I ween if ye stood at the nether end of the hole five mile beneath the midst, it would give you a pat upon the pate that it would make you claw your head, and yet should ye feel none itch at all.'

" It were too long to tell you all their disputations, for words would she none have lacked, though they should have disputed the space of seven years.   Her husband was fain to put up his sphere and leave his wife her whorl, and fall in talking of some other matter.

" Now playeth Tindale even the same part with me, and maketh an argument and a sample of the synagogue, as like to the Church of Christ for the point we speak of as the whorl was like the world, etc." *

* *English Works*, p. 628.

APPENDIX D.

(*See page* 232.)

MORE'S SPEECH ON WOLSEY'S FALL.

Although I see no reason to distrust what I have written with regard to More's speech at the opening of the Parliament of 1529, yet I am glad to quote the words of a writer who takes another view. A friendly critic of my first edition in the *Saturday Review* (May 16, 1891) writes :—

"Mr. Bridgett's attempt to discredit Hall's report of More's speech at the opening of the Parliament of 1529, when the Chancellor is said to have compared Wolsey to a 'great wether,' does not strike us as successful. On the other hand, we venture to think that Brewer's remarks on the want of 'candour, good sense, and good taste' displayed in the speech are too severe. It is difficult for us to appreciate fully the extent to which the judgments, even of the best of Henry's statesmen, were swayed by his declarations. Henry had declared his displeasure at the Cardinal's conduct, and his servants accepted his view of the case as certainly correct because it was his. And it should also be remembered that the Chancellor spoke at the opening of Parliament as the King's mouthpiece ; he declared the King's mind, the reason why he had summoned his Parliament, and the business that he expected it to do. We do not pretend that even so the speech, which we are inclined to accept as Hall gives it, is creditable to More, but we think that too much has been made of it."

APPENDIX E.

(*See page* 298.)

SIR JOHN SOME-SAY.

In the first chapter of his *Apology* Sir Thomas says: "They lay for a sample the goodly and godly, mild and gentle fashion used by him, *whosoever he was*, that now lately wrote the book of the *Division between the Temporality and the Spirituality*; which charitable mild manner, they say, that if I had used, my works would have been read both of many more, and with much better will". This gentleman, whose example was proposed, or rather opposed, to Sir Thomas, was probably well known to him; though, as he chose to be anonymous, he is merely designated as the Pacifier, or as "Sir John Some-say". He is commonly said to have been a lawyer of the Inner Temple named Christopher St. German, or Seintgerman, who had been educated at Oxford, and who died in 1540. Besides his two books, the *Pacification*, and *Salem and Bizance*, he was the author of a *Dialogue between a Doctor of Divinity and a Student on the Laws of England*. This book appeared in Latin in 1523 and 1528; the English translation has gone through more than twenty editions. *The Pacifier of Divisions* was printed by Berthelet, probably in 1530.

APPENDIX F.

SOME DESCENDANTS OF THE MARTYR.

1. THE last heir male of Sir Thomas More was Father Thomas More, S.J. He was born in 1722, and died in 1795. At the time of the suppression of the Society in 1773 he was English provincial.

2. The last male descendant of William and Margaret Roper was Edward, who died unmarried at Almanza, in Spain, in 1707, or January, 1708. His sister Elizabeth married Charles Henshaw. They had four children—a son, who died unmarried, and three daughters, co-heiresses, who were married, viz., Susanna, to Sir Rowland Wynne of Nostell, from whom the present Lord St. Oswald descends; Elizabeth, to Sir Edward Dering of Surrender Dering, ancestor of the present baronet; and Catherine, who married Sir William Strickland, but left no children.

3. As Anne Roper, Margaret's descendant in the fourth degree, married Sir Philip Constable of Everingham, the ancestor of the present Lord Herries, many Catholic families, through their relationship with the Constable-Maxwells, can thus claim descent from Blessed Thomas, through his daughter Margaret.

4. The direct representative of Blessed Thomas More is John J. Eyston, Esq., of East Hendred, who is descended through the Metcalfes from Bridget More. She had a brother, Thomas (mentioned above in No. 1), and a sister, who was prioress of the Augustinian Canonesses at Bruges. Bridget married, secondly, John Dalton, Esq., of Thurnham.

5. In the preceding generation, Mary More married Charles Waterton, Esq., of Walton Hall, whose descendant is now of Deeping Waterton.

6. There are probably innumerable other descendants of Blessed Thomas by the various female lines.

(Information given me by Rev. J. Morris, S.J., F.S.A.)

APPENDIX G.

Some of the descendants of Blessed Thomas More not only became Protestants, but even Protestant ministers. Cresacre More consoled himself by the thought that these were descended from grandchildren born after the martyr's death, and not from those to whom he gave his blessing. Of the family of More, though not a descendant, was Dr. John Donne, the well-known poet and dean of St. Paul's in the time of James I., whose life was written by Isaac Walton. His mother was Elizabeth, daughter of John Heywood, and her mother a daughter of John Rastell and of Elizabeth More, sister of Sir Thomas.

Mrs. Donne lived and died a staunch Catholic; her younger son Henry died in prison, a confessor of the faith. John apostatised, wrote against the Church, and finally became an Anglican minister. Among Protestants he has the reputation of a saint; but those who care to examine his writings will have no difficulty in discovering the cause of his loss of faith. He is generally considered the head of the metaphysical school of poets. If metaphysical means ultrabestial, I can agree; for I do not think that English literature contains anything more obscene than some of his writings. A recent editor, the Rev. Mr. Grosart, calls these "slugs on the petals of the lily," and believes that his life was pure if his pen was prurient. The poems, however, show clearly an imagination depraved by practical debauchery. One of his prose writings, *The Inthronisation of St. Ignatius in Hell*, shows that he shrank from no ribaldry and blasphemy against the Church of his parents. This came out in 1610, just after his book *Pseudo-Martyr*, in which he seeks to prove that Catholics were suffering for an evil cause. In the preface to the latter book he writes that he "is derived from such a stock and race as I believe no family (which is not of far larger extent and greater branches) hath endured and suffered more, in their persons and fortunes, for obeying the teachers of Roman doctrines, than it hath done". His conclusion seems to be, that his readers must look on it as a proof of his sincerity that he has embraced a religion which inflicted these outrages on his family, but will bestow comfort and wealth on himself!

APPENDIX H.

(See page 143.)

BLESSED THOMAS MORE'S CHAPLAIN.

I should have mentioned that Sir Thomas More's chaplain, as well as his parish priest, Blessed John Larke, suffered martyrdom for the faith. His name was John Ireland, and he died on March 7, 1544. "Eidem Moro a sacello extiterat," writes Sander (lib. i. cap. 18). He does not yet rank as "Blessed," since he was not represented among the martyrs in the series of paintings approved by Pope Gregory XIII., but he is included among the Venerables whose cause was introduced by His Holiness Pope Leo XIII. on the 9th of December, 1886.

APPENDIX I.

"FATHER THOMAS MORE, S.J., the last English provincial of the old Society, was the last male heir of the martyr. He died in 1795, and through him the family heirlooms of various relics of his blessed ancestor came to Stonyhurst College. Father More had a sister, who was superioress of the English Canonesses of St. Augustine at Bruges, and he gave her the only relic of the body of the martyr that is known to exist—excepting, of course, the head. Half of the Bruges relic is now, by the kindness of a successor of Reverend Mother More, at Manresa, Roehampton. The existence of this relic, descending in the family, speaks for the existence of a family tradition that the tomb of Blessed Thomas had been opened some time after the martyrdom.".*

A large collection of interesting relics of Blessed Thomas is preserved by the Jesuit fathers in their college of Stonyhurst. The following description is from the *Stonyhurst Magazine* of February, 1887 :—

1. THE HAT. Fr. Boone, S.J., Superior of the Brussels Residence, April 25, 1835, attests that he received it from Mlle. Thérèse Gaillard the day before her death, to be given to the English Jesuits. It was given to her, June 24, 1809, by Philippe de la Tour, parish priest of SS. Michael and

* Rev. J. Morris, S.J., in the *Month*, Feb., 1891.

(455)

Gudule, in Brussels. He took it, in the presence of Fr. Perez, S.J., of Alost, from the Brussels College Library at the Suppression. It was received by Fr. Otho Zylius, the librarian of the College at Brussels, January 15, 1654, given by Fr. Charles de Breuil, S.J., rector of the College of Roermond in Holland, by leave of Fr. John Baptist Engelgrave, S.J., the provincial. It had been given to that College by Godfrey Gilekens, chancellor of the supreme court in Guelderland, who had it for many years, and on the day on which the holy martyr died (July 6) used always to wear it in court.

2. THE SODALITY CRUCIFIX. Its inscription in Greek says that "this is a relic of St. Thomas the Apostle". Inside the cross now are bits of half-decayed paper, on which is written "St. Charles Borromeus," with some very small relics. There is also a bit of wood in a separate paper without any writing. The following is copied from the original document :—

"I, Thomas More, of the Society of Jesus, and last of the family of Sir Thomas More, lord chancellor of England, with the leave and approbation of R. F. Philip Carteret, provincial, do give unto the Sodality of our Blessed Lady in the English College at St. Omer's, this large gold cross, formerly belonging unto, and us'd or wore by Sir Thomas More himself, and since his time kept with great care in our family.

"Witness my hand, 29th June, 1755.

"THOS. MORE.

"PHILIP CARTERET, Provincial."

In a cover, on which is written : "Thomæ More Donum et authenticū Testimonium de cruce aureâ Ven. Thomæ Mori Angliæ Cancellarii pro fide passi sub Henrico 8vo ".

3. SILVER SEAL of Blessed Thomas More when sub-treasurer. Its handle is a *fleur-de-lys*. The arms are quarterly : 1st and 4th, a *chevron* engrailed between three cocks (More) ; and 2nd and 4th, a *chevron* between three unicorns' heads couped.

The crest is a Moor's head. The inscription round the seal

is "Sigillū T. More Equitis Aurati Subthesauraii Angl." With this was kept another seal, the handle of which consists of two crucifixes, back to back. The seal, engraved on a cornelian, has the inscription, " *Christiano Catholico R.*" The arms are quarterly: 1st and 4th, a *chevron* engrailed between three cocks (More); 2nd and 4th, three lions rampant (Cresacre). The heiress of the Cresacres married Sir Thomas More's only son, John, who would have impaled his wife's arms, or rather, as she was an heiress, borne them on an escutcheon of pretence. The earliest More, therefore, to whom the seal can have belonged is Sir Thomas' grandson, Thomas, who was born in 1531, and died in 1606. The seal is now in the Museum.

4. THE GEORGE : so-called because on its obverse it has, beautifully worked in gold and enamel, St. George and the Dragon. Sir Thomas was not a Knight of the Garter, so that this is not the decoration of that Order, commonly called a George. On the reverse is Our Blessed Lord sitting on the tomb stripped and surrounded by emblems of the Passion. The inscription round the rim is, "O passi graviora dabit his quoque finem". Mr. Edmund Waterton says that when the George was exhibited at the Society of Antiquaries and at the Fine Art Exhibition of 1862, the *minimum* value put upon it was £1000.

5. CAMEO—the head of the Blessed Virgin—"formerly belonging to Sir T. More". It is thus entered in the old catalogue of the Stonyhurst Museum.

6. "CAP of Sir T. More." So entered in the same catalogue, which adds : " The five preceding articles [the two seals, the George, the cameo, and the cap] were all received from Father T. More, Prov. Angl., S.J., last descendant of the family ".

7. POUNCET BOX, a shell with a silver lid, nearly plain. The catalogue says : " Presented by Revd. James Parker ". This gives us the authorship of the following note : " This box was given to Revd. Mr. Coomb by Mrs. Dalton, sister of Revd. T.

More, my provincial, at ye dissolution of ye Society by Pope
Ganganelli, who had received it from his father as a special
gift, having been used by his ancestor, Sir T. More, lord
chancellor of England, beheaded in ye reigning year [*sic*] of
King Henry VIII. I.P. " Father James Parker died at
Liverpool, October 29, 1822, *æt.* 75.

8. A silver reliquary with crystal on both sides, containing a
BONE. The inscription round the rim is " Reliquiæ Thomæ
Mori Mar. Ang. Chan." This is entered in the catalogue :
" 296. Relick of Sir T. More," and in the new catalogue this
entry is given, under the date 1826, as the gift of John Gage,
Esq. He probably also gave the next entry in the old catalogue, viz. :—

9. " 298. A GOLD CROSS which belonged to Sir T. More."
It is a small but beautifully enamelled crucifix. It is worth
noticing that the gold cord attached to it is the same as that
attached to the cornelian Cresacre seal. It is singular that the
inscription, " Presented by John Gage, Esq.," on the glass case
in which the relics have been kept in the Museum should have
attributed the gift of all to Mr. Gage, while he appears to have
given at the most two out of the ten articles the case contained
—the tenth being the Cresacre seal, still in the Museum.

Mr. J. Eyston of East Hendred, in Berkshire, possesses the can
or cup commonly used by More. " It is a pint cup, with a lid
and handle made of pieces of oak, and bound together by rings
of silver, and narrower at the top than at the bottom. It is
still perfect " (Wornum : *Holbein*, p. 203).

The Augustinian Canonesses of Abbots' Leigh, near Newton
Abbot, in Devonshire, possess the hair shirt worn by More,
and sent to his daughter Margaret the day before his martyrdom.
It was brought to them by the daughter of Margaret Clements,
the adopted child of Sir Thomas.

Letters in the autograph of Sir Thomas may still be seen in
the British Museum.

That, in spite of Morison's assertion to the contrary, Margaret

Roper really became possessed of her father's head, is confirmed
by the existence of various relics. 1. A tooth is mentioned *
as having been in the possession of the Heywood family. 2.
In the Benedictine abbey of Lamspring was a portion of a tooth,
with the following paper: "Dono dedi Rdo Arn. Ruisso,
Canonico Sⁱ Petri, Duaci, partem dentis gloriosi martyris Thomæ
Mori Angli, quem dentem obtinui a generoso Dno Guillelmo
Roper, equite aurato, præfati Mori nepote, in cujus fidem hic
nomen subscripsi 12 Julii anno 1628". This is subscribed:
Soror Maria Wysemann, priorissa monasterii divæ Monicæ,
Lovanii. (From list of Lamspring relics kept at Downside.)
3. In the monastery of the English Augustinian Canonesses at
Bruges is preserved a bone of Bl. Thomas, with the following
memorandum: "That this relic of Bl. Sir Thomas More was
delivered unto me in the year of our Lord 1645 by my cosen
Philippe Roper, to be kept in one of our † houses till better
times, and then to be restored to the Heyre of the Ropers of
Eltham, for the time being, of the name and blood. Fra. Vester
Henricus Morus Societatis Jesu Sacerdos." ‡ At the suppression of the society in 1773 this relic was given to the Prioress
of the Augustinian Canonesses at Bruges, who was herself
Mary More, the sister of the Jesuit Provincial, the last of the
direct line. It has been since divided and a part of it is venerated by the Jesuit Fathers at Roehampton. The portion at
Bruges was examined by Dr. Schram on 4th Feb., 1891. It
appeared to him to be a part of the occipital scull. If this is
the case, the inference drawn above (p. 438) regarding the
opening of the tomb will not stand.

THE CHURCH AT CHELSEA. In Feb., 1891, Rev. J. Morris,
S.J., and Mr. Bellasis, *Lancaster Herald*, examined this Church,

---

* More's *Life of More*, p. 388.

† *i.e.*, of the S. J.

‡ This H. More is the historian of the society who died in 1661.
Philip Roper was 3rd son of Thomas, eldest son of Margaret Roper.

with the kind assistance of the Rector, Rev. R. H. Davies. Father Morris writes : " It is certain that the More monument does not stand in its original place. It is now on the south of the chancel, but it must have stood in the western part of the aisle built by Bl. Thomas. The western ends of both aisles were taken down for the enlargement of the Church in 1666. In the chapel or south aisle roof there are twelve coats of arms. We were informed, however, by Mr. Surrey, to whom the Rector referred us, as his 'oldest parishioner,' that these coats are perfectly modern, having been put up by his brother several years ago. Future inquirers should therefore be warned not to build any theories upon them. Mr. Surrey further assured us that there is no truth in the current report that he had himself seen that the More vault is empty—despoiled, the rumours added, for the lead of the coffins. No one in our time has looked into the vault where, as we learn from her husband's will, Margaret Roper lies buried, and whither she translated the holy bodies from the Tower, if the story told in the Arundel MS. is true."

APPENDIX K.

MONUMENTS.

THERE has been a great readiness on the part of English-men to render justice and honour to the memory of Sir Thomas More. It would be easy to fill a long and interesting chapter with the panegyrics that have been pro-nounced upon him. Yet England has been very slow to testify her veneration by any visible memorial. Surely London, at least, ought long ago, by a public act, to have made reparation to her noblest citizen. Yet it was only within the last few years that the devotion and generosity of a Catholic gentleman, George Arnold, Esq., of Milton Hall, Gravesend, erected the first statue. This stands over a doorway of a corner house in Carey Street, Chancery Lane. In building these chambers and shops, Mr. Arnold arranged with the benchers of Lincoln's Inn to make a passage through to New Square, called More's Passage. On a slab beneath the statue is the following inscription :—

> " Sir THOMAS MORE, Knight,
> Some time Lord High Chancellor
> of England ;
> Martyred 6th July, 1535.
> The Faithful Servant
> Both of God and the King."

The houses, as well as the statue, were designed by George Sherrin, Esq., architect, and are engraved in the *British Architect* for 13th September, 1889.

CHRONOLOGICAL INDEX.

CHRONOLOGICAL INDEX.

I. LIFE.

II. WRITINGS.

LETTERS.

SUPPLEMENTARY INDEX.

(Such matters only are here mentioned as would not be sought naturally in the Table of Contents, or the previous Indices.)

Sonnets and Epigrams on Sacred Subjects. Crown 8vo, cloth, extra gilt, bevelled boards. 3s. 6d.

" The verse of the gifted author is distinguished by an easy and melodious flow, chaste imagery, simplicity, directness, and feeling deep yet reserved. The poems are redolent of the sweet spikenard of devotion, and will go far to impart it to their readers."—*Month.*

Our Lady's Dowry. How England Gained that Title. New and Revised Edition. Illustrated. Crown 8vo, cloth extra, gilt top, 506 pp. 5s.

His Eminence Cardinal Vaughan said : " The most excellent, the most interesting, and the most original work of its kind, and for its purpose, that has been published in the English language."

True Story of the Catholic Hierarchy, deposed by Queen Elizabeth, with Memoirs of its Last Two Survivors. By Rev. T. E. BRIDGETT, C.SS.R., and Rev. T. F. KNOX, D.D. Crown 8vo, cloth. 7s. 6d.

" We gladly acknowledge the value of this work on a subject which has been obscured by prejudice and carelessness."—*Saturday Review.*

Suppliant of the Holy Ghost : a Paraphrase of the "Veni Sancte Spiritus." Composed by Rev. R. JOHNSON, of Louvain, in the Seventeenth Century. Edited by Rev. T. E. BRIDGETT, C.SS.R. 32mo, neat cloth, 207 pp. 1s. 6d.

Souls Departed : Being a Defence and Declaration of the Catholic Church's Doctrine touching Purgatory and Prayers for the Dead. By His Eminence CARDINAL ALLEN. Edited by Rev. T. E. BRIDGETT, C.SS.R. New and Cheaper Edition. Fcap. 8vo, 400 pp., cloth. 3s. 6d.

Characteristics from the Writings of Cardinal Wiseman. Selected by Rev. T. E. BRIDGETT, C.SS.R. Crown 8vo, cloth. 6s.

" It is with unfeigned pleasure that we welcome this collection. The extracts are arranged under five headings—Polemical, Doctrinal, Moral, Devotional, and Miscellaneous. Father Bridgett has been careful to give us passages not only of considerable beauty, but of an interest which still lingers in present controversies."—*Tablet.*

BURNS & OATES, LTD., 28 ORCHARD STREET, LONDON, W.

A SELECTION FROM
BURNS & OATES'
PUBLICATIONS

28 ORCHARD STREET
LONDON
W.

Telegrams:
Burns Oates London

Telephone:
2706 Mayfair

HOME FOR GOOD. By Mother MARY
Loyola, of the Bar Convent, York. Edited
by Father Thurston, S.J. With Frontispiece.
3s. 6d. net (postage 4d.).

Father Thurston, S.J., *says*:

THE time of leaving school, as all will agree, is a critical
period for both girls and boys, and it is often a period
of great difficulty for their fond and anxious parents.

Mother Mary Loyola has surely done well to emphasise
the importance of this critical time, and to encourage children
who are yet at school to look forward to it and to prepare for
it. All who know Mother Loyola's other books will be
familiar with her happy touch in facing practical difficulties
of conduct and suggesting remedies. They will be prepared
for the insistence with which she waives aside pretences and
concentrates attention upon the sense of responsibility and
upon the solid formation of characters. Even from early
years she cautions them wisely against the false promises of
self-assertive allurements of pleasure and excitement and
popularity. It will not be her fault if they do not learn to
appreciate what is best and highest.

THE BOND OF PERFECTION. By
Father P. M. Northcote, O.S.M. Price 2s.
net (postage 3d.).

CONTENTS: The Author of Charity. What is Charity?
Charity towards our neighbour. The Specialities of
Charity. Patience. Kindness. Envy. Perverse Dealing.
Pride and Ambition. Selfishness. Anger. Evil Thinking.
Extreme Perversion. Appreciation of the Good and True.
The Greatest Gift.

THE SCHOOL OF DEATH. Outlines
of Meditations. Edited in Italian by the
Right Rev. Luigi Lanzoni, Provost-General of
the Institute of Charity. Translated by the
Rev. George Elson, I.C. Demy 32mo, cloth,
1s. 6d. net ; cloth, extra gilt, 2s. 6d. net
(postage 2d.).

OUR LADY'S TUMBLER. A Legend
of the Middle Age. From the Old Twelfth
Century French. Versified by Rev. George
Cormack, I.C. Wrapper, 6d. net (postage 1d.).

ANCIENT CATHOLIC HOMES OF
SCOTLAND. By Dom ODO BLUNDELL, O.S.B.
With an Introduction by the Hon. Mrs. MAX-
WELL SCOTT, of Abbotsford. Crown 8vo, cloth,
extra gilt, 3s. 6d. net (postage 4d.).

THIS work, which in copiously illustrated, deals with the
history of some of the old Scotch Houses, which were
the centres of Catholicity during the three hundred years
between 1550 and 1850. The author gives an insight into
the sufferings undergone by those who remained true to the
old faith, and shows their devoted adhesion to the House of
Stuart, which involved them in the risings of 1715 and 1745.

The progress of Catholicity is also traced from the days
when Mass was celebrated in secret, with scouts watching
the approaches, to the happier times which have seen the
restoration of much which was ruthlessly swept away in the
sixteenth century. Each of the ten chapters affords pleasant
reading, the more serious narrative being enlivened by
anecdotes, which yet help to impress their own lesson on
the mind. This is also the case with the forty illustrations,
which are partly in the text and partly separate. Every
effort has been made to secure the best workmanship, and
also to keep the price within the most moderate limits.

SISTER MARY OF THE DIVINE
HEART. DROSTE ZU VISCHERING, Religious
of the Good Shepherd, 1863-1899. By the
Abbé LOUIS CHASLE. Translated from the
French by a Member of the Order. New and
revised edition. With Illustrations. 6s.

THIS is one of the most attractive and most important
spiritual biographies published for many years.—*Irish
Monthly*.

THE FATHERS OF THE DESERT.
Translated from the German of the Countess
Hahn-Hahn by EMILY F. BOWDEN. With a
Chapter on the Spiritual Life of the First Six
Centuries. By JOHN BERNARD DALGAIRNS,
Priest of the Oratory. A New Edition. With
a Reproduction of the Picture of St. Simon
Stylites on his column, by FRANK BRANGWYN,
A.R.A. In two volumes. Crown 8vo, cloth, 8s.

THE WAY OF THE CROSS OF
THE SACRED HEART OF JESUS. Translated from the French of Exupère de Prats-de-Mollo (Capuchin), by LEONORA L. YORKE SMITH. With a Preface by Father SEBASTIAN BOWDEN. F'cap 8vo, 2s. 6d. net (postage 3d.).

THE idea contained in this little book is a happy one, and should be suggestive to many. It takes a soul along the road marked by the Stations of the Cross; at each Station it sets down the matter for meditation, and then suggests the meditation itself in the shape of a dialogue between Christ and the soul, the former telling what He would have us derive from the Station, the latter acknowledging and accepting the lesson. Thus the Stations are made in continuous colloquy—and how could they be made better?—*Tablet.*

MEMOIRS AND CORRESPONDENCE
OF COVENTRY PATMORE. By BASIL CHAMPNEYS. New Edition. Two Volumes, 8vo, with Portrait by Mr. SARGENT. 15s.

THOMAS WILLIAM ALLIES (1813-
1903). By MARY H. ALLIES. With Portraits and other Illustrations. Cr. 8vo, 3s. 6d. net (postage 4d.).

THIS volume supplies what may be called a typical spiritual romance from the Rectories of England during the great era of the earlier Victorian conversions. Mr. Allies was the friend of Newman, Faber, Father Ignatius Spencer, Manning and Aubrey de Vere; and, in addition to his own relation of his religious experiences, this volume contains a number of hitherto unpublished letters of Cardinal Newman, in some particulars more important and self-revealing than any that have yet appeared in print. The whole work makes a most deeply interesting and edifying chapter in the story of the resurrection of the Catholic Church in England.

4

A SPIRITUAL RETREAT. By Father H. REGINALD BUCKLER, O.P. Author of "The Perfection of Man by Charity," &c. Crown 8vo, cloth, 3s. 6d. net (postage 4d.).

"A SPIRITUAL RETREAT" is a distinct gain in the line of Catholic manuals of solid and attractive piety. . . . In plan, in matter and in style it takes high place in the class of retreat manuals. It may also be used very profitably as a book of spiritual reading.—*Universe.*

MADAME ROSE LUMMIS. By DELIA GLEESON. 2s. 6d. net (postage 3d.).

FIFTY years ago, in the Northern American States, the name of Madame Rose Lummis was one to conjure with. Born of a high and wealthy family, she decided to devote her life to the poor, and in the telling of her life story Delia Gleeson relates a tale of wonderful pathos and bravery. Madame Lummis's story reads like a romance, but one that breathes tenderness and piety in every page. Her life story should be one of the most treasured possessions on the bookshelves of lovers of pure, interesting, and well-written literature.—*Irish Independent.*

WATERS THAT GO SOFTLY: or, Thoughts for time of Retreat. By JOSEPH RICKABY, S.J. Crown 8vo, cloth 2s. 6d.

THIS is a remarkable book by a remarkable man, and is, all things considered, the best half-crown's worth of spiritual reading we have met with in a search of many years.—*Catholic Times.*

LIST OF APPROVED CHURCH MUSIC FOR THE ARCHDIOCESE OF WESTMINSTER. Published by Authority. Price 2s. 6d. net (postage 2d.).

CONTENTS : Masses. Incidental Mass Music. Requiem Music. Vespers. Compline. Benediction. Music for Occasional Offices. For Holy Week. Solemn Te Deum. Sequences. Offertories and Motets. Solemn Reception of a Bishop. Miscellaneous.

A TUSCAN PENITENT : Being the Life and Legend of St. Margaret of Cortona. By Father CUTHBERT, O.S.F.C. Illustrated. 4s. 6d. net (postage 4d.).

ST. MARGARET'S story is of peculiar interest and belongs to all time, not to one century or place. In the end she was given exceptional grace, but for twenty-six years her life was that of only too many girls of ardent temperament and not too much judgment. . . . It is one of the most beautiful stories ever written; fresh and tender in its old-world dressing, fascinating by its truth and naturalness.—*Tablet*.

CONFERENCES FOR CHILDREN ON THE GOSPEL OF ST. JOHN. By Sister MARY TERESA, O.S.B., of Princethorpe Priory. With a Preface by the Right Rev. OSWALD SMITH, O.S.B., Abbot of Ampleforth. 2s. 6d. net (postage 3d.).

THE ABBOT OF AMPLEFORTH *says* :

THE Christian child cannot begin too early to study the life of our Lord, and to assimilate the lesson of that life. It is by appreciation of the value of the example of our Lord that the soul is led to approach to the perfection of life manifested by our Lord. To waken this appreciation in the child's mind is the object of these simple Conferences.

The authoress has concerned herself for the most part with the homely virtues taught by word and example by our Lord, and it is well that she has done so, for these are the virtues which are especially dear to the Sacred Heart.

FRIDAY FARE. Over One Hundred Recipes for Days of Abstinence or Fasting. By Mrs. CHARLES MARSHALL, M.C.A. Wrapper, 1s. net (postage 1d.).

IT gives a large variety of fish, vegetarian and cheese dishes, a great many of which would be of much assistance to those who are taking up the modern idea of a meatless diet. The recipes are clear and very practical.—*The Queen*.

JESUS OF NAZARETH. The Story
of His Life Told to Children. By Mother
MARY LOYOLA, of the Bar Convent, York.
Edited by Father THURSTON, S.J. Large
crown 8vo, with 24 full-page Illustrations, 5s.
net (postage 4d.).

M Y heart was delighted on reading the proof sheets of
Jesus of Nazareth, by Mother Mary Loyola. The
book is eminently practical, simple, unctuous and interesting.
It will make a powerful impression on the minds of the
children. In fact, no one can read it without loving God
more, and therefore becoming better. Parents, teachers,
and instructors will find Mother Loyola's works very useful
in the difficult task of forming the minds of children to a
life of virtue. We should be glad to see a copy of *Jesus of
Nazareth* in every household in the land. We wish it God-
speed in going out on its great mission.—*Cardinal Gibbons*.

MEMOIR OF FATHER DIGNAM, S.J.
Revised with Preface by Father EDWARD
IGNATIUS PURBRICK, S.J. New and Cheaper
Edition, 5s. net (postage 4d.).

A DAILY THOUGHT. From the
Writings of Father Dignam. New edition,
32mo, leather, gilt edges, 2s.

FATHER GALLWEY. A Sketch, with
some Early Letters. By PERCY FITZGERALD,
M.A., F.S.A. 2s. net (postage 3d.).

A MODERN PILGRIM'S PROGRESS.
With an Introduction on the Prevailing Unrest
by Father SEBASTIAN BOWDEN, of the Oratory.
Second Edition. 6s.

THE FLOWER OF THE MIND. A

Choice among the Best Poems made by ALICE
MEYNELL. Printed on antique paper by Messrs.
T. and A. Constable. With a Cover Design
by L. HOUSMAN. 4s. 6d. net.

A BEAUTIFUL volume, rendered still more beautiful by
all the delights of clear type on excellent paper.—
Westminster Gazette.

THOUGHTS AND FANCIES. Verses

on the Madonna, Sonnets and Sacred Thoughts.
By the Rev. F. C. KOLBE, D.D. 2s. 6d. net
(postage 3d.).

THERE is about all a sincerity of thought, and a kind of
chaste serenity of expression which is often extremely
pleasing.—*Times.*

A SELECTION FROM THE VERSES

OF JOHN B. TABB. 2s. 6d. net (postage
3d.).

THIS selection from the poems of Father Tabb proves
conclusively that he is the greatest living master of
epigram in verse.—*Daily Chronicle.*

THE GARDEN OF ROSES OF OUR

LADY. The Excellences of the Rosary and
the Best Method of Reciting it. By Father
MESCHLER, S.J. Demy 16mo., 2s. 6d.

A NICE little devotional book treating from the spiritual
point of view of the excellences of the Rosary. The
author works in very practical instructions on prayer and
meditation.—*Tablet.*

FREE WILL AND FOUR ENGLISH

PHILOSOPHERS: Hobbes, Locke, Hume
and Mill. By Father JOSEPH RICKABY, S.J.
3s. 6d. net (postage 3d.).

CARDINAL NEWMAN. By Wilfrid Meynell. New and revised edition. With fifteen Illustrations, 2s. 6d.

THE story of the development of Newman's Religious Opinions is here told mainly as he told it; and it will be conceded to this little "Life" that it contains more of his own words, and also a greater number of facts concerning himself, his friends and his affairs, than have yet been brought together in so brief a space. An unhampered use of the pages of the *Apologia* gives to the narrative not merely a present authenticity but a finality of statement that can never be disturbed.—*Extract from Preface.*

HOLY WISDOM (*Sancta Sophia*). Directions for the Prayer of Contemplation, etc. By the Ven. F. Augustin Baker, O.S.B. Edited by Abbot Sweeney, D.D. New Edition, cloth, 3s. 6d.; or handsomely bound with leather back, 5s.

TO lovers of prayer and meditation it will be a most acceptable guide and friend.—*Tablet.*

RELIGIOUS WORSHIP, AND SOME DEFECTS IN POPULAR DEVOTIONS. By Mgr. Bonomelli, Bishop of Cremona. With the Author's Portrait. 2s. 6d. net (postage 3d.).

MARY IN THE GOSPELS : or, Lectues on the History of our Blessed Lady as recorded by the Evangelists. By the Very Rev. J. S. Canon Northcote, D.D. New Edition, pp. 344, 3s. 6d.

We cordially commend these devout and persuasive lectures.—*Month.*

One of the clearest and best treatises on the subject we have seen.—*Tablet.*

THE LITTLE OFFICE OF OUR
LADY. A Treatise, Theoretical, Practical, and Exegetical. By ETHELRED TAUNTON, Priest of the Diocese of Westminster. Demy 8vo, strongly bound, leather back, 10s. net.

THIS work is a guide to the Spiritual Life based upon the Liturgical Prayer of the Church. Its spirit is large, wide, and essentially Catholic. It will be useful to those just beginning the Spiritual Life as well as for those who, for many years, have consecrated themselves to God's service, for it contains in one volume the gist of the greatest, holiest, and most learned writers.

SPIRITUAL CONFERENCES OF
ST. FRANCIS DE SALES. Translated into English from the new and authentic Edition of the Saint's Works, with several Additions and Supplementary Notes, under the supervision of ABBOT GASQUET, O.S.B., and the late Dom BENEDICT MACKEY, O.S.B. 6s.

DECREES OF THE VATICAN
COUNCIL. Edited, with an Introduction, by the Rev. VINCENT McNABB, O.P. Demy 8vo, 2s.

"I AM THE WAY." A Treatise for
Followers of Christ. Translated by the Hon. A. WILMOT, M.L.C., from a French edition of *L'Esprit du Christianisme, ou la Conformité du Chrétien avec Jésus-Christ*, by Father NEPVEU, S.J. With a Preface by the ARCHBISHOP OF WESTMINSTER. 2s. 6d. net (postage 3d.).

ECCLESIA : THE CHURCH OF

CHRIST. A planned Series of Papers by Dom GILBERT DOLAN, O.S.B.; Father BENEDICT ZIMMERMAN, O.D.C. ; Father R. H. BENSON, M.A.; Dom JOHN CHAPMAN, O.S.B.; Dom J. D. BREEN, O.S.B.; A. H. MATHEW, and Father PETER FINLAY, S.J. 3s. 6d. net (postage 3d.).

THIS volume, prepared by high authorities, provides a concise and clear exposition of the Origin, Notes, and Prerogatives of the Church of Christ ; and supplies a specially suitable Manual to place in the hands of non-Catholics. To Catholics themselves it offers a particularly valuable armoury of information and assistance in the conduct of their discussions with inquirers or opponents.

TYBURN CONFERENCES : Oxford,

Douay, Tyburn. Conferences on the Martyrs of the English Seminaries. Delivered at Tyburn Convent by Dom BEDE CAMM, O.S.B. With Frontispiece. 2s. 6d. net (postage 3d.).

WITH his accustomed power of description, Father Camm has given us a very vivid picture of the scenes of suffering and of triumph that were so often witnessed at the historic spot close to which these Conferences were delivered.—*Ushaw Magazine.*

THE RELIGION OF THE PLAIN

MAN. By FATHER ROBERT HUGH BENSON, M.A. With the Author's Portrait. 2s. 6d. net (postage 3d.).

THIS is a book which sets forth in a plain, simple way the reasons for submitting to the authority of the Church. It is not a learned treatise, but a simple common-sense explanation of the need we have of a guide in religious matters, and of who that guide is.—*Tablet.*

THE CHURCH AND KINDNESS

TO ANIMALS. 1. Condemnation of Bull-Fights ; 2. Animals in the Lives and Legends of Saints ; 3. A Cloud of Modern Witnesses. Crown 8vo, Illustrated, 2s. 6d. net (postage 3d.).

THIS work, which has received the blessing of Pius X., contains delightful reproductions of Old Master Pictures of Animals and Saints.

SAINT BENEDICT JOSEPH LABRE

(Votary of Holy Poverty and Pilgrim). By C. L. WHITE. With Portrait and other Illustrations. 2s. 6d.

THIS charming little book will help its readers to understand the spirit of one who, though in the world, was not of the world, and whose life was deeply hidden with Christ in God.—*Catholic Weekly*.

THE APOCALYPSE, THE ANTI-

CHRIST, AND THE END. By J. J. ELAR. 5s.

The whole book deserves study by those who reverence Holy Scripture.—*Tablet*.

A sober, thoughtful, ably-written treatise, which will, we feel sure, be prized by Biblical students.—*Catholic Times*.

THE RELIGION OF OUR FORE-

FATHERS. By the Rev. VINCENT HORNYOLD, S.J. 214 pages. In wrapper, 6d. (postage 2d.) ; cloth, 1s. 3d. (postage 3d.) ; or in Seven Parts at 2d. each (postage ½d.).

Part VIII., " The Church in England, Past and Present," and Part IX., " Catholic Orders and Anglican Orders," are published separately in pamphlet form only (post free 2½d. each), and are not contained in the volume.

FAITH AND FOLLY. By the Right Rev. Mgr. JOHN S. VAUGHAN. New and Revised Edition. 5s. net (postage 4d.).

JUST the very book for meeting the new combination of hostile attack upon revealed religion. We deliberately recommend it as the most *readable* book of the kind we have ever met.—*Catholic Times.*

THE HOLY CATHOLIC CHURCH: Her Faith, Works, Triumphs. By a CONVERT. 3s. 6d.

IT has been a pleasure to read this handy guide to the truth concerning the Kingdom of God on earth. The work shows clear signs of originality in its arrangement and of diligent inquiry after unhackneyed materials. Its aim is not to make a man a Christian, but to show him what Scripture and the Church mean by being one.—*Tablet.*

MANUAL OF SCRIPTURE HISTORY. By the Very Rev. Dr. RICHARDS. New and Improved Edition. 415 pp., with Maps, etc. 2s. 6d. net (postage 4d.).

BEING a complete analysis of the historical books of the Old Testament. Adopted as a text book in our colleges and training schools.

ST. JOHN BAPTIST DE ROSSI. Translated from the Italian by Lady HERBERT. With the renowned Introduction on Ecclesiastical Training and the Sacerdotal Life by Cardinal VAUGHAN. With a Portrait of the Saint. A New Edition. 8vo. 5s. net.

ST. CATHERINE DE' RICCI : Her Life, her Letters, her Community. By F. M. CAPES. Introduced by a Treatise on the Mystical Life by Father BERTRAND WILBERFORCE, O.P. With a Portrait of the Saint, a Facsimile Letter, and other Illustrations. 7s. 6d. net.

PERIODICALS.

THE DUBLIN REVIEW. Edited by Mr. WILFRID WARD. Published Quarterly. Single copy, 5s. 6d. net. Advanced Yearly Subscription, £1 1s., post free.

CHURCH MUSIC. Issued By-Monthly. With Musical Supplements in every copy. Annual Subscription, 6s. 6d. per annum, post free. Single numbers, 1s. 3d. net each.

THE NEW YORK REVIEW. A Journal of Ancient Faith and Modern Thought. Issued every two months. Terms, 12s. 6d. a year. Single Copies, 2s. 6d. net.

Messrs. BURNS & OATES *receive Subscriptions to any of the Reviews, Magazines, or Weekly Papers published in the United Kingdom or America. Subscriptions may commence at any time, but cannot be received for less than six months; or in the case of those published abroad, twelve months. A Selected List sent on request.*

CATHOLIC STANDARD LIBRARY.

PRICE 12s. EACH VOLUME.

EDMUND CAMPION. By RICHARD SIMPSON.

THE GREAT COMMENTARY ON THE GOSPELS. By CORNELIUS à LAPIDE. Eight Volumes.

COMMENTARY ON THE HOLY GOSPEL OF ST. MATTHEW. By JOHN MALDONATUS, S.J. Two Volumes.

EXPOSITION ON ST. PAUL'S EPISTLES. By BERNARDINE à PICONIO. Three Volumes.

THE HISTORY AND FATE OF SACRILEGE. By Sir HENRY SPELMAN, Kt.

EDWARD VI. AND THE BOOK OF COMMON PRAYER. Its Origin, illustrated by hitherto unpublished documents. With Facsimile pages of MS. by ABBOT GASQUET, D.D., O.S.B., and EDMUND BISHOP.

THE WORKS OF ST. BERNARD. Translated into English from the Edition of Dom Joannes Mabillon. Vols. I. and II. containing the Letters of St. Bernard; Vol. III., Sermons and Letters.

HISTORICAL PORTRAITS OF THE TUDOR DYNASTY AND THE REFORMATION PERIOD. By S. HUBERT BURKE. Four Volumes.

Bibles and Prayer Books.

HOLY BIBLE. *Octavo Edition* (9 by 6 inches).
Cloth, red edges, 5s.; and in a great variety of leather
bindings, at 8s., 10s., 15s., 18s., 30s., and 35s. each.

> *Pocket Edition* (size 5¼ by 3¼ inches). Embossed
> cloth, red edges, 2s. 6d.; and in leather bindings at
> 4s. 6d., 6s. 6d., and 7s. 6d.

NEW TESTAMENT. *New Large Type Edition.*
With annotations, references, and an historical and
chronological index. Crown 8vo (size 7½ by 5 inches).
500 pp. Cloth, 2s.; and in leather bindings at 4s. 6d.
and 8s. 6d.

> *Pocket Edition.* Limp cloth, 6d. net (postage 2d.).
> leather bindings, 1s., 1s. 6d., 3s. and 4s. 6d.

MANUAL OF PRAYERS FOR CONGREGA-
TIONAL USE. With Epistles and Gospels. Pocket
Edition, 6d. net, or with Enlarged Appendix, 1s. to
7s. 6d.

THE CHILD'S MASS BOOK. By Hon. Mrs.
Kavanagh. Popular Edition. Cloth, 6d. Revised
Edition, with Sixteen Coloured Illustrations. Cloth, gilt,
1s.; leather, 2s. 6d.

GARDEN OF THE SOUL. Five Editions. 6d.
to 10s. 6d.

KEY OF HEAVEN. Three Editions. 6d. to 5s.

THE PATH TO HEAVEN. The Cheapest and
Most Complete Book of Devotions for public or private
use ever issued. Upwards of 1,000 pages (size, 5⅝ by
3⅝ inches). Cloth, 2s.; best cloth, red edges, 2s. 6d.;
roan, grained, 3s.; smooth grain roan, gilt edges, 4s.;
French Morocco, full gilt, with clasp, 4s. 6d.; Persian
calf, 4s. 6d.; Rutland, limp, 6s.; calf or Morocco
bindings, 7s. 6d.; German calf or Morocco, soft cushioned,
8s. 6d. each.

MANUAL OF CATHOLIC PIETY. Three
Editions. 6d. to 5s.

BIBLES AND PRAYER BOOKS (*continued*).

PAX VOBISCUM. A Large-Type Book of Devotions, compiled by a Religious, which, besides containing the usual prayers for daily use, is adapted in an especial manner to the wants of Sick Persons and Invalids. 18mo, cloth, 2s. 6d. net. Limp leather, 4s. net (postage 3d.).

CATHOLIC'S VADE MECUM. Leather, 3s. 6d. to 21s.

FLOWERS OF DEVOTION. New Edition, with Ordinary of the Mass in Large Type. 1s. 6d. to 6s.

THE GOLDEN MANUAL. The most complete Prayer Book. 6s. to 30s.

CATHOLIC'S DAILY COMPANION. 1s. to 5s.

MISSAL FOR THE LAITY. 6d. net to 5s.

CHURCH MANUAL. With Epistles and Gospels. In leather bindings. 2s., 3s. 6d., 5s. each.

SPIRIT OF THE SACRED HEART. 3s. 6d., 5s. 6d., 8s. 6d. and 12s. 6d. 700 pages, printed in LARGE clear type.

ROMAN MISSAL. With all the new Offices, and the Propers for England, Ireland, Scotland, the Society of Jesus, and the Order of St. Benedict. Size, $5\frac{7}{8}$ by $3\frac{5}{8}$in. Leather bindings, 5s. to 30s.

THE IMITATION OF CHRIST. By THOMAS à KEMPIS. Authorised Translation. In three sizes, and in numerous styles of bindings. 6d. net to 15s.

SPIRITUAL COMBAT. Pocket Edition. 6d. net to 4s. 6d. Larger Edition, 1s.

TREASURY OF PRAYER. A Manual of Popular Devotion for the frequenters of the Oratory of St. Philip Neri. With Epistles and Gospels. 16mo, cloth, 2s. 6d.; roan, 4s.; calf or morocco boards, 7s. 6d. each; calf or morocco, limp, 7s. 6d. each.

Illustrated List of Bibles, Prayer Books, Devotional Manuals, Hymn Books, etc., sent free on application.

Burns & Oates,
28 ORCHARD STREET, LONDON, W.